The Language of the
Foreign Book Trade

JERROLD ORNE

The Language of the Foreign Book Trade

ABBREVIATIONS

TERMS

PHRASES

Third Edition

American Library Association / Chicago 1976

Library of Congress Cataloging in Publication Data
Orne, Jerrold, 1911–
  The language of the foreign book trade.
  1. Book industries and trade—Dictionaries—Polyglot.
2. Bibliography—Dictionaries—Polyglot. 3. English
language—Dictionaries—Polyglot. 4. Bibliography—
Abbreviations. I. Title.
Z1006.07 1976   010'.3   76-11748
ISBN 0-8389-0219-7

Ref

Z
1006
07
1976

Printed in the United States of America

CONTENTS

PREFACE   vii

Czech   1

Dano-Norwegian   20

Dutch   52

Finnish   74

French   87

German   108

Hungarian   142

Italian   174

Polish   198

Portuguese   219

Romanian   239

Russian   259

Spanish   289

Swedish   316

PREFACE

The fundamental purpose of this third edition of *The Language of the Foreign Book Trade*, as of its earlier editions, remains unchanged. It is designed to provide a working tool for librarians and personnel in the book trade who may not have sufficient acquaintance with one or more of the languages included to serve their needs. With today's rapid expansion of communications and pressures for trade, the need for some aid in understanding basic terms, abbreviations, and phrases used in the book trade in many countries is great. This book is a multilingual glossary in fifteen of the major languages of western and central Europe, Latin America, and the USSR. Three new languages, Finnish, Hungarian, and Romanian, have now been added to the twelve of the second edition. The text for each of the latter group has been considerably enlarged to include many additional terms representing new materials or marketing terminology, as well as those resulting from a stable base list now applied to every language.

As before, the first principle of selection for inclusion of terms, abbreviations, and phrases is current usage, based mainly upon evidence of use in booksellers' catalogs. For all of western Europe, Latin America, and Scandinavia (excepting Finland), these catalogs are abundant and provide a wealth of examples. For Finland, the east European countries, and the USSR this is not true, and we have searched national bibliographies and other relevant tools for guidance. In order to assure adequate representation for these languages, we have drawn more heavily upon our native professional colleagues, providing them with the basic list of common terms found in one or more of the lists already completed. Because of this necessary change in method, all of the languages are more consistently represented, without in any way prejudicing the complete representation of those languages where there is a natural, large, international trade. Currency is in every case assured by the use of current catalogs and the expertise of native librarians and book dealers.

The third edition of *The Language of the Foreign Book Trade* contains over 26,000 entries, as compared with approximately 16,000 in the second edition. The Finnish text is short, just over 1,000 entries, due to the agglutinative character of the language. Most of the remaining texts include 1,700 or more entries, German again being the largest, with almost 2,800 listings. There are a number of new trade name entries for binding materials, more listings of business instruction terms, and, in some cases, monetary designations growing out of recent exchange and value problems. Not every term is limited to the book trade; some have a more general application but are used so frequently in the book trade they must be included. When a term has several possible meanings, only the meaning relevant to the book trade appears here. Cognate terms are freely included, if for no other reason than to give confidence to the wary user venturing into a strange tongue. The definitions are always the shortest and most specific possible, with no pretension to scholarly lexicography. These definitions are not for the linguist; they are for simple comprehension. When several defining words are given, each may serve; when two different meanings are appropriate they are separated by a semicolon rather than a comma.

The arrangement of the book is planned for maximum utility. The languages are each in a separate list, following one another in alphabetic order. As earlier, the Danish and Norwegian languages are combined in one text since there are only minor differences in spelling. Within each language the entries are alphabetized word by word and letter by letter, disregarding all diacritical marks and particular alphabetical custom. All abbreviations, terms, and phrases are combined thus in one alphabetical arrangement. This may give offense to a lexicographer or a native who finds his alphabet not arranged as he is accustomed to find it, but it will not confuse the nonlinguist user who knows nothing of a language or the values of its diacritical symbols. This arrangement has proved its efficacy in earlier editions and is continued here.

Many of the problems noted in earlier editions have continued to this time. Language lives and is subject to change, just as is any living object. Changes occur in government, in methods of production and distribution, in communications and transportation, and all of these and others affect the vocabulary in one country or another. It is because of the rapid rate of change in our time that it seemed useful to prepare a new edition of this book.

The basic texts of the second edition are a credit to the numerous contributors that edition enjoyed. The new languages have added to that distinguished company others no less able or generous with their talents. Some of the revisions also led to the involvement of more young, earnest, and linguistically talented professionals, all of whom have added considerably to the quality of the book.

Since this edition is based extensively upon the texts of its predecessor, due credit must again be given for the notable contributions made earlier by a notable list of librarians, linguists, and book trade people. From the

University of North Carolina, Mrs. Angele Avizonis, Dr. Harry Bergholz, Mrs. Helena Gerasimowicz, Sra. Esmeralda Javens, Mrs. Margareta Kirschner, Mr. Stephan Prociuk; from Duke University, Mrs. Gert Hall; from Elon College, Dr. Konstantinus Avizonis; from the U.S. Department of State, Dr. David Griffin; from the U.S. Department of Agriculture, Miss Leila Moran; from Kraus-Thomson, Messrs. Frederick Altman and Jens J. Christofferson; from Martinus Nijhoff, Mr. Hugo B. Corstius. My enduring appreciation of their valued contributions to the 1962 edition, carried over into this, is here recorded. Further indications of their attributes are represented in the preface to that earlier edition.

Additions to this distinguished company for the third edition begin with the new languages added. Mr. Esko Hakli, Deputy Librarian of the Helsinki University Library, together with a number of unnamed staff members of the Finnish National Bibliography have made major contributions to the Finnish text; for close-at-hand consultation and definition verification, I have relied upon Mr. Karl E. Olsoni of the National Science Foundation who revised successive editions of the Finnish text. The Hungarian revisions are principally the work of Messrs. Tamas Keri and Emery Koltay of R. R. Bowker Company; Mr. Leslie Pap of Arno Press, Inc.; and Dr. François Kertesz of Société Internationale de Technologie, Paris, France. A very considerable contribution was made by Mr. Erik Vajda, Deputy Director of the Hungarian Central Technical Library and Documentation Center, and his staff in Budapest, Hungary. Mrs. Ildiko Trombitas of Burroughs Wellcome Company also read the final text and made useful suggestions. The Romanian text had three principal readers, Messrs. François Kertesz and Emery Koltay, mentioned above, and Mrs. Margaretta Leon of the New York Public Research Library.

Additional expertise was found for major revisions of some of the languages of the last edition. A very intensive review was given the Spanish by Dra. Berta Becerra, Librarian for Latin American Studies at the University of North Carolina. The Swedish text had thorough review in Sweden by Mr. Arvid J. Ahlin and a number of his colleagues in the Swedish National Standards Commission. The Polish text was amplified and carefully revised by Mrs. Helena Gierasimowicz, now Planning Librarian at the University of North Carolina. A preliminary review of the Russian text was made by Prof. Michael Zarechnak of Georgetown University; however, the major task of expansion, revision, and editing is wholly credited to Mr. David P. Rose, Librarian for Slavic Studies at the University of North Carolina. Inevitably there are those contributors who through diffidence or determined anonymity are not mentioned.

A special tribute is due Mrs. Sylvia Royt, Publishing Services, American Library Association, for boundless patience, intelligent questions, and extraordinary competence as publisher's editor of this volume. Her judicious selection of native readers to give each text one more knowledgeable reading provided the final assurance of its reliability and accuracy. Her own rigorously disciplined scrutiny and acute comprehension of a very complex text merit my admiration and appreciation.

My utmost appreciation is here recorded for the encouragement and generous support of Dr. Edward G. Holley, Dean of the School of Library Science at our University, who made it possible for me to have the available time of my two talented research assistants for this work. These young people, Mrs. Mary Anne Fox and Mr. Damon Hickey, were wholly responsible for the production, proofreading, and preliminary editing of the reams of copy necessary for the numerous stages of various texts. The accuracy and reliability of the final copy is a tribute to their intelligence and endurance. Their perseverance and extraordinary devotion to this burdensome task speaks well for their future professional growth.

The quality of the revisions and new texts is largely due to the contributions of all of these named and unnamed colleagues who have shared my work. Where there are errors or omissions, these are surely my own responsibility, since I have always reserved for myself the final determination of form and content. It remains my lasting hope that my working colleagues in libraries and in the book trade will find this book useful and will find me ever grateful for such praise or criticism as my work may evoke.

JERROLD ORNE

School of Library Science
University of North Carolina
Chapel Hill, N.C.

Czech

a jiní: and others
a tak dále: and so forth, etc.
abecední: alphabetical
abecední rejstřík: alphabetical index
abecední uspořádání: alphabetical order
abecední věcný rejstřík: alphabetical subject index
abonent(i): subscriber(s)
abonnement: subscription
abonovaný: subscribed
adaptace: adaptation
adresa: address
adresář(e): directory(ies)
adresát: addressee
aj. *see* a jiní
akademie: academy
akademik: academic
aktovka(y): portfolio(s)
akvarel(y): watercolor(s)
akvarelový: watercolored
akvatint(y): aquatint(s)
alba: albums, books of plates
album: album, book of plates
aldinka: Aldine
almanach(y): almanac(s)
alternativní název: alternate title
americký: American
anály: annals
analytický: analytical
anastatický: anastatic
anglický: English
anonymně: anonymously
anonymní: anonymous

anonymní dílo(a): anonymous work(s)
anotace: annotation(s)
anotovaný katalog: annotated catalog
antedatovaný: antedated
antikva: antiqua, roman type
antikvář: antiquarian bookseller
antikvariát: secondhand bookstore
antikvární kniha: secondhand book
antologie: anthology
apokryf(y): apocrypha, apocryphal book(s)
arabeska(y): arabesque(s)
arabská(é) číslice: Arabic numeral(s)
arch(y): sheet(s), folio(s)
archiv: archives, records
archiválie: archives, records
archivní materiál: archives, documents
atd. *see* a tak dále
atlas(y): atlas(es)
atlasový format: atlas folio
aukce: auction
aukční katalog: auction catalog
autentický: authentic
autobiografický: autobiographical
autobiografie: autobiography(ies)
autograf(y): autograph(s)
autor: author, writer
autoreferát: author's summary
autoři: authors, writers
autorisované vydání: authorized edition

autorisovaný překlad: authorized
  translation
autorské právo: copyright
autorství: authorship
až do: until

b.m. *see* bez místa
b.m.a.r. *see* bez místa a roku
b.r. *see* bez roku
báchorka(y): fairy tale(s)
bádání: research
bajka(y): fable(s)
barev. *see* barevný
barevná(é) ilustrace: illustration(s)
  in color
barevná litografie: chromolithography
barevná(é) rytina(y): color
  engraving(s)
barevné(á) vyobrazení: illus-
  tration(s) in color
barevný: in color
barevný dřevoryt: woodcut in
  color
barevný kamenotisk: chromolithography
barevný tisk: color printing
barva: color
barva citronu: lemon-colored
barva fialová: violet
barva karafiátová: pink
barva levandulová: lavender
barva lososová: salmon
barva olivová: olive
barva oranžová: buff
barvitý: colored
barvotisk: color printing
barvy měděné: copper-colored
barvy pomerančové: orange
báseň: poem
básně: poems
básnictví: poetry
bavlna: cotton
beletrie: belles lettres, fiction
bez: without
bez barvy: colorless
bez copyrightu: without copyright

bez data: undated
bez hříchu: impeccable
bez lesku: lusterless
bez místa: no place of publication
bez místa a roku: no place and
  no date
bez názvu: no title
bez podpisu: unsigned
bez poplatku: duty free
bez poskvrny: immaculate
bez roku: no year, no date
bez titulního listu: title page
  missing
bez vady: flawless
bezcenný: worthless
bezdřevný papír: wood-free paper
běžná cena: current price
běžné číslo: current issue
běžné záhlaví: running title
bezplatně: without charge, free
bezplatný výtisk: free copy
bezvýznamný: insignificant,
  unimportant
bianco: blank
bibliofil: bibliophile
bibliofilské vydání: bibliophile
  edition
bibliografická informace: bibliographic information
bibliografická(é) práce: bibliographic work(s)
bibliografická(é) vzácnost(i): rare
  book(s)
bibliografický(é) seznam(y): bib-
  liography(ies)
bibliografický(é) soupis(y): bibliographic list(s)
bibliografie: bibliography(ies)
biblový papír: Bible paper
bílý: white
biograf: biographer
biografický: biographic
biografie: biography(ies)
blízko: nearly
blízký: near
bohatě: richly
bohatý: rich

bordura(y): border(s)
breviář(e): breviary(ies)
briliant: brilliant
brokát: brocade
brokátový: brocaded
bronz: bronze
bronzová barva: bronze-colored
brož. *see* brožovaný
brožovaná(é) kniha(y): booklet(s),
   paperbound book(s)
brožovaný: sewed, stitched
brožura(y): pamphlet(s), unbound
   book(s)
brzo, brzy: soon
bukinista: dealer in secondhand
   books
bulharský: Bulgarian

č. *see* číslo
čára(y): line(s)
čárová(é) mědirytina(y): line
   engraving(s)
časný: early
časopis(y): journal(s), periodical(s)
časopisectví: periodical press,
   periodical publishing
část(i): part(s), section(s)
celková: total
celokožená vazba: full-leather
   binding
celoplátěná vazba: cloth binding
celoroční předplatné: annual
   subscription rate
celostránková(é) ilustrace: full-
   page illustration(s)
celostránkové(á) vyobrazení: full-
   page illustration(s)
celý: entire, whole
cena: price, value
cena netto: net price
ceník(y): price list(s)
censura: censorship
censurované vydání: expurgated
   edition
centrální: central
černý: black
červené natřený: rubricated

červený: red
český: Czech
cestovní deník(y): travel diary(ies)
cetkaný: spangled
cetky: spangles
chyba(y): mistake(s), error(s)
chybí: missing, wanting, lacking
chybí konec: end missing
chybí začátek: beginning missing
čínský: Chinese
čís. *see* číslo
ciselovaná: chased
číslo(a): number(s), issue(s)
číslo svazku ve sbírce: serial
   number, series number
číslovaná(é) stránka(y): numbered
   page(s)
číslování: numeration
číslovaný(é) list(y): numbered
   leaf(ves)
číslovaný(é) výtisk(y): numbered
   copy(ies)
čistý: clean
citace: quotation
čítanka(y): reader(s)
citát(y): quotation(s)
čitelný: legible
citovaný: cited
cizozemský: foreign
článek: article, section
články: articles, sections
členství: membership
čmárati: scribble
črta(y): sketch(es)
čtrnáct(ý): fourteen(th)
čtrnáct dní: fortnight
čtrnáctideník: fortnightly,
   biweekly
čtrnáctidenně: fortnightly,
   biweekly
čtvereční: square
čtvrtletně: quarterly
čtvrtletník: quarterly
čtvrtý: fourth
čtyři: four
čtyřicátý: fortieth

čtyřicet: forty
cyrilice: Cyrillic alphabet

data: dates
datování: dating
datovaný: dated
datum: date
defekt: imperfection
definitivní vydání: definitive
   edition
délka: length
deník(y): diary(ies)
denně: daily
desátý: tenth
deset: ten
deska(y): cover(s)
dětská(é) kniha(y): children's
   book(s), juvenile book(s)
devadesát(ý): ninety(ieth)
devatenáct(ý): nineteen(th)
devátý: ninth
devět: nine
diagr. *see* diagram
diagram(y): diagram(s)
diář(e): diary(ies), journal(s)
díl(y): part(s), volume(s)
dílo(a): work(s)
dílo básnické: work of poetry
dílo na pokračování: work to be
   continued, publication in
   installments
dílo poctěné cenou: prize-winning
   work
dílo v jednom svazku: one-volume
   work, omnibus volume
dílo více původců: work by
   several authors
disertace: dissertation(s),
   thesis(es)
diskonto: discount
distributor knih: book distributor
divadelní hra: play, drama
dobová vazba: contemporary
   binding
dobový: contemporary
dobrodružná literatura: adventure
   books

dobrý: good
dočasně: temporarily
dočasný: temporary
dodatečný: additional
dodatek: appendix, supplement
dodatky: appendixes, supplements
dodávka: delivery
doklad(y): document(s), act(s)
dokonaný: finished
dokumentace: documentation
dokumentární: documentary
dolní ořízka: bottom edge, lower
   edge
domácí: domestic
doplavné: shipping costs
doplněk: supplement
doplněné vydání: enlarged edition
doplnitý: completed
doplňkový(é) sešit(y): supplementary part(s)
doplňkový(é) svazek(svazky): supplementary volume(s)
doplňky: supplements
dopravený: forwarded
doslov: epilogue
doslovný: literal
doslovný překlad: literal
   translation
dostatečně: sufficiently
dostatečný: sufficient
dovoz: import
dovozní právo: import regulations
dražba: auction
dřevěný: wooden
dřevořez(y): woodcut(s)
dřevoryt(y): wood engraving(s)
druhý: second, other
druhý titul knihy: bastard title
dubleta(y): duplicate(s),
   duplicate copy(ies)
duplikát(y): duplicate(s),
   duplicate copy(ies)
dva: two
dvacátý: twentieth
dvacet: twenty
dvanáct(ý): twelve(twelfth)
dvanácterka: duodecimo

dvojí: double
dvojjazyčný: bilingual
dvojnásobný(é) opis(y):
    duplicate(s), duplicate copy(ies)
dvoubarevný: bicolored
dvouměsíčník: bimonthly
dvouročník: biennial
dvousloupcový: in double
    columns

edice: edition(s)
ediční plán: publishing plan
email: enamel
encyklopedie: encyclopedia(s)
epigraf(y): epigraph(s)
epilog: epilogue
epocha: epoch
erb(y): coat(s) of arms,
    escutcheon(s)
exemplář(e): copy(ies), issue(s)

faksimilovaný(é) přetisk(y):
    facsimile reproduction(s)
faktura(y): invoice(s)
falcování: folding
falsifikát(y): falsification(s),
    forgery(ies)
fascikl(y): fascicule(s)
fiktivní autor: fictitious author
filigránový: filigreed
foliant(y): large volume(s),
    folio(s)
folie: gold leaf
formát: format
fotografický otisk: photographic
    copy
fotografický přetisk: photographic
    facsimile, photoprint
fotografie: photograph(s)
fotogravura(y): photoengraving(s)
fotokopie: photocopy(ies)
fotolitografie: photolithography
fotostat(y): photostat(s)
francouzský: French
franko: postpaid
fysická mapa: physical map

geografický: geographic
glosa(y): gloss(es)
glosář(e): glossary(ies)
gotické písmo: Gothic script,
    Old English
grafický(é) list(y): engraving(s),
    print(s)
grafika(y): graphic art; engrav-
    ing(s), print(s)

hadrový papír: rag paper
hedvábí: silk
hedvábný papír: silk paper
heliogravura: heliogravure,
    phototypography
heslo(a): catchword(s), heading(s)
hezký: handsome
hladká(é) ořízka(y): cut edge(s),
    smooth edge(s)
hlava(y): chapter(s)
hlavní název: main title
hlavní názvy: main titles
hlavní redaktor: editor in chief
hlazený: polished
hledané: sought
hledání: search
hlubotisk(y): intaglio print(s)
hnědý: brown
hodnota: value, price
hojně: abundantly, copiously
hojný: abundant, copious
horní okraj stránky: head margin,
    top margin
horní ořízka: top edge
hřbet knihy: back, spine
hromadný: collective
hrubě: coarsely
hrubozrnný: rough-grained
hrubý: coarse

identický: identical
identifikace: identification
iluminace: illumination
ilustrace: illustration(s)
ilustrace v textu: illustrations in
    the text

ilustrátor: illustrator
ilustrovaná obálka: illustrated cover
ilustrované vydání: illustrated edition
ilustrovaný: illustrated
informace: information
iniciála(y): initial(s), initial letter(s)
inkoustem: in ink
inkunábule: incunabulum(a)
interpretace: interpretation
italský: Italian

jaro: Spring
jasně: clearly
jasnost: clarity
jasný: light, clear
jazyk(y): language(s)
jeden: one
jedenáct(ý): eleven(th)
jedině: singly
jediné vydání: only edition
jedinečný: unique
jediný: only, single
jednobarevné vyobrazení: monochrome illustration
jednosvazkové dílo: one-volume work
jednosvazkový výbor z děl: selected works in one volume
jednotlivé(á) číslo(a): separate issue(s)
jelenice: buckskin
jemnost: fineness, rarity
jemný: fine, rare
jemný mušelín: muslin
jen: solely
ještě nevyšlo: not yet published
jízvy: scars
jmenný rejstřík: index of persons
jméno: name, appellation
jméno původce: name of author
jubilejní sborník: festschrift, jubilee publication
jubilejní vydání: jubilee edition

k disposici: available, at the disposal
kalendář(e): calendar(s)
kaligrafie: calligraphy
kaliko: calico
kamej: cameo
kamenotisk: lithograph
kamzičí kůže: chamois skin
kanafas: canvas
kancionál(y): hymnal(s)
kapesní atlas: pocket atlas
kapesní formát: pocket-size
kapesní slovník: pocket dictionary
kapesní vydání: pocket edition
kapitálka: headband
kapitola(y): chapter(s)
karikatura(y): caricature(s)
kartografie: cartography
karton: pasteboard
kartuš(e): cartouche(s)
kaštanová barva: chestnut-colored, maroon
katalog: catalog
každoroční: yearly
každý: each, every
klasický: classic
kniha(y): book(s)
knihkupec: bookseller, book dealer
knihkupectví: bookstore
knihomol: bookworm
knihopisné poznámky: annotations
knihovna: library
knihovnice: woman librarian(s)
knihovník(níci): librarian(s)
knihtiskárna: printing house, printing office
knihvazač: bookbinder
knihvazačství: bookbinding
knížečka(y): booklet(s)
knížka(y): small book(s), booklet(s)
knižní aukce: book auction
knižní obchod: book trade
knižní výzdoba: book decoration
knižní značka(y): bookplate(s), *ex libris*
kolace: collation

kolektiv autorů: collective authorship, joint authors

kolektivní dílo: collective work, joint work

kolem: about, approximately

kolibří kniha(y): miniature book(s)

kolofon: colophon

kolorování: illumination

kombinovaná vazba: half binding, half-bound

kombinovaný: combined

komentář(e): commentary(ies)

komentované vydání: annotated edition

komise: committee

kompilace: compilation(s)

kompilátor: compiler

kompilovaný: compiled

komplet: complete set

konec: conclusion, end

konference: conference

konfiskované vydání: seized edition

konkordance: concordance

konspekt: outline, syllabus

kopie: copy, transcript

korduán: cordovan

korigovaný: corrected

koutové ozdoby: corner pieces

kování: clasps, metal ornaments

kožená vazba: leather binding

koženka: leatherette, imitation leather

kozina: kidskin

kozinka: goatskin

kozlí kůže: kidskin

krása: beauty

krásná literatura: belles lettres

krásně: beautifully

krásný: beautiful

krasopis: calligraphy

krasopisec: calligrapher

krasopisný: calligraphic

krátce: concisely

krátký: short, brief

křehký: brittle

kreslicí papír: bristol board

křídový papír: glazed paper, glossy paper, coated stock

křivý: crooked

kronika(y): chronicle(s)

kuriosa: curiosa

kursiva: cursive, italics

kůže: leather

laciný: cheap, inexpensive

lakuna: lacuna

latinisované jmeno: Latinized name

latinka: roman type

legenda(y): legend(s), caption(s)

lepenka: cardboard, pasteboard

lepenková vazba: hard cover

lept(y): etching(s)

leptaný: etched

leštěný: burnished

léta: years

leták(y): broadside(s), handbill(s)

léto: summer

letopis(y): annals, chronicle(s)

levné vydání: cheap edition

lichá(é) stránka(y): odd page(s)

lidové vydání: popular edition

lilie: fleur-de-lys

linka(y): line(s)

linkovaný: lined

lis: press

list(y): leaf(ves), sheet(s), folio(s)

lístek: leaflet

listina(y): document(s)

listina sepsaná vlastní rukou: holograph

lístkové vydání: loose-leaf edition

lit. *see* literatura

literární dílo(a): literary work(s)

literární pozůstalost: work unpublished at the death of a writer

literatura: literature

literatura pro mládež: juvenile literature

litografie: lithography

lučavka: aquafortis, nitric acid

maďarský: Hungarian
magazin(y): magazine(s)
malebný: picturesque
malý: little, small
mapa(y): map(s), chart(s)
mapa světa: world map
marginálie: marginal notes,
   marginalia
marokén: morocco leather
masové vydání: popular edition
mastná skvrna: grease spot
měd': copper
mědiryt(y): copperplate
   illustration(s)
mědirytectví: chalcography, line
   engraving
mědirytina(y): copperplate
   engraving(s)
měditiskařství: copperplate
   printing
měkký: soft
memoary: memoirs
menší: less
měsíčně: monthly
měsíční zpráva: monthly report
měsíčník: monthly publication,
   monthly
mezera(y): gap(s)
mezi: among, between
meziřádkový: interlinear
mikrofilm: microfilm
mikrofilmová kniha: book on
   microfilm
mikrofilmování: microfilming
miniaturní kniha(y): miniature
   book(s)
ministerstvo: ministry
místní vydání: local edition
místo tisku: place of printing
místo vydání: place of publication
mistrovské dílo: masterpiece
mnohobarevný: polychrome
mnohobarvý: multicolored
mnohojazyčný: multilingual
modernizovaný: modernized
modrý: blue
monografie: monograph(s)

monumentální: monumental
mosaikový: mosaic
mosaz: brass
mp. *see* mapa
mramorovaná ořízka: marbled
   edges
mramorovaný: grained
mramorovaný papír: marbled
   paper
mylně: erroneously
mylný: erroneous

na novo: anew
na pokračování: to be continued
na př. *see* příklad
na příklad: for example
na rubu: verso
na skladě: in stock
na ukázku: on approval
na žádost: by request
nabídka(y): offer(s), tender(s)
načervenalý: reddish
nad: above
nadepsání: superscription
nadmíru: exceedingly
nadmíru zachovalý: in a good
   state of preservation
nadpis(y): superscript(s);
   caption(s)
nahnědlý: brownish
nahoře: above
náhradní výtisk(y): replacement
   copy(ies)
náklad(y): edition(s)
nakladatel: publisher
nakladatelská obálka: publisher's
   cover, original cover
nakladatelská sbírka: publisher's
   series
nakladatelská vazba: publisher's
   binding
nakladatelská značka: publisher's
   mark, signet
nakladatelské družstvo: publishing
   cooperative
nakladatelské knihkupectví: publishing and bookselling firm

nakladatelské údaje: imprint
nakladatelství: publishing house,
  publishing firm
nakupený: cumulated
nákupní cena: purchase price
naléhavě: urgently
naléhavý: urgent
nálepka(y): label(s)
nápis(y): inscription(s)
naprosto rozdílný: disparate
národní bibliografie: national
  bibliography(ies)
nárožnice: corner(s)
následovně: consecutive
následující: following
nastávající: imminent
nástin: outline, layout
naučný slovník: encyclopedic
  dictionary
nazelenalý: greenish
název: title
název kapitoly: chapter title,
  chapter heading
název na vazbě: binder's title
název sbírky: series title
název série: series title
název svazku: volume title
nažloutlý: yellowish
nazvaný: entitled
názvy: titles
neautorisované vydání: unauthorized edition
neautorisovaný překlad: unauthorized translation
nečíslovaná(é) stránka(y): unnumbered page(s)
nečíslovaný: unnumbered
nečíslovaný(é) list(y): unnumbered
  leaf(ves)
nečitelný: illegible
nedatovaný: undated
nedokončené vydání: unfinished
  edition
nedokončený: unfinished
nedostatečný: defective,
  unsatisfactory
nedostatky: defects

nedotčený: intact
nehlazený: unpolished
nejasný: blurred, not clear
nejlepší: best
nejnižší: lowest
nejnovější číslo: latest issue
  (of a periodical)
nejpřednější: foremost
někde jinde: elsewhere
neklížený papír: unsized paper
několik málo: a few
německý: German
nemožný: impossible
není k disposici: not available
neobyčejný: uncommon, unusual
neocenitelný: invaluable, priceless
neokrášlený: undecorated
neoprávněný: unauthorized
neoříznutá kniha: uncut book
neoříznutý okraj stránky: uncut
  edge, untrimmed edge
neozdobený: unadorned
nepatrný: diminutive
nepoškozená kniha: a book in good
  condition
nepoškozený: undamaged
nepotřebný výtisk: surplus copy
nepravý: imitation, spurious
nepřetržité číslování: consecutive
  numbering
nepřetržité stránkování: consecutive pagination
neprůhledný: opaque
nerevidovaný: unrevised
nerozdílný: inseparable
nerozřezaná kniha: book with
  leaves uncut
nesčíslný: innumerable
nesešitý: unstitched
nespárovaný: unmatched
nespočtený: unnumbered
nestránkováno: unpaginated
netto: net price
neúplný: incomplete, odd
neupravený: untrimmed
neúřední: unofficial
neužitý: unused

nevázaná kniha: unbound
nevydaná díla: unpublished works
nevydaný: unpublished
nezaskvrněný: spotless
nezkrácený: unabridged
nezměněné vydání: unchanged
   edition
neznámý: unknown
nikdy: never
notace: notation(s)
nové vydání: new edition, reissue
novela(y): novelette(s), short
   novel(s)
nový: new, recent

oba: both
obal(y): book jacket(s), wrapper(s)
obalená kniha: book with jacket
obálka: cover, envelope
obálka knihy: cover of a book
obálkový název: cover title
obchod knihkupecký: book trade
obchodní: commercial
obchodník: dealer
obdélný: oblong
obkličitý: encircled
obmezený: limited
obnovený: renewed
obrácený: obverse
obratný: skillful
obraz(y): picture(s), illustration(s)
obrázek: illustration
obrázková kniha: picture book
obrázky: illustrations
obrazová příloha: illustrated
   supplement
obsah: table of contents, summary
obsahovati: comprise
obsažný: condensed, comprehensive
obtížný: difficult
obyčejný: ordinary, usual
ocelorytina(y): steel engraving(s)
ocenění: appraisal, evaluation
ochotník: amateur
očividně: apparently
od začátku do konce: cover-to-
   cover, from top to bottom

odbarvený: discolored
odděleně: separately
oddělený: separate, detached
oddíl(y): section(s), division(s)
odhad: estimate, appraisal
odkaz(y): reference(s)
odložený: delayed
odpovědný redaktor: editor-in-
   charge
odříznouti: cut away, cut off
odstavce: paragraphs, items
odstavec: paragraph, item
odtrhnouti: torn off
ohebný: flexible
ohnutý roh listu: dog-eared
ohořelý: burned, scorched
okraj(e): margin(s)
okrašlený: embellished
oktáv: octavo
omezený náklad: limited edition
opatřený komentářem: commented
opatrný: discreet
opětné vydání: reissue
opis(y): copy(ies)
opotřebovaná kniha: used book,
   worn book
oprava: correction; repair,
   restoration
opravené vydání: revised edition
opravený: corrected
orig. *see* originál
originál: original
ořízka(y): edge(s)
oříznutá kniha: trimmed book
oříznutý okraj stránky: trimmed
   edge
oslabení: weakening
oslabený: weakened
oslí ucho: dog-eared
osm: eight
osmdesát: eighty
osmdesátý: eightieth
osmerka: octavo
osmnáct(ý): eighteen(th)
osmý: eighth
osobní: personal

osobní jméno: first name, given
name
otisk(y): copy(ies), print(s)
otrhaný: ragged
otupený: dulled
ovčina: sheepskin
ověření: verification
ověřiti: authenticate
ozdoba(y): decoration(s),
ornament(s)
ozdobený: ornate
ozdobné: fancy
označení: designation, mark
oznámení: announcement, notice
oznamovatel(e): bulletin(s),
gazette(s)

padělek: forgery, falsification
padesát(ý): fifty(ieth)
palcové písmeno: uncial letters
památná kniha: commemorative
volume
paměti: memoirs, recollections
pamflet(y): lampoon(s)
papír: paper
paragraf(y): paragraph(s),
paragraph mark(s)
pastelová kresba: pastel drawing
patisk(y): counterfeit edition(s),
forgery(ies)
patitul: bastard title, half title
patnáct(ý): fifteen(th)
pátý: fifth
pečet': seal
pečetní vosk: sealing wax
pěkně: neatly
pěkný: neat
pergamen: parchment
pergamenová vazba: vellum
binding
pergamenový papír: parchment
paper, vellum paper
periodicita: frequency
periodicky: serially
periodika: periodicals
periodikum: periodical
péro: pen

perokresba(y): pen and ink
drawing(s)
perová vazba: loose-leaf binding
pestrobarevný: varicolored
pevná cena: fixed price
pět: five
písemnictví: literature
písmeno: letter, type
písmo: writing, handwriting
plachtovina: sailcloth
plagiát: plagiarism
plastický: plastic
plátěná vazba: cloth binding
plátno: cloth
platný: available
plavý: fawn-colored
plesnivý: washed, mildewed
plíseň: mildew, mold
plnomocný: authoritative
plný prachu: dusty
plochý: flat
plochý hřbet: flat back
ploskořezba: bas-relief
po smrti: posthumous
po sobě: successive
počet stránek: number of pages
počet svazků: number of volumes
pochybný: dubious
pod názvem: under the title
podepsaný: signed
podle pořadí let: chronological
podložený: superimposed
podnázev: subtitle
podobizna(y): portrait(s)
podobný: alike, similar
pododíl(y): subdivision(s)
podpis(y): signature(s)
podrobný: detailed
podtrhávati: to underline
podzim: Autumn, Fall
poesie: poetry
pohádka(y): fairy tale(s)
pohádka o vílách: fairy tale
pojednání: treatise(s), essay(s)
pokračovací dílo: publication
appearing in parts, continuation
pokračování: continuation, sequel

pokradmý: clandestine
polemika: polemical writing, polemics
polokožená vazba: half-leather binding
pololetně: semiannually
polopergamenová vazba: half-vellum binding
poloplátěná vazba: half-cloth binding, half-linen
polotýdenní: semiweekly
poloúřední tiskovina: semiofficial publication
polský: Polish
poměrný: comparative
popis: description
popisný: descriptive
populární: popular
pořadí: sequence, arrangement
porfyr: porphyry
porovnání: collation
porovnatý: collated
portrét(y): portrait(s)
poškodit: to damage
poškození: damage, injury
poškozený výtisk: damaged copy, defective
poskvrněný: speckled
poskvrnitý: blurred
poslední: last, latest
poslední autorisované vydání: definitive edition
poslední vydání: last edition, latest edition
posmrtné vydání: posthumous edition
pošta: mail
poštovné: mailing charges, postage
potištěná stránka: printed page
potřebný: necessary, needed
potvrzen: confirmed
potvrzení: confirmation
pouzdro: case, box
povídka(y): tale(s), short story(ies)
povinný výtisk: legal deposit copy
požádání: demand

požadavek: desiderata
pozn. *see* poznámka
poznámka(y): note(s), footnote(s)
poznámka(y) na okraji: marginal note(s)
poznámka(y) pod čarou: footnote(s)
poznámka(y) vydavatelova: publisher's note
pozoruhodný: noticeable
práce: work(s), transaction(s)
Praha: Prague
pramen(y): source(s)
právě vyšlo: just published
právo nakladatelské: copyright
prázdný list: flyleaf
před názvem: before the title
předběžná cena: probable price, approximate price
předběžné vydání: preliminary edition
předběžný: preliminary
předešlý: anterior
předmluva: foreword, preface
přednázev: bastard title, half title
předplacení: advance payment, subscription
předplatitel(é): subscriber(s)
předplatné: subscription payment
předpokládaný autor: probable author
předposlední: penultimate
přehled(y): survey(s), outline(s)
přehlédnuté vydání: revised edition
překlad(y): translation(s)
překladatel(é): translator(s)
přeložiti: to translate
přemístění: rearrangement
přenosný: portable
přepis: transcription, transliteration
přepracované dílo: reworked book
přepracované vydání: rewritten edition
přepracování: rewriting, adaptation

přepychová vazba: deluxe binding
přepychové vydání: deluxe edition
přesně: minutely
přesný: minute, exact
přestalo vycházet: ceased publication, publication completed
přestavění: rearrangement
přetisk(y): reprint(s)
přetisk zakázán: copyright
převázaný: rebound, recased
přibližný: approximate
příjemný: pleasing
příjmení: surname
příl. *see* příloha
přílišný: excessive
příloha(y): supplement(s), appendix(es)
přímý: straight
přípisek: postscript
příručka(y): handbook(s), reference book(s)
příruční knížka: textbook
příruční slovník(y): pocket dictionary(ies)
přísně: exactly
příspěvek: contribution
příspěvky: contributions
přistřižený: cropped
přítažlivý: attractive
přívazek: bound together with
privilej: charter; privilege
pro služební potřebu: for official use
prodej: sale
prodejní cena: retail price, catalog price
proložený: interleaved
proslov: prologue
proslulý: famous, renowned
prospekt: prospectus
prostřední: mediocre
prostý: simple
protilehlý: opposite
proza: prose
prozatimní vazba: temporary binding

prozatimní vydání: provisional edition
průhledný: transparent
průměr: average
průsvitka: paper mark, watermark
průvodce: guidebook, directory
první: first
první jméno: forename
první vydání: first edition, first printing
prvotisk(y): incunabulum(a)
půlročník: semiannual publication
puncovaná(é) rytina(y): stippled engraving(s)
půvabný: charming
původ: origin, provenience
původce(i): author(s)
původní: original, authentic
původní název: original title
původní vydání: original edition

rabat: discount
řada: series, set
ražení: tooling, embossing
razítko: stamp, signet
razítko bibliotékařské: library stamp
recense: review
recensní výtisk: review copy
redakce: editing, editorial office
redakční: editorial
redaktor: editor
redigoval: edited by
referát: abstract, report
rejstřík(y): index(es), list(s)
rekreační literatura: light reading
reorganisovaný: reorganized
reprodukce: reproduction(s), copy(ies)
restaurace: restoration(s)
resumé: résumé, synopsis
revidované vydání: revised edition
revise: revision
revue: review, critique

řezaná kožená vazba: goffered-
  leather binding
řídký: rare
roč. *see* ročně
ročenka(y): yearbook(s), annual(s)
ročně: yearly, annually
ročník(y): annual volume(s)
rodové jméno: family name,
  last name
rok(y): year(s)
rok tisku: year of imprint, date of
  printing
rok vydání: year of publication,
  date of publication
román(y): novel(s)
romanopisec(pisci): novelist(s)
rovný: plain, smooth
roz. *see* rozebráno
rozebraná kniha: out-of-print
  book
rozebráno: out-of-print
rozedraný: tattered
rozkošný: delightful
rozličný: different
rozměr knihy: size of book, format
rozměr listu: size of leaf
rozmnoženo: mimeographed copy,
  processed copy
rozmnožený strojopis: mimeographed copy, processed copy
rozřezané knihy: cut pages
rozřezané stránky: tear sheets
rozsah: extent, scope
rozšířené vydání: enlarged edition
rozšířený: enlarged
rubrika(y): rubric(s)
ruční papír: hand-laid paper
rudý: red
rukopis(y): manuscript(s)
rukovět'(i): handbook(s),
  outline(s)
rumunský: Romanian
ruský: Russian
různé: miscellaneous, diverse
rydlo: drypoint
rytci: engravers
rytec: engraver

rytectví: engraving
rytina(y): print(s), engraving(s)
rytý drahokam: intaglio

s názvem: entitled
safián: crushed morocco
šagrinová kůže: shagreen
samet: velvet
satinový papír: glazed paper
sběratel(é): collector(s)
sbírka(y): collection(s), series
sbírka knih: book collection
sbírka ve sbírce: subseries
sbírka(y) zákonů: collection(s)
sborník: collective work,
  commemorative volume
schází: missing, wanting
schválené vydání: approved
  edition
schválení: approval
schváleno k tisku: approved for
  publication
sebrané spisy: collected works
šedesát(ý): sixty(ieth)
šedivý: gray
sedm: seven
sedmdesát(ý): seventy(ieth)
sedmnáct(ý): seventeen(th)
sedmý: seventh
šedý: gray
sekce: section(s)
seřazení: arrangement
série: series
sešit(y): issue(s), part(s),
  section(s)
šest: six
sestavovatel: compiler
šestnáct(ý): sixteen(th)
šestý: sixth
seznam(y): list(s), index(es)
seznam ilustrací: list of
  illustrations
seznam tiskových omylů: errata
  list
seznam vyobrazení: list of illustrations, table of illustrations
signální výtisk: advance copy

signatury: signatures
signet: printer's device, signet
simulovaný: simulated
šířka: width
šířka knihy: width of a book
šíti: sewing, stitching
škatulka: box
skizza: sketch
sklad knih: bookstore, book stock
škoda: damage
školní vydání: school edition
skonfiskovaný: suppressed
skoro: almost
skvostný: costly, superb
skvrnitý: stained
skvrny: stains
slabikář: primer, first reader
slabý: slight, weak
slaměná: straw-colored
sleva: discount
sloupec: column
slovesnost: literature
slovník(y): dictionary(ies),
    lexicon(s)
smetanový: cream-colored
smíšený: miscellaneous
souběžný: parallel
souborný název: collective title
souborný rejstřík: general index,
    composite index
současný: contemporary, current
soudobý: contemporary, current
souhlasný: suitable
souhrn: summary, résumé
soukromý tisk: privately printed
soupis(y): list(s), roster(s)
souvislý: continuous
španělský: Spanish
speciální: special
špinavý: dirty
spirální: spiral
spisek: opuscule
spisovatel(é): writer(s)
spisovatel životospisů: biographer
spisovatelka(y): woman writer(s)
spodek: bottom

spodní okraj stránky: bottom of
    a page, lower margin
spoluautor: coauthor, joint author
spolupráce: cooperation,
    collaboration
spolupracovnictví: collaboration
spolupracovník(níci): collabo-
    rator(s)
spolupůsobení: cooperation
správnost: correctness
správný: correct
sr. *see* srovnej
srnčí kůže: doeskin
srovnej: to compare
starý: aged, old
starý(é) tisk(y): old print(s),
    old book(s)
stejný: uniform, equal
štíhlý: tall
štírci knihoví: bookworms
štírek knihový: bookworm
štítek: label, lettering piece
štítky: labels, lettering pieces
sto: one hundred
stoletý: centennial
str. *see* strana
strakatě: mottling
strakatý: mottled
strana(y): page(s)
stránka(y): page(s)
stránkování: pagination
střed: center
středisko: center
stříbrný: silver
strojopis: typescript
stručný: concise
stručný výtah: compendium
studie: essays, studies
stý: one-hundredth
subskribent(i): subscriber(s)
subskripce: subscription(s)
subskripční cena: subscription
    price
surový: crude
sv. *see* svazek
svazečky: fascicles
svazek: volume, tome, fascicle

svazky: volumes, tomes, fascicles
světlo: bright
synopse: synopsis
synoptický: synoptic
systematický rejstřík: classified
 index

tabulky: tables
tajný(é) tisk(y): clandestine
 publication(s)
technický: technical
tečkovaný: dotted
teletina: calfskin
tenký: thin
textový: textual
též: also
thesa(y): dissertation(s), thesis(es)
tisíc: thousand
tisk: print, printing
tisk z hloubky: intaglio print
tisk z výšky: relief print
tiskárna: printing establishment
tiskařská značka: printer's mark,
 printer's device
tiskařské údaje: imprint
tiskařský lis: letterpress
tištěno jako rukopis: privately
 printed
titul(y): title(s)
titulní list: title page
titulní stránka: title page
titulní vinětka: headpiece
tlustý: thick
tmavý: dark
transkripce: transcription
transliterace: transliteration
třetí: third
tři: three
třicátý: thirtieth
třicet: thirty
třináct(ý): thirteen(th)
třísloupcový: in three columns
tržní cena: current price
tučné písmo: boldface type
tuhé plátno: buckram
tuzemský: domestic
tužka: pencil

týdeník: weekly
typografie: typography, printing

ubývání: decrease
učebnice: textbook(s), manual(s)
ukazatel(é): register(s), index(es)
ukázkové(á) číslo(a): sample
 issue(s)
umělecká literatura: fiction
umělecké vydání: art edition
umělý: artificial
unikát(y): unique copy(ies)
unikátní: unique
úplně: completely
úplné nové a revidované vydání: a
 new edition thoroughly revised
úplné vydání: complete edition
úplný: complete, thorough
úprava knihy: book decoration
úpravně: elegantly
úpravný: elegant
úřední oznamovatel: gazette
úřední tiskovina(y): official
 publication(s)
úřední vydání: official edition
úryvek: fragment
úspěšná kniha: best-seller
uspořádání: arrangement, order
ústřední: central
utrhačný: libelous
úvaha(y): dissertation(s),
 thesis(es)
úvod: introduction, foreword
úvodný: introductory
užitečný: useful
užitý: used

v: in
v. *see* viz
v pořádku abecedním:
 alphabetically
v.t. *see* viz též
v tisku: in press, in print
vadný: výtisk: defective copy,
 damaged copy
vady: blemishes
varianta(y): variant(s)

váz. *see* vázaný
vázaná kniha: bound book
vázaný: bound
vazba: binding
vazba s dřevěnými deskami:
    wooden boards
vazba z telecí kůže: calfskin
    binding
vážný: serious
včetně: including
vědecká(é) společnost(i): learned
    society(ies)
vědecké(á) pojednání: treatise(s),
    study(ies)
vedlejší název: alternative title
vedoucí redaktor: editor in chief
velikost: size, format
velikost knihy: size of book,
    format
velín: vellum
velké(á) písmeno(a): capital
    letter(s)
velkolepě: magnificently
velkolepý: magnificent, splendid
velkoobchod: wholesale
velký: large
velmi vážený: highly esteemed
věnovací výtisk: presentation
    copy
věnování: dedication
věnovaný: dedicated
vepřová kůže: pigskin
vepřovice: pigskin
věrný: faithful
věstník(y): bulletin(s), journal(s)
více nevyšlo: no longer published,
    all published
vícebarevná(é) ilustrace: colored
    illustration(s)
vícebarevné(á) vyobrazení: poly-
    chrome illustration(s)
vícebarevný: multicolored,
    polychrome
vícejazyčné dílo: multilingual work
vícesvazkový: in several volumes,
    multivolume
viněta(y): vignette(s)

viz: see
viz na rubu: see verso
viz též: see also
vkusný: tasteful
vlastní životopis: autobiography
vlastník: owner
vlastním nákladem: published by
    the author
vlastnoruční podpis(y): auto-
    graph(s)
vlhkost: humidity, moisture
vlhký: damp
vlnitý: wavy
vložené zápisky: insertions
vložka(y): insert(s), inset(s)
vnitřně: internally
vnitřní: inner, internal
vodová barva: watercolor
vodové znamení: watermark
vodoznak(y): watermark(s)
volný: loose
volný list: loose-leaf
volný překlad: free translation
volný výtisk: free copy
vpisek: interpolation
vročení: date of imprint, year of
    issue
všední: common
všeobecná díla: general works
všeobecně: universally
vsutý: intercalated
vtlačený nápis: tooling, embossing
výběr: selection
vybledlé: faded
výbor: selections, anthology
výborný: distinguished
vybrané spisy: selected works
vybraný: choice, exquisite
vyčerpávající bibliografie: com-
    prehensive bibliography
vycházeti: to appear, to be
    published
vyčistiti: to expurgate
vyčnělý: extant
vyd. *see* vydání
vydal: edited by
vydání: edition(s)

vydání pro mládež: edition for children

vydání s poznámkami: variorum edition

vydávaný: published by

vydavatel(é): publisher(s)

vydavatelské právo: right of publication, copyright

vydavatelský arch: publisher's sheet, publisher's signature

vydavatelství: publishing house, publishing firm

vyhlazení: excision

vyhlazený: excised

vyjde v nejbližší době: to appear soon

výjimečný: exceptional

vyjmouti: exclude

vykládati: inlay

vymazání: deletion

vymazati: delete, obliterate

vynechání: omission(s)

vyobrazení: illustration(s)

vyplaceně: postpaid

vypouklá práce: embossing

výroční den: anniversary

výroční zpráva(y): annual report(s)

vyšívání: embroidery

výška knihy: height of the book

vyškrabaný: crossed out, deleted

vyškrtnoutí: erase

vyškrtnutí: erasure

výstava: exhibition

vystrčiti: eliminate

vysvětl. *see* vysvětlivka

vysvětlení: comment

vysvětlivka(y): footnote(s), explanatory note(s)

výt. *see* výtah

výtah: abstract, abridgment

vytečkovaný: stippled

vytisk(y): copy(ies), issue(s)

vytrhnutý: torn out

výzdoba knihy: book decorations

vzácné knihy: rare books

vzácný: precious

vzácný(é) tisk(y): rare book(s)

vzpomínky: memoirs

zabarvení: coloring

zabavené vydání: confiscated edition

zachovalá kniha: in good condition, as new

zachovaný: preserved

zachovávání: conservation

zachovávati: conserving

žádaný: desired

záhlaví: heading(s), caption(s)

zahraniční: foreign

zahrnuje: including

zahrnutý: included

zakázané: forbidden

zakázané knihy: prohibited books, censored books

zakázané vydání: banned edition

zákoník: codex

zaniklý časopis: discontinued periodical

zápisky: memoirs

zaplacení: payment

zařazovati: to insert, interpolate

žargon: jargon

zářící: brilliant

zaskvrněný: spotted

zašpiněný: dirtied

zastaralý: antiquated, out of date

zastavený(é) časopis(y): discontinued periodical(s)

zastaviti: discontinue

zatemniti: darken

závěr: conclusion

závěrná vignetta: tailpiece

zavříti: conclude

záznam(y): entry(ies), item(s)

zaznamenati: quote

zcela: altogether, entirely, wholly

zcela přepracované vydání: completely revised edition

zdarma: no charge, free

zdobící: decorative

zejména: namely

zeměpisný: geographical

zhoršiti: deteriorate
zima: Winter
životopis(y): biography(ies)
životopisec: biographer
životopisný slovník: biographical
　dictionary
zkomolení: mutilation
zkonfiskovaný: confiscated
zkrácené vydání: abridged edition
zkrácení: abridgment
zkratka(y): abbreviation(s),
　contraction(s)
zlacení: gilding
zlatiti: to gild
zlato: gold
zlatý: golden
zlepšený: improved
zlomek: fragment
zlomkovitý: fragmentary
zlomky: fragments
žlutý: yellow
zmačkaný: crumpled
značka(y): mark(s)

značně: considerably, extensively
značný: considerable, extensive
znak(y): mark(s), sign(s)
znamenitý: excellent
znovu otisknouti: to reprint
zodpovědný: responsible
zpěvník(y): songbook(s)
zprac. *see* zpracovaný
zpracování: arrangement,
　adaptation
zpracovaný: elaborated
zpráva: report, account
zprávy: proceedings
zrevidovaný: revised
ztracený: lost
ztráta: loss
žurnalista: journalist
žurnalistika: journalism
zvláště jemný: superfine
zvláštní otisk(y): special reprint(s),
　offprint(s)
zvláštní vydání: special edition
zvláštnosti: curiosa, specialties

Dano-Norwegian

a. *see* andre
aaben: open
aar: year
aarg. *see* aargang
aargang: year, volume
aarh. *see* aarhundrede
aarhundrede(r): century(ies)
aarlig: annual
aarsberetning(er): annual report(s)
abonnement: subscription
adskillige: several
aegte bind: raised bands
aeldre: older, earlier
aeldste: oldest
aendrede: changed, revised
aendret: changed, revised
aeseløre: dog-ears
aeske: box
afbildn. *see* afbildning
afbildning(er): illustration(s),
    picture(s)
afbleget: faded
afbrudt: interrupted, irregular
afd. *see* afdeling
afdeling(er): part(s), section(s),
    volume(s)
afhandling(er): essay(s), paper(s),
    treatise(s)
aflang: elongated
afpudset: trimmed
afrevet: torn off, torn out
afrundet: dulled, rounded
afskåret: cut off, excised
afskrabning(er): scratch(es),
    chafing
afslidt: dulled, rounded

afsluttet: concluded, completed
afsnit: section(s), paragraph(s)
aftryk: printing(s), edition(s)
ajourfører: modernizer,
    modernizing
aktmaessig: documentary
aktmessig: documentary
aktstykke(r): document(s)
akvarel(ler): watercolor(s)
akvatinta: aquatint
alle: all
alle slags: all sorts of
alm. *see* almindelig
almanak: almanac
almenfattelig: popular
almindelig: common, ordinary
alminnelig: common, ordinary
alt det udkomne: all published
alt i alt: altogether
alt som udkom: all published
alt som utkom: all published
alt udk. *see* alt udkomne
alt udkomne: all published
amatør: amateur, collector
amatørbind: amateur binding
anastatisk: anastatic
and. *see* andre
anden: second, other
andre: others
anerkendt(e): recognized
anerkjent: recognized
anetavle: genealogical table
anføre: mention, indicate
anført: listed, indicated
angitt(e): indicated
angivne: indicated

anmaerkning(er): note(s)
anmeldelse(r): review(s)
anmerkning(er): note(s)
anmode: inquire, request
anmodning(er): request(s)
anmrkn. *see* anmerkning
annoncer: advertisements
annonser: advertisements
anonym: anonymous
antaget forfatternavn: pseudonym
antal: number
antall: number
antikva skrift: roman type
antikvar: antiquarian book dealer
antikvariat: antiquarian dealer's
  shop
antikvarisk: used, secondhand
antologi: anthology
anvisning: instruction
aquatinte: aquatint
aquatintstik: aquatint(s),
  etching(s)
år: year
arabesk: arabesque
arb. *see* arbeid
arbeid(er): work(s)
årbog(bøger): yearbook(s)
årg. *see* årgang
årgang: year, annual volume
århr. *see* århundrede
århundrede(r): century(ies)
ark: quire(s), signature(s), sheet(s)
arkiv: archives
arksignatur: signature
årstal: year
årstallet: year
artikler: articles
association-exsemplar: association
  copy
atlasbind: atlas volume(s)
åtte(nde): eight(h)
atten(de): eighteen(th)
auka: augmented
auktion: auction sale
autograf: autograph, signature
autotypi(er): halftone engraving(s)
avbildende: showing, representing

avbildn. *see* avbildning
avbildning(er): illustration(s),
  picture(s)
avd. *see* avdeling
avdeling: part, section
avhandling(er): essay(s), treatise(s)
avis(er): newspaper(s)
avisanmeldelse(r): newspaper
  review(s)
avissaertrykk: reprint from
  newspaper
avisudklip: newspaper clipping(s)
avisutklipp: newspaper clipping(s)
avkl. *see* avklippet
avklippet: clipped off
avlang: oblong
avrevet: torn off
avslutning: conclusion, end
avslutte: conclude, complete
avsnitt: section(s)
avtrykk: printing(s), edition(s),
  impression(s)
avvikende: differing
avviker: differs, deviates

b. *see* begge, bind
baandvaerk: scrolls, tracery
baerer: contains
bag: back, rear
bagerst: at the very end
bagomsl. *see* bagomslag
bagomslag: back wrapper
bagside: verso
bak: back
bakerst: at the very end
bakgrunn: background
bakomsl. *see* bakomslag
bakomslag: back wrapper
bakperm: back cover
bakside: verso
balacron: a patented book cloth
bånd(s): tie(s)
banderole: lettered scroll
bare: only, somewhat
bastardskrift: bastard type
bearb. *see* bearbeidet, bearbejdet
bearbeidelse: adaptation

bearbeidet: revised, adapted
bearbejdelse: adaptation
bearbejdet: revised, adapted
bedårende: delightful
bedste: best
begge: both, either
begraenset: limited
begrenset: limited
begyndelse: beginning
begyndelseblad: preliminary
  leaf(ves)
begynnelse: beginning
beklippet: clipped, trimmed
bemaerkn. *see* bemaerkninger
bemaerkninger: notes, remarks
bemerkninger: notes, remarks
beregnet: calculated, intended
beretning: report
berømt: famous
berører: affects, touches
besk. *see* beskadiget, beskåret
beskaaret: trimmed, cropped
beskad. *see* beskadiget
beskadiget: damaged, broken
beskåret: trimmed, cropped
beskrevet: described
beskrivelse: description
beskrivende: descriptive
beskyttelsesbind: protective
  binding, protective cover
beslag: decoration
beslaglagt: confiscated, suppressed
besørget: executed
bestaar: consists
bestående av: consisting of
består: consists
beste: best
bestemt: destined
bestilling: order, ordering
betydelig: considerable, important
betydningsfuld(e): remarkable,
  significant
betydningsfuld(este): (most)
  remarkable
bevaret omslag: wrappers
  preserved, bound in
bib.b. *see* biblioteksbind

bibliofiludgave: deluxe edition
bibliofilutgave: deluxe edition
bibliogr. *see* bibliografi
bibliografi: bibliography
bibliografisk: bibliographic
bibliotek: library
bibliotekar: librarian
biblioteksbind: library binding
biblioteksstempel: library stamp
bidr. *see* bidrag
bidrag: contribution(s)
bidragyder(e): contributor(s)
bilag: annex, supplement
bill. *see* billede(r)
billedbilag: pictorial appendix,
  supplement
billedbog: picture book
billedbok: picture book
billede(r): illustration(s), picture(s)
billedfladen: picture leaves
billedraekke: series of pictures
billedside(r): picture page(s)
billedtavler: pictorial plates
billedtekst: caption, legend
billig: cheap, inexpensive
billigbok: paperback
bind: volume(s), binding
bindebånd: ties
bindfarge: color of binding
bindfarve: color of binding
bindflade(r): side(s) of binding
bindflate(r): side(s) of binding
bindnummer: volume number
bindside(r): side(s) of binding
bindsignatur: volume number
bindtitelblad: binding title page
biografi(er): biography(ies)
biografisk: biographical
bl. *see* blad, blank
bl.o. *see* blankt omslag
bl.omsl. *see* blankt omslag
blå: blue
blaa: blue
blad: leaf, sheet; journal
blade: leaves, sheets; journals
blader: leaves, sheets; journals
bladmotiv: page motif

bladornament(er): scrollwork
bladrand(e): page margin(s)
blaek: ink
blaekklat: ink stains
blaeknotater: notes in ink
blaekplet: ink spot
blågrått: blue-gray
blandede: mixed, miscellaneous
blandet: mixed, miscellaneous
blandinger: miscellany
blandt: among
blank(t): blank
blankt omslag: blank wrapper
blekk: ink
blekkflekk(er): ink spot(s)
blind-dekor: blind tooling
blindpreg. *see* blindpregning
blindpregning: blind tooling
blindpresning: blind tooling
blindpressing: blind tooling
blindtr. *see* blindtrykt
blindtryk: blind tooling
blindtrykk: blind tooling
blindtrykt: blind-stamped,
   blind-tooled
bll. *see* blade
blodt: blood red
blokbog: block book
blokka: blocks
blokker: blocks
blomster-dekor: floral design
blomstermotiv: floral design
blomsterornament: floral design
blyansnot. *see* blyansnotater
blyansnotater: pencil notations
blyant: pencil
blyantsindstreget: pencil scored
blyantsindstregn. *see*
   blyantsindstregning
blyantsindstregning(er): pencil
   scoring(s)
blyantsmaerke(r): pencil mark(s)
blyantsmrk. *see* blyantsmaerke
blyantsskrevet: penciled
blyantstrek(er): pencil mark(s)
blyantsunderstregninger: pencil
   underscoring

bog: book
bogbind: binding, bookbinding
bogbinder: binder
bogblok: body of a book
bogdekoration: book decoration
bogejermaerke(r): *ex libris*
bogelsker: booklover
bøger: books
bogform: format
bogfortegnelse: bibliography
bogh. *see* boghandel
boghandel: book trade; bookstore
boghandler(e): book dealer(s)
bogillustrationskunst: art of book
   illustration
bogkunstner: illustrator
bogladepris: list price
boglomme: pocket
bogmaleri: illumination
bogsamling: collection of books,
   private library; lot
bogstav(er): letter(s)
bogtr. *see* bogtryk, bogtrykt
bogtryk: print, printing; letterpress
bogtrykarbejde: example of
   printing
bogtrykker: printer
bogtrykkeri: printing firm
bogtrykkermaerke(r): printer's
   mark(s), device(s)
bogtrykt: printed
bogudsalg: book sale
bogudstyr: book design
bogven(ner): bibliophile(s)
bøjelig: flexible, limp
bok: book
bok-: for further compounds
   beginning with "bok" *see also*
   entries beginning with "bog"
bøker: books
bokmål: special form of literary
   Dano-Norwegian
bokmålsutgave: bokmål edition
boksamling: collection of books;
   lot
bokutsalg: book sale

bølgete: curled, warped
bord(er): border(s), decoration(s)
bordeauxfarvet: wine-colored
bordure: border, decorative
   framework
bordyre(r): border(s)
børnetegn. *see* børnetegning
børnetegning(er): child's scribbling
bortkommet: lost, gone
bortraderet: erased
bortradert: erased
bortset fra: apart from, except
bortskåret: cut off, excised
borttaget: obliterated
bøttepapir: hand-laid paper
bra: nice, fair
brandskade: burn
bred: wide
bredde: width
brev: letter, correspondence
breve: letters, correspondence
brever: letters, correspondence
brevfacsimile: facsimile letter
brevsamling: collection of letters
brevveksling: correspondence
brist: defect
brocheret: paperbound, in
   wrappers
brochure: pamphlet, booklet
broderet: embroidered
broget: varicolored
broncespaender: bronze clasps
bronzeret: reddish-brown
brosjert: paperbound, in wrappers
brosjyre(r): pamphlet(s)
brud: break
brugsspor: trace(s) of use
brukket: broken
brun: brown
brunet: browned
brunflekket: foxed, browned
brungull: dark gold
brunlilla: dark lilac, mauve
brunplettet: foxed, browned
brunskjold. *see* brunskjoldet
brunskjoldet: foxed
bukkalv: goatskin

bundet: bound
burgunderrødt: burgundy red

cartouche: cartouche
censur: censorship
chagr. *see* chagrin
chagrin: shagreen
ciseleret: chased, finely tooled;
   chiseled
ciselering: tooling, goffering

d. *see* del
dagbog(bøger): diary(ies)
dansk: Danish
dårlig: worthless, poor
dater: dates
dateret: dated
datert: dated
dato: date
debutbog: first book
debutbok: first book
ded. *see* dedikation
dediceret: dedicated, inscribed
dedik. *see* dedikasjon
dedikasjon: dedication, inscription
dedikation: dedication, inscription
defekt: defective, imperfect
deilig(e): lovely, charming
dejlig(e): lovely, charming
dekkel(kler): board(s)
dekor. *see* dekorasjon, dekorativ
dekorasjon(er): decoration(s)
dekoration(er): decoration(s)
dekorativ: decorative, ornamental
dekoreret: decorated
del: part
dele: parts
deler: parts
dels: in part, partly
delt: divided
deltitel: part title
delv. *see* delvis
delvis: partly
denteller: dentelle
deraf: of which
derav: of which
derefter: thereafter

deretter: thereafter
deriblandt: including
dessuten: in addition
desuden: in addition
desvaerre: unfortunately
det udk. *see* det udkomne
det udkomne: all published
detailleret: detailed
detailtegning(er): detail drawing(s),
  diagram(s)
detaljert: detailed
devise: device, motto
diag. *see* diagram
diagram(mer): diagram(s)
differerende: differing, varying
digt(e): poem(s)
digterverker: poetic works
digtsamling: collection of poems
dikt(e): poem(s)
diktning: creative writing(s),
  poetry
diskr. *see* diskret
diskret: discreet
disp. *see* disputats
disputats: dissertation, thesis
disputatsudgave: thesis edition
diss. *see* disputats
div. *see* diverse
diverse: several, various
dobbeltbind: double bands
dobbeltblad: double sheet
dobbeltsid. *see* dobbeltsidig
dobbeltsidig: two-sided,
  double-page
dobbeltspaltet: two-column,
  double-column
doktoravhandling: doctoral thesis
doktordisp. *see* doktordisputats
doktordisputats: doctoral
  dissertation
dokument(er): document(s)
dokumentarisk: documentary
dr.avh. *see* doktoravhandling
drevet: embossed
duodez: duodecimo
dupliceret: mimeographed
duplik. *see* duplikeret

duplikeret: mimeographed
dybrødt: dark red
dybtryk: offset printing
dybtryksgengivelse(r): reproduc-
  tion(s) by offset
dybtrykshaefte(r): issue(s) with
  offset illustrations
dyptrykk: offset printing
dyr: expensive

een: one
efterår: Fall, Autumn
efteråret: Fall, Autumn
eftergjordt: artificial
efterl. *see* efterladt
efterladt(e): posthumous
efterord: postscript
efterskr. *see* efterskrift
efterskrift: postscript, postface
eftersøgt: sought after, rare
efterspill: epilogue
efterspurgt: in great demand,
  sought after
eftertragtet: sought after
eftertryk: pirated edition, reprint
egenhaendig: autograph, in one's
  own handwriting
egenhendig: autograph, in one's
  own handwriting
eget forlag: published by the
  author
egne: own, personal
egnet: suitable, appropriate
egtraesplade(r): oak board(s)
ei: one
eks. *see* eksemplar
eksempelsamling(er): collection(s)
  of examples
eksempl. *see* eksemplar
eksemplar(er): copy(ies)
eksempler: examples
ekspedere: to forward, to send
ekspl. *see* eksemplar
ekstranummer: special issue,
  edition
el. *see* eller
eleg. *see* elegant

elegant: elegant, elegantly
elfenbenpergament: ivory vellum
elfte: eleventh
ell. *see* eller
eller: or, otherwise
ellers: or, otherwise
elleve: eleven
ellevte: eleventh
emaljebind: enamel binding
emner: subjects
en: a, one
en del: some
en fals svag: a weak hinge or joint
endast: additional, increased
endel: somewhat, some
endelig: final
endelige udgave: definitive edition
endvidere: further
enestående: unique
eneste: only
engelsk bind: limp binding
enhvert: every, each one
enk. *see* enkelt
enkelt: single; plain, rustic
enkelte: a few
enkelthefte(r): separate issue(s)
enkeltvis: singly, separately
enkeltvis saelges: sold separately
ens. *see* ensartet
ensartet: uniform
ensfarget: of one color
ensformig: uniform
er: has been, was
er utsendt: has been released,
   sent out
erindringer: memoirs
erratablad: errata sheet
erstattet med: replaced by
eske: box
et: a, one
et par: a few, a couple
ethvert: every, each one
ett: a, one
etter: after
etterlatte skrifter: posthumous
   works
etterspurt: sought for

ettertraktet: sought after
eventuelle: possible, possibly
eventyr: tale(s)
exlibris: bookplate
expl. *see* eksemplar

f.eks. *see* for eksempel
få: few
faa: few
faareskind: sheepskin
fabl. *see* fablea
fablea: imitation leather
facsimileaftryk: facsimile reprint
facsimilia: facsimiles
faellesbd. *see* faellesbind
faellesbind: bound together, series
   binding
faellesomsl. *see* faellesomslag
faellesomslag: wrappers for series
faellespublikation: companion
   publication
faellesregister: general index
fagmessig: professional(ly)
faks. *see* faksimile
faksimile: facsimile
faksimile-avtrykk: facsimile
   reprint
faksimilebilag: supplement
faksimileret: reproduced in
   facsimile
faksimiletryk: facsimile printing
falmet: faded
fals(e): hinge(s), joint(s); guard(s)
fåreskb. *see* fåreskindbind
fåreskindbind: bound in sheepskin
farge(r): color(s)
fargefaksimile: color facsimile
fargeillustrasjon(er): color
   illustration(s)
fargepapir: colored paper
farve(r): color(s)
farvebilag: color plate(s)
farvefot. *see* farvefotografi
farvefoto(s): color photograph(s)
farvefotografi(er): color
   photograph(s)
farveillustr. *see* farveillustration

farveillustration(er): color
 illustration(s)
farvelagt: colored, in colors
farvelitografi(er): color
 lithograph(s)
farvetavle(r): colored plate(s)
farvetr. *see* farvetryk
farvetryk: color print, color
 printing
farvetrykk: color print, color
 printing
farvetrykt: printed in color
farvetvl. *see* farvetavle
fastgjort: affixed
fastklaebet: reglued
favørpris: special price
fbl. *see* friblad
fedtplet(ter): grease stain(s)
feilpag. *see* feilpagina
feilpagina: page wrongly numbered
fellesbind: bound together,
 series binding
fellestitelblad: series title page
felt(er): panel(s)
fem: five
femte: fifth
femten(de): fifteen(th)
femti(ende): fifty(ieth)
ferdig: ready
festskrift: commemorative volume
fig. *see* figur
figur(er): figure(s), illustration(s)
filet(er): fillet(s)
fineste: finest, best
fingeret: fictitious
fingermerker: finger marks
finstilt: in small print
fint: neatly
fiolett: violet
fire: four
firkant: square, quadrangle
firma-merket: company label,
 stamp
firti(ende): forty(ieth)
fjerde: fourth
fjernet: removed, erased
fjorten(de): fourteen(th)

fl. *see* flekk, flere, flyblad, flygeblad
flade ophøjede bind: flat raised
 bands
flammet: marbled
flekk(er): spot(s)
flekket: spotted
flere: more, several
flerfarvet: multicolored
fleste: most
fletvaerk: interlacings
flexibel: flexible
flg. *see* følgende
fløjl: velvet
fløjlsagtig: velvetlike
fløjlsbind: velvet binding
fløjlsforet: velvet-lined
flonel: flannel
flosset: frayed
flot: elegant
flott: elegant
flotte: profuse
fløyelsbind: velvet binding
fløyelsforet: velvet-lined
flybl. *see* flyblad
flyblad: flyleaf
flygeblad: leaflet, **pamphlet**
flyveblad: flyleaf; pamphlet
flyveskrift(er): pamphlet(s),
 broadside(s)
foderal: slipcase
fol. *see* folio
folder: folder, portfolio
foldet: folded
følge: series, sequence
følgende: following, succeeding
folieret: foliated
foliering: foliation
folio: folio
foliovaerk: folio work
folkebog: popular book, chapbook
folkelig: popular
folkeudgave: popular edition
før: before, prior to
for det meste: mostly
for eksempel: for instance
for hånden: present

for- og bagomslag: front and back
  wrappers
for- og bagperm: front and back
  cover
for- og bakdekkel: front and back
  cover
for oven: on top
for.s. *see* forfatterens
forandret: altered, changed
foranstående: preceding
forår: Spring
forarbejdet: prepared
foråret: Spring
forbedring(er): correction(s),
  improvement(s)
forbehold: with reservation
fordansket: put into Danish
fordanskning: Danish version
fordekkel(kler): front cover(s)
fordekl. *see* fordekkel
fordybet: embossed
fored: lined
foregående: preceding
forelaesning(er): academic
  lecture(s)
foreløbig: preliminary, interim
førende: leading, first class
foreste: front, foremost
forestillende: representing
foret: lined
foretaget: executed; practiced
forf. *see* forfatter, forfatterens
  forlag
forf.s. *see* forfatterens
forfalskning: forgery
forfatter: author
forfatterens: of the author
forfatterens forlag: published by
  the author
forfatterrettighed: copyright
forfatterskab: authorship
forfattet: written, authored
forgyldning: gilt decoration(s)
forgyldt: gilt, decorated with gold
forhandlinger: proceedings
forhøjning(er): raised decoration(s)
fork. *see* forkortet

forklaring: explanation
forkommende: found, occurring
forkort. *see* forkortelse
forkortelse(r): abbreviation(s)
forkortet: abridged
forkortet titel: short title
førkrigsudgave: prewar edition
forl. *see* forlag
forlaegger: publisher
forlaengst: a long time ago
forlag: publishing firm
forlagsbind: publisher's binding
forlagsrett: copyright
forlagt: published
format: format
formered: enlarged
formering: edge of book cover
formindsket: reduced in size
forneden: at the foot, below
fornem(t): exquisite(ly)
fornyet: restored, renewed
forøgede: enlarged
forøget: enlarged
forøk. *see* forøket
forøket: enlarged
foromsl. *see* foromslag
foromslag: front wrapper
forord: preface
foroven: on top
forøvrig: at the top, above
forperm: front cover
forreste: front, foremost
forreven: torn
forrevet: torn
forrige: previous, last
fors. *see* forsats
forsaavidt: insofar as
forsalg: advance sale
forsats: flyleaf, endpaper(s)
forsatsbl. *see* forsatsblad
forsatsblad: flyleaf, endpaper
forsatspapir: flyleaf
forside: front; front page
forsk. *see* forskellig
forskell. *see* forskellig
forskellig(e): various, different
forskjellig(e): various, different

forsnit: fore edge
forsøg: essay, essays
forstaerket: reinforced
forstaerkning: reinforcing
første: first
førstetryk: first impression
førstetrykket: first impression
førsteudgave: first edition
forsynede: furnished, provided; supplied
forsynet: furnished, provided; supplied
fort. *see* fortitel
fortaelling(er): short story(ies), tale(s)
fortale: preface
fortegn. *see* fortegnelse
fortegnelse(r): catalog(s), list(s)
fortiden: the past
fortil: in front
fortitel: half title
fortløbende: continuous, running
fortraeffelig: excellent
fortrinlig: excellent
fortrolig: confidential
fortryk: preprint, advance copy
fortsaettelse bindende: buyer agrees to continue subscription
fortsat: continued, to be continued
foruden: besides
foruten: besides
fot. *see* fotografi
foto: photograph
fotogr. *see* fotografi, fotografisk
fotografi(er): photograph(s)
fotografisk: photographic
fotogravure(r): photoengraving(s)
fotokopi: photostat
fotolitografi: photolithograph(y)
fr. *see* friblad
frakturskrift: black-letter type
frbl. *see* friblad
fremmed: foreign
fremragende: outstanding
fremstillet: produced, printed; related, told
fremstilling: production; account

fribl. *see* friblad
friblad: flyleaf
frise(r): frieze(s), border(s)
frisk: fresh
friskhed: freshness
friskt: fresh
front. *see* frontispice
frontisp. *see* frontispice
frontispice: frontispiece
frynset: frayed
fugtpl. *see* fugtplettet
fugtplet(ter): damp stain(s)
fugtplettet: damp-stained, foxed
fugtrand(e): damp stain(s)
fugtskj. *see* fugtskjold
fugtskjold(er): damp stain(s)
fugtskjoldet: damp-stained
fuldført: completed
fuldst. *see* fuldstaendig
fuldstaendig(t): complete(ly)
fuldt: entirely
fullkommen: perfect
fullstendig(t): complete(ly)
futteral: slipcase
fyldig: copious, ample
fylt: filled

gaaet tabt: lost
gået ind: discontinued
gamalnorsk: Old Norwegian
gamle: old
gammelrosa: old rose-colored
gammelt: old
ganske: quite
gav ut: edited
gave: gift
gedechagrin: shagreen
gedeskind: goatskin, morocco
geiteskinn: goatskin, morocco
genfortalt: retold
gengivelse: reproduction
gengivet: reproduced
genindbundet: recased
gennemarbejdet: reworked, adapted
gennemgående: throughout
gennemgang: review

gennemillustr. *see* gennemillustreret
gennemillustreret: illustrated
throughout
gennemset: edited, slightly revised
gennemsk. *see* gennemskudt
gennemskudt: interleaved
gennemslagspapir: thin copy paper
genoptryk: reprint
genudgivelse: new edition; reissue
gjengivelse: reproduction
gjennemgående: throughout
gjennomskutt: interleaved
gjetskbd. *see* gjetskindbind
gjetskindbind: sheepskin binding
gl. *see* glat, glittet
glanset: polished
glanspapir: fancy paper
glat: smooth
glatpoleret: smooth, polished
glatt: smooth
glimrende: excellent, brilliant
glittet: coated, polished
glosar: glossary, word list
glose(r): gloss(es)
gnavet: gnawed
godt: good, fine
gotisk: Gothic
gråblå: blue-gray
graf(er): graph(s)
grafisk: graphic
grålilla: lilac-gray
granitol: a patent book cloth
granskning: research
grav. *see* graveret
graveret: engraved
gravert: engraved
grøn: green
grønn: green
groteskskrift: block letter
grov: rough, rustic
grundlaeggende: basic,
fundamental
grundtraek: basic outline
gruppe: group
gul: yellow
guld: gold

gulddek. *see* gulddekoration
gulddekoration: gold decoration
guldfileter: gold fillets
guldlinier: gold fillets
guldpraegning: gold stamping
guldpresset: gold-stamped
guldsn. *see* guldsnit
guldsnit: gilt edges
guldtrykt: printed with gold
gull: gold
gulldekor: gold tooling
gullrosetter: gold rosettes
gullskimmer: gold sheen
gullsnitt: gilt edges
gullstjerner: gold stars
gulltoppsn. *see* gulltoppsnitt
gulltoppsnitt: gilt top edge
gulnet: yellowed
gulplet: foxing
gulplettet: yellow-spotted, foxed
gulvpap: heavy gray paperboard
gummistempel: rubber stamp

h. *see* halv, hefte
haandb. *see* haandbog
haandbog(bøger): handbook(s)
haandgjort: handmade
haandindbundet: handmade
binding
haandkoloreret: hand-colored
haandskrevet: handwritten
haandskrift: manuscript, handwriting
haandtegning: sketch, drawing
haefte(r): part(s), fascicle(s),
issue(s); pamphlet(s)
haefteomslag: wrappers
haeftesubskription: parts issued
to subscribers
haeftet: sewed
haiskinn: sharkskin
hajskind: sharkskin
hajskindbind: sharkskin binding
halv: half
halv pris: half price
halvårlig: semiannual
halvb. *see* halvbind

halvbind: half volume; half
    binding
halvbuckrambind: half-buckram
    binding
halvdel: half
halvfablea: half fablea, an
    imitation leather
halvfrans: half-calf
halvhundre: fifty
halvlaeder: half-leather
halvlaerred: half-cloth
halvmaanedskrift: semimonthly
    publication
halvmånedlig: semimonthly
halvpergament: half-vellum
halvpluviusin: half-leatherette,
    fabrikoid
halvsaffian: half-morocco
halvsh. *see* halvshirting
halvshirting: half-cloth
halvtonaetsning: halftone
    engraving
halvtreds: fifty
halvtredsindstyve: fifty
halvtres: fifty
halvtresinstyve: fifty
hånd. *see* håndinbundet
håndb. *see* håndbog
håndbog: handbook
håndbok: handbook
håndbundet: hand-bound
håndg. *see* håndgjort
håndgj. *see* håndgjort
håndgjort: handmade
håndinbundet: hand-bound
håndkoloreret: hand-colored
håndmalede: hand-painted
håndskrevet: handwritten,
    autographed
håndskrift(er): manuscript(s)
håndtrykket: hand-printed
hardt: severely
haves også separat: also available
    separately
hefte(r): part(s), fascicle(s),
    issue(s); pamphlet(s)
hefteomslag: wrappers

hefteskrift: publication issued in
    parts
heftet: stitched, sewed
heftn. *see* heftning
heftning: stitching
helbalycronbd. *see* helbalycronbind
helbalycronbind: full-balycron
    binding
helbind: full binding
helbuckrambd. *see* helbuckrambind
helbuckrambind: full-buckram
    binding
hele vaerket: complete work
helfabl. *see* helfabrikoidlaederbind
helfableabind. *see* helfabrikoid-
    laederbind
helfabrikoidlaederbind: imitation
    leather binding
helgranitolbd. *see* helgranitolbind
helgranitolbind: imitation leather
    binding
hellaeder: full leather
hellaederspejlbind: full-leather
    paneled binding
hellaerred: full cloth
hellaerredsmappe: full-cloth
    portfolio
helldr. *see* hellaeder
hellerretsbind: full-cloth binding
hellrd. *see* hellaerred
helmaroquin: full morocco
helpergament: full vellum
helplastb. *see* helplastikbind
helplastikbind: full-plastic binding
helpluv. *see* helpluviusin
helpluviusin: full leatherette,
    fabrikoid
helruskindbind: full-suede binding
helsaffianbd. *see* helsaffianbind
helsaffianbind: full-morocco
    binding
helsh. *see* helshirting
helshirting: full cloth
helside(s): full page
helsidesbilde: full-page illustration
helsidesplanche(r): full-page
    plate(s)

helsjirtb. *see* helsjirtingsband
helsjirtingsband: full-cloth binding
helskb. *see* helskindbind
helskind. *see* helskindbind
helskindbind: full-leather binding
helstrieb. *see* helstriebind
helstriebind: full-buckram binding
helt: all, entirely
helt skinnbind: full-leather
  binding
helvti: half
henved: approximately, nearly
her: here, with this item
her og der: in some places
heraf: of which, of this, of these
herav: of which, of this, of these
heri: in which, in this, in these
herunder: under this heading
hf. *see* hefte, heftet
hft. *see* hefte, heftet
hftr. *see* hefter
hidtil: so far
hist. *see* historisk
historisk: historical
hittil: so far
hj. *see* hjørne
hjørne(r): corner(s)
hjørnebeslag: cornerpieces
hjørneroset(ter): corner rosette(s)
hjørnestempler: corner decorations
hjorteskind: buckskin, doeskin
hlaeder. *see* halvlaeder
hldr. *see* halvlaeder
hlvlrd. *see* halvlaerred
hlvpluv. *see* halvpluviusin
høj: high
hollandsk: Dutch
høst: Fall, Autumn
høsten: Fall, Autumn
høstnr. *see* høstnummer
høstnummer: Fall issue
hov. *see* hoved
hoved: head, principal
hovedpart: the majority, most of
  which; main part
hovedparten: the majority, most
  of which; main part

hovedredaktør: editor in chief
hovedregister: general index
hovedsagelig: principally
hovedtitel: main title
hovedvaerk: principal work, main
  work
hovedverk: principal work, main
  work
høyre: right-hand
hpluv. *see* halvpluviusin
hprgt. *see* halvpergament
hsh. *see* halvshirting
hshirt. *see* halvshirting
hul(ler): hole(s)
hullet: holed
hundreaarige: centennial
hundred(e): hundred(s)
hundrede: hundredth
hver: each
hver enkel: each one separately
hvert enkelt: each one separately
hvid: white
hvidt: white
hvitt: white
hvoraf: of which
hvorav: of which
hvormed: with which, together
  with
hvorpå: upon which

i alt: altogether
i anl. *see* i anledning
i anledn. *see* i anledning
i anledning: on the occasion
i gammel hånd: in old handscript
i kassette: in a box
i samtidens stil: in contemporary
  style
i teksten: in the text
i tidens stil: in contemporary
  style
iagttagelser: observations
ialt: altogether
ib. *see* indbundet
identisk: identical
ifølge: according to
ikke almindelig: uncommon

ikke i boghandelen: not for general
sale, privately printed
ikke i bokh. *see* ikke i boghandelen
ikke i handelen: not for general
sale, privately printed
ill. *see* illustrasjon, illustreret
illum. *see* illuminerede
illuminerede: illuminated, colored
illumineret: illuminated, colored
illustr. *see* illustrasjon
illustrasjon(er): illustration(s)
illustration(er): illustration(s)
illustrationsmateriale: illustrations,
illustrative material
illustrator: illustrator
illustreret: illustrated
illustrert: illustrated
imidlertid: however, still
imit. *see* imiteret
imiteret: imitated
imitert: imitated
imod: against
imot: against
imponerende: impressive
indbinding: binding
indbindningspris: binding price
indbøjet: folded in
indbundet: bound
indeholder: contains
indenfor: within, inside
inders. *see* inderside
inderside: inner side
indgående: extensive, extensively
indgik i: merged with
indheftet: bound in
indhold: contents
indholdsfortegnelse: index
indholdsfortgn. *see* indholdsfortegnelse
indholdsregister: table of contents
indklaebet: tipped in
indl. *see* indlagt, indledning
indlagt: laid in; enclosed
indledning: introduction
indledningsord: prefatory note
indmalet: painted in
indrammet: framed

indramning: framing
indre: inner, inside
indsat: inserted
indskrift: inscription
indskudt: inserted
indstr. *see* indstreget
indstreget: underlined, scored
indstregninger: underscoring
indtil: until, up to
indtrykt: printed in, embossed
indvendig: inside
init. *see* initial
initial(er): initial letter(s)
inkunabel(bler): incunabulum(a)
inl. *see* inledning
inledning: introduction
inledningsark: first signature
innb. *see* innbundet
innbinding: being bound, binding
innbundet: bound
inneh. *see* inneholder
inneholder: contains
innhold: contents
innholdsfortegnelse: index
innklebet: pasted in
innl. *see* innledning
innlagt: laid in; enclosed
innledn. *see* innledning
innledning: introduction
innrammet: framed
innsiden: inside
innskudt: inserted
innslag: flap
innvendig: inner, inside
inst. *see* institutt
institutt: institute
interf. *see* interfolert
interfolert: interleaved
istandsat: remade, renewed
itu: broken

jaevn: ordinary
jansenistbind: Jansenist binding
japanpapir: Japanese paper
jevnfør: compare, see
jfr. *see* jevnfør
jordslaaet: mildewed, foxed

jub.skrift. *see* jubilaeumsskrift
jubilaeumsbog: jubilee book
jubilaeumsskrift: jubilee publication
jubileumsbok: jubilee book
julebog(bøger): Christmas gift
book(s)

kaliko: calico, cloth
kalv: calf
kalveskind: calfskin
kalveskinn: calfskin
kammarmorsnit: marbled edge(s),
combed edge(s)
kantet: edged, bordered
kantforgylning: gilding on edges
of covers
kap. *see* kapitael
kapitael: capital letter
kapitaelbånd: headband
kapitel: chapter
kapitelinitial(er): chapter initial
letter(s)
kapitler: chapters
karduskart. *see* karduskartonnasje
karduskartonnasje: board covers
covered with blank paper
kardusomslag: blank wrapper
karikatur(er): caricature(s)
karikatyr(er): caricature(s)
kart. *see* kartonert, kartonnasje
kart(er): map(s), chart(s)
kartbilag: map supplement
kartnbd. *see* kartonbind,
kartonbundet
kartografi: cartography
karton. *see* kartonert
karton: boards, pasteboard;
slipcase
kartonbd. *see* kartonbind
kartonbind: board binding
kartonbundet: bound in boards
kartonert: bound in boards
kartong: boards, pasteboard;
slipcase
kartonnage: slipcase
kartonnasje: board covers

kartonneret: bound in boards
kartouche: cartouche
kartskiss(er): sketch map(s)
kartuche: cartouche
kartusche: cartouche
kassette: slipcase
katalog(er): catalog(s)
kemityperet: engraved in zinc
kender(e): expert(s), connoisseur(s)
kgl. *see* kongelig(e)
kildehenvisn. *see* kildehenvisning
kildehenvisning(er): reference(s)
to sources
kildehistorisk: based on original
sources
klaebet op: pasted up
klebet inn: pasted in
klipp: clipping
klippet: clipped
kludepapir: rag paper
klumme(r): column(s)
klutepapir: rag paper
knap: button, knob
knapp(er); button(s), knob(s)
knipl. *see* kniplingsmønster
kniplingsmønster: lacelike pattern
knop(per): boss(es)
knudestempel(pler): nodular
stamp(s)
knytebånd: fastening ribbon
kobb. *see* kobber
kobber(e): copper engraving(s)
kobberplade(r): copperplate(s)
kobberst. *see* kobberstik
kobberstik: copper engraving(s)
kobberstukket: copper-engraved
kobberstukne: copper-engraved
kobbertavler: engraved plates
kobbertr. *see* kobbertrykt
kobbertrykt: copperplate printing
kodeks: codex
kol. *see* koloreret
kold: cold, drypoint
koldnaalsradering(er): drypoint
etching(s)
kollationering: collation
kolofon: colophon

kolor. *see* koloreret
koloreret: colored
kolorering: coloring
kolorert: colored
komb. *see* kombineret
kombineret: combined
kommentar(er): commentary(ies)
kommenteret: commented
kommentert: commented
komp. *see* komplet, komponeret
kompilation: compilation
kompilator: compiler
komplet: complete
komplett: complete
komponeret: composed, designed
komponeret bind: original publisher's decorated binding
komposisjon(er): composition(s)
komposition(er): composition(s)
konfiskeret: confiscated
konfiskert: confiscated
kongelig(e): royal
kongl. *see* kongelig
konkordans: concordance
kontant: cash
konto: account
kontrast: contrast
kopperstikk: copper engravings
kort: map(s), chart(s); brief
kortbilag: supplement of maps
kortblade: map sheets
kortfatt. *see* kortfattet
kortfattet: concise, brief
kortmappe: portfolio of maps
kortplancher: map plates
kostbareste: most expensive
kostede: cost, sold for
kostet: cost, sold for
kostumekobber: engraved plates
  of costumes
kpl. *see* komplet
kplt. *see* komplet
kraftig: forceful, heavy
krideret: fine-coated (paper)
kritik(er): review(s)
kritiker(e): reviewer(s)
krøllet: crushed, crinkled

krønike(r): chronicle(s)
kronologisk: chronological
krusedulle: flourish, paraph
kse. *see* kassette
kundskab: knowledge, study
kunst: art
kunstbilag: art supplement
kunstbog(bøger): art book(s)
kunstgengiv. *see* kunstgengivelse
kunstgengivelse(r): art reproduc-
  tion(s)
kunstlaeder: imitation leather,
  leatherette
kunstlaer: imitation leather,
  leatherette
kunstner(e): artist(s)
kunstnerisk: artistic
kunstpergament: art vellum
kunsttr. *see* kunsttryk
kunsttryk: art printing
kunsttrykpapir: art paper, fine-
  coated paper
kunstudgave: deluxe edition
kuriøs: curious, quaint
kursiv: italics
kvadratisk: square
kvart: quarto
kvartalskrift: quarterly publication
kvartark: quarto sheet
kvarto: quarto
kvartside: quarto page
kyndig: experienced, expert

laeder: leather
laederkapitael: leather headband
laedermosaik: inlaid leatherwork
laederryg: leather back
laedertitelfelt: leather title piece
laenkebind: chained binding
laer: leather
laerde selskaber: learned societies
laerde selskaper: learned societies
laerebog: textbook
laerebok: textbook
laerredsbd. *see* laerredsbind
laerredsbetrukket: cloth-covered
laerredsbind: cloth binding

laerredsbundet: cloth-bound
laerredsfals(e): cloth joint(s),
　guard(s)
laerredskant(er): cloth edging(s)
laerredsryg: cloth back
laerredsside(r): cloth cover(s)
laerrygg: cloth back
laesebog: reader, textbook
landkart: map(s)
landkort: map(s)
landtoning(er): view(s)
lang: long
langnarvet: long-grained
langs: along
lap: patch
lapp: patch
lappet: patched
latinske bogstaver: roman script
lav: low
ldrryg. *see* laederryg
ldrtitelfelt. *see* laedertitelfelt
ledet: directed
ledsaget: accompanied
lejlighedsdigt: occasional poem
leksikon: encyclopedia, dictionary
lerret: canvas, cloth
lerretsovertr. *see* lerretsovertraekket
lerretsovertraekket: cloth-covered
lesebok: textbook
leselig: legible
let: slight, slightly
letlaeseligt: easily legible
lett: slight, slightly
lette: light, slight
leveres: be furnished, delivered
levering: delivery; fascicle, part
lex.-8vo. *see* lexikon-octavo
lexikon-octavo: large octavo
liden: small
lidt: a few, a little
lige: straight
lige side: verso
lige utkommet: just published
ligeledes: likewise
liggeled: also, likewise
lilje(r): fleur(s)-de-lys
lille: short, small

lille smule: a little
limbånd: raised bands
linie(r): line(s)
linieforgyldn. *see* linieforgyldning
linieforgyldning: gold fillets
linieret: lined, ruled
linietaelling: marginal line numbers
linje(r): line(s)
linjemønster: pattern of lines
linoleum-snit: linoleum-cut plate
linosnit: linoleum-cut plate
lit. *see* litografi
liten: small
litograferet: lithographed
litografert: lithographed
litografi: lithographed plate,
　lithography
litografisk: lithographic
litt: slightly
litteraturheft(e): bibliographic
　issue(s)
livserindringer: memoirs
livsskildring: biography
lødig: fine
lødigste: finest
lomme: pocket
lommebog: pocketbook, almanac
løs: loose, unstuck
løs i bindet: loose in binding
løs-ryg: hollow back
løse ark i mappe: loose signatures
　in portfolio
løst monteret: loosely mounted
luksusudg. *see* luksusudgave
luksusudgave: deluxe edition
lydefri: perfect, flawless
lydefrit: perfect, flawless
lys: light-colored, pale
lysebrun: light brown
lyst: light-colored, pale
lystryk: photolithograph(s),
　photolithography
lystryksgengiv. *see* lystryksgen-
　givelse
lystryksgengivelse(r): reproduc-
　tion(s) in photolithography

m.fl. *see* med flere
m.m. *see* med mere
maanedsskrift: monthly
maerke(r): mark(s)
maerkelig: strange, unusual
makuleret: damaged
makulert: damaged
maleri(er): painting(s)
malet: painted
månedlig: monthly
månedsskrift: monthly
mange: many, numerous
manglende: missing
mangler: lacking, missing
manuskript: manuscript
manuskriptsamling: collection of
  manuscripts
mappe(r): portfolio(s)
margen(er): margin(s)
margin-notater: marginal notes
marginalnotater: marginal notes
marinblå: marine blue
markedet: market
markspist: worm-eaten
marm. *see* marmoreret
marmor. *see* marmoreret
marmoreret: marbled
marmorering: marbling
marokin: morocco
maroquin: morocco
maroquinbind: morocco binding
maroquintitelfelt: morocco title
  piece
maskinbeskåret: machine trimmed
maskinmanuskript: typescript
maskinopsk. *see* maskinopskåret
maskinopskåret: trimmed by
  machine
maskinskr. *see* maskinskrevet
maskinskrevet: typed
maskinskript: typescript
mat: tarnished, without luster
med flere: with several others
med hvide blade: interleaved
med kyndig hand: by an expert
  craftsman
med meget: et cetera

med mere: among others, inter alia
medaillon: medallion
medaljong: medallion
medarb. *see* medarbeider
medarbeider: collaborator
medbundet: bound with, bound in
medforfatter: coauthor, joint
  author
medindbd. *see* medindbundet
medindbundet: bound with
medl. *see* medlem
medlem(mer): member(s)
medt. *see* medtaget
medtaget: damaged, worn
medtatt: damaged, worn
medvirkning: collaboration,
  cooperation
meget pent: nice copy
meget sjaelden: very rare
meget sjelden: very rare
mellem mangt: among others
memoirer: memoirs
merke: mark
messingsbeslag: brass decorative
  ornamentation
messingspaende(r): brass clasp(s)
metalspaender: metal clasps
mg. *see* mange
mgl. *see* mangler
middelalder: Middle Ages
middelalderen: Middle Ages
middelalderlig: medieval
middelmaatig: mediocre
midte: center
midtre: central
mimeograferet: mimeographed
mindealbum: commemorative
  album
mindeskrift: commemorative
  volume
mindeudg. *see* mindeudgave
mindeudgave: commemorative
  edition
mindre: smaller, minor, less
miniaturebog: miniature book
minneskrift: commemorative
  volume

minneutgave: commemorative
edition
misfarvet: discolored
mjuk: limp, flexible
modsat: opposite
moms: sales tax
monografi: monograph
monteret: mounted
montert: mounted
mørkeblå: dark blue
mørkebrun: dark brown
mørkegrøn: dark green
mørkere: darker
morsomt: nice
mosaik: mosaic, inlaid
motiv(er): motif(s)
motsatt: opposite
motto: motto, epigraph
ms. *see* manuskript
mskript. *see* manuskript
mugplet: mildew spot
multigr. *see* multigraferet
multigraferet: multigraphed
mus. *see* notetrykk
myke: flexible
mykt: flexible

n.p. *see* nedsat pris, ny pris
n.p.fribl. *see* navn på friblad
n.p.o. *see* navn på omslag
n.p.s. *see* navn på en side, navn
på smudsbladet
n.p.smt. *see* navn på smudstitelblad
n.p.t. *see* navn på titelblad
n.ptbl. *see* navn på titelblad
naest: next to, after
naesten: almost
naestnyeste: penultimate, next to
the last or latest
naestsidste: penultimate, next to
the last or latest
naevnt: mentioned
narv(er): grain, scoring
naturfarvet: natural color
navn: name
navn på en side: name on a page

navn på friblad(et): name on
flyleaf
navn på omslag(et): name on
wrapper
navn på smudsbladet: name on
flyleaf
navn på smudstitelblad: name on
half-title page
navn på titelblad: name on title
page
navne- og sagregister: index of
names and subjects
navne- og sakregister: index of
names and subjects
navneliste: list of names
navnetrekk: signature
nederste: bottom, lower
nedkratset: disfigured by scribbling
nedre: bottom, lower
nedsat pris: reduced price
neste: next
nettopris: net price
nevnt: mentioned
ngl. *see* nogle
ni: nine
niende: ninth
niger: morocco
nigerskind: morocco
nitten(de): nineteen(th)
nitti(ende): ninety(ieth)
no. *see* nummer
nodebilag: music supplement
noder: notes
nodetillaeg: music supplement
nødtørfdig: not strong, flimsy
noe: some, somewhat, a little
noen: some
noget: some, somewhat, a little
nogle: some
nøgleroman: *roman à clef*
nøjagtig: exact
norsk: Norwegian
notater: notes
note(r): annotation(s)
notemateriale: annotations
notesbog: notebook
notetrykk: printed music

notitser: notes
noveller: short stories, tales
nr. *see* nummer
nu: now
nulevende: contemporary
numm. *see* nummereret
nummer: number
nummereret: numbered
nummerering: numbering, pagination
nummerert: numbered
nummr. *see* nummereret
nusset eksemplar: dirty copy
nusset ekspl. *see* nusset eksemplar
nutidig: modern, present-day
ny: new
ny pris: list price
nyd. *see* nydelig
nyd. ekspl. *see* nydelig eksemplar
nydelig: nice
nydelig eksemplar: nice copy
nyere: newer, more recent
nyerhvervelse(r): recent acquisi-
 tion(s)
nyeste: newest, most recent
nyindkøb: recent acquisitions
nynorsk: New Norwegian
nyt: new
nytaarsbog: New Year publication
nytryk: reprint(s), reprinting
nytt: new

o. *see* omslag, over
o.a. *see* og andre
o.m. *see* også med
o.m.a. *see* og mange andre
o.o. *see* originalt omslag
o.s.v. *see* og så videre
oase. *see* oaseged
oaseged: deep-grained morocco
ødelagt: destroyed
off. *see* offentlig
offentlig: public
officiel(t): official(ly)
offisiell: official(ly)
offset: offset
offsettryk: offset printing

ofte: often
og andet: and others
og andre: and others
og mange andre: and many others
og så videre: et cetera
også: also
også med: (bound) together with
ohellaerr. *see* originalhellaerret
ohfablea. *see* originalhelfabrikoidlaeder
ohldr. *see* originalhellaeder
øjensynlig: obvious
okart. *see* originalkartonnage
oksehud: oxhide
omarb. *see* omarbeidet, omarbejdet
omarbeidet: revised
omarbejdet: revised
ombundet: rebound
omfattende: comprehensive
omfatter: comprises
omgitt (av): surrounded (by),
 framed (with)
omgivet (af): surrounded (by),
 framed (with)
omhandler: deals with
omhdl. *see* omhandler
omhyggelig(t): careful(ly)
omkranset: framed, surrounded
omkring: around, about
omredigeret: revised, reedited
omredigering: revision
omrids: outline
omriss: outline
oms. *see* omsett
omsett: translated
omsl. *see* omslag
omslag: wrapper
omstillet: transposed
omtr. *see* omtrykt
omtrent: approximately
omtrykt: reprinted
ønsket: desired
opdrive: to find
ophøjede bind: raised bands
ophøjninger: raised bands
opkl. *see* opklaebet
opklaebet: mounted

opl. *see* oplag
oplag: printing, edition
oplagstal: number of copies printed
opluv. *see* originalpluviusin
oplysende: explanatory
oplysing(er): explanatory note(s)
oplysn. *see* oplysning
oplyst: explained, interpreted; enlightened
oppbd. *see* originalpapbind
oppdrive: to find
oppforet: fully lined
opph. *see* opphøyde
opphøjde: raised
opphøyde: raised
oppklebet: mounted
oppl. *see* opplag
opplag: printing, edition
opprinnelig: original
oppslagsbok: reference book
opptrykk: reprint
opr. *see* oprindelig
oprindelig: original
opsiktsvaekkende: startling, sensational
opskaaren: opened (with paper knife)
opslagsvaerk: reference work
optegnelser: notes
optr. *see* optryk
optryk: reprint
optrykt: reprinted
or. *see* original
ordbog: dictionary
ordbok: dictionary
orden: order (sequence)
ordliste: vocabulary, word list
ordnede: arranged
ordnet: arranged
ordre: order (purchase)
ordsamling: vocabulary, word list
organ: publication
orienterende: exploratory
orig.bd. *see* originalbind
orig.skb. *see* originalskindbind
origb. *see* originalbind
orig-ms. *see* original-manuskript

original: original
originalbind: original binding
originalgrafik: original engravings, etchings
originalhelfabrikoidlaeder: original full imitation leather
originalhellaeder: original full leather
originalhellaerret: original full cloth
originalkartonnage: original paper-board binding
original-manuskript: author's manuscript
originalpapbind: original boards
originalpluviusin: original fabrikoid
originalradering(er): original etching(s)
originalshirting: original cloth
originalskindbind: original leather binding
originalt omslag: original wrapper
originaludgave: original edition
originalutgave: original edition
orm(e): worm(s)
ormaedt: worm-eaten
ormehul(ler): wormhole(s)
ormstukken: worm-eaten
ornert: decorated
oshirt. *see* originalshirting
osv. *see* og så videre
otte(nde): eight(h)
otti(ende): eighty(ieth)
ov. *see* over
oven. *see* foroven
ovenfor: above
ovennaevnte: above-mentioned
ovenstående: above
over: over, about, of
overalt: universally
overdaadigt: abundantly; exquisitely
overdådig: abundantly; exquisitely
overordentlig: extraordinary
overs. *see* oversat, oversigt
oversaettelse: translation
oversaetter(e): translator(s)

oversat: translated
oversatt: translated
oversetter(e): translator(s)
oversigt: summary, survey
oversigtstavle: synoptic table
oversikt: summary, survey
overskrift: superscription, heading
oversnit: top edge
øverste: upper
overstemplet: stamped over
overstreget: crossed out, canceled
overtrekk: lined out
overtrekkspapir: lined paper
overtrukket: covered, coated
øvre: upper
øvrige: remaining, others

p. *see* pagina
p.t.bl. *see* på titelblad
på lager: in stock, available
på prøve: on approval
på stort papir: on large paper
på titelblad: on the title page
paa forlangende: on request
paa hovedet: upside down
paany: again, anew
påbegyndt: started
paent: neat, nice
pag. *see* pagineret, paginering
pagina(ae): page(s)
pagineret: paginated, numbered
paginering: pagination
påklaebet: pasted on, mounted
påklistret: pasted on, mounted
pamflet: pamphlet
påny: again, anew
pap: cardboard
papaeske: pasteboard box
papbd. *see* papbind
papbind: boards
papir(er): paper(s)
papirbind: paperbound
papkart. *see* papkartonnage
papkartonnage: box, slipcase
papomslag: paperboard covers
papp: cardboard
pappb. *see* pappbind

pappbind: boards
pappermer: cased binding
paraferet: initialed
paralleltekst: parallel text
påsat: affixed, superimposed
påsatt: affixed, superimposed
påtrykt: printed on, imprinted
pen: neat, fine
pene: neat, fine
pennetegning(er): pen and ink
  drawing(s)
pent: neat, fine; good copy
penteksemplar: fine copy
pentekspl. *see* penteksemplar
perfekt: perfect
pergament: parchment, vellum
pergamentforstaerkning(er): vellum reinforcing(s)
pergamenthåndskrift(er): vellum
  manuscript(s)
pergamentryg: parchment back(s)
pergt. *see* pergament
perkal: calico
perkalin: buckram
perm: side
personal- og real-register: index
  of persons and subjects
personliste: list of names, persons
personregister: index of names,
  persons
pirattryk: pirated publication(s)
pjece: pamphlet, booklet
pl. *see* plettet, planche
plan(er): map(s), plan(s)
planche(r): plate(s)
plano: unfolded
plansje(r): plate(s)
plast. *see* plastic
plastic: plastic
plastryggb. *see* plastryggbind
plastryggbind: plastic back
  binding
pletfri: spotless
plettet: spotted
plettfri: spotless
plommefarvet: plum-colored
pluv. *see* pluviusin

pluviusin: leatherette, fabrikoid
pol. *see* polert
poleret: polished, calendered
polert: polished, calendered
polykrom: multicolored
pompøs: grandiose, impressive
porfyr: porphyry
port. *see* portraet
porto: postage
portofrit: prepaid
portr. *see* portraet
portr.-stik. *see* portraetstik
portraet(ter): portrait(s)
portraetstik: engraved portrait
portraettegninger: portrait draw-
    ings
portrett(er): portrait(s)
pr. *see* pro
praeget: stamped, tooled
praegtig: magnificent, splendid
pragteksemplar: beautiful copy
pragtfuld: splendid
pragtvaerk: deluxe work
praktutgave: deluxe edition
praktverk: deluxe work
prektig: splendid
presset: tooled, stamped
pris(er): price(s)
prisaendringer: price change(s)
prisbelønnet: prize-winning
priv. *see* privat
privat: private, privately
privatbind: three-quarter binding
privattryk: privately printed
privilegium: permit to publish
pro: per, each
prospekt(er): view(s)
prøve(r): specimen(s), sample(s)
proveniens: provenance
prøveoversaettelse: tentative
    translation
provinstryk: provincial publication
prydet: adorned
prydinitial(er): ornamental
    initial(s)
pseud. *see* pseudonym
pseudonym: pseudonym

publ. *see* publikasjon
publikasjon(er): publication(s)
publikation(er): publication(s)
punkteret: stippled

quartal: quarter

r. *see* rekke
raakant: deckled edges
rabat: discount
radering(er): etching(s)
raekke(r): series
ramme: frame, border
rand: edge, margin
randbemaerkning(er): marginal
    note(s)
randbemerk. *see* randbemerkning
randbemerkning(er): marginal
    note(s)
randforsiring: ornamental border
randnotater: marginal notes
rankemønster: leafy pattern,
    design
rankemotiv: leafy motifs
rankevaerk: scrolls, interlaced
    pattern
raritet: rarity
ratebetaling: installment payment
recension: review
red. *see* redaksjon, redaktør,
    redigeret
redaksjon: editorship
redaktion: editorship
redaktør: editor
redegørelse: report
redigeret: edited
redigert: edited
referat: report
registerbind: index volume
rekke(r): series
remme: ties
ren: clean
renset: expurgated
renskrift: fair copy
rep. *see* repareret
reparation: repair
repareret: repaired

reparert: repaired
reproduceret: reproduced
reprodusert: reproduced
rest: the balance, the rest
restaureret: restored, repaired
restaurering: restoring, repair
restoplag: remainders
resumé: summary
ret: rather
rettelse(r): correction(s)
rettleiing: introduction
rev. *see* revideret
revet: torn
revideret: revised
revidert: revised
revne: crack, split
revnet: split
rift(er): tear(s)
rig: rich
rigt: richly
rik: rich
rikt: richly
rk. *see* raekke
rocaille: shell-like pattern
rød: red
rødkridtet: marked with red pencil
rødlig: reddish, fawn-colored
rødt: red
roman: novel
røskener: fleurons
rovtryk: pirated publication(s)
rubr. *see* rubriceret, rubrik
rubriceret: rubricated
rubrik: rubric, heading
rubrisert: rubricated
rudeformet: lozenge-shaped
rudemønstret: checkered design
rulle(r): scroll(s)
ruskind: suede
ruskindbd. *see* ruskindbind
ruskindbind: suede binding
ruslaeder: Russian leather
rustplet(ter): foxing
rustplettet: foxed
ryg: back, spine
rygdekoration: ornamentation on
  spine

rygfals: back joint
rygfelt(er): panel(s) on back or
  spine
rygforg. *see* rygforgyldning
rygforgyldn. *see* rygforgyldning
rygforgyldning: gold tooling on
  back
rygg: back, spine
ryggdekor. *see* ryggdekoration
ryggdekoration: ornamentation
  on spine
ryggstrimmel: butt
rygskilt: label, lettering piece
rygtitel: spine title

s. *see* side
s/hv. *see* sort/hvitt
s.p.t. *see* stempel paa titelblad
saaledes: thus, in this condition
sådan: in this condition
saelges: sold, available
saelges separat: sold separately
saerdeles: especially
saerlig: special
saernummer: special issue
saerpraeget: unusual
saertilbud: special offer
saertr. *see* saertryk
saertryk: separate, reprint
saerudg. *see* saerudgave
saerudgave: special edition, deluxe
  edition
saerutgave: special edition, deluxe
  edition
saet: set
saffian: morocco
saffiansryg: morocco back
saffiansrygg: morocco back
sagregister: subject index
sakregister: subject index
salaer: salary
således: thus, in this state
salg: sale
samarb. *see* samarbeid
samarbeid: collaboration
saml. *see* samlet, samling
samlebind: collective work

samlede: collected, compiled
samlede verker: collected works
samler(e): collector(s)
samlet: collected, compiled
samlevaerk: composite work
samling(er): collection(s)
samlingsverk: collective work
samme: same
sammelbind: collective volume
sammen med: together with
sammenbragt: gathered
sammenbundet: bound together
sammendrag: abstract
sammenfold. *see* sammenfoldet
sammenfoldet: folded
sammenlagt: laid together
sammenlignende: comparative
sammenstykket: mended
samt: and, together with
samt. *see* samtidig
samt.-bd. *see* samtidig-bind
samtid. *see* samtidig
samtidig: contemporary
samtidig-bind: contemporary
  binding
samtlig: entire, complete
sarsenett: book cloth
sart(e): delicate
schatteret: hatched
scholier: scholia, critical notes
se: see
segl: seal
seks: six
seksten(de): sixteen(th)
seksti(ende): sixty(ieth)
selskab(er): society(ies)
selskap(er): society(ies)
selvbiografi: autobiography
selvportraet: self-portrait
selvskrevet: autograph, in one's
  own handwriting
selvstaendig: independent
semsket: chamois
senere: later
sennepsgul: mustard color
sep. *see* separat
separat: separate, separately

sepia: sepia
sepiafarvet: sepia-colored
serie: series
serpr. *see* serprent
serprent: separate, offprint
sett: set
shb. *see* shirtingsbind
shirt. *see* shirting
shirting: cloth
shirtingrygg: cloth spine, half-
  cloth
shirtingsbd. *see* shirtingsbind
shirtingsbind: cloth binding
shirtingsomslag: cloth wrapper
shirtomsl. *see* shirtingsomslag
shr. *see* shirtingrygg
side: page, side
sideforgyldning: gold tooling on
  sides
sideløbende: facing, opposite
sider: pages, sides
sidetal: number of pages, pagination
sidetitel: cover title
sidste: last, final
sidstnaevnt: last mentioned
sign. *see* signeret
signatur: signature; letter or
  number denoting signature
signeret: signed
signert: signed
silke: silk
silkebind: silk binding
silkeforsats: silk endpapers
silkemoiré: watered silk, tabby
simpel: simple, unpretentious
siselert: goffered
siste: last, final
sjaeld. *see* sjaelden
sjaelden: seldom found, rare
sjaeldenhed: rarity
sjaeldneste: rarest
sjagr. *see* sjagreng
sjagreng: shagreen
sjelden: rare
sjeldenhet: rarity
sjette: sixth

sjirting: cloth
sjøgrønt: sea green
skadet: damaged
skaeg: bearded edge(s)
skaev: askew, crooked
skb. *see* skindbind
skema: schema
skildring(er): description(s)
skimmelplet: mildew
skind: leather
skindafstødning(er): rubbing
  damage(s) to leather
skindbind: leather binding
skindforstaerkninger: leather
  reinforcing
skindindlaeg: leather intarsia
skindkanter: leather edges
skindkapitaeler: leather capital
  letters
skindkassetter: leather slipcases
skindryg: leather back
skindtit. *see* skindtitel
skindtitel: leather title piece
skinn: leather
skinnbind: leather binding
skinnrygg: leather spine, half-
  leather
skisse(r): sketch(es)
skitse(r): sketch(es)
skizze(r): sketch(es)
skjev: askew, crooked
skjold(er): satin(s)
skønhedsfejl: blemish(es)
skønnlitteratur: fiction, belles
  lettres
skr. *see* skinnrygg
skrab. *see* skrabet
skrabet: scratched, scraped
skramme: scratch
skrammet: scratched, scraped
skrapet: scratched, scraped
skravering: azure tooling
skrevet: written
skrift(er): work(s), writing(s)
skriftmaal: literary language
skrivepapir: writing paper, ledger
  paper

skriver(e): writer(s), scribe(s)
skrivter: works, writings
skrotstik: dotted print(s)
skuespil: play, drama
skygget: hatched
slaegtstavle(r): genealogical
  table(s)
slapp: weak
slidt: worn, frayed
slitt: worn, frayed
slutning: end, conclusion
slutt: end
sluttede: closed up, ended
slutvignet: tailpiece
slyngning(er): tracery, scroll(s)
sm. *see* smukt
sm.t. *see* smusstitel
smaapletter: small spots
smaaskrifter: miscellanea
smaedeskrift(er): lampoon(s)
småflekker: small spots
småfliset: slightly flaked
småfortaelling(er): short story(ies)
smagfuld: tasteful
smakfull: tasteful
smal: narrow, thin
smårifter: small tears
småskr. *see* småskrifter
småskrifter: miscellanea
smt. *see* smudstitel
smudset: dirty, soiled
smudsig: dirty, soiled
smudsomslag: dust jacket
smudstitel: half title, bastard title
smudstitelblad: half-title page
smuk: nice
smukkest(e): nicest
smukt: handsomely
smusset: dirty, soiled
smussig: dirty, soiled
smussomslag: dust jacket
smusst. *see* smusstitel
smusst.bl. *see* smusstitelbladet
smusstitel: half title, bastard title
smusstitelbladet: half-title page
smykket: adorned
snart: almost

snavset: dirty, soiled
snit: edges
snitmaleri: fore-edge painting
snitt: edges
søgt: sought
søkort: chart(s)
sol. *see* solid
solgt: sold
solid: strong, well-made
sølv: silver
sølvspaender: silver clasps
som altid: as always
som ny: as new
som regel: as a rule, in general
som vanlig: as usual
sommer: Summer
sommeren: Summer
sørgespil: tragedy
sort: black
sort/hvitt: black and white
sortkunst: mezzotint process
spaende(r): clasp(s)
spaenderest(er): remnant(s) of
    clasps
spaettet: speckled
spalte(r): column(s)
special: special
specielt: especially
spejl: panel work; lining
spejlbind: leather binding with
    panel designs, "mirror" binding
spejlmonogram: "mirror" mono-
    gram
spenner: clasps
spesiell: special
spesielt: especially
spiralheftet: spiral binding
splitt: split, cracked
splittet: split, cracked
spor: trace(s)
spr. *see* sprukket
spraengt: sprinkled
spraenkt: sprinkled
sprukket: cracked
ss. *see* sider
st. *see* stempel
st.hft. *see* stift heftet

st.p.omsl. *see* stempel på omslag
st.p.smt. *see* stempel på smusstitel
st.p.t. *see* stempel paa titelblad
staalstik: steel engraving(s)
stadig: stable, steady
staerkt: strongly, considerably
staffage: adornments
stålst. *see* stålstikk
stålstikk: steel engraving(s)
stamtavle(r): genealogical table(s)
stand: state, condition
standardudgave: standard edition
standset: ceased
steintrykk: lithograph, lithography
stempel(pler): stamp(s), mark(s)
    left by a stamp, stamping tool
stempel på omslag: stamp on
    wrapper
stempel på smusstitel: stamp on
    half-title page
stempel paa titelblad: stamp on
    title page
stemplet: stamped
stens. *see* stensilert
stensilert: mimeographed
stensiltrykt: printed by stencil
stentrykt(e): lithographed
sterk: strongly, greatly
sterkt: strongly, greatly
stift heftet: boards
stik: engraving(s)
stikk: engraving(s)
stikordskatalog: subject catalog
stikordsregister: subject index
stilfuld: stylish, tasteful
stivheftet: boards
stødt: mutilated, crushed
stoffbind: cloth binding
stor: large
storartet: excellent
storhefte(r): large part(s),
    fascicle(s)
større: larger, greater
størrelse: size
største: largest, greatest
størstedelen: the largest part
stort: large

støvet: dusty
støvfylt: dust-filled
støvskjoldet: dust-stained
stregbordure: gilt lines, fillets
stregfilet(er): line fillet(s)
stregforgyldning: gold tooling in
   line designs, fillets
streker: lines, marks, markings
striemappe: canvas portfolio
strieryggb. *see* strieryggbind
strieryggbind: canvas binding
strimmel: wrapper
strip(er): strip(s)
stukket: engraved
stukne: engraved
styg: ugly, bad
stygg: ugly, bad
stykke(r): part(s), piece(s)
subskript. *see* subskription
subskription: subscription
subskription er bindende for hele
   vaerket: subscribers contract
   for entire work
superexlibris: ownership stamp
suppl. *see* supplement
supplement: supplement
supplementshefte: supplementary
   issue
supplerende: supplementary
supplert: supplemented
supprimert: suppressed
svaert: heavy, thick
svag: slight
svak: slight
svensk: Swedish
svinelaeder: pigskin
svineskind: pigskin
sytten(de): seventeen(th)
sytti(ende): seventy(ieth)
syv(ende): seven(th)

t.b. *see* titelblad
t.bl. *see* titelblad
tab. *see* tabel
tab: loss
tabel(ler): table(s)
tabelvaerker: collections of tables

tallrik(e): numerous
talr. *see* talrig
talrig(e): numerous
tap: loss
tavle(r): plate(s)
tb. *see* tabel
tegn. *see* tegning
tegnede: drawn
tegner(e): artist(s), illustrator(s)
tegnet: drawn
tegngr. *see* tegning
tegning(er): drawing(s)
teikning(ar): drawing(s)
tekst: text
tekstbd. *see* tekstbind
tekstbilag: text supplement
tekstbind: text volume
tekstbl. *see* tekstblad
tekstblad: text page
tekstfigurer: illustrations in the
   text
tekstforklaring(er): textual
   explanation(s)
teksthefte: text part; issue
tekstkritisk(e): critical
tekstrettelse(r): correction(s) in
   the text
teksttab: loss of text
teksttap: loss of text
temmelig: rather, fairly
textbidrag: textual contribution(s)
textrevision: revision of text
ti(ende): ten(th)
tiaar: decade
tiår: decade
tidebog: book of hours
tidl. *see* tidlig
tidlig: early
tidligst: earliest, first
tidsskr. *see* tidsskrift
tidsskrift(er): journal(s),
   magazine(s), periodical(s)
tidsskriftraekke: run (of a journal)
tidstypisk: typical of the time
tiende: tenth
til bogladepris: at list price
til minde om: in commemoration of

til priser: at prices
tilblivelse: origin
tilbud: offer
tilbyde: offer
tildels: partly
tilegnelse: dedicatory note
tilegnet: dedicated to
tilføjelse(r): addition(s)
tilføyde: added
tilføyelse(r): addition(s)
tilhørende: belonging to
tilhørt: belonged to
tillaeg: supplement, appendix
tillaegsbind: supplementary
   volume
tilleg: supplement, appendix
tilligemed: together with
tilrettelagt: arranged
tilsammen: together, in all
tilskrift(er): handwritten note(s)
tilskrivn. *see* tilskrivning
tilskrivning: handwritten notes
tilsmudset: soiled
tilstand: state
tilstede: extant, present
tilstraekkelig: sufficient
tit. *see* titel
titel: title
titel–etiket: title label
titelbilde: frontispiece
titelbillede: frontispiece
titelbl. *see* titelblad
titelblad: title page
titelfelt: title piece, label
titelkobber: engraved frontispiece;
   engraving on title page
titelskilt: label on spine
titelvignett: vignette on the title
   page
to: two
tolv(te): twelve(twelfth)
tomefelt: volume label
tonede: shaded, tinted
tonet: shaded, tinted
tontryk: tint(s)
tontrykkplansjer: color plates
topp: top

toppsnit: top edge
tospaltet: two-column
totalopplag: whole edition
tr. *see* trykkeri, trykt
traepermer: wood boards
traeplade(r): wood board(s)
traesk. *see* traeskårne
traeskårne: woodcut
traesn. *see* traesnit
traesnit: woodcut(s)
traesnitvignetter: woodcut
   vignettes
traktat: treatise
tre(dje): three (third)
tredive: thirty
tredivte: thirtieth
tredjedel: third
treliniet: three-line
trepermer: wooden boards
tresidet: three-sided
tresnittillustrasjoner: woodcut
   illustrations
tretten(de): thirteen(th)
trist: sad
tryk: printing, prints
trykfejl: misprint(s)
trykk: printing, prints
trykkefriheden: freedom of the
   press
trykkeri: printing office
trykkfeil: typo, misprint
trykning: printing
trykpapireksemplar: copy made on
   printer's stock, usually for work
   copy
trykpapirekspl. *see* trykpapireksemplar
trykt: printed
tsd. *see* tusind
tus. *see* tusen
tuschmanér: chiaroscuro
tusen: thousand(s)
tusende(r): thousand(s)
tusind: thousand(s)
tusinde(r): thousand(s)
tv. *see* tvaer
tvaer: oblong

tvaerfolio: oblong folio
tvende: two
tverr: oblong
tvl. *see* tavle
tvlr. *see* tavle
tyding: translation
tyk: thick, heavy
tykk: thick, heavy
tykkelse: thickness
tynd: thin
tyndpapir: bible paper
tynn: thin
tynt: thin
type(r): type
tysk: German
tyve(nde): twenty(ieth)

u. *see* uddrag
u.a. *see* uden aar, uden aarstal
u.å. *see* uden år, uden trykkeår
u.st. *see* uden sted, uden trykkested
u.st.o.å. *see* uden trykkested og år
uafsluttet: unfinished
ualmindeligt: unusual, uncommon
ualminnelig: unusual, uncommon
ubedret: unimproved
uberørt: untouched, intact
ubesk. *see* ubeskaaret
ubeskaaret: untrimmed, with
    deckled or rough edge
ubeskåret: untrimmed, with
    deckled or rough edge
ubet. *see* ubetydelig
ubetydelig: insignificant, slight
ubrugt: unused, as new
udarb. *see* udarbejdet
udarbejdet: compiled
udateret: undated
udatert: undated
udbedret: repaired
udbedring: repair, correction
udbudt: offered
udbyde: offer
uddr. *see* uddrag
uddrag: extract(s), selection(s)
uddragne: selected, excerpted
uden aar: without date

uden aarstal: without date
uden år: without date
uden dato og år: without date or
    year
uden sted: without place
uden teksttab: without loss of text
uden trykkeår: without date
uden trykker: without printer
uden trykkested: without place of
    publication
uden trykkested og år: without
    place or date
udfoldeligt: folding
udfoldningskobbere: folded
    engravings
udførlig: detailed
udførligt: detailed
udført: executed
udg. *see* udgave, udgivet
udgave(r): edition(s)
udgave for ungdommen: juvenile
    edition
udgivelse: publication, issuance
udgiver: editor, publisher
udgivet: edited
udhug: excision
udk. *see* udkom
udkast: draft
udkom: published
udkommer ikke mere: no longer
    published
udkommer om kort tid: to appear
    shortly
udm. *see* udmaerket
udmaerket: excellent, distinguished
uds. *see* udsolgt
uds.i.b. *see* udsolgt i boghandelen
udsalg: sale
udsdt. *see* udsendt
udsendelse: issuing, distribution
udsendt: issued, distributed
udskaering: excision
udskåret: cut out, carved
udslettet: erased
udsmykket: adorned, ornamented
udsmykning: decoration
udsn. *see* udsnit

udsnit: excerpt, excised portion
udsøgt: choice
udsolgt: out of print
udsolgt i boghandelen: out of print
udtog: excerpt, abstract
udtømmende: exhaustive
udtvaering: rubbing
udv. *see* udvalg, udvalgt
udvalg: choice, selection
udvalgt: chosen, selected
udvendig: external
udvidet: increased, enlarged
uens. *see* uensartet
uens: unlike, differing
uensartet: disparate, not uniform
ufarget: uncolored, natural
ufarvet: uncolored, natural
uforandret: unchanged
ufriskt: soiled
ufuldendt: unfinished
ufullstendig: incomplete
ugeblad: weekly
ugeskrift: weekly
uhyre: exceedingly
uib. *see* uindbundet
uillustr. *see* uillustreret
uillustreret: without illustrations
uillustrert: without illustrations
uindbundet: unbound
uinnb. *see* uinnbundet
uinnbundet: unbound
ujaevnt: uneven
ukeblad: weekly publication
ukendt: unknown, unlisted
ukentlig: weekly
ukjent: unknown, unlisted
uklanderlig: sloppy
ukolorert: uncolored
ukomplet: incomplete
ulastelig: impeccable, irreproach-
    able
ulike: unlike, dissimilar, not alike
ums. *see* umsett
umsetjing: translation
umsett: translated
umulig: impossible
umvølt: translated, adapted

under medv. af *see* under med-
    virkning af
under medvirkning af: with the
    collaboration of
under trykken: in press
under udgivelse: in course of
    publication
underskønt: magnificent
underskrift: signature
undersnit: bottom edge
undersøgelse(r): investigation(s),
    study(ies)
undersøkelse(r): investigation(s),
    study(ies)
understr. *see* understreget,
    understregning
understreget: underlined
understregning(er): underlining(s)
understrek. *see* understrekning
understrekning(er): underlining(s)
undertitel: subtitle
undertrykt: suppressed
ungdomsudgave: juvenile edition
unumm. *see* unummereret
unummereret: unnumbered
uops. *see* uopskaaret
uopskaaret: unopened, uncut
uopskr. *see* uopskaaret
upag. *see* upagineret
upagineret: with pages unnum-
    bered
upg. *see* upagineret
usedv. *see* usedvanlig
usedvanlig: unusual, unusually
usigneret: unsigned
usynl. *see* usynlig
usynlig: imperceptible
utal: multitude
utarb. *see* utarbeidelse, utarbeidet
utarbeidelse: preparation, editing
utarbeidet: prepared, edited
utdrag: extract(s)
utført: executed
utg. *see* utgave, utgit, utgiver
utgave: edition
utgit: published, edited
utgitt: published, edited

utgiver: editor
utgjevi: edited
utgjevne: edited
utgjør: constitutes, comprises
utk. *see* utkommer
utklippsbok: scrapbook
utkommer: is (are) published
utrykt: unpublished
utsendt: sent out, released
utsolgt: out-of-print
utstilling: exhibition
utv. *see* utvalg
utvalg: selection
uundvaerlig: indispensable
uunnvaerlig: indispensable
uvurderlig: invaluable

våben: coat(s) of arms
våbenskjold(e): coat(s) of arms
vaelskbd. *see* vaelskbind
vaelskbind: half-sheepskin binding
  with corners
vaerdi: value
vaerdifuld: valuable
vaerdig: worthy
vaerk(er): work(s)
vakker: beautiful, handsome
vakkert: beautiful, handsome
vandbeskadiget: water-damaged
vandmaerke: watermark
vandskjold(er): water stain(s)
vandskjoldet: stained by water
vanligt: usual
vannmerke: watermark
vannskjold(er): water stain(s)
vanskelig: difficult
vår: Spring
våren: Spring
variant(er): variant(s)
variation(er): variation(s)
vasket: washed
vat: sales tax
vedføjet: added, written in

vedhaengende: attached
vedlagt: accompanying, added,
  enclosed
vejledn. *see* vejledning
vejledning: introduction, directions
velbev. *see* velbevaret
velbevaret: well-preserved
velbevart: well-preserved
velh. *see* velholdt
velholdt: well-preserved
velin. *see* velinpapir
velinpapir: vellum paper
venstre: left-hand
verdi: value
verdifull: valuable
verdifullt: valuable
verdiløs: worthless
verk(er): work(s)
versalbogstav(er): capital(s)
vetenskapelig: scientific, scholarly
videnskabelig: scientific, scholarly
vidner: witnesses
vidunderlig: marvelous
vign. *see* vignet
vignet(ter): vignette(s), head-
  piece(s)
vignetkobber: engraved vignette
vigtig: important
vigtigst(e): most important
vinrødt: wine-colored
vinter: Winter
vinteren: Winter
virkningsfuld: striking, impressive
vuggetryk: incunabulum(a)
vurdering: evaluation

xylograferet: woodcut

yderligere: additional
yderst: extremely
ydre: outer, external
ypperlig: outstanding
ytre: outer, external

Dutch

aanbieding: offer
aangeb. *see* aangeboden
aangeboden: offered
aangekondigd: announced
aangenaam: pleasing
aangev. *see* aangevuld
aangevuld: increased, supplemented
aanhaling: citation, quotation
aanhangsel: appendix, supplement, annex
aanhangselen: appendixes, supplements, annexes
aanhangsels: appendixes, supplements, annexes
aant. *see* aantekening
aantal: number
aantek. *see* aantekening
aantekening(en): annotation(s), note(s)
aantrekkelijk(e): attractive
aanvraag: request
aanvulling(en): addition(s), supplement(s)
aanvullings: additional, supplementary
aanwezig: extant, available
aanwinst: acquisition
aardig: attractive
ab. *see* abonnement
abc-boek: primer
abonn. *see* abonnement
abonnement: subscription
academisch: academic
acht(ste): eight(h)
achtenswaardig: respectable, worthy

achterkant: back side, overleaf
achterplat(ten): back cover(s)
advertentie: advertisement
afb. *see* afbeelding
afbeelding(en): illustration(s)
afbestellen: cancel
afbn. *see* afbeeldingen
afd. *see* afdeling
afdeling(en): part(s)
afdruk: printing
afgebroken: broken off
afgeknaagd: gnawed
afgescheurd: torn off
afgeschuurd: abraded
afgesneden: trimmed, opened
afgeweekt: loose, unstuck
afkorting: abridgment, abbreviation
afl. *see* aflevering
aflev. *see* aflevering
aflevering(en): part(s), issue(s)
afmeting: size, format
afneembaar: detachable, removable
afschr. *see* afschrift
afschrift(en): copy(ies)
afschuring: abrasion
afzonderlijk: separate(ly), detached
album: album
algemeen: general, generally
alleen: alone
alleenverkoop: exclusive distribution
alles wat verscheen: all published
alles wat verschenen is: all published
almanak: almanac

alphabetisch: alphabetical
als nieuw: as new
analytisch: analytical
anastatisch: anastatic
ander: other, another
anders: otherwise
annalen: annals
annotatie(s): annotation(s)
anon. *see* anoniem
anoniem: anonymous
antiquaar: antiquarian bookseller
antiquariaat: antiquarian book
  shop
aquarel: watercolor
aquatint: aquatint
arabesk: arabesque
archief: archives
art. *see* artikel
artikel: article, essay
artikelen: articles, essays
artikels: articles, essays
artistiek: artistic
atlas: atlas
auteur: author
auteursrecht: copyright
authentiek: authentic
autobiographie: autobiography
autobiografisch: autobiographical
autograaf(grafen): autograph(s)
autotypie: halftone engraving
azuurblauw: azure-colored

b.v. *see* bij voorbeeld
balacron: a patent book cloth
band(en): binding(s), cover(s),
  wrapper(s)
bandnummer: volume number
bandstempel: binder's tool
bedreven: skillful
beginletter: initial
behalve: except, besides
beide: both
beknopt: concise
bekrabbeld: disfigured by
  scribbling
bekroond: prizewinning
belangrijk: important, outstanding

bellettrie: fiction
ben. *see* benevens
benedenmarge: lower margin
benevens: together with, including
bep. *see* beperkt
beperkt: limited
beredeneerd: commented
bericht(en): report(s)
beroemd: famous, renowned
besch: *see* beschadigd
beschad. *see* beschadigd
beschadigd: damaged
beschadiging: damage, injury
beschreven: described
beschrijving: description
besluiten: concluded
besmeurd: soiled
besprenkelen: sprinkling
bestelformulier: order form
bestellen: to order, to place an
  order
bestelling: order
betaling: payment
betr. *see* betreffende
betreffende: concerning
bevat: contains
bevestigd: confirmed
bevestiging: confirmation
bevredigend: satisfactory
bew. *see* bewerkt
bewerker: editor
bewerking: version, adaptation
bewerkt: edited, arranged, adapted
bewonderenswaardig: admirable
bez. *see* bezorgd
bezaan: sheepskin
bezorgd: edited
bibl. *see* bibliotheek
bibliofiel: bibliophile
bibliografie: bibliography
bibliografisch: bibliographic
bibliothecaris: librarian
bibliotheek: library
bibliotheekstempel: library mark,
  library stamp
biblst. *see* bibliotheekstempel
bij elkaar: together

bij gelegenheid: occasionally
bij int. *see* bij intekening
bij intekening: by subscription
bij jaargang: by year
bij jrg. *see* bij jaargang
bij voorbeeld: for example
bijdr. *see* bijdrage
bijdrage(n): contribution(s)
bijeengezocht: collected
bijeenverzameld: collected
bijgeb. *see* bijgebonden
bijgebonden: bound in
bijgev. *see* bijgevoegd
bijgevoegd: added, appended
bijl. *see* bijlage
bijlage(n): appendix(es), supplement(s)
bijnaam: surname
bijvoegsel: supplement, appendix
bijvoegselen: supplements, appendixes
bijvoegsels: supplements, appendixes
bijzonder: special
binder: bookbinder
binnenkort: shortly
binnenlands: domestic
binnenrand: inside margin
binnenspiegel: lining, doublure
biograaf: biographer
biografisch: biographical
blad(en): leaf(ves), page(s)
blad van het voorwerk: preliminary leaf
bladmotief: leafy scroll
bladnummering: foliation
bladwijzer: index, table of contents
bladz. *see* bladzijde
bladzijde(n): page(s)
blanco: blank
blauw: blue
blazoen: coat(s) of arms
blind: blank, unadorned
blinddr. *see* blinddruk
blinddruk(ken): blind tooling
blindgestempeld: blind-tooled
blindstempel: blind tooling

bloemenvignet(ten): floral vignette(s)
bloemlezing: anthology
bloemornament(en): floral ornament(s)
bloempje(s): floret(s)
bloemstempel: floral design used in tooling
blokboek: block book
blz. *see* bladzijde
blzz. *see* bladzijden
bnd. *see* band
boek(en): book(s)
boekband: binding
boekbinder: bookbinder
boekdeel(delen): volume(s)
boekdrukker: printer
boekenstalletje: small secondhand bookstore
boekhandel: book shop, book trade
boekhandelaar: book dealer
boekje(s): booklet(s), small book(s)
boekliefhebber: bibliophile
boekomslag: book jacket, dust wrapper
boeksneden: edges of a book
bont: multicolored
bordure: ornamental border
bovenaan: at the top
bovendien: in addition
bovenkant: top edge
bovenrand: upper margin
bovenste: uppermost
brandgat: burn
breedte: width
breuk: break, crack
briefwisseling: correspondence
brochering: stitching, sewing
brochure(s): small book(s), brochure(s), pamphlet(s)
brokaat: brocade
bronnen: sources
bruikbaar: useful
bruin: brown
bruinrode: reddish-brown
buckr. *see* buckram

buckram: buckram
buigzaam: flexible, limp
buiten de tekst plaat: not in the
text
buitengewoon: uncommon
buitenlands: foreign
buitenrand: outside margin
buitentekstplaat(platen): plate(s)
not in the text
buitentekstpltn. *see* buitentekst-
platen
bundel(s): collection(s), volume(s)

calicot: calico
caricatuur: caricature
cartographie: cartography
cartonnage: cased binding
cartouche: cartouche
cassette: case, container
cat. *see* catalogus
catalogus(sen): catalog(s)
catalogusprijs: list price
censuur: censorship
chagrijnleder: shagreen
chagrinleer: shagreen
citroenkleurig: lemon-colored
clandestiene uitgave: clandestine
printing
col. *see* colophon
collatie: collation
collationeren: collate
collectie: collection
colophon: colophon
comment. *see* commentaar
commentaar: commentary
compendium: abridgment
compilatie: compilation
compilator: compiler
compl. *see* compleet
compleet: complete, completely
concordantie: concordance
condities: terms
contributie: membership fee
copie: copy, imitation
correctie(s): correction(s)
couv. *see* couvert
couvert(en): cover(s)

cplt. *see* compleet
critisch: critical
cursief: in italics
custode: catchword

d. *see* deel
dagboek: diary
datum van verschijnen: date of
publication
de meeste: the majority of, the
greater part
deel: part, volume
deelnummer: volume number
deels: partly
deeltje: small volume
defect: defective
definitief: definitive
delen: parts, volumes
delicaat: delicate
derde: third
dertien(de): thirteen(th)
dertig(ste): thirty(ieth)
devies: device, motto
diagr. *see* diagram
diagram(men): diagram(s)
dichtheid: thickness
dichtwerken: poems, poetical
works
dikte: thickness
diss. *see* dissertatie
dissertatie(s): dissertation(s)
dissertatiethesis: dissertation thesis
dln. *see* delen
dltje. *see* deeltje
dof: dull, lusterless
door: throughout
door bemiddeling van: through the
intermediary of
doorgestreept: crossed out,
canceled; effaced
doorlopend: continuous, consecutive
doorschieten: interleave
doorschoten: interleaved
doorstrepen: to cross out, cancel;
to efface
doorzichtig: transparent

doos: box
dr. *see* druk
drie: three
driemaandelijks: quarterly
droge naald: drypoint
druk(ken): print(s), edition(s)
drukfout(en): misprint(s), printing error(s)
drukker: printer
drukkerij: printing firm
drukkersmerk: printer's mark
drukpers: press
drukproef: proof copy
drukvermelding: imprint
dubbel: double
dubbelbl. *see* dubbelblad
dubbelblad: double page or leaf
dubbeldruk: double-striking
dubbelen: duplicates
duidelijk: obvious
duimgreep: thumb index
duizend(ste): thousand(th)
dun: thin, of poor quality
dundruked. *see* dundrukeditie
dundrukeditie: thin paper edition

e.a. *see* en andere
e.v.a. *see* en vele anderen
echt: genuine
ed. *see* editie
editie: edition
een: one
een boekdeel: single volume
een weinig: a little
eenjarig: yearly, of one year
eenkleurig: monochrome
eenvormig: uniform
eerste: first
eerste druk: first printing, first edition
eerste uitgave: first edition
eeuw: century
eeuwse: century
eigenh. *see* eigenhandig
eigenhandig: autograph, in one's own hand
eigennaam: proper name

einde: end
eindvignet: tailpiece
elf(de): eleven(th)
elk: each, every
emendaties: emendations
en andere: and others, among others
en vele anderen: and many others
enig: any, some
enig bekende: only one known
enig exemplaar: unique copy
eniglijk: solely
enigsz. *see* enigszins
enigszins: somewhat, a little
enkele: a few
enz. *see* enzovoort
enzovoort: and so forth
epiloog: epilogue, postface
etiket: label
ets(en): etching(s)
ex. *see* exemplaar
ex.-l. *see* ex-libris
ex-libris: *ex libris*, bookplate
exceptioneel: exceptional
exempl. *see* exemplaar
exemplaar(aren): copy(ies)
expl. *see* exemplaar
extra mooi: superfine
exx. *see* exemplaren
ezelsoor: dog-ear

fabel(s): fable(s)
facs. *see* facsimile
facsimile: facsimile
facsimile-uitgave: facsimile edition
factuur: invoice
facultatief: optional
feestbundel: volume of tributes
feilloos: impeccable
fig. *see* figuur
figuren: figures, diagrams
figuur: figure, diagram
figuurwerk: scrollwork
filet(s): fillet(s)
fluweel: velvet
fluwelig: velvetlike

foedraal: box, slipcase
fol. *see* folio
foliëring: foliation
folio: folio
formaat: format, size
forse: sturdy
foto(s): photograph(s)
fotocopie: photocopy, photostat
fotogr. *see* fotografie
fotografie: photograph
fotografisch: photographic
fotogravure: photogravure
fotolithografie: photolithography
fr. *see* fraai
fraai: handsome, handsomely
franco: postpaid, prepaid
franse titel: half-title page
frappant: striking
fris: fresh
frisheid: freshness
front. *see* frontispies
frontisp. *see* frontispies
frontispies: frontispiece
fustein: fustian

gaaf: sound, in perfect condition
gaatjes: small holes
gaufreren: goffer
geannoteerd: annotated
geannuleerd: canceled
geaquareleerd: hand-colored
gearceerd: hatched
geb. *see* gebied, gebonden
gebied: area, subject
geblakerd: scorched
gebogen: curved
gebonden: bound
geborduurd: embroidered
gebr. *see* gebruikt
gebrek: defect
gebrekkig: defective, imperfect
gebrocheerd: sewed
gebroken: split
gebronsd: reddish-brown
gebruikssporen: traces of use
gebruikt: used, worn
gebruind: browned

gec. *see* gecartonneerd
gecart. *see* gecartonneerd
gecarton. *see* gecartonneerd
gecartonneerd: bound in boards
gecensureerd: censored, suppressed
geciseleerd: chiseled, goffered
gecommentarieerd: commented
gecompleteerd: completed
geconserveerd: preserved
gecycl. *see* gecyclostileerd
gecyclostileerd: multigraphed
ged. *see* gedeelte, gedurende
gedat. *see* gedateerd
gedateerd: dated
gedeelte(n): part(s), section(s)
gedeeltelijk: part(ly)
gedenkboek: commemorative volume
gedenkschrift: commemorative volume
gedicht(en): poem(s)
gedr. *see* gedrukt
gedreven: embossed
gedrukt: printed
gedrukte omslag: printed cover
gedurende: during
geel: yellow
geelachtig: yellowish
geelbruin: fawn-colored, tawny
geëmailleerd: enamel(ed)
geest: spirit
geëtst: etched
geëtste plaat: etching
gefacsimileerd: reproduced in facsimile
gefactureerd: invoiced
gefolieerd: foliated
gegevens: data
geglansd: calendered
gegr. *see* gegraveerd
gegrav. *see* gegraveerd
gegraveerd: engraved
geh. *see* geheel
geheel: full, whole, entirely
gehoogd: heightened
geill. *see* geillustreerd

geills. *see* geillustreerd
geillumineerd: illuminated
geillustr. *see* geillustreerd
geillustreerd: illustrated
geillustreerd omslag: illustrated
cover
gejasperde sneden: sprinkled edges
gekl. *see* gekleurd
gekleurd: colored
geknaagd: gnawed
gekrast: scratched
gekreukeld: wrinkled
gekuist: expurgated
gel. *see* gelegenheid
gelegenheid: occasion, opportunity
gelezen: read
gelijk: equal, same, similar
gelijke band: uniform binding
gelijkluidend: identical text
gelijktijdig: contemporary
gelijmd: glued
gelinieerd: ruled, lined
gelithografeerd: lithographed
gemarmerd: marbled
gemarmerde sneden: marbled
edges
gematigd: moderate
gemutileerd: mutilated
genumm. *see* genummerd
genummerd: numbered
geornamenteerd: decorated
gepagin. *see* gepagineerd
gepagineerd: paged
geparafeerd: initialed
geplakt: pasted, mounted
geplet: crushed
gepointilleerd: stippled
gepolijst: polished, burnished
gerangschikt: arranged, classified
geredigeerd: directed
gereduceerd: reduced
geregleerd: ruled, lined
gerep. *see* gerepareerd
gerepareerd: repaired
gereserveerd: reserved
gerestaureerd: mended, repaired

geribd: ribbed, grained; bound
with raised bands
gerubriceerd: rubricated
geruit: checkered
gesatineerd: glazed
gesch. *see* geschept
geschaafd: rubbed, scratched
geschat: esteemed
geschatte prijs: estimated price
gescheiden: separate, single
geschenkboek(en): gift book(s)
geschept: handmade
gescheurd: torn
geschilderd: painted
geschreven: written, composed
geschrift(en): pamphlet(s),
paper(s)
gesign. *see* gesigneerd
gesigneerd: signed
gesleten: worn
gespikkeld: speckled
gestaakt: discontinued
gestempeld: stamped, tooled
gestenc. *see* gestencild
gestencild: mimeographed,
duplicated
getal: number
getekend: drawn
getint: tinted
getiteld: entitled
gevl. *see* gevlekt
gevlamde zijde: watered silk
gevlekt: spotted
gevouwen: folded
gewaardeerd: esteemed
gewassen: washed
gewijd aan: dedicated to
gewijz. *see* gewijzigd
gewijzigd: altered
gewoon: ordinary, usual
gezet: composed, set
gezocht: sought after, rare;
searched
gids: guide
giganten-paperback: large format
paperback

gigantische paperback: large
   format paperback
glad: smooth
gladde snede: smooth edge,
   trimmed edge
glansloos: dull, lusterless
glossarium: glossary
glosse: gloss
goed: good
goedkoop: cheap, inexpensive
gothisch: Gothic
goud: gold
gouden: gilt, decorated with gold
goudst. *see* goudstempel
goudstempel: gold stamping
goudstempeling: gilt-stamped
gr. *see* gravure
grafiek(en): graph(s)
grafische voorstelling(en):
   representation(s), graph(s)
graph. *see* graphiek
graphiek(en): graph(s)
grav. *see* gravure
gravure(s): engraving(s)
grijs: gray
grijsachtig rood: roan
groen: green
groenachtig: greenish
grof: coarse, rough
groot: large
groot papier: large paper
groothandel: wholesale
grootte: size
grote: large
grotendeels: mostly
groteske: block letter

h. *see* half
half: half
halfband: half binding
halfjaarlijks: semiannual
halfleder: half-leather, half-calf
halfleer: half-leather, half-calf
halflinnen: half-cloth
halfmaandelijks: fortnightly
halfmarokijn: half-morocco
halfperkament: half-vellum

hand: hand
handboek: manual
handel: trade
handelaar: dealer
handeling(en): paper(s), trans-
   action(s)
handgekleurd: hand-colored
handig: handy
handingekl. *see* handingekleurd
handingekleurd: hand-colored
handleiding: manual
handschr. *see* handschrift
handschrift(en): manuscript(s)
handt. *see* handtekening
handtekening(en): hand drawing(s),
   signature(s)
haveloos: dilapidated
helft: half
heliogravure: photogravure
herdr. *see* herdruk
herdruk(ken): reprint(s)
herdrukt: reprinted
herfst: Fall, Autumn
herhaaldelijk: frequently
herinneringen: memoirs
herkomst: provenance
herstelbaar: repairable
hersteld: repaired
herstellen: repair
herstelling: repair
hertenleer: buckskin, doeskin
herz. *see* herzien
herzien: revised
herziene uitgave: revised edition
herziener: reviser
herziening: revision
hetz. *see* hetzelfde, hetzelve
hetzelfde: the same
hetzelve: the same
hier en daar: here and there,
   occasional
hierbij: hereby
hiermede: herewith
hled. *see* halfleder
hlf. *see* half
hlflinn. *see* halflinnen
hlinn. *see* halflinnen

hln. *see* halflinnen
hoek(en): corner(s)
hoesje(s): dust wrapper(s)
honderd(en): hundred(s)
honderdste: hundredth
hoofd: superscript
hoofdje: rubric, heading
hoofdletter(s): capital(s)
hoofdstuk(ken): chapter(s)
hoog: high
hoogst: extremely
hoogte: height
hout: wood
houtblok: wood block
houten: wooden
houtgravs. *see* houtgravures
houtgravure(s): wood engraving(s), woodcut(s)
houtsn. *see* houtsnede
houtsnede(n): woodcut(s)
houtvrij: wood-free
houtworm: woodworm
H.S. *see* handschrift
hs. *see* handschrift
hss. *see* handschriften
hulpboekjes: auxiliary book
huls: slipcase

i.d.t. *see* in de tekst
i.h.b. *see* in het boek
identiek: identical
ieder: each, every
iets: somewhat
ietw. *see* ietwat
ietwat: somewhat
ill. *see* illustratie
illegaal: unauthorized
illuminatie: illumination
illust. *see* illustratie
illustr. *see* illustratie
illustratie(s): illustration(s)
imitatie: imitation
imitatieleer: imitation leather
impressum: imprint
in aflev. *see* in aflevering
in aflevering: in parts
in beslag genomen: confiscated

in cassette: in case, container
in de tekst: in the text
in het boek: in the book
in overeenstemming met: in agreement with
in samenwerking met: in collaboration with
in vellen: in sheets
in voorbereiding: in preparation
incompleet: incomplete, defective
incunabel(en): incunabulum(a)
ing. *see* ingebonden
ingebonden: bound in
ingekl. *see* ingekleurd
ingekleurd: in colors, colored
ingel. *see* ingeleid
ingelast: intercalated
ingelegd: laid in
ingeleid: introduced
ingelijmd: glued in, reglued
ingelijst: framed, bordered
ingen. *see* ingenaaid
ingenaaid: sewed
ingeperst: embossed
ingeplakt: pasted in
ingescheurd: torn
ingevoegd: inserted
inh. *see* inhoud
inhoud: contents
inhoudsopgave: table of contents
init. *see* initiaal
initiaal(alen): initial letter(s), initial(s)
inkoop: purchase
inkt: ink
inl. *see* inleiding
inlegblad: interleaved page, loose leaf
inleid. *see* inleiding
inleidend: preliminary
inleiding: introduction
inlichting: inquiry
inschrift: inscription
inscriptie: inscription
insnijding: scoring
integral: integral
inteken. *see* intekenaar

intekenaar: subscriber
intekenaarster: subscriber
intekenen: to subscribe
intekening: subscription
intekenprijs: subscription price
interpoleren: interpolate
interpretatie: interpretation
inwendig: internal, inner
inzage. *see* ter inzage
ivoorperk. *see* ivoorperkament
ivoorperkament: ivory vellum

jaar: year
jaarbericht(en): annal(s),
   transaction(s)
jaarboek: annual, yearbook
jaarboekje: yearbook
jaargang: year
jaarlijks: annual
jaartal: date
jaarverslag: annual report
jansenistenband: Jansenist binding
jrg. *see* jaargang
juchtleer: Russian leather
juweel: gem

k. *see* kaart
kaart(en): map(s), chart(s)
kaartje(s): small map(s), chart(s)
kaft: dustcover
kalfsleer: calf
kalfsleren band: calf binding
kant(en): margin(s)
kanttekening(en): marginal note(s)
kantwerk: lacework
kapitaal: capital letter
kapitaalband: headband
karton: cardboard, pasteboard
kartonnage(s): pasteboard bind-
   ing(s)
kartonnen band: bound in boards
kastanjebruin: chestnut color
kastanjekleurig: chestnut-colored
katern(s): quire(s)
katoen: cotton, cotton cloth
keerzijde: verso
kettingband: chained binding

keurig(e): exquisite, neat, clean
keus: selection
keuze(n): selection(s)
kinderboek: children's book
kl. *see* klein, kleur
klamp(en): clasp(s)
klassiek: classic
klein: small
klemband(en): clip binder(s), ring
   binder(s)
kleur(en): color(s)
kleuren-reproductie(s): color
   reproduction(s)
kleurendr. *see* kleurendruk
kleurendruk: color print
kleurenkaart(en): colored map(s)
kleurenplaten: color plates
kleurillustraties: color illustrations
kleurloos: colorless
kleurrijk: colorful
klrn. *see* kleuren
kneep: joint
knop(pen): boss(es)
kol. *see* kolom
kolom(men): column(s)
kolomtitel: headline
kop: top edge
kop verguld: gilt top
kopen: to buy
koper: copper
kopergr. *see* kopergravure
kopergrav. *see* kopergravure
kopergravure: copper engraving
koperlichtdruk: photoengraving
kopij: copy
kopijrecht: copyright
koptitel: heading, title
kopvignet: headpiece
kort: short, brief
korting: discount, reduction
kortstondig: ephemeral
kostbaar: costly, expensive
krabbels: scribbles
kras: scar, scratch
kroniek(en): chronicle(s)
krt. *see* kaart
krtjes. *see* kaartjes

krtn. *see* kaarten
krulornament: arabesque
krulwerk: scrollwork
kunstdrukpapier: coated paper
kunstfoto(s): art photograph(s)
kunstled. *see* kunstleder
kunstleder: imitation leather
kunstleer: imitation leather
kunstmatig: artificial
kunstzijde: artificial silk
kwadraat: square
kwaliteit: quality
kwart: quarter, one-fourth
kwartaal: quarter(ly)
kwartaalblad: quarterly

l. *see* licht, linnen
laatst: last
laatstverschenen: current, latest
lacune: gap
langw. *see* langwerpig
langwerpig: oblong
lasterlijk: libelous
lavendel: lavender
ldr. *see* leder
led. *see* leder
leder: leather
lederen: leather
leer: leather
leerboek: textbook
leerkapitaal: leather headband
leersnede: leather-cut
leesbaar: legible
leiding: direction
leikleurig: slate-colored
lelie: fleur-de-lys
lengte: length
lente: Spring
les(sen): lecture(s)
letter(en): letter(s)
letterkunde: literature
letterlijk: literal
levensbeschrijving: biography
leverbaar: available, in stock
levering: delivery
levertijd: delivery date
lexicon: thesaurus

lezing(en): lecture(s), reading(s)
licht: slightly
licht beschadigd: slightly damaged
lichtbruin: light brown
lichtdr. *see* lichtdruk
lichtdruk: photoengraving,
  phototype
lidmaatschap: membership
liefelijk: lovely
liefhebber: collector, amateur
lijn(en): line(s)
lijnenspel: pattern of lines
lijst: list; border
linkerhand: left-hand
links: left
linn. *see* linnen
linnen: cloth
lint(en): tie(s)
literatuur: literature
litho. *see* lithografie
lithogr. *see* lithografie
lithografie: lithograph, lithography
lithografisch: lithographic
ln. *see* linnen
lnn. *see* linnen
loffelijk: praiseworthy
lompenpapier: rag paper
loofwerk: leafy scroll decoration
lopende deel: current volume
los: detached, loose
los in band: loose in its covers
losbladig: loose-leaf
lovertje(s): spangle(s)
lr. *see* leder, leer
luchtfoto(s): aerial photo(s)
luxe: deluxe
luxe-editie: deluxe edition
luxe-uitgave: deluxe publication
luxueus: luxurious

m. *see* met
maandblad: monthly publication
maandelijks: monthly
maandschr. *see* maandschrift
maandschrift: monthly, monthly
  magazine
mager: thin, fine-faced

map(pen): portfolio(s), pocket(s)
mar. *see* marokijn
marge(s): margin(s)
marmer: marbling, marbled
marmering: marbling
marokijn: morocco
marokijnleer: morocco
marokko. *see* marokijn
marron: maroon
matig: mediocre
meander: lacelike pattern
medaillon: medallion
mede-auteur: joint author
mededeling(en): communication(s)
medew. *see* medewerking
medewerker(s): collaborator(s),
   contributor(s)
medewerking: collaboration
meer: more
meerdere: several
meerderheid: majority
meertalig: polyglot
meestal: mostly, generally
meeste *see* de meeste
meesterstuk: masterpiece
mengelwerk(en): miscellany(ies)
merend. *see* merendeels
merendeels: greater part
merkbaar: noticeable
merkwaardig: noteworthy
met: with
met inbegrip van: including
met opdracht auteur: with the
   author's dedication
met verwijzing naar: with reference to
microfoto(s): microphotograph(s)
middeleeuwen: Middle Ages
middelmatig: mediocre, moderate
midden: center
mimeogr. *see* mimeographeerd
mimeographeerd: mimeographed
minder: less
miniatuur: miniature
mod. *see* modern
mod. gec. *see* modern gecartonneerd

modern: modern
modern gecartonneerd: modern
   cased-board binding
moiré: moiré
moirézijde: watered silk
monografie: monograph
monster: pattern, specimen
monumentaal: monumental
mooi: fine, beautiful, handsome
motief: design, pattern
mozaïek: mosaic
muziek: music

n.v.v. *see* niet verder verschenen
naam: name
naamlijst: register, list of names
naamloos: anonymous
naar aanleiding van: with reference
   to
naast: next to
nabootsing: imitation, copy
nadruk(ken): reprint(s)
nagel. *see* nagelaten
nagelaten: posthumous
nagenoeg: almost
nagezien: examined, inspected
namaak: imitation, fake
namelijk: namely, viz.
naslagwerk: reference work
nauwelijks: hardly, scarcely
nauwkeurig: exact
nawoord: epilogue
negen: nine
negende: ninth
negentien(de): nineteen(th)
negentig(ste): ninety(ieth)
net: nice, neat
niet in de handel: not for general
   sale, privately printed
niet meer verschenen: no more
   published
niet verder verschenen: no more
   published
nieuw(e): new
nl. *see* namelijk
no. *see* nummer
nodig: necessary

nooit: never
noot: note
noten: notes
notulen: proceedings, transactions
novelle: novelette, short story
nummer(s): number(s), item(s)
nummering: pagination
nummert door: continuous paging
nw. *see* nieuw

o. *see* origineel
o.a. *see* onder andere
o.m. *see* onder meer
o/snee. *see* op snede
obl. *see* oblong
oblong: oblong
oblongformaat: in oblong format
oker: ochre
olijfgroen: olive green
omgevouwen: folded
omgew. *see* omgewerkt
omgewerkt: revised, rewritten
omgezet: inverted
omlijst: framed, bordered
omlijsting: frame, border
omsl. *see* omslag
omslag: cover
omstreeks: circa, about
onafgesn. *see* onafgesneden
onafgesneden: uncut
onbed. *see* onbeduidend
onbedrukt: blank
onbeduidend: insignificant,
  insignificantly
onbekend: unknown
onbelangrijk: insignificant
onbeschadigd: undamaged
onbeschr. *see* onbeschreven
onbeschreven: blank, unused
onbevlekt: immaculate, spotless
onbevredigend: unsatisfactory
onbruikbaar: unusable
onder: under
onder andere(n): among others
onder meer: among others
onder rembours: cash on delivery
onderaan: at the bottom

onderdrukt: suppressed
ondergrond: background
ondermarge: lower margin
onderschrift: legend, caption
ondersteuning: support
onderstreept: underlined
onderstrepen: to underline
onderstreping(en): underlining(s)
ondert. *see* ondertitel
ondertekend: signed
ondertekening: signature
ondertitel: subtitle
onderweg: in transit
onderwerp: subject
onderzocht: investigated
onderzoek: inquiry, investigation
ondoorschijnend: opaque
onfr. *see* onfris
onfris: not fresh, worn
ongebruikelijk: unusual
ongebruikt: unused
ongedr. *see* ongedrukt
ongedrukt: unprinted, unpublished
ongeëvenaard: matchless
ongehecht: unstitched
ongekuist: unexpurgated
ongelijk: disparate
ongelukkig: unfortunate
ongenoegzaam: insufficient
ongenummerd: unnumbered
ongeoorloofd nadrukken: pirated
  edition
ongeopend: unopened
ongepagineerd: unpaged
ongepolijst: unpolished
ongeschonden: untouched,
  undamaged
ongeveer: approximately
ongewijzigd: unchanged
ongewoon: exceptional
onlangs: recently
onleesbaar: illegible
onopengesneden: unopened, uncut
onrechtmatig: unauthorized,
  pirated
onregelmatig: irregular
onschatbaar: priceless

ontbr. *see* ontbreekt
ontbreekt: lacking, missing
ontelb. *see* ontelbaar
ontelbaar: innumerable, numerous
ontst. *see* ontstaan
ontstaan: originate
ontw. *see* ontworpen
ontworpen: designed
onuitgeg. *see* onuitgegeven
onuitgegeven: unpublished
onv. *see* onveranderd
onveranderd: unchanged, unrevised
onverk. *see* onverkort
onverkort: unabridged
onverminkt: undamaged, un-
mutilated
onversierd: plain, undecorated
onvolledig: defective, incomplete
onvoltooid: incomplete
onvoorstelbaar: exceptional
ook: also
oorkonde(n): document(s),
charter(s)
oorlogsjaren: war years
oorspr. *see* oorspronkelijk
oorsprong(en): origin(s), source(s)
oorspronkelijk: original
oorspronkelijke uitgave: original
edition
op aanvraag: on request
op snede: on the edge
op zicht: on approval
opdr. *see* opdracht
opdracht: dedication
opdruk: tooling
opeenvolgend: consecutive, successive
openbare les: inaugural address
opengesn. *see* opengesneden
opengesneden: cut open
opg. *see* opgave
opgave: table, table of contents
opgehelderd: clarified
opgeplakt: pasted up, mounted
opgespoord: traced
opgezet: set up, mounted

opl. *see* oplaag
oplaag(lagen): edition(s)
opmerkelijk: noticeable, remarkable
opmerkenswaardig: noteworthy
opn. *see* opnieuw
opnieuw: again, anew
opschrift: inscription
opstellen: works, miscellanea
optie given: to give the first
refusal
opvouwbaar: folding
or. *see* origineel
orig. *see* origineel
origin. *see* origineel
origineel: original
ornament(en): ornament(s)
oud: old
overdr. *see* overdruk
overdruk: reprint, offprint
overgeb. *see* overgebonden
overgebonden: rebound
overgedrukt: reprinted
overgegaan in: continued as
overgeplakt: pasted over
overgezet: translated
overige: remaining
overvloedig: copious
overzetting: translation
overzicht: abstract, synopsis,
survey

p. *see* pagina
p.d. *see* per deel
p.dl. *see* per deel
paar: a few
paarlemoer: mother-of-pearl
pagina('s): page(s)
pagineerd: paged
paginering: pagination
pamflet(ten): pamphlet(s)
paneel: panel
paperback: paperback
papier: paper
paraaf: paraph, flourish
parodie: parody

particuliere uitgave: privately
  printed
pennenaam: pseudonym
pentekening(en): pen and ink
  drawing(s)
pentk. *see* pentekening
per deel: each part, volume
per jaarg. *see* per jaargang
per jaargang: for the year
per kruisband: by book post
perforatie: perforation
perforeren: perforate
periodiek: periodical
perk. *see* perkament
perkament: parchment, vellum
perkt. *see* perkament
pers: press
photogr. *see* photographie
photographie(s): photo(s)
pl. *see* plaat
plaat: plate
plaatje: small plate
plaatpapier: plate paper
plaats: place
plaats van herkomst: place of
  origin; provenience
plaatsregister: list of places
plagiaat: plagiarism
plan: plan, project
plannen: plans, projects
plano: in sheets
plaquette: plaque
plat(ten): side(s) of a book
platen: plates, illustrations
platenalbum: album of illustrations
platenatlas: atlas of plates, book
  of plates
platenregister: index to plates
platina: platinum
platte ribben: flat bands
plattegr. *see* plattegrond
plattegrond(en): plan(s), map(s)
pltn. *see* platen
poezie: poetry
polychroom: multicolored
porfier: porphyry

portef. *see* portefeuille
portefeuille: portfolio
port: postage
porto: postage
portr. *see* portret
portret(ten): portrait(s)
portrn. *see* portretten
posthuum: posthumous
postpakket: postal parcel
postscriptum: postscript
potlood: pencil
potloodaant. *see* potloodaante-
  kening
potloodaantekening(en): pencil
  note(s)
potloodstrepen: pencil underscoring
potloodtekening: pencil drawing
pp. *see* pagina's
prachtband: deluxe binding,
  ornamental binding
prachtig: splendid, magnificent
prachtuitgave: deluxe edition
preliminair(en): preliminary(ies)
prent(en): engraving(s), print(s)
prentenboek: picture book
presentexemplaar: presentation
  copy
prijs: price
prijs bij intekening: prepublication
  price
prijs nog onbekend: price not yet
  known
prijslijst: price list
prijsopgaaf: quotation
prijsverlagingen: reduced price
prijswijzigingen: price changes
prijzen: prices
prijzen op aanvraag: prices upon
  request
privédruk: privately printed
proefnummer(s): specimen
  copy(ies)
proefschrift: thesis
proloog: prologue
prospectus: prospectus
provisioneel: provisional

provisorisch: interim, temporary
pseudoniem: pseudonym
publicatie(s): publication(s)
punteerwerk: stippling
purperen: purple

quantiteit: quantity

rand(en): margin(s), border(s)
randglosse(n): marginal note(s)
randversiering(en): ornamental
  border(s)
randwerk: ornamental border
rankwerk: scrollwork
recht van terugzending: option of
  return
rechts: right
recto: recto, front side
red. *see* redactie
redacteur: editor
redactie: editorship
redactiecommissie: editorial
  committee
rede: speech, address
redelijk: reasonable
reeks: series, set
reg. *see* register
regel: line
regelnummers: line numbers
register: index
registerdeel: index volume
rein: clean
rekening: account, bill
reliëfkaart: relief map
repertorium: list, index;
  reference work
repr. *see* reproductie
reprod. *see* reproductie
reproductie(s): reproduction(s)
rest: remainder
restant: remainders
restauratie: repair
ribben: raised bands, edges
ribbenband(en): ribbed binding(s)
riemen: laces, straps
rijk: rich, richly
rijkelijk: copious

rijstpapier: rice paper
roestkleurig: rust-colored
roestvlek(ken): rust spot(s), foxing
roestvlekje(s): small rust spot(s)
roestvlekkig: foxed
roman: novel
romeins: roman type
ronde gotische letter: bastard type
rood: red
roodachtig: reddish
roodbruin: russet color
roodsn. *see* roodsneden
roodsneden: red edges
rose: pink
rozet: rosette
rubriceren: classify; rubricate
rubricering: classification; rubrication
rubriek(en): heading(s), section(s)
rug(gen): back(s)
rugschild: back label
rugschildje: small back label
rugtitel: back title piece
rugveld(en): panel(s) on spine
rugzijde: back of a book, spine
ruil: exchange
ruiling: exchange
ruim: liberally, more than
ruit: lozenge
ruiten: checkered pattern
ruitformig: lozenge-shaped
rustiek: rustic
ruw: raw, rough

samen: together
samengeb. met *see* samengebonden
  met
samengebonden met: bound with
samengebracht: compiled
samengesmolten: merged
samengest. *see* samengesteld
samengesteld: compiled
samengevoegd: merged
samensteller: compiler
samenvatting: summary
samenvoegen: to merge
samenw. *see* samenwerking

samenwerking: collaboration
satijn: satin
satinet: sateen
schaafplek: scratch, chafed spot
schaal: scale
schaapleer: sheepskin
schaars: scarce, rare
scharn. *see* scharnier
scharnier: hinge, joint
schenking: gift
schets: sketch
schetskaart(en): sketch map(s),
   outline map(s)
scheur(en), crack(s), tear(s)
schild: medallion
schilderachtig: picturesque
schilderij(en): picture(s)
schimmelvlek(ken): mildew
   spot(s)
schoon: clean
schotschrift: libelous pamphlet
schr. *see* schrijver
schram: scar, scratch
schrift: handwriting, hand
schrijver: author, writer
schrijver-uitgever: privately
   published
schroeivlek: burn
schuifdoos: slipcase
schuilnaam: pen name, pseudonym
schutbl. *see* schutblad
schutblad: endpaper, flyleaf
segrijn: shagreen
serie: series
sierlijk: neat, elegant
sierlijst: ornamental border
sierrand: ornamental border
signat. *see* signatuur
signatuur(turen): signature(s)
simili. *see* similigravure
similigravure: halftone engraving
slap(pe): flexible, limp
slappe band: flexible binding
slecht: bad, badly
slechts: only, merely
sleuteroman: *roman à clef*
slijtage: traces of wear

slordig: tattered
slot: end, conclusion
slot(en): clasp(s)
slotvignet: tailpiece
sluitornament: tailpiece
smaadschrift: lampoon
smaak: taste
smaakvol: tasteful
smal: narrow
smoezel. *see* smoezelig
smoezelig: dirty, smudged
snede(n): edge(s)
snee. *see* snede
soepel: limp, flexible
soepele band: flexible binding
solide: durable
sommige: some
soms: sometimes, in some instances
spatiëren: space
spec. *see* speciaal
speciaal: special, separate
specialiteit: specialty
spikkelig: speckled
spiraalband: spiral binding
spleet: split
spoed: rush, haste
spoedig: prompt
sporen: traces, marks
spotprent(en): caricature(s)
spreukband: lettered scroll,
   legend
sprokkelingen: collectanea
sprookje(s); fairy tale(s)
st. *see* stempel, stuk
staalgr. *see* staalgravure
staalgravs. *see* staalgravures
staalgravure(s): steel engraving(s)
staat: condition, state
standaardwerk: standard work
steen: lithograph
steendruk: lithography
steendrukkerij(en): lithographer(s)
stekig: wormholed
stel: set
stempel: stamp, tool
stempelband: tooled binding
stereotiepe: stereotype

sterk: strong
sterrekaart: celestial chart
stichter: founder
stijf: stiff
stijl: style
stippel vergulding: gilt dots
stkn. *see* stukken
stn. *see* stukken
stoer: sturdy
stof: cloth
stoffig: dusty
stofomsl. *see* stofomslag
stofomslag: cloth cover, dust jacket
strokleurig: straw-colored
strook: guard
stud. ab. *see* studenten abonnement
studenten abonnement: student
  subscription
stuk: piece, volume
stukje: small piece, pamphlet
stukken: pieces, volumes
stuks: pieces, volumes
suppl. *see* supplement
supplement: supplement
supra-exlibris: book stamp(s)
systematisch: systematic

t. *see* tekst
t/m. *see* tot en met
taal: language
tab. *see* tabel
tabel(len): table(s), list(s)
tachtig(ste): eighty(ieth)
tal van: a great number of
talloos: innumerable
talr. *see* talrijk
talrijk: numerous
tamelijk: rather
te koop: for sale
teek. *see* tekening
teekening: *see* tekening
tek. *see* tekening
teken. *see* tekening
tekening(en): drawing(s)
tekn. *see* tekening
tekst: text

tekstafb. *see* tekstafbeeldingen
tekstafbeeldingen: illustrations in
  the text
tekstfig. *see* tekstfiguren
tekstfiguren: illustrations in the
  text
tekstgravures: engravings in the
  text
tekstillustraties: illustrations in
  the text
tekstueel: textual
tekstverlies: loss of text
telkens: each (every) time
ter ere: in honor
ter inzage: on approval
ter perse: in press
terugzending: return
tez. *see* tezamen
tezamen: together
tien(de): ten(th)
tijd: time
tijdelijk: interim, temporarily
tijdschrift: periodical, journal
tint: shade, tint
tit. *see* titel
titel(s): title(s), title page(s)
titel en inhoud niet verschenen:
  title page and index not done
titelafb. *see* titelafbeelding
titelafbeelding: illustrated title
titelblad: title page
titelgravure: engraved title
titelp. *see* titelpagina
titelpag. *see* titelpagina
titelpagina: title page
titelpl. *see* titelplaat
titelplaat: frontispiece
titelpr. *see* titelprent
titelprent: frontispiece
titelvignet: headpiece
toegel. *see* toegelicht
toegelicht: explained
toegevoegd: added
toel. *see* toelichting
toelichting: explanation
toestand: condition
toestemming: permission

toevoegsel: addendum
toezicht: supervision
toneelstuk: play
toongravure: chiaroscuro
tot en met: through, up to and
  including
totaal: total, in all
traceerwerk: tracery
traktaat: tract, treatise
tussen: between
tussentijd: interim
tussentijdse verkoop voorbehouden:
  subject to previous sale
twaalf(de): twelve(twelfth)
twee(de): two (second)
tweedehands: secondhand
tweejarig: biennial
tweemaandelijks: semimonthly
tweetalig: bilingual
tweevoud: duplicate
twintig(ste): twenty(ieth)
typisch: typical
typografisch: typographical
typographie: typography

uit de band: binding loose
uit de tijd: obsolete, outdated
uit dezelfde tijd: contemporary
uitdr. *see* uitdrukking
uitdrukking(en): expression(s)
uitg. *see* uitgegeven
uitgaaf: edition, publication
uitgave. *see* uitgaaf
uitgebr. *see* uitgebreide
uitgebreide: enlarged
uitgeg. *see* uitgegeven
uitgegeven: published
uitgekn. *see* uitgeknipt
uitgeknipt: cut out
uitgescheurd: torn out
uitgesneden: cut out, excised
uitgesteld: deferred
uitgever: publisher
uitgeversband(en): publisher's
  binding(s)
uitgevershuis: publishing firm
uitgevoerd: executed

uitgewerkt: elaborated, developed
uitkomen: to appear
uitlegging: commentary
uitsl. *see* uitslaand
uitslaand: unfolding
uitsluitend: exclusive
uitst. *see* uitstekend
uitstekend: excellent
uitstellen: postpone
uittreksel: excerpt
uitv. *see* uitverkocht
uitverk. *see* uitverkocht
uitverkocht: out of print
uitvoerig: detailed
uitvouwbaar: unfolding
uitwissen: efface, erase
unciaal: uncial
uniek: sole, unique
unif. *see* uniform
uniform: alike, in a uniform style

v.d.tijd. *see* van dezen tijd
vaardigheid: skill
vakken: sections
vals: false
van dezen tijd: contemporary
varia: miscellanies
variatie: variation
varkensleer: pigskin
vaste bestelling: standing order
veel: many, much
veelbetekenend: significant
veelkleurig: varicolored
veertien(de): fourteen(th)
veertig(ste): forty(ieth)
veiling: auction sale
veilingsvoorwaarden: conditions
  of sale
vel(len): leaf(ves), sheet(s),
  gathering(s)
veld(en): panel(s)
vele: many
velijn: vellum
velijnpapier: vellum paper
veranderd: altered
verb. *see* verbeterd
verbeterd: improved, corrected

verbetering: correction
verboden: suppressed
verder: further, otherwise
vereenvoudiging: reduction
verfrommeld: crushed, crinkled
verg. *see* verguld, vergulding
vergeeld: yellowed
verguld: gilt, decorated with gold
vergulde binnenrand: inside
   dentelle
vergulde sneden: gilt edges
vergulding: decorations in gold
vergunning: permit
verhaal: narrative, story
verhalen: narratives, stories
verhandelingen: proceedings
verhoogd: enhanced
verificatie: verification
verkieselijk: preferable
verkl. *see* verkleurd
verklaard: explained
verklar. *see* verklarend
verklarend: explanatory
verklaring: commentary, explanation
verkleind: reduced
verkleurd: faded, discolored
verkleuring: discoloration
verkocht: sold
verkoop: sale
verkoping: sale, auction
verkort: abridged
verkorte titel: short title
verkorting: abridgment
verkrijgbaar: available
verlegen: shopworn
verlucht: illuminated
verluchting: illumination
verm. *see* vermeerderd
vermaard: renowned
vermeerderd: enlarged, augmented
vermeerderde uitgave: enlarged
   edition
vermiljoenrood: vermilion
vernieuwd: restored
verouderd: aged, obsolete
verpakking: packing

verplicht: under obligation
verrijken: enrich
verrukkelijk: delightful
vers. *see* versierd
versch. *see* verscheen, verscheiden
verscheen: appeared, issued
verscheiden: several, various
verschenen: published
verschijnt binnenkort: to appear
   shortly
verschoten: faded
versierd: decorated
versiering: decoration, ornamentation
verslag: report
versleten: worn, tattered
versterkt: reinforced
vert. *see* vertaling
vertaald: translated
vertaling: translation, version
vertolking: interpretation
vertraagd: delayed
vervallen: dilapidated, in poor
   condition
vervalsing: falsification, forgery
vervangen door: replaced by
vervolg: continuation, sequel
vervolgwerk: serial publication
verwant: related
verz. *see* verzameld
verzamelaar: collector
verzamelaarsband: three-quarter
   binding
verzameld: compiled, collected
verzameld werk: collective work
verzameling: collection, compilation
verzameltitel: collective title
verzamelwerk: collective work
verzen: verse, poems
verzendkosten: shipping costs
verzonden: forwarded
verzorgd: produced
vier(de): four(th)
vierkant: square
vign. *see* vignet
vignet(ten): vignette(s)

71

vijf(de): five (fifth)
vijfig(ste): fifty(ieth)
vijftien(de): fifteen(th)
violet: violet
vl. *see* vlekkig
vlek(ken): spot(s), stain(s)
vlekje(s): small spot(s)
vlekkeloos: spotless, immaculate
vlekkig: foxed, spotted
vliegend blad: flyer, leaflet
vlugschrift: pamphlet
vocht: moisture
vochtigheit: humidity, moisture
vochtvl. *see* vochtvlekkig
vochtvlekken: damp spots
vochtvlekkig: damp-stained
voegzaam: proper, suitable
voet: bottom
voldoende: sufficient
volgend: following, subsequent
volgwerk: serial publication
volksboek: chapbook
volksuitgave: popular edition
voll. *see* volledig
volled. *see* volledig
volledig: complete, completely
volrandig: with margins uncut
volumineus: voluminous
voor rekening van: charged to,
  for account of
voorbeeld: example
voorbereid: prepared
voorbereiding: preparation
voorbericht: foreword, preface
voordracht(en): talk(s), speech(es),
  lecture(s)
voorhanden: available
voorjaar: Spring
voorkomen: appearance
voorlaatst: penultimate
voorlopig: interim, temporary
voornaam: distinguished
voornamelijk: mainly
voorplaat: front cover
voorraad: stock
voorrede: introduction, preface
voorsnede: fore edge

voorst. *see* voorstelling
voorste: foremost
voorstel. *see* voorstelling
voorstelling(en): representation(s),
  illustration(s)
voortgezet door: continued by
voortitel: half title
voortreff. *see* voortreffelijk
voortreffelijk: excellent, outstanding
voortzetting: continuation
vooruitbetaald: prepaid
voorw. *see* voorwoord
voorwaarde(n): condition(s)
voorwerk: preliminary pages,
  front matter
voorwoord: foreword, preface
voorzijde: face, front side
vouw: fold
vracht: freight
vrij van rechten: duty free
vrijblijvend: without commitment
vrnl. *see* voornamelijk
vroeger: formerly
vuil: soiled, dirty

waard(e): value, worth
waardeloos: worthless
waarderen: value
waardevol: valuable
waaronder: among which
waarop: on which
waarvan: of which
wapen: arms
wapenboek: book of arms
wapencartouche: cartouche containing a coat of arms
wapenpl. *see* wapenplaten
wapenplaten: plates of coats of
  arms
wapenschild: coat of arms
wat: somewhat, slightly
watermerk: watermark
watervl. *see* watervlekken,
  watervlekkig
watervlekken: water stains
watervlekkig: stained by water

weekblad: weekly
weervl. *see* weervlekkig
weervlekkig: weather-stained
weggeschrapt: effaced, erased
weinig: a little, little
wekelijks: weekly
werk(en): work(s)
werkje: opuscule, pamphlet
wetenschap: learning, science
wetenschappelijk: scientific
wiegedruk(ken): incunabulum(a)
winter: Winter
wit(te): blank, white
wonderschoon: wonderful
woord vooraf: preface
woordenboek: dictionary
woordenlijst(en): vocabulary(ies)
wordt niet herdrukt: will not be
   reprinted
worm(en): worm(s), wormed
wormgaatje(s): small wormhole(s)
wormstekig: wormed

z.j. *see* zonder jaartal
z.p. & j. *see* zonder plaats en jaar
z.pl. *see* zonder plaats
zaak- en plaatsregister: index of
   subjects and places
zaakregister: subject index
zak: pocket
zakformaat: pocket-size
zalmkleurig: salmon-colored
zamen. *see* tezamen
zeer: very, exceedingly
zegel: seal, signet

zegellak: sealing wax
zeldz. *see* zeldzaam
zeldzaam: rare
zelfd(e): same
zelfportret: self-portrait
zending: shipment
zes(de): six(th)
zestien(de): sixteen(th)
zestig(ste): sixty(ieth)
zeven(de): seven(th)
zeventien(de): seventeen(th)
zeventig(ste): seventy(ieth)
zijde: side; silk
zincographisch: zincographic
zoekgeraakt: lost, mislaid
zojuist verschenen: just published
zomer: Summer
zonder: without
zonder band: unsewn
zonder jaartal: without date of
   publication
zonder plaats: without place of
   publication
zonder plaats en jaar: without
   place or date
zonder titel: without title page
zw. *see* zwart
zw/w *see* zwart/wit
zwaar: heavy, severely
zwak: weak
zwart: black
zwart/wit: black and white
zwarte kunst: mezzotint
zwijnsleer: pigskin

Finnish

aapistaulu: hornbook
äärimmäinen: extreme
abstrakti: abstract
aika: time
aikakauskirja: periodical, journal
aikakauslehti: periodical, journal
ainoa: unique, only
ainokaisnidos: odd volume
aistikas: elegant
aito: real, genuine, actual
aivan: quite, altogether
ajankohta: date
akateeminen: academic
akatemia: academy
akvatinta: aquatint
alanimeke: subtitle
alaviite: footnote
alaviitteet: footnotes
albumi(t): album(s)
alempi: lower
alennettu: reduced
alennus: discount
alkeiskirja: primer
alku: beginning
alkukirjaimet: initial letters
alkukirjain: initial letter
alkukirjoitus: introduction
alkukuva: frontispiece
alkulause: preface, prefatory note
alkulehti: flyleaf, title page
alkuperä: origin
alkuperäinen: original, authentic
alkuperäiskansi: original cover
alkuperäissidos: original binding
alkusanat: foreword, preface,
  introduction

alkuteos: original work
allekirjoitus: signature
alleviivattu: underlined
alleviivaus: underlining
almanakka: almanac
anonyymi: anonymous
antiikva: roman type
antikvaarinen: antiquarian
antikvariaatti: antiquarian book
  shop
antologia: anthology
apuraha: subsidy, allowance
arabeski: arabesque
arkisto: archives
arkit: sheets
arkki: sheet
arkkijärjestyksen tarkistus:
  collation
arkkiveisu: broadside
artikkeli(t): article(s)
asiahakemisto: subject index
asiakirjat: documents, file
asuurikoriste: azure-tooled
aukileikkaamaton: uncut
autenttinen: authentic
autografi: signature
avopainate: broadside
avustaja: collaborator, contributor

bastardikirjasin: bastard type
bibliofiili: bibliophile
bibliografia: bibliography
bibliografinen: bibliographical
bukrami: buckram

defekti: defective

diagrammi: diagram
draama: drama

edellinen: preceding
ei kirjakaupassa: not available in
  bookstores
elämäkerrat: biographies
elämäkerta: biography
emalisidos: enamel binding
enemmistö: majority
enimmät: most
ennen: earlier, previously
ennenmainittu: above-mentioned
ensi: first
ensimmäinen painos: first edition
ensipainos: first edition
entinen: old, previous
epätäydellinen: incomplete,
  defective
erilainen: different, differing
erillistutkimus: monograph
erinomainen: excellent
eripainokset: offprints, reprints,
  separates
eripainos: offprint, reprint,
  separate
erittäin: particularly, especially
erittäin harvinainen: very rare
erityinen: special
esinimeke: half title
esinimiö: half-title page
esiökuva: frontispiece
esipuhe: preface, prologue,
  foreword
esite: prospectus
esitelmä: lecture
espartopaperi: esparto paper
essee: essay
etu-: front
etukannet: front covers
etukansi: front cover
etulehti: flyleaf
etupaperi: endpaper
etusivu: front page, title page
etusyrjä: fore edge

foliokoko: folio

formaatti: format, size
fotogravyyri: photogravure
fotolitografia: photolithography
fotostaattikopio(t): photostatic
  copy(ies)
fraktuura: black letter, gothic type
friisi(t): frieze(s)
frontispiisi: frontispiece

goottilainen kirjasin: Gothic type
groteskikirjasinlaji(t): block
  letter(s)

haalistunut: faded
hakanen: clasp
hakaset: clasps
hakemisto: directory, index
hakemistokirjaukset: headings
hakemistokirjaus: heading
haljas(nahka): split (leather)
hankauma(t): abrasion(s)
hankautunut: chafed
hankittu: furnished
harvat: few
harvinainen: rare
harvinaisen: extraordinary, very
  exceptional
harvinaisesti: rarely
harvoin: seldom
hävitetty: destroyed
heikko: weak
heikosti: weakly
hellittänyt: loosened
henkilöhakemisto: index of persons
hento: slight, weak
hetkikirja: book of hours
hieno: fine
hienojakoinen: close
hienosti: elegantly
himmeä: lusterless, dull
hinnasto: price catalog
hinta: price
home: mildew
homepilkku: mildew stain
homepilkut: mildew stains
huomautukset: annotations, notes
huomautus: annotation, note

huutokauppa: auction sale
huvinäytelmä: comedy
huvittava: entertaining
hyvä: good
hyväksytty: authorized, approved
hyvin tehty: well-made

i.p. & v. *see* ilman painopaikkaa
ja vuotta
i.v. *see* ilman painovuotta
ilman: without
ilman painopaikkaa ja vuotta:
without place or date
ilman painovuotta: without date
ilman sivunumeroita: unnumbered
ilman tekijännimeä: anonymous
ilmeinen: obvious
ilmestyä painosta: be off the press
ilmestymispaikka: place of
publication
ilmestymispäivä: date of publication
ilmestynyt: published
ilmoitus: advertisement, notice
initiaali(t): initial(s)
inkunaabeli(t): incunabulum(a)
irrallaan: covers loosened
irtopäällykset: dust wrappers
irtopäällys: dust wrapper
isokokoinen paperi: large paper

ja niin edespäin: et cetera, and
so forth
jäännöserä(t): remainder(s)
jakso: set, series
jäljelle jäänyt: remaining
jäljennökset: copies
jäljennös: copy
jäljennöspainos: facsimile edition
jäljet: traces
jäljittely: imitation, copy
jälkeen: after, behind
jälkeisteos: posthumous work
jälki: trace
jälkimmäinen: the latter
jälkipainos: reissue, reprint,
republication

jälkipuhe: postscript
japaninpaperi: Japanese vellum
jäsen: member
jatkettu: continued
jatkojulkaisu(t): continuation(s)
johdanto: introduction
jokakuukautinen: monthly
jokapäiväinen: daily
jokaviikkoinen: weekly
jokavuotinen: annual
jokin: some, any
juhlajulkaisu: festschrift
juhlakirja: festschrift
juhtinahka: Russian leather
julkaisematon: unpublished
julkaisija: publisher
julkaista: to publish
julkaistu: published
julkaisu: edition, publication
julkaisupaikka: place of publication
julkaisusarja: series
julkaisut: proceedings, transactions
julkaisutiedot: imprint
juuri ilmestynyt: just published

käännetty: translated
käännös: translation
kääntäjä: translator
kääntöpuoli: verso
kääntösivu: verso
kaava (kartta): design
kahdeksan: eight
kahdeksankymmentä: eighty
kahdeksantoista: eighteen
kahdeksas: eighth
kahdeksaskymmenes: eightieth
kahdeksastoista: eighteenth
kahdeskymmenes: twentieth
kahdestoista: twelfth
kaikkiaan: in all
kaiverre: print
kaiverrettu: engraved
kaiverrus: engraving
kaivertaja: engraver
kaiverteet: prints

kaksi: two
kaksikymmentä: twenty
kaksinkertainen: double
kaksitaitteinen: folio
kaksitoista: twelve
kaksitoistataitteinen: duodecimo
kalenteroitu: calendered
kallisarvoinen: valuable
kannatus: support
kannet: covers
kansanpainos: popular edition,
    people's edition
kansi: board, cover
kansikannet: binding covers
kansikuva: cover design, front
    picture
kansilehti: front cover, frontispiece
kansinasta(t): boss(es)
kansinimiö: cover title
kansio: album
kansipeili: doublure
kansisidonta-ainekset: covering
    materials
kansitaipeet: joints
kansitaive: joint
kansivuoraus: cover paper
kanssa: including, with
kantapainos: first edition,
    editio princeps
kapea: narrow, thin
kapiteelinauha: headboard
kappale(et): copy(ies)
karikatyyri: caricature
kartanpiirustus: map drawing
kartasto(t): atlas(es)
kartografia: cartography
kartonki: cardboard
kartta: chart, map
karttaja: charts, maps
karttaluonnos(okset): sketch
    map(s)
kartussi(t): cartouche(s)
käsikirja: handbook, manual
käsikirjoitus: manuscript
käsikirjoitusten koristelu:
    illumination

käsikirjoitusten somistus:
    illumination
käsin valmistettu: handmade
käsin valmistettu paperi: hand-
    made paper
käsinkirjoitettu: handwritten
käsinväritetty: hand-colored
käsipainin: handpress
käsky(t): decree(s), order(s)
kassa: cash
katkaista: cut off
katkelma: extract, fragment
katsoen: concerning
kaunis: beautiful
kaunokirjallisuus: belles lettres
kaunokirjoitus: calligraphy
käypä hinta: market price
kehys: border, frame
keittokirja(t): cookbook(s)
kellastunut: yellowed
keltainen: yellow
kera: with
kertoja: narrator
kertomus: story, tale
kesä: Summer
keski: middle
keskiaikainen: medieval
keskinkertainen: mediocre
keskustelut: transactions
ketjukirja: chained binding,
    chained book
kevät: Spring
kevyt: light, lightly
kielet: languages
kieli: language
kieltää: banned, forbidden
kiilloton: lusterless
kiilto: luster
kiiltopaperi: glazed paper
kiistakirjanen: lampoon; pamphlet
kilpikirjoitus: shield inscription
kirja(t): book(s)
kirja on painossa: being reprinted
kirjailtu: embroidered
kirjakauppa: bookstore
kirjakauppias: book dealer,
    bookseller

kirjake: character, type
kirjakotelo: slipcase
kirjaleimasin: book stamp
kirjallisuusluettelo: bibliography
kirjanen: pamphlet
kirjanhakanen: book clasp
kirjankansi: book cover
kirjankustannusliike: publishing
  house
kirjankustantaja: publisher
kirjanlehdet: leaves
kirjanlehti: leaf
kirjanpainajanmerkki: printer's
  mark
kirjanselkä: back of a book, spine
kirjansidonta: binding
kirjansidontaklootti: calico
kirjansitoja: bookbinder
kirjansivu(t): leaf(ves)
kirjanystävä: bibliophile
kirjapaino: printing shop, printer
kirjasin: character, type
kirjasto: library
kirjastoleima(sin): library stamp
kirjastonhoitaja: librarian
kirjastopainos: library edition
kirjauutuudet: new books, new
  publications
kirje(et): letter(s)
kirjepaperi: letter paper
kirjoittamaton: clean, unmarked
kirjoitus: article, paper
kirjoituspaperi: writing paper
kirkas: clear
kivipainaja: lithographer
kivipainanta: lithography
kivipainate: lithographs
kivipainatteet: lithographs
klootti: cloth
kloottinahka: full-cloth binding
kloottisidos: cloth binding
koirankorva: dog-eared
koko: size
kokoelma: collection
kokonaissumma: total, sum total,
  a total of
kokooja: compiler

kokoomanimilehti: collective title
  page
kokoomasidos: collective volume
kokositeet: raised bands
kokosivun: full page
kokosivun kuva(t): full-page
  illustration(s)
kolmas: third
kolmaskymmenes: thirtieth
kolmastoista: thirteenth
kolme: three
kolmekymmentä: thirty
kolmetoista: thirteen
kolofoni: colophon
komedia: comedy
kommentaari(t): commentary(ies)
kompendi: compendium
kompilaatio: compilation
konferenssi: conference
konkordanssi: concordance
koodeksi: codex
kookas: large, tall
koostaja: compiler
kootut: collected
kootut teokset: collected works,
  complete works
koristaminen: ornamentation
koristekehys: ornamental border
koristeltu selkä: decorated on
  spine
koristeselkä: decorated spine
koristettu: decorated
koristeviiva(t): fillet(s), line(s)
korjaaminen: correction
korjattu painos: corrected edition
korjatut painokset: corrected
  editions
korjaukset: mended, repaired
korjauksia: corrections
korjauslipuke: repair shop
korotettuun: increased
korupainos: deluxe edition
kostuma(t): damp stain(s)
kostumatäpläinen: damp-spotted
kostunut: damp-stained, damp-
  spotted
kotelo: case

kova: hard
kromolitografia: color lithography
kronikat: annals, chronicles
kronikka: chronicle
kuivaneula: drypoint
kullattu: gilded
kulma(t): corner(s)
kulma korjattu: corner repaired
kulmahelat: metal corners
kulmat korjattu: corners repaired
kulmat vahingoittuneet: corners damaged
kulta: gold
kultakoristeselkäinen: gilded on spine
kultareunainen: gold-bordered
kultasyrjä(t): gilt edge(s)
kultaus: gilding
kulunut: worn
kumpikin: either, each
kustannuspaikka: place of publication
kustantaa: to edit, to publish
kustantaja: publisher
kustantamo: publishing firm
kuudes: sixth
kuudeskymmenes: sixtieth
kuudestoista: sixteenth
kuukausilehti: monthly
kuusi: six
kuusikymmentä: sixty
kuusipeuran nahka: doeskin
kuusipeuran vasikka: fawn
kuusitoista: sixteen
kuva(t): illustration(s), picture(s), figure(s)
kuvakirja: picture book
kuvaliite muotokuva(t): portrait plate(s)
kuvateksti: caption
kuviollinen: graphic
kuvioton: plain
kuviteltu: fictitious
kuvitettu: illustrated
kuvittaa: to illustrate
kuvittaja: illustrator
kuvitus: illustration

kvartto: quarto
kyhmy(t): boss(es), knob(s)
kymmenen: ten
kymmenes: tenth
kysytty: sought after

laaja: extensive
laajennettu: enlarged
laajennettu painos: enlarged edition
laajuus: width
laakaleimasin: flat stamp
laatia: compile
lähde: source
lähteet: sources
laitokset: issues
laitos: issue
laivastonsininen: navy blue
lampaannahka: sheepskin
langaton: loose, unstitched
läpi-: through
lastenkirja(t): children's book(s)
laulukirja(t): songbook(s)
legenda: legend
lehden kääntöpuoli: verso
lehden numero: foliation
lehden takasivu: verso
lehdennumeroilla varustettu: foliated
lehdet: leaves, pages
lehti: leaf, page
lehtinen: broadside
leikattu: cut, trimmed
leike: clipping
leikkaamaton: uncut
leikkaamattomat syrjät: untrimmed edges
leikkaukset: cut edges
leikkaus: cut edge
lentokirjanen: pamphlet, brochure
leveäreunainen: with wide margins
liima: glue
liimata: to paste, to glue
liimautua: glued
liisteröity kartonki: pasteboard
liite: appendix
liiteet: appendixes

liitekuva: plate
likaantunut: very dirty
likimain: about, approximately
lisäksi: in addition
lisäksi tuleva: additional
lisälehdet: added leaves
lisälehti: added leaf
lisänide: additional volume
lisätty: added, enlarged
lisävihko: appendix, supplement
lisävihkot: appendixes, supplements
lisäyksiä: addenda
lista: list
litografia: lithograph
loistava: splendid
loisto: deluxe
loistopainos: deluxe edition
loistosidos: fine binding, deluxe binding
loistoteos: deluxe edition
loistoton: dull, without luster
loppu: end
loppukoriste: tailpiece
loppunut varastosta: out of stock
loppusivu: colophon
loppusumma: amount, total, sum total
loppuvinjetti: colophon
lopullinen: definitive
lovi: cut, notch
luennot: lectures
luento: lecture
luettelo: catalog
luettelohinta: list price
luku: chapter
lukuisa: numerous
lukuunottamatta: apart from
lumppupaperi: rag paper
luukku: hatched
luvunotsikko: chapter heading
luvut: chapters
lyhenne: abbreviation
lyhennetty: abridged
lyhentää: abridge
lyhentämätön: unabridged
lyhentäminen: abridgment

madonreiät: wormholes
madonreikä: wormhole
madonsyömä: wormholed
mahdollisesti: possibly
mainio: excellent
mainokset: advertisements
mainos: advertisement
majuskeli(t): capital letter(s)
marginaali(t): margin(s)
marmori: marbled
marmoroitu: marbled
marmoroitu paperi: marble paper, marbled paper
marokiini: morocco
marokonnahka: morocco
matala: low
medaljonki: medallion
melkein: almost
memoaarit: memoirs
merkit: traces
merkitsevä: significant
merkityksetön: insignificant
merkki: trace
mezzotintopiirros: mezzotint
miellyttävä: pleasant
mimeografi: mimeographed
miniatyyri: miniature
molemmat: both
moni: many
monikielinen: polyglot
monistaminen: reproduction
moniste: reproduction
monivärinen: multicolored
monografia: monograph
motto: motto
muinainen: old
muistelmat: memoirs
muistelmateos: memoirs
muistikirja(t): notebook(s)
muistuttaa: commented
muistutukset: comments, notes
muistutus: comment, note
mukaelma: adaptation
mukailla: arranged
mukailu: imitation
mukaisesti: in accordance with
muotokuva(t): portrait(s)

muotopuoli: irregular
musiikki: music
musta: black
muun muassa: among others
muutamat: a few
muuttumaton: unchanged
myöskin: also

nahka: leather
nahkakannet: leather bindings
nahkakansi: leather binding
nahkakantinen: full-leather binding
nahkanide: leather binding
nahkaselkäsidos: quarter-bound
nahkasidos: leather-bound
näköispainokset: facsimile editions, reprints
näköispainos: facsimile edition, reprint
näky: view
näyte: example, sample
näytelmä: play
näytteet: examples, samples
neljä: four
neljäkymmentä: forty
neljännesvuosijulkaisu: quarterly
neljäs: fourth
neljäskymmenes: fortieth
neljästoista: fourteenth
neljätoista: fourteen
nettohinta: net price
neuvonta: information
nide: volume
nidonta: stitching
nidottu: stitched; bound in paper covers
niinkuin: as, like
nimeke: title
nimekkeet: titles
nimetön: anonymous
nimi: name, title
nimihakemisto: index of names
nimikirjoitus: signature
nimikirjoituskoukero: paraph, flourish
nimiö: title
nimiökuva: frontispiece

nimiölehti: title page
nimiölehti puuttuu: title page missing
nimiösivu: title page
niteet: volumes
nitoa: to sew, to stitch
nitomaton: sheet of text
nitomattomat: in sheets, sheets of text
nitominen: stitching
noin: circa, ca.
novelli(t): short story(ies)
nuhraantunut: used, soiled
numero: number, part
numeroidut sivut: paginated
numeroitu sivu: numbered page
nuotit: notes
nuotti: note
nyhälaitainen: gnawed
nykyinen: present, modern
nyt: now

offset: offset
ohut: thin
ohutkansinen: with thin covers
oikaisulipuke: errata slip
oikea: right-hand
oktaavo: octavo
omaelämäkerta: autobiography
omistajanleima: owner's stamp
omistajanmerkit: marks of ownership
omistaminen: possession
omistettu: dedicated
omistuskirjoitus: inscription
omistussanat: inscription
oppikirja(t): textbook(s)
oranssi: orange
osa: part, volume
osaksi: partly
otaksuttava: presumable
otaksuttavasti: presumably
ote: extract
otsikko: rubric
otsikkokoriste: headpiece(s)
otsikkovinjetti: headpiece
otsikoitu: rubricated

pääasiallisesti: mainly
päällä: above, on
pahvi: cardboard
pahvikannet: hard covers
pahvikansi: hard cover
paikkahakemisto: gazetteer
painaa: print
painama: impression, imprint
painatteet: printed matter
painettu: printed
painettu kirja: printed book
paino: press
painopaikka: place of publication
painos: edition
painosmäärä: run, number of
　copies printed
painossa: in press
painotarkastus: censorship
painotiedot: imprint
painotuotteet: printed matter
painovirhe: misprint
painovuosi: date of publication
päivä: day
pakotettu: embossed
paksu: thick
palanut: burned
paljous: quantity
palkinto: prize
palsta(t): column(s)
pari: couple
pergamentti: vellum
pergamenttiselkä: vellum back
pergamenttisidokset: vellum
　bindings
pergamenttisidos: vellum binding
perustaa: constitutes
pidennetty: elongated
pienoiskoko: miniature
pienoiskuva: miniature
pienoismaalaus: miniature
pienoispainos: miniature book
　edition
piirustettu: drawn
piirustukset: designs, drawings,
　sketches
piirustus: design, drawing, sketch
pikku: little, small

pikkukirjanen: pamphlet
pilakuva(t): caricature(s)
pilkku: spot
pilkukas: spotted
pisteitetty: dotted
pitkä kirja: tall book
pitsikehys: dentelle frame
plagiaatti: plagiarism
pohja: bottom
poikittais: oblong
poikkeuksellinen: exceptional
poiminto: extract
poistaa: cross out, delete
postuumi: posthumous
pöytäkirja: proceedings
prospekti: prospectus
puhdas: spotless, clean
puhdistettu: cleansed
pukinnahka: buckskin
punainen: red
puolikloottisidos: half-cloth
　binding
puolimarokkosidos: half-morocco
　binding
puolinahka: half leather
puolinahkasidos: half-leather
　binding
puolinidokset: half issues
puolinidos: half issue
puolipergamenttisidos: half-vellum
　binding
puolisidos: half binding
puolivasikka: half-calf
puolivasikkasidos: half-calf
　binding
puolivuosi: half year
puolivuotinen: semiannual volume
puukannet: wooden sides
puupainate(et): block book(s)
puupiirros: woodcut
puutteellinen: defective
puuttuvat: missing, lacking

raaputettu: erased
raaputus: erasure
rajoitettu: limited
rajoitettu painos: limited edition

rakentaa: compile
rasteripainatus: halftone
reijät: holes
reikä: hole
repeytynyt: torn
reunahuomautus: marginal note
reunusnauha: headband
reunustetut: bordered
revityt: torn out
rikas: rich
romaani(t): novel(s)
rosoreuna: deckle edge
runo: poem
runous: poetry
runovalikoima: poetry anthology
ruskea: brown
ruskopilkkuinen: foxed
ruskotäpläinen: foxed
ruudullinen: checkered design
ryhmä(t): group(s)
ryppy: wrinkled
ryysyinen: tattered

saatavissa: available
saattaa: accompanies
šabloni: pattern
sadas: hundredth
šagriini: shagreen
säilynyt: preserved
salanimi: pseudonym
salkku: portfolio
salkut: portfolios
sama: same
samalla: together with
samanaikainen: contemporary
samanmuotoinen: similar
samaten: also
sametti: velvet
sanakirja(t): dictionary(ies)
sanaluettelo: glossary
sananlasku(t): proverb(s)
sanasto: glossary, vocabulary
sanomalehti: newspaper
sarja: series, set
sata: hundred
savu: smoke
sävyleikkaus: chiaroscuro

sävypiiros: chiaroscuro
seitsemän: seven
seitsemänkymmentä: seventy
seitsemäntoista: seventeen
seitsemäs: seventh
seitsemäskymmenes: seventieth
seitsemästoista: seventeenth
sekajulkaisu: miscellanea
sekuntiosoitin: second-hand
selänpään reunus: headcap
selitykset: annotations
selityksiä: commentaries
selityksineen: with annotations
selitys: commentary, interpretation
selkäkentät: panels on spine
selkäkirjannimi: back title
selkänimeke: title on spine
selkänimiö: title on spine
selkäpuoli: verso
seloste: review
sensuuri: censorship
siannnahka: pigskin
sidoksestaan irtaantunut: loose in binding
sidokset: bindings, volumes
sidos: binding, volume
sidottu: bound
siirtokopio: photocopy
siirtokopiot: photocopies
siisti: neat
siivota: expurgated
sileä: smooth
silotettu: smoothed
silotettu marokonnahka: crushed morocco
simultaaninen: simultaneous
sinetti: seal
sinimusta: blue-black
sininen: blue
sisä: inner
sisällinen: internal
sisällys: contents, table of contents
sisältää: comprised, included
sisäreuna: inner edge
sisimmäinen: innermost
sisuste: lining

sitäpaitsi: besides
sitoa: bind
sitomaton: unbound
sivu: leaf, page
sivunumero: page number
sivunumerointi: paging
sivunumeroton: without pagination
sivuteksti(t): page(s) of text
skitsi: sketch
sokkopuristus: blind tooling
sommitella: compile, sketch
suhteellinen: relatively
suojanasta(t): boss(es)
suojapäällys: book jacket, dustcovers
suora: direct, straight
suoraan: directly
suoritaa: executed
suoritettu: edited
supistelma: abridgment
suuraakkonen: capital letter(s), uppercase letters
suuresti: highly
suuri: great, large
syksy: Autumn, Fall
synopsis: synopsis
syntyperä: provenance
syrjä(t): edge(s)

tahraantunut: soiled
taipuisa: flexible
taipuisa side: flexible binding
taitteinen: folded
taka: back
takakansi: back cover
takaosa: rear
takavarikoitu: confiscated, suppressed
talvi: Winter
täpläpainanta: stippled
tarina(t): short story(ies)
tarkistettu painos: revised edition
tasasiteet: flat bands
tasku: pocket
taskupainos: pocket edition
taskusanakirja: pocket dictionary

tasoitettu: trimmed
tässä: here
taulu: plate
taulukko: table
taulukot: tables
tavallinen: ordinary
täydellinen sarja: all published, complete series
täydellisesti: altogether, completely
tekijä: author
tekijäkumppani: joint authors
tekijänoikeus: copyright
tekonahka: imitation leather, leatherette
teksti: text
tekstikuva: illustration in the text
tekstin: textual
teokset: works
teos: work
teräskaiverrus: steel engraving
teräskynäpiirrokset: steel engravings
teräskynäpiirros: steel engraving
tietosanakirja(t): encyclopedia(s)
tiivistetty: abridged
tilaukset: orders, subscriptions
tilaus: order, subscription
tili: account
toimitettu: compiled
toimittaa: to edit
toimittaja: editor
toimittanut: edited
toimitukset: proceedings, transactions
toinen: additional, second
toisenlainen: different
toisin: otherwise
tomuinen: dusty
transkriptio: transcription
tuhat: thousand
tulivahinko: fire damage
tummennettu: darkened
tuntematon: unknown
tuskin milloinkaan: hardly ever
tutkielma(t): essay(s), treatise(s)
tyhjälehti: flyleaf

typistetty: abbreviated, abridged
tyypillinen: typical

ulko: outer
unsiaali: uncial
uudet tarkastukset: new revisions
uusi: new
uusi painos: new edition
uusi sarja: new series
uusi tarkastus: new revision
uusintapainos: new edition,
  revised edition

vaakuna: coat of arms
väärä: erroneous, wrong
vaatesidonta: cloth covers
vähä: minor
vähemmän: less
vähempi: minor
vahingoittunut: damaged
vahva: strong
vahvistettu: reinforced
vaihtuva sivuotsikko: running title
väitöskirja: dissertation, treatise
vajanainen: defective
väliaikainen: preliminary,
  temporary
väliaikaissidos: temporary binding
valikoima: selection
välilehdet: interleaved pages
välilehditetty: interleaved
valinta: choice
valitut: selected
valkoinen: white
valmistava: introductory
valokopio: photocopy
valokuva(t): photograph(s)
valokuvaus: photographic
vanha: old, older
varaspainos: pirated edition
varastossa: in stock
väri(t): color(s)
väriliite: color plate, supplement
väriliitteet: color plates, supplements
värilitografia(t): color lithograph(s)
värillinen: colored

väritön: pale, colorless
väritys: coloring
varovainen: careful
vasikannahka: calfskin
vasikannahkasidos: calf binding
vasikka: calf
vaskipiirros: copper engraving,
  etching
vastuunalainen: responsible
vertailla: compare
vesileima: watermark
vesiväri(t): watercolor(s)
viat: defects
vierasmaalainen: foreign
vierus: margin
vierusnumero: marginal numbers
vihanta: green, verdant
vihko: booklet, issue, part
vihkot: booklets, issues, parts
vihreä: green
viideskymmenes: fiftieth
viidesosa: fifth
viidestoista: fifteenth
viikkolehti: weekly
viisi: five
viisikymmentä: fifty
viisitoista: fifteen
viitteillä varustettu: annotated
viivoitettu: ruled
vika(t): defect(s)
vinjetit: vignettes
vinjetti: vignette
violetti: violet
vuodet: years
vuorattu: lined
vuosi: year(s)
vuosikerrat: annual volumes, years
vuosikerta: annual volume, year
vuosikirja(t): annual(s), year-
  book(s)
vuosikirjat: annals
vuositilaushinta: annual subscription
vuotuinen: annual, yearly

yhdeksän: nine
yhdeksänkymmentä: ninety

yhdeksäntoista: nineteen
yhdeksäs: ninth
yhdeksäskymmenes: ninetieth
yhdeksästoista: nineteenth
yhdessä: together
yhdestoista: eleventh
yhteisnimeke: collective title
yhteistyö: collaboration
yksi: one
yksitoista: eleven
yksityinen: several

yksityiskohtainen: detailed
yksityispainos: privately printed
yläsyrjä: top margin
yleinen: public
yleiskatsaustaulukko: synoptic
   table
yli: over, more than
ylimittainen: oversize
ylinnä: at the top
ynnä muita: et cetera

French

à: to, with
a. *see* acier, année, avec
à c. *see* à coins
à coins: with corners, cornerpieces
à comp. *see* à compartiments
à compartiments: in squared
  patterns
à décor linéaire: with linear
  design decoration
à dent. *see* à dentelle
à dentelle: in dentelle design
à divers: in some
à double page: two-page
à fermoirs: with clasps
à fond: thoroughly
à fond criblé: with dotted background
à fr. *see* à froid
à froid: blind tooling
à grain écrasé: crushed grain
à grain long: straight-grained
à grande échelle: in large scale
à l'encre: in ink
à la charge de: at the expense of
à la fin: at the end
à la grotesque: in grotesque style
à la main: by hand
à lanières: with laces, ties
à larges mors: with wide joints
à long grain: straight-grained
à paraître: to appear
à part: aside, separate
à peine: scarcely
à petit nombre: in small number
à pleine page: full-page
à préciser: to be specified

à recouvrement: re-covered
à relier: to be rebound
à restaurer: to be restored
à suivre: to follow
à toutes marges: with full
  margins, untrimmed
ab. *see* abîmé, absent
abîm. *see* abîmé
abîmé: damaged, in poor condition
abond. *see* abondamment
abondamment: abundantly
abonn. *see* abonnement
abonné: subscriber
abonnement: subscription
abrégé: abridged
abréviation: abbreviation
abs. *see* absent, absolument
absent: lacking, missing
absol. *see* absolument
absolument: absolutely
abt. *see* abonnement
acc. *see* accident
accid. *see* accident
accident(s): damage(s)
accroc: tear
achevé *see* achevé d'imprimer
achevé d'imprimer: completion of
  printing note
acier: steel
adapt. *see* adaptation, adapté
adaptation: adaptation
adapté: adapted
addenda: addenda
additif: additional
adr. *see* adresse
adresse: address

agr. *see* agréable
agréable: appealing
agrémenté: ornamented, decorated
airain: brass, bronze
ais: binder's board(s)
ais de bois: wood board(s)
ajouté: added
alb. *see* album
album: album
alfa: esparto paper
alinéa: paragraph
allongé: long, elongated
almanach: almanac
amande: almond-colored
amarante: amaranthe, a soft
  reddish-purple color
amateur: collector
amphore(s): vase(s), design
  representing vase(s)
ample: considerable
an. *see* ancien, anneé
anc. *see* ancien
ancien: old, former
angle: angle
annales: annals
année: year
annexe: attached supplement
annot. *see* annotation, annoté
annotation: annotation
annoté: annotated
annuaire: annual, yearbook
annuel: annual, once a year
anon. *see* anonyme
anonyme: anonymous
ant. *see* antiqué
anthologie: anthology
antiqué: tooled
app. *see* appendice
apparition: appearance
append. *see* appendice
appendice: appendix
apprêté: polished, calendered
approximatif: approximate
aqu. *see* aquarelle
aquarelle: watercolor
aquarellé: painted in watercolors
aquatinte: aquatint, watercolor

arabesque: arabesque
archives: archives, records
ardoise: slate, color of slate
ardoisé: slate-colored
argenté: silvered
armes: armorial designs
armoiries: heraldic designs
armorié: decorated in heraldic
  designs
arraché: torn off, torn out
artificiel: artificial
assurance: insurance
atlas: atlas
attaches: ties
atteinte: damaged
attrayant: attractive
au comptant: for cash
au début: at the front
au pointillé: stippled
au ras du texte: at the edge of
  the text
au total: in all
aubergine: eggplant-colored
augm. *see* augmenté
augmenté: enlarged
aut. *see* auteur, autographe,
  autour
auteur: author
autobiographie: autobiography
autog. *see* autographe
autogr. *see* autographe
autographe: autograph
autographié: autographed
autor. *see* autorisé
autorisé: authorized
autour: around
aux armes: with armorial designs
aux petits fers: with small, fine-
  designed tooling
av. *see* avec
avant-propos: preface, introduction
avec: with
avec témoins: with witnesses
avertissement: notice
azuré: azured, tooled in close
  parallel lines

b. *see* bois, broché
balafre: scar, scoring
bande: band, strip pattern
bandeau(x): border strip(s)
banderole: ornamental band,
 scroll
barbes: deckled edge
bariolé: variegated
barré: canceled
bas. *see* basane
bas de page: foot of the page
basane: sheepskin
bâtarde: bastard type
beau: fine, beautiful
beige: beige-colored
bel: beautiful, fine
belle: beautiful, fine
bibl. *see* bibliothèque
bibliographie: bibliography
bibliographique: bibliographical
bibliophile: book lover
biblioth. *see* bibliothèque
bibliothécaire: librarian
bibliothèque: library
biffé: lined through, erased
bigarré: variegated
bilingue: bilingual
biographie: biography
bistre: dark brown, sepia
bl. *see* blanc
blanc: blank, white
blas. *see* blason
blason: armorial shield
bleu: blue
bleu ardoise: slate blue
bleu clair: clear blue, light blue
bleu lavande: lavender blue
bleu marine: marine blue
bleu nuit: midnight blue
bleu sombre: dark blue
bleuté: blued
blond: blond
bois: woodblock, woodcut
boîtage éd. *see* boîtage éditorial
boîtage éditorial: publisher's
 boxing
boîte: box

boîtier: slipcase
bon: good
bon état: in good condition
bord: edge
bord. *see* bordure
bordeau: border design
bordure: ornamental border
bouquin: used book of small value
bouquinerie: secondhand bookstore
bouton(s): knob(s), boss(es)
br. *see* bradel, broché
bradel: bradel, a cased binding
brique: brick-colored
brisé: broken
bristol: bristol board
broch. *see* broché
brochage: stitching, stitched
 binding
broché: stitched, sewed
brochure: pamphlet, pamphlet-
 style binding
brodé: embroidered
bronze: bronze-colored
brûlure: burn
brun: brown
brunâtre: brownish
bruni: browned, burnished
bulletin: bulletin
burin: steel engraving tool

c. *see* cassé, coins
cabochon(s): knob(s), boss(es)
cachet: stamp, seal
cachet de bibliothèque: library
 stamp
cachet de colportage: agent's
 stamp
cadre: frame, design forming a
 frame
cahier: quire, signature; notebook
caissons: line designs forming
 square or oblong frames
calendrier: calendar
calligraphié: handwritten, in fine
 style
calque: tracing
camaieu: chiaroscuro

capsule: slipcase, container
car. *see* caractère, carré
caractère(s): letter(s), type
carnet: notebook
carré: square
cart. *see* carton, cartonnage,
  cartonné
cart-croq. *see* carte-croquis
cart. d'éd. *see* cartonnage de
  l'éditeur
cartable: cardboard cover, carrying
  case
carte: map
carte-croquis: sketch map
cartographie: cartography
carton: cardboard, pasteboard
carton. *see* cartonnage, cartonné
cartonn. *see* cartonnage
cartonnage: board binding
cartonnage de l'éditeur: publisher's
  board binding
cartonnage de protection: protective cover
cartonné: bound in boards
cartouche: ornamental oval frame,
  cartouche; inset map
cassé: broken
cassure: break
cdé. *see* cordé
censure: censorship
cent: one hundred
cent. *see* centimètre
centimètre(s): centimeter(s)
centre: center
cerise: cherry red
cerne: ring, circle
ch. *see* chaque, chiffré
chacun: each
chag. *see* chagrin
chagr. *see* chagrin
chagrin: shagreen
chagriné: made to resemble
  shagreen
chaînette: chainlike design used
  in decorating bindings
chamois: chamois
chansonnier: songbook

chapitre: chapter
chaque: each
charn. *see* charnière
charn. écl. *see* charnière éclatée
charn. éclat. *see* charnière éclatée
charnière(s): hinge(s), joint(s)
charnière éclatée: broken joint
chef-d'oeuvre: masterpiece
chemise: wrapper, usually of cloth
  or paper
chemise à cordonnets: wrapper
  with ties
chemise-étui: slipcase
chevrette: kidskin
chevronné: chevroned
chg. *see* chagrin
chgr. *see* chagrin
chif. *see* chiffré
chiffon: rag, rag paper
chiffré: numbered
chiffres en manchette: marginal
  numbers
chrestomathie: anthology
chromo. *see* chromolithographie
chromol. *see* chromolithographie
chromolithographie: lithograph in
  color
chronique(s): chronicle(s)
cinq(uième): five(fifth)
cinquante(ième): fifty(ieth)
cis. *see* ciselé
ciselé: chiseled
ciselures: chiseling
citron: citron, lemon-colored
clair: clear, light-colored
clair-obscur: chiaroscuro
clef: key
co-auteur: coauthor
codex: codex
coiffe(s): headband(s), leather
  rollover at top and bottom of
  spine
coins: corners, corner designs
col. *see* colonne, coloré
coll. *see* collection
collation: collation
collé: glued

collection: collection
colonne: column
colophon: completion of printing note
color. *see* coloré, colorié
coloré: colored
colorié: colored
coloris: coloring
com. *see* commerce
comm. *see* commentaire, commenté
commande: order
commande ferme: firm order
comment. *see* commentaire
commentaire: commentary
commenté: annotated
commerce: trade
comp. *see* compartiments, complet
compart. *see* compartiments
compartiments: panel sections
compilateur: compiler
compilation: compilation
compl. *see* complet
complet: complete
comportant: comprising
comporter: comprise, include
comprenant: including
comptant *see* au comptant
compte: account
compte-rendu: proceedings
concordance: concordance
conforme: the same as
cons. *see* conservé
conserv. *see* conservé
conservation: preservation
conservé: preserved
considérablement: considerably
consolidé: reinforced, strengthened
cont. *see* contenant
conte: tale
contemp. *see* contemporain
contemporain: contemporary
contenant: containing
contenu: content
continuation: continuation
contre-garde: page opposite flyleaf

contrefaçon: counterfeit, pirated edition
copie: copy
coquille: misprint
cordé: with bands
cordon: cord
cordonnets: ties, cords
corr. *see* corrigé
corrigé: corrected
corrigenda: corrigenda
couché: *see* papier couché
coul. *see* couleur
couleur: color
coupe(s): cut(s), edge(s)
coupé: cut, opened
coupure: cut
cour. *see* courant
courant: running
couronne: crown
couronné: approved, awarded a prize or some special honor
court de marges: narrow margins
cousu: sewn
couv. *see* couvert, couverture
couv. cons. *see* couverture conservée
couv. muette *see* couverture muette
couvert: covered
couverture: cover
couverture conservée: cover preserved
couverture de protection: protective cover
couverture(s) muette(s): blank cover(s)
couverture rigide: hard cover
couvre-livre: book cover
cramoisi: deep red
craqué: cracked
crayonnage: pencil marks
crème: cream-colored
crétonne: cretonne
criblé: dotted
croq. *see* croquis
croquis: sketch
cuir: leather

cuir de Russie: Russian leather
cuivre: copper, copper engraving
cul-de-lampe: tailpiece
curieux: curious

d. *see* dans, date, demi, doré, dos
d.c. *see* dos conservé
d. et c. *see* dos et coins
d. et h.t. *see* dans et hors texte
d.l.t. *see* dans le texte
d. parch. *see* demi-parchemin
d.-r. *see* demi-reliure
d.-rel. *see* demi-reliure
d.s.t. *see* doré sur tranches
d. veau *see* demi-veau
dactylographié: typewritten
daim: buckskin, doeskin
damassé: linen damask
damiers: checkered designs
dans: in
dans et hors texte: in and not in the text
dans le texte: in the text
date: date
de: of, from, with
de bonne tenue: in good state
de l'époque: contemporary
de luxe: deluxe
de prochaine publication: soon to be published
de relai: alternative, substitute
déboîté: loosened in the joints
débr. *see* débroché
débroché: unstitched
déch. *see* déchiré, déchirure
déchir. *see* déchiré, déchirure
déchiré: torn
déchirure: tear, torn place
décollé: unglued
décoloré: discolored
décor: decoration, design
décoré: decorated
découpé: cut off, cut out
découpure: cut
décousu: unsewn
dédicace: dedication note
dédicacé: with dedication note

dédicatoire: dedicatory
déf. *see* défectueux, défectuosité
défaut(s): defect(s)
défect. *see* défectueux
défectueux: defective, damaged
défectuosité(s): defect(s)
définitif: definitive
défr. *see* défraîchi
défraîchi: shopworn, faded
délié: with binding loosened
demandé: sought, wanted
demi: half
demi-chagrin: half-shagreen binding
demi-parchemin: half vellum
demi-rel. *see* demi-reliure
demi-reliure: half binding
demi-soie: half silk
demi-veau: half calf
dent. *see* dentelle
dentelle: lacelike design used in tooling bindings
dentelle de pampres: leafy vine design
dentelle intérieure: inside lace design
dép. *see* dépliant
dépl. *see* dépliant
dépliant: unfolding, folding
déplier: to unfold
dérel. *see* dérelié
dérelié: with binding gone
dern. *see* dernier
dernier: last
des. *see* dessin
dess. *see* dessin
dessin: drawing, design
dessiné: drawn, designed
dét. *see* détaché
détachable: detachable
détaché: detached, loose
déteint: faded, discolored
détérioré: deteriorated
deux(ième): two(second)
devise: motto, inscription
diagr. *see* diagramme
diagramme: diagram

diff. *see* différent
différent: different
dim. *see* dimension
dimension: dimension, size
disloqué: disjointed
disponible: available
dissert. *see* dissertation
dissertation: dissertation
dix(ième): ten(th)
dix-huit(ième): eighteen(th)
dix-neuf: nineteen
dix-neuvième: nineteenth
dix-sept(ième): seventeen(th)
doc. *see* document
docum. *see* document
document: document
dor. *see* doré, dorure
doré: gilt, decorated with gold
doré sur témoins: with gilt on
    uncut edges
doré sur tranches: with gilt edges
dorure: gilding, decoration in gold
dos: back of a book
dos à compartiments: back with
    sections
dos à nerfs: back with raised
    bands
dos conservé: back preserved
dos et coins: back and corners
dos factice: imitation back
dos refait: rebacked
doubl. *see* doublure
double: double, liner
doublé: lined
double-couronne: double crown
double emboîtage: double slipcase
double(s) garde(s): double end-
    paper(s)
double page: double page
doubles-planches: double plates
doublure: lining
douze(ième): twelve(twelfth)
droit: straight
ds. *see* dans
ds. et h.t. *see* dans et hors texte
ds. le t. *see* dans le texte

é. *see* état
é.o. *see* édition originale
eau-f. *see* eau-forte
eau-forte: etching
éb. *see* ébarbé
ébarb. *see* ébarbé
ébarbé: trimmed
ébauche: draft
éc. *see* écaille
écaille: scalelike design, mottled
échelle: scale
écl. *see* éclaté
éclat. *see* éclaté
éclaté: broken, burst
écoinçon(s): corner design(s)
écorch. *see* écorché
écorché: skinned
écorchures: skinned spots
écorné: with corners broken
écrasé: crushed
écriture: writing
écru: natural-colored
écusson: armorial shield
écusson de tomaison: volume-
    number label
éd. *see* éditeur, édition
édit. *see* éditeur, édition
édit. orig. *see* édition originale
éditeur: publisher, editor
édition: edition
édition collective: anthology,
    collected works
édition originale: original edition
édition populaire: ordinary edition
édition princeps: editio princeps
eff. *see* effacé
effacé: effaced
égratignure: scratch
él. *see* élégant
élég. *see* élégant
élégant: elegant
éliminé: eliminated
ém. *see* émail
émail: enamel
émargé: trimmed, margins cut
    down
émaux: enamels

emb. *see* emboîtage
emboît. *see* emboîtage
emboîtage: case
emboîté: cased, bound
émeraude: emerald-colored
émouss. *see* émoussé
émoussé: dulled, rounded
en: in
en boîte plastique: in a plastic box
en couleur: in color
en double: duplicated, repeated
en fasc. *see* en fascicules
en fascicules: in fascicules
en feuilles: in sheets
en ff. *see* en feuilles
en long: the long way
en marge: on the margin
en mauvais état: in bad condition
en noir: in black
en partie: in part, partly
en pleine page: in full page
en pochette: in pocket
en quadrichromie: in four colors
en regard: opposite, facing
en réimpr. *see* en réimpression
en réimpression: being reprinted
en sachet plastique: in a plastic
  bag
en similé: in facsimile
en souscription: on subscription
en sus: additional, above
en taille-douce: in copperplate
en tête: at the front
en-tête: heading, headpiece
en tête de page: at the top of the
  page
enc. *see* encadrement
encadr. *see* encadrement
encadré: framed
encadrem. *see* encadrement
encadrement: frame, border
encadt. *see* encadrement
encart. *see* encartage
encartage: insertion
encastré: inset
enchères: auction
encollé: pasted, mounted

end. *see* endommagé
endommagé: damaged
enfoncé: embossed
enlacé: entwined
enlevé: missing, removed
enluminé: illuminated, decorated
  with colors by hand
enluminure: illumination
enrichi: enriched
ens. *see* ensemble
ensemble: together, group
ent. *see* entièrement
entamé: slightly damaged
entièr. *see* entièrement
entièrement: entirely
entièrement refondu: entirely
  reworked
entoilé: cloth-covered
entredeux: space between two
  designs, design used to fill that
  space
entrelacs: interlaced fillets, interlacings
entrenerfs: panels between raised
  bands
env. *see* environ, envoi
env. aut. *see* envoi autographe
envir. *see* environ
environ: about
envoi: dedicatory note or
  inscription
envoi autographe: autograph
  inscription
envoi ordinaire: surface mail
envoi par avion: air mail
envoi signé: signed inscription
ép. *see* époque
épaisseur: thickness
éparse: scattered
épid. *see* épidermé, épidermure
épidermé: with surface of skin
  scraped off
épidermure: place where skin has
  been scraped
épigraphe: epigraph
épis: grain, design representing
  grain

époq. *see* époque
époque: time, period, contemporary
épr. *see* épreuve
épreuve: proof
épuisé: exhausted, out-of-print
érafl. *see* éraflure
éraflé: scraped
éraflure: scraped spot
erreur: error
escarboucle: carbuncle
esquisse: sketch
essai: essay
est. *see* estampe
estampe: print, engraving
estampé: stamped, embossed
estampille: stamp
estimé: esteemed
ét. *see* état, étude
état: condition, state
état de conservation: condition
état de fraîcheur: state of freshness
état de neuf: as new
étiq. *see* étiquette
étiquette: label
étoffe: cloth
étr. *see* étranger
étranger: foreign
étroit: narrow
étude: study
étui: case, container
étui-boîte: slipcase
étui de l'éditeur: publisher's case
étui gainé: closed slipcase
étui-reliure: binding with case
ex. *see* exemplaire
ex-libris: bookplate
exceptionnellement: unusually
exemp. *see* exemplaire
exempl. *see* exemplaire
exemplaire(s): copy(ies)
exemplaire d'auteur: author's copy
exemplaire nominatif: copy designated for a person
explic. *see* explication
explicatif: explanatory

explication: explanation
exposé: summary
ext. *see* extérieur
extérieur: exterior
extr. *see* extrait
extrait: extract
exx. *see* exemplaires

f. *see* faux, feuille, filets
f. *see* franc
f.b. *see* franc belge
f.-t. *see* faux-titre
fac. *see* faculté
facs. *see* facsimilé
facsim. *see* facsimilé
facsimilé: facsimile
fact. *see* factice
factice: artificial, imitation
facture: bill, invoice
faculté: faculty
faible: feeble, weak
fané: faded
fant. *see* fantaisie
fantaisie: fancy, imagination
fasc. *see* fascicule
fascic. *see* fascicule
fascicule: fascicule, part
fat. *see* fatigué
fatig. *see* fatigué
fatigué: worn
fauve: fawn-colored
faux: false, imitation
faux nerfs: imitation cords
faux-titre: half or bastard title
fc. *see* franco
fco. *see* franco
fend. *see* fendu
fendu: split
fente(s): break(s), split(s)
fer: tool
ferm. *see* fermoirs
fermoir(s): clasp(s)
feuillages: foliagelike patterns
feuille(s): sheet(s)
feuille de garde: endpaper
feuille volante: broadside
feuillet(s): sheet(s), leaf(ves)

feuillet d'errata: errata sheet, leaf
feuillet(s) de garde: endpaper(s)
feuillet(s) mobile(s): looseleaf
   sheet(s)
feuillets chiffrés: numbered sheets,
   leaves
feuillets non chiffrés: unnumbered
   sheets
ff. *see* feuilles, feuillets
ff.ch. *see* feuillets chiffrés
ff.nch. *see* feuillets non chiffrés
ficelles: laces
fig. *see* figure
figg. *see* figures
figure(s): illustration(s),
   diagram(s)
figuré: figured
fil. *see* filets
fileté: decorated with fillets
filets: fillets, line or band
   decorations
filets brisés: broken lines
filets courbes: curved line patterns
filets droits: straight line patterns
filets gras: heavy, thick fillets
filets maigres: thin fillets
filets ondulés: wavy line patterns
filigrane: watermark
fin de chapitre: ornamental design
   at end of chapter
finesse: fineness, high quality
fl.d.l. *see* fleur-de-lys
fleur. *see* fleurons
fleur-de-lys: lily design
fleurdelisé: decorated with fleur-
   de-lys
fleurette: small floral design
fleuronné: having a floral design
fleurons: large floral design
fleurons d'angle: corner floral
   designs
fleurons de titre: floral design
   included in a title page
fol. *see* folio
folio: folio
folioté: foliated
foncé: deep, dark

format: format
format de poche: pocket-size
format rogné: trimmed size
fort: thick, strong
fort estimé: highly esteemed
fr. *see* français, à froid
fragile: fragile
fraîche: fresh
fraîcheur: freshness
frais: fresh
franc(s): franc(s)
franc(s) belges: Belgian franc(s)
français: French
franco: prepaid, shipping costs
   paid
frappé: stamped, tooled
frappé à froid: blind-tooled
froissé: wrinkled
froissures: wrinkles, wrinkling
front. *see* frontispice
frontisp. *see* frontispice
frontispice: frontispiece
frott. *see* frotté
frotté: scraped, roughened
frottis: light discoloration, smear
fusains: charcoal drawings
fx. titre *see* faux-titre

g. *see* gravé
gaine: slipcover
gainé: slipcovered
gamme: gamut
garde(s): endpaper(s)
gauf. *see* gaufré
gaufré: goffered
gaufrure: goffering
gd. *see* grand
genre: type
glacé: glazed, coated
glands: acorns, designs representing acorns
glose: gloss
glossaire: glossary
goth. *see* gothique
gothique: Gothic
gouaché: painted in gouache
gouttière: fore edge

gr. *see* grain, grand, gravé, gravure
gr. au trait. *see* gravure au trait
gr.s.bois. *see* gravure sur bois
grain: grain
grain écrasé: crushed grain
grand: large
grand de marges: large margins
grandeur: size
granit. *see* granité
granité: colored to resemble
   granite
granulé: small-grained
graphique: line design, line
   drawing
gras: thick, heavy
grattage: scratch
gratté: scratched
grav. *see* gravé, gravité, gravure
gravé: engraved
graveur: engraver
gravité: seriousness
gravure: engraving, print
gravure au trait: line engraving
gravure sur bois: wood engraving,
   woodcut
grd. *see* grand
grecque: ornamental border design
grège: raw
grenat: pomegranate-colored
griffé: scratched
griffonné: with scribblings
gris: gray
gris souris: mouse-colored
gros: large, thick
grotesque: grotesque
guilloché: with a checkered pattern
guillochures: checkered patterns
guirl. *see* guirlande
guirlande: garland

h. *see* hors
h.c. *see* hors commerce
h.com. *see* hors commerce
h.t. *see* hors-texte
habituel: usual
hachure: hatching, shading
haut: top, upper part

haut. *see* hauteur
hauteur: height
havane: light brown
hebdomadaire: weekly
hectographié: hectographed
hélio. *see* héliogravure
héliochromie: color engraving
héliogr. *see* héliogravure
héliograv. *see* héliogravure
héliograve: photoengraved
héliogravure: photoengraving
héliotypie: photoprinting
historié: historiated, ornamented
Hol. *see* Hollande
Hollande: Holland paper
hommage de l'auteur: gift of the
   author
hors: outside
hors commerce: not for sale,
   privately printed
hors-texte: not in the text
huit(ième): eight(h)
humidité: moisture

ident. *see* identique
identique: uniform, identical
ill. *see* illustration, illustré
illisible: illegible
illustr. *see* illustration, illustré
illustrateur: illustrator
illustration: illustration
illustré: illustrated
immaculé: immaculate
imp. *see* imprimé, imprimerie,
   imprimeur
impeccable: impeccable
impr. *see* imprimé, imprimerie,
   imprimeur
impression: printing
imprim. *see* imprimé, imprimerie
imprimé: printed, printed matter
imprimerie: printing, printing firm
imprimeur: printer
in-fol. *see* in-folio
in-folio: folio
in-plano: in sheets; broadside
in-t. *see* in-texte

in-texte: in the text
inclus: inclusive, enclosed
incunable: incunabulum
inéd. *see* inédit
inédit: unpublished
inégalable: unmatched
inexpurgé: unexpurgated
inf. *see* inférieur, infime
infér. *see* inférieur
inférieur: lower
infime: very small, minute
init. *see* initiale
initiale(s): initial letter(s)
inscr. *see* inscription
inscription: inscription
insign. *see* insignifiant
insignif. *see* insignifiant
insignifiant: insignificant
int. *see* intérieur
intégral: complete
intér. *see* intérieur
interc. *see* intercalé
intercalé: intercalated
interfolié: interleaved
intérieur: interior, inner
interligné: interlinear
interversion: transposition
interverti: transposed
intitulé: entitled
intr. *see* introduction
introduction: introduction
introuvable: impossible to find
irréprochable: irreproachable
isolé: single
isolément: singly
italique: italics
ivoire: ivory-colored

j. *see* Japon
jans. *see* Janséniste
jansén. *see* janséniste
janséniste: Jansenist, an
    unornamented style of binding
Japon: Japan paper
jaquette: book jacket, wrappers
jaquette couleur: colored wrapper
jasp. *see* jaspé

jaspé: marbled, sprinkled
jaune: yellow
jauni: yellowed
jaunissures: yellowed marks, foxing
jésus: paper of approximately
    superroyal size
jeu de filets: line pattern
joints: joints
jonquille: jonquil-colored, pale
    yellow
journal: newspaper, periodical
jouxte: next to
jumelés: paired, reinforced
justifié: justified

l. *see* largeur, lettre, lieu
l.a. *see* lettre autographe
lâche: weak
lanières: laces
larg. *see* largeur
largeur: width
lav. *see* lavallière
lavable: washable
lavall. *see* lavallière
lavallière: russet-colored
lavé: washed
lavis: wash, wash drawing
lég. *see* léger, légèrement
légende: legend, caption
léger: slight, light
légèrement: slightly
légt. *see* légèrement
lettre: letter
lettre autographe: autograph letter
lettres bâtardes: slanting type
    letters
lettres rondes: round type letters
lettrine: reference letter, decorated
    initial letter
lexique: lexicon
lib. *see* libraire, librairie
libelle: lampoon, small libelous
    work
libr. *see* libraire, librairie
libraire: bookseller
librairie: bookstore
lie de vin: purplish-red

lieu: place
ligne: line
ligné: lined
lilas: lilac
lim. *see* liminaire, limité
limin. *see* liminaire
liminaire: preliminary, prefatory
limité: limited
lin: linen
linéaire: line pattern, linear
lisible: legible
lisse: smooth, trimmed
listel: a border fillet
lith. *see* lithographie, lithographié
litho. *see* lithographie, lithographié
lithogr. *see* lithographie,
   lithographié
lithographie: lithograph
lithographié: lithographed
livr. *see* livraison
livraison: part, issue
livre: book
livre d'heures: book of hours
livre(s) d'occasion: secondhand
   book(s)
livre(s) épuisé(s): out-of-print
   book(s)
long: lengthwise, long
longueur: length
losange: diamond-shaped pattern
losangé: tooled in a diamond-
   shaped pattern
lourd: heavy
luxe: deluxe

m. *see* marbré, maroquin
mac. *see* maculé
maculature: mackle, waste sheet
maculé: spotted, soiled
maigre: thin
majuscules: capital letters
man. *see* manuscrit
manchette(s): marginal note(s)
manq. *see* manquant
manquant: lacking
manque: lacks, is missing
manuscrit(s): manuscript(s)

maquette: specimen volume
mar. *see* maroquin
mar. noix. *see* maroquin noix
Marais: a fine paper
marb. *see* marbré, marbrure
marbré: marbled
marbrure: marbling
marg. *see* marge, marginal
marge(s): margin(s)
margin. *see* marginal
marginal: marginal
maroq. *see* maroquin
maroquin: morocco
maroquin noix: nut-brown
   morocco
maroquiné: made to resemble
   morocco, with morocco finish
marque d'imprimeur: printer's
   mark
marron: maroon, chestnut-colored
mastique: mastic
mat: with mat finish
mauv. *see* mauvais
mauvais: bad
médaillon: medallion, inset
médiocre: mediocre
mélange: miscellany
mém. *see* mémoire
mémoire(s): memoir(s), report(s)
men. *see* menu
mensuel: monthly
menu: minor
métallique: metallic
meurtri: damaged, bruised
mi-marges: half margins
mi-maroquin: half morocco
mi-page: half page, near
mi-souple: semiflexible
milieu: center
mille: thousand
mince: thin
minime: extremely small
minuscule: extremely small in size
mis à jour: brought up to date,
   revised
mis en vente: offered for sale

mise en page: layout of printed page

mll. *see* mouillure

mobile: movable

mod. *see* moderne

moderne: modern

moire: moiré, a watered fabric, usually silk

moisissure: mildew

monogr. *see* monogramme

monogramme: monogram

monographie: monograph

monté: mounted

morceau(x): piece(s), selection(s)

mordoré: bronzed

mordorés: bronzed

mors: joint

mosaïqué: decorated in mosaic patterns

mosaïque(s): mosaic(s), mosaic pattern(s)

motif: design, pattern

mouch. *see* moucheté

moucheté: speckled, spotted

mouil. *see* mouillé, mouillure

mouill. *see* mouillé, mouillure

mouill. marg. *see* mouillures marginales

mouillé: stained by dampness, moisture

mouillure: stain caused by moisture

mouillure(s): damp spot(s)

mouillures marginales: marginal damp spots

mousse: soft-finished

mouton: sheepskin

mq. *see* manque

mquant. *see* manquant

mque. *see* manque

ms. *see* manuscrit

mss. *see* manuscrits

mst. *see* manuscrit

muet: blank, undecorated

muette: blank, undecorated

multigr. *see* multigrafié

multigrafié: multilithed

mutilé: mutilated

n. *see* nom

n.c. *see* non chiffré

n.ch. *see* non chiffré

n.chiffr. *see* non chiffré

n.é. *see* non ébarbé

n. identifié *see* non identifié

n.r. *see* non rogné

n.s. *see* nouvelle série

nacré: colored in mother-of-pearl

naturel: natural

nbr. *see* nombre

nch. *see* non chiffré

nelle. *see* nouvelle

nerfs: raised bands, cords

nerfs plats: flat bands

neuf: new, nine

neuve: new

neuvième: ninth

ni: neither

nlle. *see* nouvelle

no. *see* numéro

noix: nut-brown

nom: name

nom de plume: pen name, pseudonym

nomb. *see* nombreux

nombr. *see* nombreux

nombre: number

nombreux: numerous

non chiffré: unnumbered

non coupé: uncut

non ébarbé: untrimmed

non identifié: not identified

non mis dans le commerce: not offered for sale

non numéroté: unnumbered

non paginé: not paginated

non rogné: untrimmed

non signé: not signed

not. *see* notice

notice(s): brief summary(ies), annotation(s)

nouv. *see* nouveau

nouveau: new

nouvelle: new

nouvelle série: new series
num. *see* numéro, numéroté
numér. *see* numéroté
numéro: number
numéro double: double number
numéro isolé: single number
numérotation: numbering
numéroté: numbered

o. *see* original
obl. *see* oblong
oblong: oblong
occ. *see* occasion
occasion: bargain
ocre: ocher
oeuvre: work, opus
oeuvres choisies: selected works
olive: olive-colored
ombré: shaded
onciales: uncial letters
ondulé: wavy
onglets: tabs, binding strips
onze(ième): eleven(th)
opuscule: small work
or. *see* original
orange: orange-colored
ordin. *see* ordinaire
ordinaire: common, ordinary
orig. *see* original
origin. *see* original
original: original
orn. *see* orné
orné: decorated
ornem. *see* ornementé
ornement: ornament
ornementé: decorated
os: bone
ouv. *see* ouvrage
ouvr. *see* ouvrage
ouvrage: work
ouvrage saisi: seized work

p. *see* page, pièce
p. de t. *see* pièce de titre
p. de tom. *see* pièce de tomaison
p. de tomaison *see* pièce de
 tomaison

p. de tr. *see* peau de truie
p.f. *see* petits fers
page(s): page(s)
page de garde: endpaper
pages non chiffrées: unnumbered
 pages
pagination: pagination
pagination suivie: continuous
 pagination
paille: straw-colored
pailleté: spangled
paillettes: spangles
pâle: pale
pâli: paled, faded
pallette(s): small T-shaped
 design(s)
palmette: palm-leaf design
pampres: leafy vine design
pap. *see* papier
papier: paper
papier bible: Bible paper
papier chamois: buff-colored paper
papier couché: laid paper
papier de couleur: colored paper
papier(s) de garde: lining
 paper(s), endpaper(s)
papier de riz: rice paper
papier glacé: coated paper,
 glazed paper
papier Japon: Japan paper
papier mince: thin paper
papier moiré: watered paper
papier pailleté: spangled paper
papier surfine: extra fine paper
papier vergé: laid paper
paquet-poste: parcel post
par places: in places
parafé: initialed
paragraphe: paragraph
paraître: appear
parch. *see* parchemin
parchem. *see* parchemin
parchemin: parchment, vellum
parcheminé: parchmentlike
parf. *see* parfait
parfait: perfect
part *see* à part

particulier: individual
partie: part
paru: appeared, published
parution: appearance, publication
parution courante: now coming out
passé: worn, faded
pastiche: imitation, copy
peau: leather, skin
peau de chamois: chamois skin
peau de chèvre: goatskin
peau de porc: pigskin
peau de truie: pigskin
peau de vélin: vellum
peau suédée: sueded leather
péga. *see* pégamoîd
pégamoîd: imitation parchment
peigne: combed edges
peigné: grained
peint: painted
perc. *see* percaline
percal. *see* percaline
percale: percale
percaline: book cloth, buckram
percaline grège: raw book cloth
perforé: perforated
périodique: periodical
perlé: ornamented with small
    vignettes
perte de texte: loss of text
pet. *see* petit
petit: small
petits fers: small pattern designs
peu: little, few
peu connu: little known
phot. *see* photographie, photo-
    graphique
photo *see* photographie
photocopie: photocopy
photog. *see* photographie,
    photographique
photogr. *see* photographie,
    photographique
photographie: photograph, photo-
    graphic illustration
photographique: photographic
photograv. *see* photogravure
photogravure: photoengraving

photot. *see* phototypie
phototypie: phototype
pièce: piece, part
pièce d'armes: armorial piece
pièce de milieu: centerpiece
pièce de titre: title label
pièce de tomaison: volume label
pièces: volume and title labels
piq. *see* piqué, piqûre
piqq. *see* piqûres
piqué: with small holes
piqué de vers: wormholed
piqûre(s): hole(s)
piqûre de vers: wormhole
pl. *see* planche, plat, plein
pl. parch. *see* plein parchemin
plaisant: attractive
plan: map, chart
planche(s): plate(s), illustration(s)
plaq. *see* plaquette
plaque: medallion, shield bearing
    a design
plaquette: booklet, pamphlet
plat(s): side(s) of a book, flat
    surface(s)
plat(s) de couverture: side(s) of
    the cover
plat inférieur: back cover
plat supérieur: front cover
platiné: decorated in platinum
plchs. *see* planches
plein: full
plein parchemin: full vellum
pli: fold
pliant: folding
plié: folded
pll. *see* planches
plus. *see* plusieurs
plusieurs: several
pochette: pocket, strong envelope
pochoir: stencil
pointe: point
pointe sèche: drypoint
pointillé: stippled
poli: polished, burnished
polych. *see* polychrome
polychr. *see* polychrome

polychrome: multicolored
polycopié: duplicated
porc: pigskin
porph. *see* porphyre
porphyre: porphyry
port: shipping costs
port. *see* portrait
port.-front. *see* portrait-
frontispice
portef. *see* portefeuille
portef. avec étui *see* portefeuille
avec étui
portefeuille: portfolio
portefeuille avec étui: portfolio
in slipcase
porto: shipping costs
portr. *see* portrait
portrait: portrait
portrait-frontispice: frontispiece
portrait
post. *see* postérieur
poste ordinaire: regular mail
postér. *see* postérieur
postérieur: of a later date; back
postface: epilogue
posth. *see* posthume
posthume: posthumous
poussiéreux: dusty
pp. *see* pages
pp.n.ch. *see* pages non chiffrées
précieux: precious
précis: summary
préf. *see* préface
préface: preface, foreword
prél. *see* préliminaire
prélim. *see* préliminaire
préliminaire: preliminary
prem. *see* premier
premier: first
premier tirage: first printing
première émission: first issue
prép. *see* préparation
préparation: preparation
prés. *see* présentation
présentation: presentation
presse: press
prisé: prized

priv. *see* privilège
privilège: privilege, permit to
publish
prix: price
prix public: retail price
prochainement: soon
propre: clean
propriété littéraire: copyright
provenance: provenance, source
prune: plum-colored
pseudonyme: pseudonym
pt. *see* petit
pub. *see* publication, publié
publication: publication
publié: published
pur: pure
pur chiffon: pure rag

q. *see* quelques
qq. *see* quelques
qques. *see* quelques
quadrille: checkered
quarante(ième): forty(ieth)
quatorze(ième): fourteen(th)
quatre(ième): four(th)
quatre-vingt(ième): eighty(ieth)
quatre-vingt-dix(ième):
ninety(ieth)
quelq. *see* quelques
quelques: some, a few
queue de paon: peacock's tail
queue du dos: foot of the back
quinze(ième): fifteen(th)

r. *see* relié
rabais: discount
rabat: flap
rac. *see* raccommodage, raciné
raccommodage(s): repair(s)
raciné: tooled in a design resembling tree roots
raisin: paper approximately royal
size
raisonné: systematic
ramages: branch and flower design
rapiécé: mended
rappel: recall, repetition

rapport: report
rare: rare
rareté: rarity
rarissime: extremely rare
ravissant: ravishing
recherché: in great demand
récit: tale
recollé: reglued
rectification: correction
recto: recto, front side
recueil: collection
rédacteur: editor
rédaction: editorship
rédigé: compiled, edited
réduit: reduced
rééd. _see_ réédition
réédition: new edition
refait: remade, made over
refondu: reorganized, recast
réglé: ruled, lined
reh. _see_ rehaussé
rehaussé: decorated, enhanced
réimp. _see_ réimpression, réimprimé
réimposé: reimposed
réimpr. _see_ réimpression
réimpres. _see_ réimpression
réimpression: reprint, reprinting
réimprimé: reprinted
rel. _see_ relié, reliure
rel. éditeur _see_ reliure éditeur
rel. époque _see_ reliure époque
rel. mod. _see_ reliure moderne
rel. tardive _see_ reliure tardive
relai _see_ de relai
relevé: set off
relevés: charts
relié: bound
relieur: binder
reliure: binding
reliure à anneaux: loose-leaf binding
reliure à spirale: spiral binding
reliure amateur: half binding with corners
reliure de l'époque: contemporary binding

reliure éditeur: publisher's binding
reliure en spirale: spiral binding
reliure enchaînée: chained binding
reliure époque: contemporary binding
reliure moderne: modern binding
reliure postérieure: later binding
reliure romantique: binding tooled in the romantic style
reliure tardive: delayed binding
remanié: reworked, revised
remboîté: rebound, recased
remise: discount
remonté: renewed
rempl. _see_ remplié
remplié: folded on itself
renf. _see_ renforcé
renforcé: reinforced
renouvelé: renewed
rép. _see_ réparé
répar. _see_ réparation
réparat. _see_ réparation
réparation: repair(s)
réparé: repaired, mended
répertoire: list, index
repl. _see_ replié
replié: folded on itself
repoussé: stamped in by hand, embossed
repr. _see_ reproduction
reprod. _see_ reproduction
reproduction: reproduction
rest. _see_ restauré
restaurable: repairable
restauration(s): restoration(s)
restauré: restored
résumé: abstract, summary
retiré du commerce: withdrawn from sale
réunion: assemblage
rev. _see_ revu
révisé: revised
revu: revised
revue: periodical, review
richem. _see_ richement
richement: richly

rinceau: branchlike design,
    foliated scroll
r° *see* recto
rocaille: encrusted pattern
rog. *see* rogné
rogn. *see* rogné
rogné: trimmed, cut
rom. *see* romantique
roman: novel
romant. *see* romantique
romantique *see* reliure romantique
ronéotypé: duplicated
rongé: gnawed, eaten
rongures: gnawed spots
rosace: ornament resembling a
    rose, rosette
rosacé: decorated with rosettes
rouge: red
rouge et noir: printed in red and
    black; rubricated
rouille: rust
roul. *see* roulette
roulette: circular design, fillet
rouss. *see* rousseurs
rousseurs: red spots, foxing
roussi: foxed, browned
rss. *see* rousseurs
ruban: ribbon, bookmark
rubrique: rubric
rubriqué: rubricated
rustique: rustic, unpolished

s. *see* sans, siècle, sur
s.a. *see* sans année
s.b. *see* sur bois
s.c. *see* sans couverture, sur cuivre
s.d. *see* sans date
s.éd. *see* sans éditeur
s.l. *see* sans lieu
s.l.n.d. *see* sans lieu ni date
s.p. *see* sans prix
sain: in good condition
sale: dirty
sali: dirtied
salissures: dirty spots
sans: without
sans année: without year

sans couverture: without cover
sans date: without date
sans éditeur: without publisher
sans gravité: unimportant
sans lieu: without place of
    publication
sans lieu ni date: without place or
    date of publication
sans perte de texte: without
    loss of text
sans prix: without price
satin: sateen
sauf: except
saumon: salmon-colored
sceau(x): seal(s)
scolies: critical notes
se dépl. *see* se dépliant
se dépliant: folding
se détachant: coming loose
seize(ième): sixteen(th)
semestriel: semiannual
semis: scattering
séparé: separated, detached, single
sépia: sepia
sept(ième): seven(th)
sér. *see* série
série: series
sertis: background, setting
seul. *see* seulement
seul paru: the only one published
seulement: only
siècle: century
signalé: indicated
signat. *see* signature
signature: signature
signé: signed
signet(s): marker(s), tassel(s)
simili: facsimile, imitation
simili-Japon: imitation Japan
    paper
similicuir: imitation leather
similigrav. *see* similigravure
similigravure: halftone engraving
similipeau: imitation leather
simulé: simulated
six(ième): six(th)

skivertex: a patented leather book cloth
soigné: carefully done
soixante(ième): sixty(ieth)
soixante-dix(ième): seventy(ieth)
solide: solid
souffert: injured, damaged
souillures: soil marks
souligné: underlined
soulignure(s): underlining(s)
souple: flexible
sous: in, under
sous couverture: in covers
sous couverture rempliée: in slipcase
sous emboîtage: in container
sous portefeuille: in portfolio
sous presse: in press
sous-titre: subtitle
souscripteur: subscriber
souscription: subscription
sp. *see* spécial
spéc. *see* spécial
spécial: special
spécimen: sample, specimen
spirale: spiral
ss. *see* sous
strié: striated
suédé: sueded
suite: series
sup. *see* supérieur, supplément
super. *see* supérieur
super-ex-libris: ownership mark on outside cover
superfin: superfine
supérieur: top, upper
suppl. *see* supplément
supplément: supplement
supprimé: suppressed, censored
supralibros: property stamp
sur: on
sur acier: on steel
sur bois: on wood
sur cuivre: on copper
sur demande: on request
surfin: superfine

t. *see* tête, texte, titre, tome
t.d. *see* taille-douce

tabac: tobacco-colored
tabis: watered silk, tabby
tabl. *see* tableau
table: index, table
table de matières: table of contents
tableau: picture, table
tache: spot, stain
taches d'humidité: damp spots
tacheté: spotted
taille-douce: copperplate, copper engraving
taupe: taupe
teinte: color, tint
teinté: tinted
tel que paru: as it appeared
tel quel: as is
tellière: paper, approximately foolscap size; large foolscap
témoins: witnesses, untrimmed edges
terni: tarnished
têt. *see* tête
tête: head of a book, top edge
tête-de-chapitre: chapter head
tête-de-nègre: dark brown
tête-de-page: head of page
tête de série: first of series
tétrachromie: four-color print
texte: text
thèse: thesis
timb. *see* timbré
timbré: stamped
tir. *see* tirage
tirage: edition, printing
tirage à part: separate, reprint
tirage à petit nombre: limited edition
tirage restreint: limited edition
tiré: printed
tiré à petit nombre: limited edition
tirés à part: offprints
tissu: woven material
tit. *see* titre
titre: title, title page
titre courant: running title
titre de relais: alternate title
titre-frontispice: title frontispiece

toile: cloth
toilé: cloth-covered
toile de lin: linen cloth
toile de soie: silk
toile écrue: unbleached cloth
toile granitée: grained cloth
toile moderne: modern cloth
tom. *see* tomaison
tomaison: volume numbering
tome: tome, volume
ton(s): shade(s)
torsade: spiral or cablelike design
totalisant: totaling
touché: lightly damaged
toute toile: full cloth
tr. *see* traduction, traduit, tranche, travail
tr. de v. *see* travail de vers
tr. jaspée *see* tranche jaspée
tr. marbrée *see* tranche marbrée
traces: marks, traces
traces de colle: traces of glue
traces d'humidité: traces of dampness
traces d'usure: traces of wear
trad. *see* traduction, traduit
traducteur: translator
traduction: translation
traduit: translated
traînée(s): trace(s)
trait: line
traité: treatise
tranche: trench, hollow edge
tranche jaspée: sprinkled trench
tranche marbrée: marbled trench
tranchefile(s): headband(s)
trav. de vers *see* travail de vers
travail: work, piece of work
travail de vers: signs of worms
trèfle: trefoil
tréflé: trefoiled
treize(ième): thirteen(th)
trente(ième): thirty(ieth)
très: very
très usagé: badly worn
trimestriel: quarterly
triple: triple
trois(ième): three(third)

trou(s) de vers: wormhole(s)
truie: pigskin
typ. *see* typographique
typographique: typographic

un: one
une: one
uni: smooth, even
uniformément: uniformly
unique: unique, sole
us. *see* usagé, usé
usag. *see* usagé
usagé: worn
usé: worn
usure: wear, worn spot

v. *see* veau, vélin
variante(s): variant(s)
veau: calf
vél. *see* vélin
vélin: vellum
vélin pur fil: fine thread parchment
velours: velvet
velouté: velvetlike, with velvet surface
vendu: sold
vente: sale
verdâtre: greenish
vergé: laid paper
vermiculé(s): vermiculated
vers: worms
verso: verso, back side
vient de paraître: just published, just out
vign. *see* vignette
vignette: vignette
vingt(ième): twenty(ieth)
viol. *see* violet
violet: violet
violine: purple-violet
v° *see* verso
volume: volume
volute(s): scroll(s)
vue(s): view(s)

zincotypie: zinc engraving

German

A. *see* Auflage, Ausschnitt
A.d.W. *see* Akademie der
  Wissenschaften
a.d.Zt. *see* aus der Zeit
ab sofort: immediately
Abb. *see* Abbildung
Abbild. *see* Abbildung
Abbildgn. *see* Abbildung
Abbildung(en): illustration(s)
Abbr. *see* Abbreviatur
Abbreviatur(en): abbreviation(s)
Abdr. *see* Abdruck
Abdruck(e): copy(ies), offprint(s)
abgebildet: reproduced
abgeblättert: come off, peel
abgedr. *see* abgedruckt
abgedruckt: printed, reprinted
abgegriffen: worn
abgelöst: detached
abgen. *see* abgenutzt
abgenutzt: worn
abgerissen: torn off
abgeschabt: scraped
abgeschn. *see* abgeschnitten
abgeschnitten: cut away
abgesehen: except for
abgesetzt: sold
abgew. *see* abgewetzt
abgewetzt: chafed
Abh. *see* Abhandlung
Abhandlung(en): transaction(s),
  treatise(s)
Abkürzung(en): abbreviation(s)
Abnahmeverpflichtung: subscribers
  must contract for the entire
  series

Abonnement: subscription
Abriss: synopsis
Abschn. *see* Abschnitt
Abschnitt(e): section(s)
Abschürfung(en): abrasure(s)
Abt. *see* Abteilung
Abteilung(en): part(s)
Abtl. *see* Abteilung
abweichend: different, differing
  from
Abzug(züge): copy(ies)
acht(e): eight(h)
achtzehn(te): eighteen(th)
achtzig(ste): eighty(ieth)
Ahnentafel(n): genealogical table(s)
Akad. *see* Akademie
Akad.W. *see* Akademie der
  Wissenschaften
Akademie: academy
Akademie der Wissenschaften:
  Academy of Science(s)
Alben: albums
Album: album
alles Erschienene: all published
alles was erschien(en): all that
  was (were) published
allg.verst. *see* allgemeinverständlich
allgemeinverständlich: popular,
  easy to understand
alphabetisch: alphabetical(ly)
als Handschrift gedruckt: privately
  printed
als Manuskript gedruckt: privately
  printed
alt: old
Altersspur(en): trace(s) of aging

altkol. *see* altkoloriert
altkoloriert: colored long ago
Altkolorit: old coloring
am Anfang: at the beginning
am Ende: at the end
amtl. *see* amtlich
amtlich: official
anast. *see* anastatisch
anastatisch: anastatic
andersfarbig: differently colored
Anf. *see* Anfang
Anfang: beginning
Anforderung: demand, request
Anfrage: inquiry, request
angeb. *see* angebunden
angebd. *see* angebunden
Angebot: quotation
angebunden: bound with
angefleckt: slightly spotted
angefressen: gnawed
angegilbt: slightly yellowed
anger. *see* angerissen
angerändert: slightly spotty along
  margins
angerandet: with beginnings of
  staining on edges
angerissen: slightly torn
angeschlagen: slightly bruised
angeschlg. *see* angeschlagen
angeschm. *see* angeschmutzt
angeschmutzt: slightly soiled
angeschnitten: slightly damaged
  by cutting
angestaubt: slightly dusty
Anh. *see* Anhang
Anhang(hänge): appendix(es)
ankol. *see* ankoloriert
ankolor. *see* ankoloriert
ankoloriert: slightly colored
Anl. *see* Anlage
Anlage(n): enclosure(s)
anlässlich: on the occasion of
Anm. *see* Anmerkung
Anmerk. *see* Anmerkung
Anmerkg. *see* Anmerkung
Anmerkgn. *see* Anmerkung
Anmerkung(en): note(s)

Anmkgn. *see* Anmerkung
Annalen: annals
anon. *see* anonym
anonym: anonymous(ly)
Anrandung(en): beginning(s) of
  stains along the edges
Ans. *see* Ansicht
anscheinend: apparently
Ansicht(en): view(s)
Ansichtenwerk: collection of views
anspruchsvoll: pretentious
anstelle: instead of
Anstreich. *see* Anstreichungen
Anstreichungen: marks
Anthologie: anthology
Antiqua: roman letters, roman
  type
Antiquar: rare book dealer
Antiquariat: secondhand book
  shop, secondhand dealer; rare
  book dealer
Anzahl: number
App. *see* Appendix
Appendix: appendix
Aquarell: watercolor
Aquatinta: aquatint
Aquatinta-Frontispiz: watercolored
  frontispiece
Aquatintakupfer: watercolored
  engraving
Arabeskenstempel: arabesque
  stamping(s)
Arbeit(en): work(s), study(ies)
Archiv: archives
Atlanten: atlases
Atlas: atlas
auf Wunsch: upon request
aufgeklebt: mounted, pasted in
aufgelegt: edited
aufgeplatzt: burst, cracked
aufgerissen: torn
aufges. *see* aufgesetzt
aufgeschnitten: opened with paper
  knife
aufgesetzt: patched, mounted
aufgewalzt: rolled on under
  pressure, laminated

aufgez. *see* aufgezogen
aufgezeichnet: recorded
aufgezogen: mounted
Aufl. *see* Auflage
Auflage: edition
Auflagenvermerk: note concerning
   edition
Auflg. *see* Auflage
Aufnahmen: photographs
Aufsätze: essays, papers
aus der Zeit: of that time
Ausbess. *see* Ausbesserung
Ausbesserung: repair
ausführl. *see* ausführlich
ausführlich: *in extenso*, detailed
Ausg. *see* Ausgabe
Ausgabe: printing, edition
Ausgabe letzter Hand: definitive
   edition
ausgeb. *see* ausgebessert
ausgebess. *see* ausgebessert
ausgebessert: repaired
ausgebrochen: broken loose
ausgefranst: worn
ausgemalt: illuminated
ausgeprägt: stamped, raised
ausgeschlagen: lined
ausgeschn. *see* ausgeschnitten
ausgeschnitt. *see* ausgeschnitten
ausgeschnitten: cut out, excised
ausgew. *see* ausgewählt
ausgewählt: selected
ausgezeichn. *see* ausgezeichnet
ausgezeichnet: excellent, in
   excellent state
Ausklapptafel(n): folding plate(s)
Ausland: foreign countries
Ausleihsp. *see* Ausleihspuren
Ausleihspuren: marks of lending
ausnahmslos: without exception
ausradiert: erased, scratched out
ausschlagbar: foldout
ausschliessl. *see* ausschliesslich
ausschliesslich: exclusive
Ausschn. *see* Ausschnitt
Ausschnitt: excision, clipping
aussen: externally

ausser: except, besides
äusserst: outermost, utmost,
   lowest (price)
Ausw. *see* Auswahl
Auswahl: selection
Auswahl-Ausgabe: selected edition
Auszug(züge): excerpt(s)
auszugweise: in excerpts
Autogr. *see* Autograph
Autograph: autograph
autographiert: autographed
autographisch: handwritten
autor. *see* autorisiert
autoris. *see* autorisiert
autorisiert: authorized
Autotypien: illustrations in
   autotype

Balacron: a patented book cloth
Ballonleinen: balloon cloth
Band: ribbon, band, tie; volume
Bändchen: small volume(s),
   pamphlet(s)
Bände: volumes
Bänder: ribbons, bands, ties
Banderole(n): narrow band(s)
Bandzahl(en): volume number(s)
Barverkauf: cash sale
Bastardschrift: bastard type
Bd. *see* Band
Bdch. *see* Bändchen
Bdchn. *see* Bändchen
Bde. *see* Bände
Bdn. *see* Bände
bdr. *see* bedruckt
bearb. *see* bearbeitet
Bearb. *see* Bearbeiter, Bearbeitung
Bearbeiter: reviser(s)
bearbeitet: reworked, revised
Bearbeitung: revision
bed.verm. *see* bedeutend vermehrt
bedeutend vermehrt: considerably
   enlarged
bedruckt: printed
Begleitheft: accompanying issue
Begleitwort(e): explanatory
   remark(s)

begr. *see* begründet
begründet: founded
beh. *see* behandelt
behandelt: deals with
beiderseitig *see* beidseitig
beidseit. *see* beidseitig
beidseitig: on both sides
Beifügung: addition
beigeb. *see* beigebunden
beigebunden: bound with
beigedr. *see* beigedruckt
beigedruckt: bound together,
    issued with
Beiheft: supplementary issue
Beil. *see* Beilage
Beilage(n): supplement(s)
beiliegt: added
Beitr. *see* Beitrag
Beitrag(träge): contribution(s)
bekleistert: pasted over, covered
    with glue
bekritzelt: scribbled on
Belletristik: belles lettres, fiction
bemerkenswert: noteworthy
ben. *see* benutzt
benagt: gnawed
benutzt: used, with traces of use
Benutzungsspuren: traces of use
ber. *see* berieben
berechnet: planned, calculated,
    estimated
berechtigt: authorized
bereinigt: expurgated
bereits erschienen: already
    published; available
Bericht(e): bulletin(s)
Berichtigung(en): correction(s)
berieb. *see* berieben
berieben: scraped
berühmt(est): (most) famous
bes. *see* besonders
besch. *see* beschädigt
beschabt: scraped
beschäd. *see* beschädigt
beschädigt: damaged
Beschädigung(en): defect(s)
bescheuert: chafed

Beschlag(schläge): mounting(s),
    decoration(s)
beschlagnahmt: seized
beschmutzt: soiled
beschn. *see* beschnitten
beschnitten: cut, trimmed
beschränkt: limited
beschrieben: inscribed, covered
    with writing
Besitzeintragung(en): note(s)
    concerning ownership
Besitzerstempel: owner's stamp
Besitzverm. *see* Besitzvermerk
Besitzvermerk: notation of
    ownership
besonders: special, separate
besorgt: edited, prepared
best. *see* bestossen
Bestellung(en): order(s)
bestoss. *see* bestossen
bestossen: bruised, injured
beweglich: movable, mobile
bez. *see* bezeichnet, bezogen
bezeichnet: designated
beziehungsweise: respectively
bezogen: covered
bezügl. *see* bezüglich
bezüglich: concerning
Bezugspreis: subscription price
Bibl. *see* Bibliographie
Bibl.-St. *see* Bibliothekstempel
Bibl.Stemp. *see* Bibliothekstempel
bibliogr. *see* bibliographisch
Bibliograph(en): bibliographer(s)
Bibliographie(n): bibliography(ies)
bibliographisch: bibliographic
Bibliothekar(e): librarian(s)
Bibliotheksausgabe: library edition
Bibliotheksband(bände): ex-library
    volume(s)
Bibliothekseinbänd(e): library
    binding(s)
Bibliothekstempel: library stamp
biegs. *see* biegsam
biegsam: flexible
Bild(er): picture(s)
Bildbeigaben: plates

Bildbeilage(n): picture
  supplement(s)
Bilderwerk: volume of plates
Bildinitialen: illustrated initial
  letters
Bildn. *see* Bildnis(se)
Bildnis(se): portrait(s)
Bildseiten: plates
Bildtaf. *see* Bildtafel
Bildtafel(n): illustrated plate(s)
Bildteil: picture section
Bindg. *see* Bindung
Bindung: binding
biogr. *see* biographisch
biographisch: biographical
bis auf: except for
bis zum Erscheinen: until it
  appears
bisher: up to now, so far
bitte anfordern: please request
Bl. *see* Blatt
blassblau: pale blue
Blatt(Blätter): leaf(ves), page(s)
Blättchen: small leaf(ves), page(s),
  leaflet(s)
blattgr. *see* blattgross
blattgross: full-page
Blattrand(ränder): margin(s)
Blattweiser: list(s) of catchwords
Blattzahl: number of sheets
Blattzählung: foliation, numbering
  of leaves, pages
blau: blue
Bld. *see* Bild
Bleianm. *see* Bleianmerkungen
Bleianmerkungen: pencil notes
Bleist. *see* Bleistift
Bleistift: pencil
Bleistiftanmerkungen: pencil notes
Bleistiftanstrich(e): pencil mark(s)
Bleistiftmarginalien: marginal
  pencil notes
Bleistiftnotiz(en): penciled note(s)
Bleistiftstriche: pencil lines
Bleistiftunterstreichungen: pencil
  underlining
Bleistiftvermerke: pencil marks

blindgepr. *see* blindgeprägt
blindgeprägt: blind-tooled
Blindpräg. *see* Blindprägung
Blindprägung: blind goffering
Blindpressung: blind tooling
Bll. *see* Blätter
Blockbuch: block book
Blumenrankenornament: interlaced
  floral ornamentation
Blumenstempel: floral stamping(s)
Blütenlese(n): anthology(ies)
blütenweiss: immaculately white
Blz. *see* Blattzahl
Bog. *see* Bogen
Bogen(Bögen): sheet(s)
Bord. *see* Bordüre
Bordüre(n): border(s), ornamental
  frame(s)
br. *see* broschiert
Br. *see* Broschur
Brandschaden: damage caused by
  burning
Braunanmalung: coloration in
  brown
braunfl. *see* braunfleckig
braunfleckig: brown-spotted
Bräunung(en): browning(s),
  browned spot(s)
breit: wide
Breite: width
breitrandig: with wide margin(s)
Brief(e): letter(s)
Brief.-Faksim. *see* Brief-Faksimile
Brief-Faksimile: facsimile letter
Briefbeil. *see* Briefbeilage
Briefbeilage(n): supplement(s) of
  letter(s)
Briefwechsel: correspondence
Bro.d.Z. *see* Broschur der Zeit
Brokatpapier: brocaded paper
Brokatpapierüberzug: brocade
  paper cover
bronziert: lustrous dark brown
brosch. *see* broschiert
broschiert: stitched, in paper covers
Broschur: brochure binding

Broschur der Zeit: brochure
binding of the time
Broschüre(n): pamphlet(s),
brochure(s)
brsch. *see* broschiert
Bruch: fold
brüchig: brittle
Bruchspuren: traces of cracking
Buchausgabe: edition in book form
Buchbinder: bookbinder(s)
Buchbinderpreis: binding cost
Buchdeckel: cover(s) of book(s)
Buchdr. *see* Buchdrucker,
Buchdruckerei
Buchdrucker: printer(s)
Buchdruckerei: printer, print shop
Buchdruckpapierüberzug: cover of
printing paper
Bücherfreund(e): bibliophile(s)
Bücherliebhaber: bibliophile(s)
Büchersammler: book collector(s)
Buchh. *see* Buchhandlung
Buchhandel: book trade, bookstore
Buchhändler: book dealer(s)
Buchhandlung: book dealer,
bookstore
Büchlein: small book
Buchschmuck: book decoration
Buckram-Leinen: buckram
Bund: band
Bünde: bands
Bunt- und Schwarzdruck: color
and black and white
Buntbilder: colored illustrations
Buntpapier: multicolored paper
Bütten: handmade paper
büttenähnl. *see* büttenähnlich
büttenähnlich: like handmade paper
Büttenpapier: handmade paper
bzw. *see* beziehungsweise

ca. *see* cirka
cellophaniert: cellophane-covered
chromolith. *see*
chromolithographiert
chromolithographiert:
chromolithographed

Chronik(en): chronicle(s)
cirka: circa

D. *see* Deckel
d.i. *see* das ist
d.Z. *see* der Zeit
d.Zt. *see* der Zeit
dabei: including, attached
dafür: in contrast
Damast: damask
dargest. *see* dargestellt
dargestellt: represented
Darst. *see* Darstellung
darstellend: representing
Darstellung(en): representation(s)
das ist: that is
dass. *see* dasselbe
dasselbe: the same
Dat. *see* Datum
datiert: dated
Datierung: dating, date
Datum: date
dazugeh. *see* dazugehörig
dazugehörend: accompanying,
matching
dazugehörig: accompanying,
matching
dazwischen: in between
Deckbl. *see* Deckblatt
Deckblatt: cover sheet
Decke: cover
Deckel: cover(s)
Deckelbezug(bezüge): covering(s)
of cover(s)
Deckelill. *see* Deckelillustration
Deckelillustration(en): cover
illustration(s)
Deckelkupfer: cover engraving
Deckelvergoldung: gilding on side
Deckelvignette: cover vignette
Deckname(n): pseudonym(s)
Ded. *see* Dedikation
Dedikation: dedication note
def. *see* defekt
defekt: damaged, incomplete
Defekt(e): deficiency(ies), flaw(s)
dekorativ: decorative, sumptuous

demnächst: in the near future
Denkschrift(en): memoir(s),
  memorandum(a);
  commemorative volume(s)
der Zeit: of that time
ders. *see* derselbe
derselbe: the same
dess. *see* desselben
desselben: of the same
Detailaufnahme(n): photograph(s)
  of details
Di. *see* Dissertation
Diagramme: diagrams
Dickdruckpapier: heavy printing
  paper
Dicke: thickness
dies. *see* dieselbe
dieselbe(n): the same
Diss. *see* Dissertation
Dissertation: dissertation
Dokumentenpapier: parchment
  paper
dopp. *see* doppelt
Doppelband: double volume
Doppelbd. *see* Doppelband
Doppelbl. *see* Doppelblatt
Doppelblatt: double page
doppelblattgr. *see* doppelblattgross
doppelblattgross: double-page size
Doppeldruck(e): double
  impression(s)
doppels. *see* doppelseitig
doppelseitig: double-page
doppelt: duplicated, double
Doppeltafeln: double plates
Dr. *see* Druck, Drucker
Drama: play(s)
drei: three
dreiseitiger Goldschnitt: three
  edges gilded
dreissig(ste): thirty(ieth)
dreizehn(te): thirteen(th)
dritte: third
Drittel: third(s)
Druck(e): print(s)
Drucker: printer(s)
Druckerm. *see* Druckermarke

Druckermarke(n): printer's
  mark(s)
Druckersignet: printer's device
Druckerzeichen: printer's mark(s)
Druckfehlerverzeichnis(se): errata
  list(s)
Druckvermerk: colophon
Dublettenstempel: stamp(s)
  designating duplicate copy(ies)
dunkelgrün: dark green
dunkelrot: dark red
dunkelviolett: dark violet
Dünndr.-Pap. *see* Dünndruckpapier
Dünndruck: thin paper, India
  paper
Dünndruckausgabe: thin-paper
  edition
Dünndruckpapier: thin paper,
  India paper
Dupl. *see* Duplikat
Duplikat(e): duplicate(s)
durchg. *see* durchgesehen
durchgearb. *see* durchgearbeitet
durchgearbeitet: revised
durchgeh. *see* durchgehend
durchgehend: throughout
durchges. *see* durchgesehen
durchgesehen: verified, reviewed
durchgestrichen: crossed out
durchgez.Bünde. *see*
  durchgezogene Bünde
durchgezogene Bünde: raised bands
durchlaufd. *see* durchlaufend
durchlaufend: consecutive,
  consecutively numbered
durchlocht: perforated
durchsch. *see* durchschossen
durchschossen: interleaved
durchstrichen: crossed out
durchweg: throughout
durchwegs: throughout

ebd. *see* ebenda
Ebd. *see* Einband
ebda. *see* ebenda
ebenda: same place
ebendaselbst: same place

ebendazu: for the same
ebenf. *see* ebenfalls
ebenfalls: also
Ecke(n): corner(s)
Eckfleuron(s): corner floral motif(s)
Eckkartusche(n): corner
  cartouche(s)
Eckstück(e): cornerpiece(s)
eigenh. *see* eigenhändig
eigenhändig: autograph,
  handwritten
eigenhd. *see* eigenhändig
eighd. *see* eigenhändig
ein: one
ein paar: a few, some
Einb. *see* Einband
Einband: binding
Einbanddecke(n): cover(s) for
  binding
Einbanddeckel: cover(s)
Einbandrücken: spine
Einbandzeichng. *see*
  Einbandzeichnung
Einbandzeichnung: binding design
Einbd. *see* Einband
Einbddecke. *see* Einbanddecke
Einblattdr. *see* Einblattdruck
Einblattdruck: broadside
Einf. *see* Einführung
einfach: simple
einfarb. *see* einfarbig
einfarbig: single color
Einfassung: frame, border
Einfassungsleiste: frame
Einführung: introduction
eingeb. *see* eingebunden
eingebunden: bound in
eingedr. *see* eingedruckt
eingedruckt: printed in text
eingef. *see* eingeführt
eingeführt: introduced, prefaced
eingegangen: no longer published,
  ceased publication
eingehängt: cased in, inserted
eingeklebt: pasted in
eingel. *see* eingeleitet
eingelassen: recessed, set in

eingelegt: inserted loosely, laid in
eingeleitet: with introduction
eingem. *see* eingemalt
eingemalt: painted in
eingeprägt: stamped in
einger. *see* eingerissen
eingerissen: torn
eingerückt: aligned
eingeschaltet: inserted,
  intercalated
eingestampft: destroyed, pulped
eingraviert: engraved
einheitl. *see* einheitlich
einheitlich: uniform
Einl. *see* Einleitung
Einlegetabelle(n): tipped-in
  chart(s)
einleit. *see* einleitend
einleitend: introductory
Einleitung: introduction
einmalig: one-time, unique
Einriss: small tear
eins: one
Einschaltblatt(blätter): inserted
  leaf(ves)
einschl. *see* einschliesslich
einschliesslich: including, inclusive
Einschluss: inclusion
Einschub(schübe): insertion(s)
einseitig bedruckt: printed on one
  side only
einseitig gedruckt: printed on one
  side only
Eintr. *see* Eintragung
Eintrag. *see* Eintragung
Eintragung: entry, note
einwandfrei: faultless
einz. *see* einzeln
Einzelausgabe: separate (edition)
Einzelband(bände): separate
  volume(s)
Einzeldarstellung(en):
  monograph(s)
Einzelheft(e): separate issue(s)
Einzeljahrgang(gänge): separate
  annual volume(s)
einzeln: separate, separately

einzelne: several
Einzelnummer: single number
Einzelpr. *see* Einzelpreis
Einzelpreis: price for each part
Einzeltitel: separate item(s)
einzig: only, unique
einzusetzen: to be inserted
elf(te): eleven(th)
Empf. *see* Empfänger
Empfänger: recipient
Endblätter: endpapers
Endpreis: final price
entf. *see* entfärbt
entfärbt: discolored, faded
entfernt: removed
enth. *see* enthält, enthalten
enthält: contains
enthalten(d): contain(ing)
Entwurf(würfe): draft(s), plan(s),
  sketch(es)
entzückend: attractive, charming
erbitte Angebote: offers requested
erg. *see* ergänzt
Erg. *see* Ergänzung
Erg.-Bd. *see* Ergänzungsband
Erg.-H. *see* Ergänzungsheft
ergänzt: supplemented,
  complemented
Ergänzung(en): supplement(s)
Ergänzungsband: supplementary
  volume
Ergänzungsheft: supplementary
  issue
Erh. *see* Erhaltung
erhalten: preserved
Erhaltung: state of preservation
Erinnerungen: memoirs
erkl. *see* erklärend, erklärt
erklär. *see* erklärend
erklärend: explanatory
erklärt: explained, clarified
Erklärung: explanation
erl. *see* erläuternd, erläutert
Erl. *see* Erläuterung
erläuternd: explanatory
erläutert: annotated
Erläuterung(en): explanation(s)

Ermässigung: reduction
erneuert: renewed, replaced
ersch. *see* erschienen
erscheint demnächst: to appear in
  the near future
erschienen: published
ersetzt: replaced
erst: not until, only
Erstausgabe: first edition
Erstdruck: first printing
erste Ausgabe: first edition
ersten Ranges: first class
erstmalig: original, for the first
  time
erstmals: for the first time
erw. *see* erweitert
erweit. *see* erweitert
erweitert: enlarged
Erz. *see* Erzählung
Erzählung: story
Eselsohren: dog-ears
Etikett(e): label(s)
Etui(s): case(s), box(es)
etw. *see* etwas
etwa: approximately
etwas: rather, somewhat
Ex. *see* Exemplar
Exempl. *see* Exemplar
Exemplar(e): copy(ies)
Exkurs(e): insertion(s),
  supplementary paper(s)
Expl. *see* Exemplar
Exx. *see* Exemplar

f. *see* fehlen, fehlt, folio
F. *see* Folge
Fächerstempel: fan-shaped
  stamp(s)
Faks. *see* Faksimile
Faksim. *see* Faksimile
Faksimile: facsimile(s)
Faksimiledruck: facsimile reprint
Faksimiletafel(n): facsimile
  table(s)
faksimiliert: copied in facsimile
fälschlich: erroneously
Fälschung: forgery, fake

Faltblatt: folding leaf
Faltbuch: accordion-folding book
Faltkarte: folded map
Faltkupf. *see* Faltkupfer
Faltkupfer: folding copperplate(s)
Falttaf. *see* Falttafel
Falttafel(n): folding plate(s)
Falttfln. *see* Falttafel
Falz: fold, joint
Familienwappen: coat(s) of arms
farb. *see* farbig
Farbabweichung: irregular,
    variant color(s)
Farbendr. *see* Farbendruck
Farbendruck: color print
Farbentafeln: colored plates
Farbentafln. *see* Farbentafeln
farbig: colored
Farblichtdruck(e): photographic
    color reproduction(s)
Farblithografie(n): color
    lithograph(s)
Farbschnitt(e): colored edge(s)
Farbtaf. *see* Farbtafel
Farbtafel(n): colored plate(s)
Fassung: version
fast: almost
Fbdr. *see* Farbendruck
Feder: pen
Federornament: featherlike
    ornamental design
Federzeichnungen: pen and ink
    drawings
fehlend: lacking
fehlerhaft: erroneous, deficient
Fehlstelle(n): deficiency(ies),
    defective spot(s)
fehlt: lacks, is missing
fein: fine, delicate
Feinleinen: fine cloth
feinst: most delicate(ly)
Feld(er): panel(s)
ferner: further, furthermore
fest: firm, solid
Festschrift: commemorative
    volume
Feucht.-Sp. *see* Feuchtigkeitsspuren

feuchtfleckig: damp-spotted
Feuchtigkeit: moisture
Feuchtigkeitsschäden: damage,
    imperfections caused by moisture
Feuchtigkeitsspuren: traces of
    moisture
ff. *see* folgend
Fig. *see* Figur
Figur(en): figure(s), diagram(s)
figürl. *see* figürlich
figürlich: figured
Fil. *see* Fileten
Fileten: fillets
fingerfl. *see* fingerfleckig
fingerfleckig: finger-marked
Fingerspuren: fingerprints, traces
    of handling
fl. *see* fleckig
Fl. *see* Fleck
flach: flat
Flechtband: lace-ribbon
    ornamental design
fleck. *see* fleckig
Fleck(e): spot(s), stain(s)
Fleckchen: small spot(s)
fleckenfrei: spotless
fleckenlos: spotless
fleckig: spotted
flex. *see* flexibel
flexibel: flexible
flexibl. *see* flexibel
fliegender Vorsatz: flyleaf
fliegendes Blatt: broadside
Florilegium: anthology
Flugblatt(blätter): broadsheet(s),
    handbill(s)
Flugschrift(en): pamphlet(s)
fol. *see* folio
Fol. *see* Foliant
Folge: series
folgend(e): following, and following
    pages
Foliant(en): folio volume(s)
foliiert: foliated
Foliierung: foliation
folio: folio, sheet
Format: size, format

Formatangabe: designation of size
fortgef. *see* fortgeführt
fortgeführt: continued
fortges. *see* fortgesetzt
fortgesetzt: continued
fortlaufend: consecutive
Forts. *see* Fortsetzung
Fortsetzung: continuation
fotogr. *see* fotografiert
Fotogr. *see* Fotografie
Fotografie(n): photograph(s)
fotografiert: photographed
fotomechanisch: photomechanical
Fotomontage(n): photomontage(s)
Fototafeln: photographic tables
Fraktur: black-letter type
franz. *see* französisch
Franzband: leather binding,
    usually calf
französisch: in French style,
    French
frisch: fresh
Frische: freshness
Front. *see* Frontispiz
Frontispiz: frontispiece
Frühdruck: early print, near
    incunabulum
Frühjahr: Spring
Frzbd. *see* Franzband
fünf(te): five (fifth)
fünfzehn(te): fifteen(th)
fünfzig(ste): fifty(ieth)
Fussnote(n): footnote(s)

G. *see* Goldschnitt
galant: risqué, erotic
ganz: entire(ly), quite
ganz wenig: very little
Ganzgoldschnitt: all edges gilt
Ganzl. *see* Ganzleinen
gänzl.umgearb. *see* gänzlich
    umgearbeitet
Ganzleder: full leather
Ganzleinen: full cloth
Ganzleinwand: full cloth
gänzlich umgearbeitet: entirely
    revised

ganzs. *see* ganzseitig
ganzseit. *see* ganzseitig
ganzseitig: full-page
Ganztafeln: full-page plates
Gbsp. *see* Gebrauchsspuren
geb. *see* gebunden
gebdn. *see* gebunden
gebr. *see* gebrochen
Gebr.-Sp. *see* Gebrauchsspuren
Gebr.-Spur. *see* Gebrauchsspuren
gebrauchsfleckig: stained through
    use
Gebrauchsspuren: marks of use
gebräunt: foxed, browned
gebrochen: broken
Gebrsp. *see* Gebrauchsspuren
gebunden: bound
Gedenkschrift: commemorative
    publication
gediegen: solid(ly), strong(ly)
gedr. *see* gedruckt
gedruckt: printed
gefalt. *see* gefaltet
gefaltet: folded
geflickt: patched
geflt. *see* gefaltet
gefranst: worn
gefüttert: lined
gegen bar: for cash
gegenüber: facing, opposite
gegenübergest. *see*
    gegenübergestellt
gegenübergestellt: facing
Gegenwart: present
gegilbt: yellowed
geglättet: smoothed, burnished
geh. *see* geheftet
geheftet: stitched, bound in
    pamphlet style
gehöht: heightened
gekl. *see* geklebt
geklebt: pasted, pasted together
geknickt: dog-eared, cracked, bent
geknittert: crumpled
gekr. *see* gekrönt
gekrönt: prize-winning
gekürzt: shortened, condensed

gelbfleckig: with yellow spots, foxed
Geleitwort: introduction, introductory note
Gelenk(e): joint(s)
gelitten: suffered, damaged
gelockert: loosened
gelöscht: canceled
gem. *see* gemalt
gemalt: hand-colored
Gemeinschaft: collaboration, cooperation
gemeinverst. *see* gemeinverständlich
gemeinverständlich: popular
gen. *see* genannt
genannt: mentioned
genarbt: grained
gepl. *see* geplant, geplatzt
geplant: planned, scheduled
geplatzt: burst, cracked
gepr. *see* geprägt, gepresst
geprägt: embossed
gepresst: stamped, tooled
gepunzt: punched out, embossed
ger. *see* gering
gerade Bandzahlen: even volume numbers
gering: unimportant, inferior, cheap
geringfügig: insignificant, slight
gerippt: ribbed
gerissen: torn
ges. *see* gesammelt
gesammelt: collected
Gesamtaufl. *see* Gesamtauflage
Gesamtauflage: entire edition
Gesamtausgabe: complete edition
Gesamtreg. *see* Gesamtregister
Gesamtregister: general index
Gesamtwerk: collected work, entire work
geschaffen: created
geschätzt: highly valued, estimated
Geschenkausgabe: gift edition
Geschenkband: gift volume
Geschenkeinband: gift binding

Geschenkexemplar: gift copy
geschichtl. *see* geschichtlich
geschichtlich: historical
geschickt: clever, skillful
geschmückt: decorated
geschn. *see* geschnitten
geschnitten: engraved, cut
geschrotet: dotted, sprinkled
gesprenkelt: sprinkled
gesprungen: cracked, broken
gest. *see* gestempelt, gestochen
gestaltet: artistically arranged
gestempelt: stamped, marked with a stamp
gestickt: embroidered
gestochen: engraved
gestrichen: crossed out, lined out
gesucht: sought after, in demand
getilgt: canceled
getönt: toned, tinted
getr.Z. *see* getrennte Zählung
getrennte Zählung: separate numbering
getuscht: tinted
gewaschen: washed
geweisst: whitened
gewidmet: dedicated to
gewöhnlich: usual(ly)
gez.S. *see* gezählte Seiten
gezählte Seiten: numbered pages
gilbfleckig: with yellow spots, foxed
Glanzfolie: glossy foil
Glanzfolieneinband: glossy foil binding
Glanzpapier: glossy paper
glatt: smooth
gleichmässig: uniform
gleichnamig: with the same name, title
gleichzeitig: at the same time
Glossar: glossary
Glwd. *see* Ganzleinwand
golddurchwirkt: gold-brocaded
Goldfil. *see* Goldfileten
Goldfileten: gold fillets

Goldfolienumschlag: gold-leaf decorated covers
goldgedr. *see* goldgedruckt
goldgedruckt: printed with gold
goldgehöht: heightened with gold
goldgeprägt: gold-stamped
Goldornament(e): gilt decoration(s)
Goldpr. *see* Goldprägung
Goldprägung: gold stamping
Goldpressung: gold stamping
Goldschmuck: gilding
Goldschn. *see* Goldschnitt
Goldschnitt: gilt edge(s)
goldverz. *see* goldverziert
goldverziert: decorated with gold
Goldverzierung: gold decoration
got. *see* gotisch
gotisch: gothic type
Gr.-Ausg. *see* Gross-Ausgabe
Gr.okt. *see* Grossoktav
graph. *see* graphisch
Graphik(en): graphic(s)
graphisch: graphic, graphical
graphische Darstellung(en): graph(s)
grav. *see* graviert
Grav. *see* Gravüre
graviert: engraved
Gravüre(n): engraving(s), etching(s)
Gross-Ausgabe: large edition
Grösse(n): size(s)
Grossoktav: large octavo
grösstenteils: mostly, largely
grosszügig: generous, grandiose
Groteskschrift: block letter(s)
grün: green
Grund: background
grundlegend: basic, fundamental
Grundr. *see* Grundriss
Grundriss(e): outline(s), compendium(ia), primer(s)
Gummistempel: rubber stamp(s)
Gutachten: expert attestation(s)
Gzld. *see* Ganzleder
Gzln. *see* Ganzleinen

gzstg. *see* ganzseitig

H. *see* Hälfte, Heft
Habilitationsschrift: thesis required for the induction of lecturers at state universities
Hadernpapier: rag paper
Halbband: half volume, divided volume
Halbfranz: half calf
Halbfranzband: half-calf binding
Halbjahrsband: semiannual volume
Halbkalbsleder: half calf
Halbleder: half leather
Halbleinen: half cloth
Halbleinwand: half cloth
Halbmaroquin: half morocco
Halbmonatsschrift: fortnightly publication
Halbperg. *see* Halbpergament
Halbpergament: half vellum
Halbschweinsleder: half pigskin
Hälfte(n): half, half volume(s)
Hand(Hände): scribe(s)
Handel: trade
Handexemplar: personal copy, reference copy
handgeb. *see* handgebunden
handgebunden: hand-bound
handgemalt: hand-painted
handgeschöpft: handmade
handgestickt: embroidered
handkol. *see* handkoloriert
handkoloriert: hand-colored
Handschr. *see* Handschrift
Handschrift: manuscript; autograph
handschriftl. *see* handschriftlich
handschriftlich: handwritten
hauchdünn: ultrathin
Hauptwerk: main work
Heft(e): part(s), issue(s), number(s)
Heften: parts, issues, numbers
Heftkante(n): edge(s) on binding side
Heftung: stitching

hektogr. *see* hektografiert
hektografiert: hectographed
Heliograv. *see* Heliogravüre
Heliogravüre: photoengraving
hell: light-colored, bright
hellblau: light blue
hellbraun: light brown
Helldunkelschnitt: chiaroscuro
heller: lighter colored
Herausgabe: editing, publication
Herausgeber: editor(s)
herausgegeben: published, edited
herausgeschnitten: cut out,
  excised
Herbst: Autumn, Fall
hergestellt: produced
herrlich: magnificent
hervorrag. *see* hervorragend
hervorragend: outstanding
Hfranzbd. *see* Halbfranzband
Hfrz. *see* Halbfranzband
Hfte. *see* Heft
Hftn. *see* Heften
Hfz: *see* Halbfranzband
Hfzbd. *see* Halbfranzband
hie und da: occasionally, in some
  places
hier und da: occasionally, in some
  places
Hilfstabellen: auxiliary tables
hinter: back, rear
hinterlegt: mounted, strengthened
Hl. *see* Halbleinen
Hldr. *see* Halbleder
Hled. *see* Halbleder
Hln. *see* Halbleinen
Hlwd. *see* Halbleinwand
Hlz. *see* Holzschnitt
hohl: hollow, curved
hohler Schnitt: hollow edge, fore
  edge
Holzdeck. *see* Holzdeckel
Holzdeckel: wooden board(s)
Holzdeckelband: binding with
  wooden boards
Holzdeckeleinband: binding with
  wooden boards

holzfleckig: foxed
holzfr. *see* holzfrei
holzfrei: free of wood, pure rag
  (paper)
Holzschn. *see* Holzschnitt
Holzschnitt(e): woodcut(s)
Holzschnitt-Bordüre(n): woodcut
  border(s)
Holzschnitt-Porträt(e): woodcut
  portrait(s)
Holzschnittfleuron(s): woodcut
  fleuron(s)
Holzschnittmarke: woodcut mark
Holzschnittumrahmung: woodcut
  border, frame
Holzstich(e): woodcut(s), wood
  engraving(s)
Holzstock(stöcke): woodblock(s)
Hpergt. *see* Halbpergament
Hpgt. *see* Halbpergament
Hprgt. *see* Halbpergament
hrsg. *see* herausgegeben
Hrsg. *see* Herausgeber
hs. *see* handschriftlich
Hs. *see* Handschrift
Hschwldr. *see* Halbschweinsleder
Hschwsldr. *see* Halbschweinsleder
hübsch: handsome
hundert(ste): hundred(th)

i.H. *see* in Heften
i.J. *see* im Jahr
identisch mit: identical to
ill. *see* illustriert
Ill. *see* Illustration, Illustrator
illuminiert: illuminated
illust. *see* illustriert
Illustrat. *see* Illustration
Illustration(en): illustration(s)
Illustrator: illustrator
illustriert: illustrated
im Druck: in press
im Erscheinen: in progress
im Erscheinen begriffen: in
  process of publication
im ganzen gut: good as a whole
im Innern: inside

im Jahr: in the year
im Stile d.Zt. *see* im Stile der Zeit
im Stile der Zeit: in the style of
  the time
im Text: in the text
im übrigen: otherwise
imit. *see* imitiert
imitiert: imitated, artificial
Impr. *see* Impressum
Impressum: imprint
in Heften: in parts
in Herst. *see* in Herstellung
in Herstellung: in preparation
in sich selbständig: complete in
  itself
in Vorbereitung: in preparation
Inh.-Verz. *see* Inhaltsverzeichnis
Inhalt: contents
Inhaltsverzeichnis: table of
  contents
Init. *see* Initialen
Initialen: initial letters
inkl. *see* inklusive
inklusive: inclusive, including
Inkun. *see* Inkunabel
Inkunabel(n): incunabulum(a)
innen: inner, inside
Innendeckel: inside cover
Innenkantenbordüre: borders on
  inner margins of covers
Innenkantenvergoldung: gilding on
  inner margins of covers
Innenspiegel: doublure, lining
Innensteg: inner fillet
Innere(s): interior, inside
Inschrift: inscription
insges. *see* insgesamt
insgesamt: all together
intakt: intact, complete
Intarsia: inlay, mosaic
Intarsie: inlay, mosaic
Interimsausgabe: provisional
  edition
irrtümlich: erroneous(ly), wrong(ly)

J. *see* Jahr
Jahr: year

Jahresabonnement: annual
  subscription
Jahresbezugspreis: annual cost,
  cost per year
Jahresg. *see* Jahresgabe
Jahresgabe: New Year's
  publication
Jahrg. *see* Jahrgang
Jahrgang(gänge): year(s),
  volume(s)
Jahrh. *see* Jahrhundert
Jahrhundert: century
jährl. *see* jährlich
jährlich: annual(ly)
Jansensteneinband: Jansenist
  binding
Japanbütten: handmade Japan
  paper
Japanpapierüberzug: handmade
  Japan paper cover
je: per volume, per item
jeder: each
jeweils: in each case
Jg. *see* Jahrgang
Jgge. *see* Jahrgänge
Jh. *see* Jahrhundert
Jhdt. *see* Jahrhundert
Jubiläumsausgabe: jubilee edition
Juchten: Russian leather
Jungfern-Pergament: virgin
  parchment

K. *see* Kustode
Kalbdrbd. *see* Kalblederband
Kalblederband: full-calf binding
kalligr. *see* kalligraphisch
kalligraphisch: calligraphic
Kaltnadel: drypoint
Kante(n): edge(s) of cover
Kantenvergoldung: gilding on
  edges of cover
Kap. *see* Kapitel
Kapital(e): headband(s),
  headcap(s)
Kapitel: chapter(s)
kart. *see* kartoniert
Karte(n): map(s), chart(s)

Kartensk. *see* Kartenskizze
Kartenskizze(n): sketch map(s)
Kartographie: cartography
Karton: pasteboard, cardboard;
  cancel
Kartonhülle: pasteboard slipcase
kartoniert: bound in boards
Kartonumschlag: pasteboard case
Kartusche(n): cartouche(s)
Kassette: box, slipcase
Kastenvergoldung: gilt frame or
  fillets
Kastenverzierung: blind frame or
  fillet tooling
käuflich: for sale
Kaufpreis: purchase price
kaum: scarcely, hardly
kenntlich: recognizable,
  characterized
Kette(n): chain(s)
Ketteneinband: chained binding
Kinderbuch(bücher): children's
  book(s)
Kinderlesebuch(bücher):
  hornbook(s), primer(s)
kl. *see* klein
klar: clear, distinct
Klbldbd. *see* Kalblederband
Kldr. *see* Kunstleder
klein: small
Kleinoffset: small offset printing
Kleinoktav: small octavo
knapp: narrow(ly)
Knick: break, crack
Knickfalte(n): bent fold(s)
Kniff(e): fold(s)
Kodex: codex
Kohlezeich. *see* Kohlezeichnung
Kohlezeichnung(en): charcoal
  drawing(s)
kol. *see* koloriert
Kol. *see* Kolophon
Kol.-titel: *see* Kolumnentitel
Kollat. *see* Kollation
Kollation: collation
kollationiert: collated
Kolophon: colophon

kolor. *see* koloriert
kolorierfähig: suitable for coloring
koloriert: colored
Kolorit: coloring
Kolumnentitel: running title
komm. *see* kommentiert
Komm. *see* Kommentar
Komment. *see* Kommentar
Kommentar: commentary
Kommentarheft: supplement of
  comments or annotations
kommentiert: commented
Komödie(n): comedy(ies)
komp. *see* komponiert
Komp. *see* Komponist
Kompilationswerk: compiled work
Kompilator: compiler
kompl. *see* komplett
komplett: complete
komplette Reihe: complete series
komponiert: composed
Komponist: composer
konform: alike, uniform
Konkordanz: concordance
Konvolut: lot
Kopf(Köpfe): head(s), top(s)
Kopfgoldschnitt: gilt top edge
Kopfleiste(n): headpiece(s)
Kopfsteg: headstick, head margin
Kopft. *see* Kopftitel
Kopftitel: headline, running title
korr. *see* korrigiert
Korrektur(en): correction(s)
korrigiert: corrected
kostbar: expensive, precious
kostenlos: free, without cost
Kpfr. *see* Kupfer
Kpfrst. *see* Kupferstich
Kpfrtaf. *see* Kupfertafel
kplt. *see* komplett
Kpr. *see* Kupferstich
Kpt. *see* Kupfertitel
kräftig: strong
Kratzer: scratch(es)
krit. *see* kritisch
kritisch: critical, critically
Kritzel: doodling(s)

Krt. *see* Karte
kt. *see* kartoniert
Kt. *see* Karte
Kte. *see* Karte
Ktn. *see* Karten
Kunstbeil. *see* Kunstbeilage
Kunstbeilage(n): supplementary
art plate(s)
Kunstblatt(blätter): art print(s),
reproduction(s)
Kunstdruck: art print
Kunstdruckanhang: supplement
of art prints
Kunstdruckbeilagen:
supplementary art plates
Kunstdruckpapier: art paper,
fine-coated glossy paper
Kunstdrucktafel(n): art plate(s)
Kunstleder: artificial leather,
leatherette
Künstler: artist(s), illustrator(s)
künstlich: artificial
Kupf. *see* Kupferstich
Kupfer: copper, copper
engraving(s)
Kupferplatte(n): copperplate(s)
Kupferstecher: copperplate
engraver
Kupferstich(e): copper
engraving(s), etching(s)
Kupfert. *see* Kupfertitel
Kupfertafel(n): copper
engraving(s), engraved plate(s)
Kupfertiefdruck: copper engraving
Kupfertiefdruckreproduktion(en):
copper-engraved reproduction(s)
Kupfertitel: engraved title page
Kupf.-Tfln. *see* Kupfertafel
Kursive: italics
Kursivschrift: italics
kurzrandig: with small margins
Kurztitel: short title
Kust. *see* Kustode(n)
Kustode(n): signature marking(s)
Kustoden: catchwords
Kustos: catchword
Kvergold. *see* Kantenvergoldung

l. *see* leicht, letzt, links
L. *see* Lage
l.fl. *see* leicht fleckig
Lackeinband: lacquered binding
läd. *see* lädiert
Ladenpr. *see* Ladenpreis
Ladenpreis: list price
lädiert: slightly damaged
Lage(n): quire(s), signature(s)
Lagebezeichnung: designation of
quires, signatures
lam. *see* laminiert
lam.Br. *see* laminierte Broschur
laminiert: laminated
laminierte Broschur: laminated
brochure binding
Landkarte(n): map(s)
langnarbig: long-grained
laufende Kolumnentitel: running
titles
Ldnpr. *see* Ladenpreis
Ldr. *see* Leder
Ldrbd. *see* Lederband
Ldrecke. *see* Lederecke
Lebensbeschreibung: biography
Led. *see* Leder
Leder: leather
Lederband: leather binding
Lederecke(n): leather corner(s)
Lederetui: leather case
Lederintarsie: leather mosaic
Lederkanten: leather edges
Ledermappe: leather portfolio
Lederrücken: leather back
Lederschl. *see* Lederschliesse
Lederschlaufe(n): leather loop(s)
Lederschliesse(n): leather clasp(s),
tie(s)
Lederschnittornamentik:
leather-cut decoration
Lederstreifen: leather strip(s)
lediglich: only
leer: blank, empty
Lehrbuch: textbook
leicht: a little, slightly
leicht fleckig: slightly spotted
leimfleckig: glue-spotted

Leimung: glueing
Leinen: cloth
Leinenband: cloth binding
Leinendecke(n): linen cover(s)
Leinenstreifen: linen strips, tapes
Leinw. *see* Leinwand
Leinwand: cloth
Leinwandband: cloth binding
Leinwandstreifen: cloth strip(s)
Leinwdbd. *see* Leinwandband
Leiste(n): border(s)
Leporello-Album: album of
　foldout pages in panorama form
Leporello-Form: foldout, panorama
　form
Lesart(en): reading(s),
　interpretation(s)
lesbar: legible
Letter(n): letter(s)
letzt: last
Lex. *see* Lexikon
Lexika: dictionaries
Lexikon: dictionary
Lfg. *see* Lieferung
Lfgn. *see* Lieferung
Lgebez. *see* Lagebezeichnung
Lgebzg. *see* Lagebezeichnung
Lichtdr. *see* Lichtdruck
Lichtdruck: photoengraving
Lichtdrucktafel(n): photographic
　plate(s)
Liebhaber: amateur(s),
　collector(s)
Liebhaberausg. *see*
　Liebhaberausgabe
Liebhaberausgabe: collector's
　edition
Liebhaberdruck: collector's
　printing
Liebhabereinband: three-quarter
　binding
Liederanhang(hänge):
　appendix(es) of songs
Liederbuch: songbook
Lief. *see* Lieferung
lieferbar: available
Lieferg. *see* Lieferung

Lieferung(en): number(s), part(s),
　fascicle(s)
Lieff. *see* Lieferung
Liefg. *see* Lieferung
Liegt bei: is included, laid in
Lilie(n): fleur(s)-de-lys
limit. *see* limitiert
limitiert: limited
limitiert und numeriert: limited
　and numbered
limitierte Auflage: limited edition
limitierte Ausgabe: limited edition
Linie(n): line(s)
liniiert: ruled
link: left-hand
links: to the left
Linolschnitt(e): linocut(s)
Lit.-Verz. *see* Literatur-
　Verzeichnis
Literatur-Verzeichnis: list of
　references, bibliography
Literaturangabe(n): reference(s)
lith. *see* lithografiert
Lith. *see* Lithografie
Lithogr. *see* Lithografie
Lithograf. *see* Lithografie
Lithografie(n): lithograph(s),
　lithography
lithografiert: lithographed
Lizenzausgabe: licensed publication
Ln. *see* Leinen
Lnb. *see* Leinenband
Loch: hole
löcherig: with holes, wormholed
Löchlein: small hole(s)
Lochung: wormholing, perforation
locker: loose
los: loose
Löschen: erasing
lose Bogen: loose leaf
lose im Einband: loose in the
　binding
lose in O Mappen: loose in the
　original portfolios
Lustspiel(e): comedy(ies)
Luxusausgabe: deluxe edition
Lw. *see* Leinwand

Lwb. *see* Leinwandband
Lwd. *see* Leinwand
Lwdbd. *see* Leinwandband

MA. *see* Mittelalter
M-A. *see* Miniaturausgabe
mager: thin, narrow
Maiblumeninitiale(n): initial(s) decorated with lilies of the valley
Maj. *see* Majuskel
Majuskel: uppercase letter
makellos: immaculate, perfect
makuliert: damaged, pulped
manch: some, a few
Manuskr. *see* Manuskript
Manuskript: manuscript, typescript
Mäppchen: little portfolio(s)
Mappe(n): portfolio(s)
Mappendeckel: portfolio cover
Mar. *see* Maroquin
Märchen: folk tale(s), tale(s), fairy tale(s)
Marginalie(n): marginal note(s)
marm. *see* marmoriert
marmor. *see* marmoriert
marmoriert: marbled
Maroq. *see* Maroquin
Maroquin: morocco
Maroquinécraséband: bound in crushed morocco
Maroquinlederband: bound in morocco
Maschinenschrift: typescript
maschinschriftlich: typewritten
massgeblich: standard, recognized
mässig: poor, moderate
Massstab: scale
matt: dull, pale
Mäusefrass: gnawing of mice
Medaillon: medallion
mehr. *see* mehrere
mehr nicht erschienen: no more published
mehrere: several
mehrf. *see* mehrfach

mehrfach: multiple, in several places, several copies
mehrfarb. *see* mehrfarbig
mehrfarbig: varicolored
Mehrwertsteuer: sales tax, VAT (value added tax)
meist: mostly
Memoiren: memoirs
Menge: a great many
merklich: noticeable
merkw. *see* merkwürdig
merkwürdig: unusual, remarkable
Messingschliessen: brass clasps
Metallbuckel(n): metal boss(es), knob(s)
Metallecke(n): metal corner(s)
Metallschliesse(n): metal clasp(s)
Metallschnitt: metal cut
min. *see* minimal
Min. *see* Miniatur, Minuskel
min.fleckig *see* minimal fleckig
Miniatur(en): miniature(s)
Miniaturausgabe: miniature edition
minimal: minimal
minimal fleckig: minimal spotting
minimal stockfleckig: minimal foxing
Minuskel(n): minuscule(s), lowercase letter(s)
Minuskelhandschriften: manuscript in lowercase letters only
Mitarb. *see* Mitarbeit
Mitarbeit: collaboration
Mitarbeiter: collaborator(s)
mitgebunden: bound with
mitgenommen: not fresh
mitsamt: together with
Mitteilung(en): communication(s)
Mittelalter: Middle Ages
mittelalterlich: medieval
mittelmässig: moderate
Mittelstück: centerpiece
Mitverfasser: joint author(s)
Mitw. *see* Mitwirkung
Mitwirkung: cooperation
MNE. *see* mehr nicht erschienen

mod. *see* modern
modern: modern
möglich: possible
Moiréseide: moiré silk
Monatsschr. *see* Monatsschrift
Monatsschrift: monthly publication
Monogr. *see* Monogramm,
  Monographie
Monogramm: monogram
Monogrammstempel: stamped
  initials
Monographie(n): monograph(s)
mont. *see* montiert
montiert(e): mounted
Motiv: pattern, design
Ms. *see* Manuskript
Muschelverzierung: shell-like
  decoration
Musikbeilage(n): music
  supplement(s)
Muster: pattern(s)
Musterbeispiel: model of its kind
Musterübersetzung: model
  translation
mutiliert: mutilated

n. *see* netto, neu
N.a.T. *see* Name auf Titelblatt
n.F. *see* neue Folge
n.i.H. *see* nicht im Handel
n.R. *see* neue Reihe
n.S. *see* neue Serie
Nachahmung: imitation
Nachbildung(en): reproduction(s)
Nachdr. *see* Nachdruck
Nachdruck: reprint, pirated edition
Nachdruckrecht: copyright
Nachf. *see* Nachfolger
Nachfolger: successor(s)
nachgeklebt: reglued
nachgelassen: posthumous
nachgeliefert: furnished later
nachgeschnitten: recut
nachgestochen: reengraved
nachgewiesen: traced, documented
nachgezogen: retraced, freshened
Nachlass: literary remains

Nachschlagewerk(e): reference
  work(s)
Nachschrift: postscript, postface
Nachstich(e): reengraving(s)
Nachtr. *see* Nachtrag
Nachtrag(träge): appendix(es)
Nachw. *see* Nachwort
nachweisbar: identifiable
Nachwort: postscript
Nagelschaden: damaged by nailing
Nagelspur(en): trace(s) of nailing
nahezu: nearly
Name auf Titelblatt: name on the
  title page
Name auf Vorsatz: name on
  endpaper
Namensstempel: name stamp
Namenszug: signature
Narbe(n): grain(s)
NaT. *see* Name auf Titelblatt
NaVorsatz. *see* Name auf Vorsatz
Nebent. *see* Nebentitel
Nebentitel: subtitle, subhead
nett: nice
netto: net
neu: new
Neuauflage: new edition
Neuausg. *see* Neuausgabe
Neuausgabe: new edition, reprint
neubearb. *see* neubearbeitet
neubearbeitet: revised
Neudruck: reprint
neue Folge: new series
neue Reihe: new series
neue Serie: new series
neuer: newer
Neuerscheinung(en): recent
  publication(s)
neuest: newest
neun(te): nine(th)
neunzehn(te): nineteen(th)
neunzig(ste): ninety(ieth)
neuw. *see* neuwertig
neuwertig: as good as new
ng. *see* nicht gezählt
nicht ganz frisch: not completely
  fresh

nicht gezählt: not counted, unnumbered

nicht im Handel: not for general sale, privately printed

nie erschienen: never published

no. *see* netto

No. *see* Nummer

Notenanhang: music appendix

Notenanhg. *see* Notenanhang

Notenbeil. *see* Notenbeilage

Notenbeilage(n): supplement(s) of music

Notenbeisp. *see* Notenbeispiel

Notenbeispiel(e): musical illustration(s)

Notizen: notes

Novelle(n): long short story(ies)

Nr. *see* Nummer

num. *see* numeriert

numer. *see* numeriert

numeriert: numbered

Numerierung: numbering, pagination

Nummer: number

Nummernschildchen: small numbered label(s)

Nummernstempel: number stamp

nur an Bibliotheken: only to libraries

o. *see* ohne

O. *see* Original

o.Dr. *see* ohne Drucker

o.Ersch.Verm. *see* ohne Erscheinungsvermerk

o.J. *see* ohne Jahr

oJ/oO. *see* ohne Jahres-bezw. ohne Ortsangabe

o.O. *see* ohne Ort

o.O.Dr.u.J. *see* ohne Ort, Drucker und Jahr

o.O.u.J. *see* ohne Ort und Jahr

o.O.u.Verl. *see* ohne Ort und Verleger

o.O.u.Vlg. *see* ohne Ort und Verlag

o.U. *see* ohne Umschlag

oben: on top

Oberrand: top margin

Oberschnitt: top edge

Obr. *see* Originalbroschur

Obro. *see* Originalbroschur

öffentlich: public

Offizin: print shop, printing office

Offsetdruck: offset printing

öfters: fairly frequently

Ohfranz. *see* Originalhalbfranz

Ohfrz. *see* Originalhalbfranz

Ohldr. *see* Originalhalbleder

Ohlwd. *see* Originalhalbleinwand

ohne: without

ohne Abzug: without discount

ohne Drucker: without printer

ohne Erscheinungsvermerk: without imprint

ohne Jahr: without year, without date

ohne Jahresangabe: without date of publication

ohne Jahres-bezw. ohne Ortsangabe: without year or place of publication

ohne Ort: without place of publication

ohne Ort, Drucker und Jahr: without place, publisher, and date

ohne Ort und Jahr: without place and date

ohne Ort und Verlag: without place and publisher

ohne Ort und Verleger: without place and publisher

ohne Umschlag: without covers

OHPergament *see* Originalhalbpergament

Ohprgt. *see* Originalhalbpergament

Old. *see* Originalleinwand

Oldr. *see* Originalleder

olivgrün: olive green

Olw. *see* Originalleinwand

Olwd. *see* Originalleinwand

Opappbd. *see* Originalpappband

Opbd. *see* Originalpappband

Opp. *see* Originalpappband

Oppbd. *see* Originalpappband
Or. *see* Original
ordentl. *see* ordentlich
ordentlich: regular
Orgmappe. *see* Originalmappe
Orhfranz. *see* Originalhalbfranz
Orig. *see* Original
Origbd. *see* Originalband
Orighleinen. *see* Original-
 halbleinen
Original: original, original binding
Originalband: original binding
Originalbroschur: original brochure
 binding
Originaleinband: original binding
Originalformat: original format
originalgetreu: authentic
originalgross: original size
Originalhalbfranz: original half calf
Originalhalbleder: original half
 leather
Originalhalbleinen: original half
 cloth
Originalhalbleinwand: original half
 cloth
Originalhalbpergament: original
 half vellum
Originalleder: original leather
Originalleinen: original cloth
Originalleinwand: original cloth
Originalleinwandband: original
 cloth binding
Originalmappe: original portfolio
Originalpappband: original boards
Originalseidenband: original silk
 binding
Originalumschlag: original wrapper
Origleinen. *see* Originalleinen
Origlwd. *see* Originalleinwand
Origumschlag. *see* Originalumschlag
Orlwd. *see* Originalleinwand
Ormappe. *see* Originalmappe
Oseidenband. *see*
 Originalseidenband
Ou. *see* Originalumschlag

P. *see* Papier

Packpapier: packing paper
Pag. *see* Paginierung
paginiert: paginated
Paginierung: page numbering
Pamphlet(e): pamphlet(s)
Pap. *see* Papier
Paperback: paperback
Papier: paper
Papierbeschädigung(en):
 damage(s) in the paper
Papierfehler: defect(s) in the paper
Papierschaden: paper defect(s)
Papiersiegel: paper seal
Papierumschlag: paper wrapper
Pappband: bound in pasteboard
 covers
Pappe: pasteboard
paraphiert: initialed
Partie(n): section(s)
Partiturbeilage(n): supplement(s)
 of music scores
Pb. *see* Pappband
Pbck. *see* Paperback
Pbd. *see* Pappband
Perg. *see* Pergament
Pergament: parchment, vellum
Pergament-Schale: parchment
 cover
Pergamentartig: imitation vellum
Pergamentband: vellum binding
Pergamentbezug: vellum covering
Pergamentpapierumschlag: vellum
 paper covers
Pergt. *see* Pergament
Perkal: calico
Perkalin: buckram
Pers.u.Ortsreg. *see* Personen- und
 Ortsregister
Personen- und Ortsregister: person
 and place index
Personenverz. *see* Personen-
 verzeichnis
Personenverzeichnis: index of
 persons
Pg. *see* Pergament
Pgt. *see* Pergament
Pgtbd. *see* Pergamentband

Phot. *see* Photographie
Photogr. *see* Photographie
Photographie(n): photograph(s)
Photogravüre: photogravure
Pl. *see* Plan
Plan(Pläne): plan(s), design(s)
Plansk. *see* Planskizze
Planskizze(n): sketch plan(s)
Plasteinband: plastic binding
Plastik: plastic
Plastikordner: plastic file
Platte(n): plate(s)
poliert: burnished
Portf. *see* Portfolio
Portfolio: portfolio
Porto: shipping costs, postage
Portr. *see* Portrait, Porträt
Portrait: portrait
Portraite: portraits
Portraits: portraits
Porträt: portrait
Porträte: portraits
Porträts: portraits
Postgebühren: costs of mailing
posthum: posthumous
postum: posthumous
Pp. *see* Pappband, Pappe
Ppbd. *see* Pappband
Pr. *see* Preis
Pr.-A. *see* Prachtausgabe
Prachtausg. *see* Prachtausgabe
Prachtausgabe: deluxe edition
prächtig: marvelous
prachtv. *see* prachtvoll
prachtvoll: wonderful, magnificent
Prägeband: goffered binding
Prägestempel: embossed stamp
Prägung: goffering
Preis: price
Preis auf Anfrage: price on request
Preis pro komplett: price for the entire work
Preisangabe(n): price quotation(s)
preisgekrönt: prize-winning
Preisschrift: prize-winning publication
Presse-Exemplar: reviewer's copy

Prgt. *see* Pergament
Priv. *see* Privatdruck
Privatdruck: privately printed
Privateinband: personal binding
Privileg: privilege, permit to publish
pro Jahr: per year, each year
pro komplett: price for the entire work
Probeabdruck: sample copy
Probeheft: sample volume
Probehefte kostenlos: free sample issues
Probeseiten: specimen pages, sample pages
Progr. *see* Programmschrift
Programmschrift: school publication
Prospekt: prospectus
prunktvoll: spurious
Pseudonym(e): pseudonym(s)
punktiert: dotted, stippled
Punktstempel: dot stamping(s)

qu. *see* quer
Qu.-Fol. *see* Querfolio
quadratisch: square
Quart: quarto
Quartal(e): quarter(s)
Quartausgabe: quarto edition
Quartband: quarto
Quelle(n): source(s)
Quellenangabe(n): source reference(s)
quer: oblong
Quer-4to. *see* Querquartband
Querfolio: oblong folio
Querformat: oblong format
Querquartband: oblong quarto
Quetschspur: pressure mark

r. *see* recto
R. *see* Reihe
R.-Tit. *see* Rückentitel
Rabatt: discount
rad. *see* radiert
Rad. *see* Radierung

Radg. *see* Radierung
Radiergn. *see* Radierung
Radierlöchern: erasure holes
Radierstelle: erasure spot
radiert: erased with knife or eraser
Radierung(en): etching(s)
Rahmenstempel: framelike
   stamping(s)
Randanmerkungen: marginal notes
Randbemerkungen: marginal notes
Randecke(n): corner(s) of margin
Randeinriss: tear in margin
Ränder: margins
Randglossen: marginal notes
Randleiste(n): border(s), frame(s)
Randnoten: marginal notes
Randnotizen: marginal notes
Randschrift(en): marginal note(s)
Randwasserfleck(e): marginal
   water stain(s)
Randwurmstich(e): marginal
   wormhole(s)
Rang: rank
Ranken: scrollwork
Rarissimum: very rare
Rasur: erasure
Ratenzahlung: on the installment
   plan
Raubdruck: pirated edition
rauhen: course, rough
rautenförmig: lozenge-shaped
Rautenwappen: lozenged coat of
   arms
rcks. *see* rückseitig
re. *see* rechts
recht: right-hand
rechteckig: right-angled, square or
   rectangular
rechtmässig: authorized
rechts: to the right
recto: recto, front side
Red. *see* Redaktion
red. *see* redigiert
Redaktion: editorship
Rede(n): speech(es), address(es)
redig. *see* redigiert
redigiert: edited

Reg. *see* Register
Register: index, table of contents
Registerband: index volume
Registerbd. *see* Registerband
Registerbl. *see* Registerblatt
Registerblatt(blätter): index
   page(s)
reichst: very rich(ly), abundant(ly)
reichvergold. *see* reichvergoldet
reichvergoldet: richly gilt
reichverziert: richly decorated
Reihe: series
Reihenfolge: order, sequence
Reinschrift: fair copy
reizend: attractive
reizvoll: charming
Rekto: front side
Reliefkarte: relief map
Reliefprägung: raised stamping
Reliefpressung: tooling in relief
rep. *see* repariert
repar. *see* repariert
repariert: repaired
Repertorium: list, index
Reprod. *see* Reproduktion
Reproduktion(en): reproduction(s)
resp. *see* respektive
respektive: respectively
Rest(e): remainder, remnant(s)
Restauflage: remainder
restauriert: restored
rev. *see* revidiert
revid. *see* revidiert
revidiert: revised
Richtigstellung(en): correction(s),
   corrigendum(da)
Riemen: leather tie(s)
Ringbindung: ring binding
Riss(e): tear(s)
Risse: plans, sketches
Rocaille(n): shell-like design(s)
rohe Bogen: unbound and unfolded
   sheets
Rohleinen: raw linen
Rollenstempel: roll stamp(s)
Roman(e): novel(s)
rose: pink

Rosette(n): rosette(s)
rostfleckig: rust-stained, foxed
rot: red
rotbraun: brick red
Rötelzeichnung(en): sanguine
   drawing(s)
rotgedr. *see* rotgedruckt
rotgedruckt: printed in red
rötlich: reddish
Rotschnitt: red edge(s)
Rotstiftmarginalien: red pencil
   notes
Rsch. *see* Rückenschild,
   Rückenschildchen
Rschild. *see* Rückenschild
Rschr. *see* Rückenschild
Rubr. *see* Rubrik, Rubrizierung
rubr. *see* rubriziert
Rubrik(en): column(s)
Rubrikator(en): rubricator(s)
rubriz. *see* rubriziert
rubriziert: rubricated
Rubrizierung: rubrication
Rückblatt: back sheet
Rückdeckel: back cover
Rücken: back, spine
Rückenfeld(er): panel(s) on spine
Rückengelenk: back joint
Rückengoldpressung: gold tooling
   on back
Rückenschild(er): back label(s)
Rückenschildchen: small back label
Rückentitel: title on spine
Rückenvergold. *see* Rücken-
   vergoldung
Rückenvergoldung: back gilding
rückseitig: on the verso
Rückvergoldg. *see* Rücken-
   vergoldung
rückw. *see* rückwärtig
rückwärtig: back, rear, backward
rückwärts: at the rear, backward
rund: approximately, roughly
Rundblick(e): panorama(s)
Rundstäben: tooled bands
Rv. *see* Rückenvergoldung
Rverg. *see* Rückenvergoldung

Rvergold. *see* Rückenvergoldung
Rvg. *see* Rückenvergoldung

s. *see* siehe
S. *see* Seite
S.A. *see* Separatabdruck
S.-A. *see* Separatabdruck
Sachregister: subject index
Saff. *see* Saffian
Saffian: morocco
Saffianband: morocco binding
Sammelband(bände): collected
   volume(s)
Sammeltitel: collective title
Sammelwerk: collective work
Sammetband: velvet binding
Samml. *see* Sammlung
Sammlg. *see* Sammlung
Sammlgn. *see* Sammlung
Sammlung(en): collection(s)
Samt: velvet
sämt. *see* sämtliche
sämtl. *see* sämtliche
sämtliche: all
Sars. *see* Sarsenetteinband
Sarsenetteinband: cloth binding
satiniert: coated
saub. *see* sauber
sauber: clean
Schabblatt(blätter): mezzotint(s)
Schabspur: trace of rubbing
Schabstelle(n): chafed spot(s)
Schachbrettmuster: checkered
   design
Schaden: damage, defect
Schäden: damages, defects
schadh. *see* schadhaft
schadhaft: damaged
Schafleder: sheepskin
Schaflederüberzug: covering of
   sheepskin
Scharniere: hinges, joints
Schattenriss: silhouette
Schatulle: box
Schaubild(er): illustration(s)
Schaudeckel: display cover

Schaudeckelvergoldung: display cover gilding
Schauspiel(e): play(s)
Schemata: diagrams
Scherenschnitt(s): silhouette(s)
Schild: label
Schildchen: small label(s)
Schildpattleder: mottled calf
Schl. *see* Schliesse
Schl.-B. *see* Schlussblatt
Schlagwort: subject heading; key word, catchword
schlecht: bad, defective
schlicht: plain
Schliessband(bänder): tie(s)
Schliesse(n): clasp(s)
Schliessenrest(e): remnant(s) of clasps
Schlussband: end volume
Schlussblatt: end leaf
Schlüsselroman: *roman à clef*
Schlussschr. *see* Schlussschrift
Schlussschrift: colophon
Schlusst. *see* Schlusstitel
Schlusstitel: colophon
Schlussvermerk: concluding note, colophon
Schlussvignette: tailpiece
Schm.bl. *see* Schmutzblatt
Schmähschrift(en): lampoon(s)
schmal: narrow, small
Schmaloktav: narrow octavo
schmiegsam: flexible, limp
schmuck: nice
Schmuckstück(e): decorative device(s)
Schmutzblatt: flyleaf
schmutzig: soiled, dirty
Schmutztit. *see* Schmutztitel
Schmutztitel: half title
Schnitt(e): edge(s) of a book; cut(s), engraving(s)
Schnörkel: flourish(es), scroll(s), paraph(s)
Scholie(n): critical note(s)
schön: beautiful, handsome
Schraffiert: azure-tooled, hatched

Schraffierung: hatching
Schrifttum: literature
Schriftwiedergab. *see* Schriftwiedergabe
Schriftwiedergabe(n): reproduction(s) of handwriting
Schuber: protective case, slipcase
Schutzhülle: protective cover, covering
Schutzumschlag: jacket, paper wrapper
schw. *see* schwarz
schwach: slight, slightly
Schwanz: tail
schwarz: black
schwarzweiss: black and white
Schweinsleder: pigskin
Schweinslederband: pigskin binding
Schweinslederbezug: pigskin covering
Schwldr. *see* Schweinsleder
Schwsldr. *see* Schweinsleder
Sd. *see* Sonderdruck
sechs(te): six(th)
sechzehn(te): sixteen(th)
sechzig(ste): sixty(ieth)
sehr selten: very rare
Seide: silk
Seidenp. *see* Seidenpapier
Seidenpapier: tissue paper
Seidenspiegel: silk doublure(s)
Seidenüberzug: silk covering
Seidenvorsatz: silk endpapers
Seite(n): page(s)
seitengross(e): full-page
Seitenwand(wände): side(s)
Seitenzahl: number of pages
Seitenzählung: pagination
selbständige Buchausgabe: separate issue in book form
Selbstbiographie: autobiography
Selbstverl. *see* Selbstverlag
Selbstverlag: published by the author
Selbstvlg. *see* Selbstverlag
selten: rare, scarce
selten angeboten: seldom offered

Seltenheit: rarity
seltenst: rarest
Sengschaden: scorch damage
Separatabdruck: separate, reprint, offprint
Separatdruck: separate, reprint, offprint
Separattafel(n): separate plate(s)
Ser. *see* Serie
Serie(n): series
Serienpreis: series price
Siebdruck: silk-screen printing
sieben(te): seven(th)
siebzehn(te): seventeen(th)
siebzig(ste): seventy(ieth)
Siegel: seal(s)
Siegellackspuren: traces of wax seals
siehe: see
sign. *see* signiert
Signet: printer's or publisher's device
signiert: signed
Silberdruck: silver printing
Silberdurchbruch: silver filigree
silbergetrieben: silver-chased
silbern: silver
Silberornament(e): silver decoration(s)
Silberprägung: silver goffering
Sitzungsberichte: proceedings
Sk. *see* Skizze
Skizze(n): sketch(es)
Slg. *see* Sammlung
so komplett selten: seldom found so complete
soeben erschienen: just out
Sommer: Summer
Sonderabdr. *see* Sonderabdruck
Sonderabdruck: separate printing, offprint
Sonderausgabe: special edition
Sonderdruck: separate printing, offprint
Sonderh. *see* Sonderheft
Sonderheft(e): special issue(s), special number(s)

Sonderpreis: special price
sonst: otherwise
sorgfältig: careful
soweit erschienen: as far as has been published
soweit fustzustellen: as far as can be ascertained
Sp. *see* Spalte
sp. *see* spaltig
Spalte(n): column(s)
spaltig: columned
später: later
Spende: gift
Spiegel: doublure(s)
Spitzenbordüre(n): lacelike border design(s)
Spitzenmuster: lacelike pattern(s)
Spottschrift(en): lampoon(s)
Spruchband(bänder): legend(s), lettered scroll(s)
Sprung(Sprünge): crack(s)
SS. *see* Seite
St. *see* Stempel, Stich
St.a.T. *see* Stempel auf dem Titelblatt
St.a.Tr. *see* Stempel rückseitig auf Titelblatt
stach: engraved
Stahlst. *see* Stahlstich
Stahlstich(e): steel engraving(s)
Stammbaum: genealogical tree
Stammbuch(bücher): *album* (*alba*) *amicorum*
Stammtafel(n): genealogical table(s)
stark: strong, heavy
stärker: stronger, heavier, relatively extensive
statt: instead of
Stehkante(n): edge(s) of cover
Stehkantenfilet(en): fillet(s) on edge of cover
Stehkantenvergoldung: gilding on edge of cover
steif: stiff
steifbr. *see* steifbroschiert

steifbroschiert: bound in stiff paper covers
Stelle(n): place(s), spot(s)
stellenw. *see* stellenweise
stellenweise: partly, occasionally
Stemp.a.Vors. *see* Stempel auf Vorsatz
Stempel: stamp
Stempel auf dem Titelblatt: stamp on the title page
Stempel auf Vorsatz: stamp on endpaper
Stempel im Text: stamp in the text
Stempel rückseitig auf Titelblatt: stamp on verso of title page
Ster.-Aufl. *see* Stereotyp-Auflage
Stereotyp-Auflage: reprint edition from stereotype plates
stereotypiert: stereotyped
stets gesucht: always in demand
Stich(e): engraving(s)
Stichwort: key word, subject heading
Stil: style
Stitext. *see* Stempel im Text
Stockfl. *see* Stockfleck
stockfl. *see* stockfleckig
Stockfleck(en): spot(s) caused by dampness
stockfleckig: foxed, spotted by dampness
stockig: molded
Streitschrift(en): pamphlet(s)
Strichätzung: line etching
Striche: lines
Stricheisen: tool for line engraving
Strichzeichnung(en): line drawing(s)
Stück(e): piece(s)
Studienausgabe: study edition
Studienführer: study guide(s)
Stundenbuch(bücher): book(s) of hours
Sub.-Pr. *see* Subskriptionspreis
Subskr. *see* Subskription
Subskription: subscription

Subskriptionspreis: subscription price
Super-Exlibris: book stamp(s)
Superlibros: book stamp(s)
Suppl. *see* Supplement
Supplement: supplement
Supplementband: supplementary volume
Sz. *see* Seitenzahl

T. *see* Tafel, Teil, Titel
T.-A. *see* Taschenausgabe
Tab. *see* Tabelle
Tabelle(n): chart(s), table(s)
tadell. *see* tadellos
tadellos: irreproachable, perfect
Taf. *see* Tafel
Tafel(n): plate(s)
Tafelband: volume of plates
Tafelserie: series of tables
Tafelwerk(e): volume(s) of plates
Tageb. *see* Tagebuch
Tagebuch: diary, journal
Taschenausgabe: pocket edition
Taschenformat: pocket-size
Tausend(e): thousand(s)
Teil(e): part(s)
teils: partly
teilw. *see* teilweise
teilweise: partly, in part
tekt. *see* tektiert
tektiert: blotted out
Textabb. *see* Textabbildung
Textabbildung(en): illustration(s) in the text
Textband: volume of text
Textbeschäd. *see* Textbeschädigungen
Textbeschädigungen: damage done to text, loss of text
Textbilder: illustrations in the text
Textfiguren: figures in the text
Textheft: text issue
Textholzschn. *see* Textholzschnitt
Textholzschnitt(e): woodcut(s) in the text
Textill. *see* Textillustration

Textillustration(en): illustration(s)
in the text
textlich: textual
Textrevision: revision of text
Textspalte(n): column(s) of text
Textteil: textual portion
Textunterschrift(en): caption(s)
under text
Textverlust: loss of text
Textvignetten: vignettes in the
text
Textzeichn. *see* Textzeichnung
Textzeichnung(en): drawing(s) in
the text
Tfl. *see* Tafel
Tfln. *see* Tafel
Theil *see* Teil
tief: deep(ly)
Tiefdruck: photogravure
Tiefdruckabbildung(en):
photogravure illustration(s)
Tiefdruckbild(er): photogravure
picture(s)
Tiefdrucktafel(n): photogravure
plate(s)
Tintenfl. *see* Tintenfleck
Tintenfleck(e): ink stain(s)
Tintenschrift: writing in ink
Tit. *see* Titel
Titel: title(s)
Titel-Zeichnung: title-page drawing
Titelaufkleber: label(s) on title
page
Titelb. *see* Titelbild
Titelbild: frontispiece
Titelbl. *see* Titelblatt
Titelblatt: title page
Titelblattrückseite: verso of title
page
Titelbordüre: border on title page
Titeldecke: title cover
Titelei: preliminaries
Titeleinf. *see* Titeleinfassung
Titeleinfass. *see* Titeleinfassung
Titeleinfassung: border on title
page

Titelholzschnitt(e): woodcut on
title page(s)
Titelkupfer: engraving on title
page
Titelradierung: etching on title
page
Titelrückseite: verso of title page
Titels. *see* Titelseite
Titelschmuck: title-page decoration
Titelschnitt: engraving on title
page
Titelseite: title page
Titelüberschrift(en): title
heading(s)
Titelvignette: vignette on title page
Tl. *see* Teil
Tle. *see* Teil
tls. *see* teils
Tondruck: chiaroscuro
Trachtenkupfer: copperplate
illustration(s) of costumes
Tragödie(n): tragedy(ies)
Traktat(e): tract(s), treatise(s)
Trauerspiel(e): tragedy(ies)
Trockenstempel: dry stamp
Ts. *see* Tausend
Tsd. *see* Tausend
Type(n): font(s) of type
typograph. *see* typographisch
typographisch: typographic

u. *see* und
U. *see* Umschlag
u.a. *see* und andere, unter anderem
u.d.T. *see* unter dem Titel
u.ff. *see* und folgende
u.s.w. *see* und so weiter
ub. *see* unbeschnitten
überarb. *see* überarbeitet
überarbeitet: revised
übereinstimmenden: conformal,
corresponding
überkl. *see* überklebt
überklebt: pasted over
übers. *see* übersetzt
Übers. *see* Übersetzer, Übersetzung

Überschrift(en): heading(s), caption(s)
Übersetzer: translator(s)
übersetzt: translated
Übersetzung: translation
Übersicht: synopsis
Übersichtstabelle(n): synoptic table(s)
übert. *see* übertragen
übertr. *see* übertragen
übertragen: translated
Übertragung: translation, version
Überzug: cover
Überzugpapier: cover paper
übrig: remaining
übs. *see* übersetzt
Übs. *see* Übersetzung
uff. *see* und folgende
Umfang: in all
umfangr. *see* umfangreich
umfangreich: comprehensive
umfasst: comprises, contains
umgearb. *see* umgearbeitet
umgearbeitet: revised
umrahmt: framed
Umrahmung: frame, border
Umschl. *see* Umschlag
Umschlag: wrapper, jacket
Umschlagbild: cover design
Umschlagblatt(blätter): cover sheet(s), paper cover(s)
Umschläge beigebunden: wrappers bound in
Umschlagränder: edges of cover
Umschlagrücken: back of cover
Umschlagseite: side of cover
Umschlagt. *see* Umschlagtitel
Umschlagtitel: external title, title on wrapper (cover)
Umschrift(en): transcription(s)
unaufgeschn. *see* unaufgeschnitten
unaufgeschnitten: uncut, unopened
unaufgezogen: unmounted
unbed. *see* unbedeutend
unbedeut. *see* unbedeutend
unbedeutend: slight(ly), insignificant(ly)

unbedruckt: plain, without printed text
unbek. *see* unbekannt
unbekannt: unknown
unbereinigt: unexpurgated
unberührt: perfect, untouched
unbeschn. *see* unbeschnitten
unbeschnitten: untrimmed
unbestimmt: not established, indefinite
und: and
und andere: and others
und folgende: and the following
und so weiter: and so forth
unfrisch: not fresh, shopworn
ungebunden: unbound
ungedruckt: unpublished
ungefähr: approximately
ungeheftet: in loose sheets
ungenau: inexact, erroneous
ungerade Bandzahlen: odd volume numbers
ungewöhnlich: exceptional(ly)
ungez.Bll. *see* ungezählte Blätter
ungezählte Blätter: unnumbered leaves
Unicum: unique item
unleserl. *see* unleserlich
unleserlich: illegible
unn. *see* unnumeriert
unnumeriert: unnumbered
unpag. *see* unpaginiert
unpaginiert: unpaginated
unregelmässig: irregularly
unsauber: soiled, dirty
unsigniert: unsigned
unt. *see* unten, unter
unten: at the bottom
unter: lower, under
unter anderem: among others
unter anderen: among others
unter dem Titel: under the title
unter Mitwirkung: with the collaboration
unterdrückt: suppressed, prohibited
Unterkante: bottom edge of cover

unterlegt: repaired; mounted
Unterrand: bottom margin
Unterschrift(en): signature(s)
Unterstr. *see* Unterstreichung
Unterstreich. *see* Unterstreichung
Unterstreichgn. *see* Unterstreichung
Unterstreichung(en): underlining(s)
Unterstriche: underlinings
unterstrichen: underlined
Untertitel: subtitle(s)
unver. *see* unverändert
unveränd. *see* unverändert
unverändert: unchanged, unaltered
unvergl. *see* unvergleichlich
unvergleichlich: incomparable
unverkürzt: unabridged
unveröff. *see* unveröffentlicht
unveröffentlicht: unpublished
unvollständig: incomplete
Unzahl: very large number
Unziale: uncial
Urausgabe: original edition
Urheberrecht: copyright
urheberrechtlich: copyright
Urkunde(n): document(s)
Urkundennachweis: references to
   documents
Ursprung: origin
Urtext: original text
Useite. *see* Umschlagseite
usw. *see* und so weiter

Variante(n): variant(s)
vb. *see* verbessert
Velinpapier: vellum paper
Velp. *see* Velinpapier
veränd. *see* verändert
verändert: revised
verb. *see* verbessert
verbessert: improved
Verbestellpreis: prepublication
   price
verbilligt: reduced in price
verbl. *see* verblichen
verblasst: faded, paled
verblichen: faded

verbunden: misbound
vereinz. *see* vereinzelt
vereinzelt: here and there
verf. *see* verfasst
Verf. *see* Verfasser
verfärbt: discolored
Verfasser: author(s)
verfasst: composed, written
verfügbar: available
verg. *see* vergilbt
vergilbt: yellowed, faded
vergleiche: see, compare
Vergleichstafeln: parallel tables
vergoldet: gilt, decorated with gold
Vergoldung: gilding, decoration in
   gold
vergr. *see* vergriffen
vergriffen: out-of-print
Verh. *see* Verhandlungen
Verhandlungen: proceedings
verk. *see* verkauft
Verkauf: sale
verkauft: sold
verkleinert: reduced
Verl. *see* Verlag, Verlust
Verl.Anst. *see* Verlagsanstalt
Verl.Ges. *see* Verlagsgesellschaft
Verlag: publishing firm
Verlagsanstalt: publishing firm
Verlagseinband: publisher's binding
Verlagsgesellschaft: publishing firm
Verlagsverzeichnis: publisher's list
verlängert: elongated
Verlegereinband: publisher's
   binding
Verlegermarke: publisher's device
verloren: lost
Verlust: loss
verm. *see* vermehrt
verm.-Ausg. *see* vermehrte-Ausgabe
vermehrt: enlarged
vermehrte-Ausgabe: enlarged
   edition
Vermerk: remark, note
vermischt: mixed, miscellaneous
vernichtet: destroyed
veröff. *see* veröffentlicht

Veröff. *see* Veröffentlichung
veröffentlicht: published
Veröffentlichung: publication
vers. *see* versehen
Versalien: capital letters
verschieden: different, varying
verschlungen: interlaced
verschm. *see* verschmutzt
verschmutzt: soiled
Verschnürung: cording,
   interlacing
verschollen: disappeared without
   trace
verschossen: paled
versehen: furnished
versehentlich: mistakenly
Versendkosten: costs of shipping
verso: verso
verst. *see* verständlich
verständlich: comprehensible
verstärkt: strengthened, reinforced
Verstärkung: strengthening,
   support
verstaubt: dusty
versteigert: sold at auction
Versteigerung(en): auction(s)
Versteigerungskatalog: auction
   sale catalog
Verstkg. *see* Verstärkung
verstümmelt: mutilated
vertieft: sunken, recessed
vervielf. *see* vervielfältigt
vervielfältigt: multigraphed
vervollst. *see* vervollständigt
vervollständigt: completed,
   supplemented
verwischt: blurred
verz. *see* verziert
Verz. *see* Verzeichnis
Verzeichnis: list, listing, index
verziert: decorated, adorned
Verzierung: decoration
Vf. *see* Verfasser
vgl. *see* vergleiche
viele: many
vier(te): four(th)
viertel: quarter(s), fourth(s)

vierteljährlich: quarterly
Vierteljahrsschrift: quarterly
   publication
vierzehn(te): fourteen(th)
vierzig(ste): forty(ieth)
Vign. *see* Vignette
Vignette(n): vignette(s)
violett: violet, mauve
Vlg. *see* Verlag
Vlgsverz. *see* Verlagsverzeichnis
Vokab. *see* Vokabularium
Vokabularium: word list
Volksausgabe: popular edition
Vollbilder: full-page illustrations
völlig: wholly, entirely
vollst. *see* vollständig
vollst.umgearb. *see* vollständig
   umgearbeitet
vollständig: complete
vollständig umgearbeitet:
   completely revised
Vollständigkeit: completeness
vollständigste: most complete
von alter Hand: by an old hand
vor allem: above all, principally
vor kurzem erschienen: recently
   published, just out
Vorabdruck(en): preprint(s)
vorauss. *see* voraussichtlich
voraussichtlich: expected to appear
Vorbereitung: preparation
Vorbertg. *see* Vorbereitung
Vorbes. *see* Vorbesitzer
Vorbesitzer: previous owner
Vorbestellpreis: prepublication
   price
Vorblatt(blätter): flyleaf(ves)
vord. *see* vorder
vorder: front
Vorder- und Rückdeckel: front and
   back covers
Vorderdeckel: front cover
Vordergrund: foreground
Vorderscharnier: front hinge
Vorderseite(n): front page(s)
vorgbdn. *see* vorgebunden
vorgeb. *see* vorgebunden

vorgebunden: bound in front
vorhanden: present, available
Vorlage(n): model(s), pattern(s)
vorläufig: temporary, interim
Vorlesung(en): academic lecture(s)
Vornehm: high class
Vorr. *see* Vorrede, Vorredner
vorrätig: in stock
Vorrede: preface
Vorredner: author of preface
Vors. *see* Vorsatz
Vorsatz(sätze): endpaper(s)
Vorsatzbl. *see* Vorsatzblatt
Vorsatzblatt: endpaper
Vorsatzpapier: endpaper(s)
Vorst. *see* Vorstücke
Vorstücke: preliminary matter
Vort. *see* Vortitel, Vortrag
Vortitel: half title
Vortrag(träge): lecture(s)
Vorw. *see* Vorwort
Vorwort: preface
Vorz.-Ex. *see* Vorzugsexemplar
vorzügl. *see* vorzüglich
vorzüglich: preeminent
Vorzugsausgabe: special edition
Vorzugsexemplar(e): preferential
  copy(ies)

W.a.T. *see* Widmung auf Titel
Wappen: coat of arms
Wappenbild: reproduction of coats
  of arms
Wappenprägung: coats of arms in
  blind tooling
Wappensupralibros: coat of arms
  used as book stamp
wasserbesch. *see* wasserbeschädigt
wasserbeschädigt: damaged by
  water
wasserfl. *see* wasserfleckig
Wasserfleck(en): water stain(s)
wasserfleckig: stained by water
wassergewellt: crinkled by water
Wasserrand(ränder): water stain(s)
wasserrandig: water-stained
Wassersch. *see* Wasserschäden

Wasserschäden: water-damaged in
  several places
Wassersp. *see* Wasserspuren
Wasserspuren: traces of dampness
wasserw. *see* wasserwellig
wasserwellig: crinkled by water
wattiert: padded
wechselnd: varying
weggerissen: torn off
weggeschnitten: cut off
weisses Blatt: blank page
weitere: additional
wellig: wavy
wen. *see* wenig
wenig: little
wenige: few
Werk(e): work(s)
Werkdruckpapier: work printing
  paper
wichtig: important
Widm. *see* Widmung
Widmg. *see* Widmung
Widmung: dedication note
Widmung auf Titel: dedication
  note on title page
Widmung des Verfassers:
  dedication note of the author
wie neu: as new
Wiedergabe(n): reproduction(s)
Wiegendruck(e): incunabulum(a)
Wildld. *see* Wildleder
Wildleder: chamois leather
Wildlederband: chamois binding
Winter: Winter
winzig: minute
wiss. *see* wissenschaftlich
Wiss. *see* Wissenschaft
Wissenschaft(en): field(s) of
  learning, science(s)
wissenschaftlich: scholarly
Wochenschrift: weekly publication
wöchentlich: weekly
wohlerhalten: well-preserved
wohlfeil: inexpensive
Wörterbuch: dictionary, word list
Wörterverzeichnis: word index
Wortlaut: wording, text

wundervoll: marvelous
wurmfrass: worm-eaten
Wurmgang(gänge): wormhole(s)
wurml. *see* wurmlöcherig
Wurmlöcher: wormholes
wurmlöcherig: wormholed
Wurmspur(en): trace(s) of worms
wurmst. *see* wurmstichig
Wurmstich(e): wormhole(s)
wurmstichig: with wormholes
Wurmstichspur(en): trace(s) of
   worms

Z. *see* Zeile
z.T. *see* zum Teil
z.Zt. *see* zur Zeit
Zahlentafeln: tables of figures
zahllos: innumerable
zahlr. *see* zahlreich
zahlreich: numerous
zart: delicate, delicately
zartrosa: pale pink
zehn(te): ten(th)
Zeichen: sign(s), mark(s)
Zeichn. *see* Zeichnung
Zeichnung(en): drawing(s)
Zeile(n): line(s)
Zeilenzählung: line numbering
Zeit: time
Zeitgen. *see* Zeitgenosse
zeitgenöss. *see* zeitgenössisch
Zeitgenosse: contemporary
zeitgenössisch: contemporary
Zeitschrift: journal
Zeittaf. *see* Zeittafel
Zeittafel(n): chronological table(s)
zellophanierte: cellophane covered
zensiert: censored
Zensur: censorship
zerbrochen: cracked
zerknittert: crinkled
zerkratzt: scratched
zerschl. *see* zerschlissen
zerschlissen: worn out

zettel: label
ziemlich: rather, fairly
Zierleiste(n): decorative border(s)
Zinkotypie(n): zincograph(s)
zirka: approximately
zis. *see* ziseliert
zisel. *see* ziseliert
ziseliert: chased, chiseled
zitiert: cited
Zs. *see* Zeitschrift
zsgest. *see* zusammengestellt
Zt. *see* Zeit
Ztsch. *see* Zeitschrift
zugeschrieben: attributed
zugleich: simultaneously
zuletzt erschienen: last published
zum Teil: partly
zur Subskription gestellt: offered
   for subscription
zur Subskription stellen: to offer
   for subscription
zur Zeit: now, at present
zus. *see* zusammen
zus. mit *see* zusammen mit
zusammen: together
zusammen mit: together with
Zusammenfassung: résumé
zusammengebunden: bound
   together
zusammengest. *see* zusammengestellt
zusammengestellt: collected,
   chosen, compiled
Zusatz(sätze): addendum(a)
Zustand: condition, state
zuverl. *see* zuverlässig
zuverlässig: reliable, authentic
zwanzig(ste): twenty(ieth)
zwei(te): two (second)
zweifarbig: two-color
zweisprachig: bilingual
zwischen: between
Zwischentitel: inserted title(s)
zwölf(te): twelve (twelfth)

Hungarian

a: the
a lap alján: at the bottom of the
   page
a margón: on the margins
abécérendi: alphabetical order
ábécéskönyv(ek): primer(s)
ábr. *see* ábra
ábra(k): figure(s), picture(s),
   illustration(s)
abrázió(k): abrasion(s), abrasure(s)
acélmetszet(ek): steel engraving(s)
adaptálás: adaptation
adaptálta: arranged, reedited
adatok nélkül: without date
adattár(ak): directory(ies)
addenda: addenda
adomány: gift
agyonfogdosott: shopworn
ajándék: gift
ajándékkönyv: gift book
ajándékkötet: gift volume
ajánlás: dedication, inscription
ajánlat: bid, offer
ajánló bibliográfia: selected
   bibliography
ajánlott: certified, registered
akad. *see* akadémia
akadémia: academy
akadémikus: academic, academi-
   cian
akvarellfestés(ek): watercolor(s)
akvatinta: aquatint
akvizício: acquisition
aláhúzás: underlining, underscoring
aláhúzott: underlined, underscored

aláírás(ok): signature(s)
aláírott: signed
aláírt: signed
aláírt levél: autograph letter signed
aláírva: signed
alap: background
alapos: solid, solidly
alapvető mű: standard
alatt: below, under
album(ok): album(s)
alcím: subtitle
aldina: Aldine
alfabetikus: alphabetic
alfabetikusan: alphabetically
alig: scarcely, hardly
alján: at the bottom
alk. *see* alkalmazta
alkalmazás: adaptation
alkalmazta: adapted by
alkalmi: occasional
alkalmi példány(ok): secondhand
   book(s)
áll valamiből: consisting, consists
   of
állandó rendelés: standing order
állapot: condition, state
állomány: stock
almanach(ok): almanac(s)
álnév: pseudonym, pen name
álnevű: pseudonymous
alnyomat: tint
alsó: lower
alsó él: lower edge
alsó margó: bottom margin
alsó rész: bottom

alsó rész él: bottom edge
alsó rész szél: bottom margin
alsó szél: tail
ált. *see* általános
általában: usual, usually
általános: general
általános mű: general work
általános mutató: general index
alternatív cím: alternate title
alternatíva: alternative
alul: on the bottom
amatőrkötés: amateur binding
analitikus: analytical
anasztatikus utánnyomás: anastatic reprint
angol: English
annotáció(k): annotation(s)
annotált: annotated
antik papír: antique finish paper
antikozott: dulled
antikva: roman type; antique
antikvár: secondhand
antikvár könyvkereskedés: secondhand bookstore
antikvár példány: secondhand
book
antikvárium: antiquarian bookseller
antológia: anthology, collection
apró: minute, small
aprólékos: meticulous
aprólékosan: minutely
aquatinta(ák): aquatint(s)
ár: price
ár nélkül: without price
arabesk(ek): arabesque(s)
arabs szám: arabic number(s)
arany cizellálás: gold-tooled
arany vaknyomás: gold-stamped,
gold stamping
aranydíszítés: gold decoration
aranydíszítésű: decorated with gold
aranyfólia: gold leaf
aranyfüst: gold leaf
aranymetszés: gilding, gilt edges
aranymetszéssel: with gilt edges
aranyozás: gilding, gold tooling

aranyozott hátsó: gilt back
aranyozva: gilt, gilded
aranyréteg: gilding, gold ornamentation
aranyvágás: gilt edge
aranyvágású: gilt edged
aranyzását vesztett: tarnished
árazott: prized
arch. *see* archivum
archivum: archives
áremelkedés: price increase
árengedmény: rebate
árjegyzék: price list
árjegyzéki ár: list price
árleszállitás: reduction in price
árny és fény játéka: chiaroscuro
árnyalat(ok): shade(s), halftone(s)
árnyalatos felvétel(ek): halftone
picture(s)
árnyalatvisszaadás(ok): halftone
reproduction(s)
árnyékos: shaded
árnyékvetés: shading
árok: trench
árusítás: sale
árváltozás: change in price
árverés: auction
árverésjegyzék: auction catalog
árverezés: auction sale
asszociáció: association
asszociáció példány: association
copy
asztaldísz: centerpiece
átalakított: remade
átdolg. *see* átdolgozás, átdolgozott,
átdolgozta
átdolgozás: adaptation, revision
átdolgozott: adapted, revised
átdolgozta: adapted by, revised by
átellenes: opposite
átfogó: comprehensive
áthajtás: book jacket, cover
áthúzott: lined through
áthúzta: lined through
átír: transcribe
átírás: transcription
átlag: average

átlapozás: collation
atlasz(ok): atlas(es)
átlátszó: transparent
átlőtt: reimposed
átnézett kiadás: pasted over
átragasztva: pasted over
átrendezés: rearrangement
átrendezett: rearranged
áttekintő táblázat: synoptic table
áttördelt: reorganized
átüt: set off
aukció: auction
aukció katalógus: auction catalog
autentikus: authentic
autografált aláírás: facsimile
autográfia: autograph
autográfia dedikáció: autographed
    dedication
autotípia: photoengraving
avult: obsolete
az: the
azelőtt: previously
azonkívül: besides
azonos: same
azóta: since
azurdíszítés: azure tooling

bagaria: Russian leather
bagariabőr: Russian leather
ballonvászon: balloon cloth
baloldali: left-hand
-ban, -ben, -on, -en, -ba, -be: in
barátkötés: monastic binding
barkás: grained
bármely: any
barna: brown
barnás: brownish
barnás foltok: foxed, foxing
barnított: browned
barnult: browned
bársony: velvet
bársonykötés: velvet binding
becslés: appraisal
bef. see befejezett
befejezés: conclusion
befejezetlen kiadvány: unfinished
    publication

befejezett: completed
befejező kötet: end volume
behajtható: foldout
behúzás: indentation
beillesztés: insert, insertion
beillesztett: inserted, inset
bejegyzés: entry, note
bejelölés(ek): mark(s)
bekarikázott: encircled
bekezdés: indentation, paragraph
bekötés: binding, cover
bekötési tábla(k): binding board(s)
beleértve: included, inclusive
bélelés: lining
bélelt: lined
belenyomtatva: printed in text
bélés: doublure
beleszámítva: including
belföldi: domestic
belőtt: interleaved, inserted
belövés: interleaving
belső: inner
belső lapszél: inner margin
belül: inside
bélyegző(k): stamp(s)
bélyegzővel ellátott: sealed,
    stamped
bemutatott: presented
benne: including
benyomódás: mottling
bepiszkolódott: soiled
bepiszkolódtak: soiled
beragasztott: pasted
beragasztva: pasted in
berakás: inlay
berakott: set in
bérmentesített: postpaid, prepaid
besz. see beszámoló
beszámoló(k): proceedings,
    report(s)
beszéd(ek): speech(es)
beszúrt: intercalated, interleaved
betekintésre: on approval
betű(k): letter(s), type
betűfajta: font, type
betűkép: typeface

betűminta: typeface
betűrend: alphabetic
betűrendes mutató: alphabetical
  index
betűről betűre másolt: copy in
  facsimile, literal copy
betűsoros: alphabetic
betűtalp: serif
betűtípus: type
betűvel jelzett burokráma:
  lettered scroll
bev. *see* bevezetés, bevezető
bevezetés: introduction
bevezető: introductory
bevezető előszó: prologue
bevonódott minta: encrusted
  pattern
bezárólag: inclusively
bibl. *see* bibliográfia, bibliográfiai
biblianyomó papír: Bible paper
bibliofil: booklover
bibliofil kiadás: bibliophile edition
bibliofil kiadvány: bibliophile
  publication
bibliofil kötés: amateur binding
bibliográfia(k): bibliography(ies)
bibliográfiai: bibliographic
bibliográfus: bibliographer
bíborfesték: purple
bilingvis: bilingual
billentyű: key
biogr. *see* biográfia
biográfia: biography
biográfiai: biographical
bírálat(ok): review(s)
birkabőr: sheepskin
biz. *see* bizottság
bizottság: committee
biztos rendelés: firm order
blokkbetű: black letter
blokkönyv: block book
bőr: leather, skin
bordaköz(ök): panel(s)
bordás gerinc: back with raised
  bands
bordázat(ok): band(s)
bordázott: raised, ribbed

bordázott gerincű: with ribbed
  spine
bordázott papír: laid paper
bőrdomborítás: leather embossing
borítás: covering, cover
boriték: book jacket
boritékcím: cover title
borító(k): cover(s)
borító zsinegekkel: wrapper with
  ties
borítócím: cover title
borítók belekötve: wrappers
  bound in
borítókarton: protective case
borítólap: jacket, wrapper
borítólap rajza: cover design
boríton: on book jacket
boríton lévő kép: cover design
borjúbőr: calf
borjúbőrkötés: calfskin binding
bőrkötés: leather binding
bőrsarkok: leather corners
borszínű: wine-colored
bőrutánzat: artificial leather,
  leatherette
bőséges: copious
bőségesen: abundantly
bőv. *see* bővített
bőv. kiad. *see* bővített kiadás
bővített: enlarged
bővített kiadás: enlarged edition
Bp. *see* Budapest
br. *see* brosúra
bradel-kötés: bradel binding
Braille-írás: braille
brokát: brocade
bronz: bronze, bronzed
bronzírozott: lustrous dark brown
brosúra(k): brochure(s), booklet(s)
brosúrakötés: brochure binding
bruttó: gross
Budapest: Budapest
bukrám: buckram
burkoló: book jacket, cover
burokráma(ák): scroll(s)
burokráma(ák) díszítő: ornamental scroll(s)

c. *see* cím
cápabőr: sharkskin
carta lucida: coated paper
cca. *see* cirka
cédula(ák): label(s)
celofán: cellophane
cenz. *see* cenzúra, cenzúrázott
cenzúra: censorship
cenzúrázatlan: unexpurgated
cenzúrázott: censored, expurgated
ceruza: pencil
ceruza aláhúzás: pencil underscoring
ceruzabejegyzések: pencil notes
ceruzajegyzetek: pencil notes
ceruzajelölések: pencil marks
ceruzarajz(ok): pencil drawing(s)
ceruzavonás(ok): pencil mark(s)
cikk(ek): article(s)
cikornya: flourish, scroll
cikornyás: richly ornamented
cím(ek): title(s)
címerek: arms
címeres kötés: armorial binding
címerkötés: armorial binding
címerpajzs: armorial design, crest
címfej: headline, masthead
címív: front matter, prelims
címjegyzet: title label
címke(ék): label(s), tag(s)
címkép: frontispiece
címl. *see* címlap
címlap: title page
címlap hátlapja: verso of title page
címlap hiányzik: title page lacking
címlap nélkül: without title page
címlap rajza: cover design
címlapon: on the title page
címlevél: title leaf
címmetszet: engraving on title
   page
címnegyed: front matter, prelims
címoldalak: front matter
címrajz: cover design
címszalag: wrapper
címszó: catchword
címtábla: frontispiece
címtár(ak): directory(ies)

című: entitled, named
címzés, postai: address
cinkográfia: zinc etching,
   zincography
cirill betűk: Cyrillic letters
cirka: circa, approximately
citromsárga: lemon yellow
citromszínű: lemon-colored
cizellálás: tooling
cizellált: chased, chiseled
cizellálva: chased, chiseled
cl. *see* címlap
colligatum: work bound with
   another
csak: only
családnév: surname
csat(ok): clasp(s)
csatolva: annexed, enclosed
csekély: unimportant
cserélhető lapokkal: with loose
   leaves
cseres juhbőr: basil
cserzetlen bőr: shagreen
csigavonal díszítés: spiral design
csillagjelzés: asterisk
csipkedíszítés: lacework
csipkeminta: lace pattern
csipkeszegély: lace border design
csipkeszerű keretdísz(ek): ornamental border(s)
csípős szatíra: lampoon
csiríz: glue, paste
csiszolás: polishing
csodálatos: marvelous
csomagolás: packing
csonkítatlan: unexpurgated
csontszínű: bone-colored
csúnya: ugly

daloskönyv: songbook
damaszt: damask
dámszarvasbőr: doeskin
darab(ok): piece(s)
db. *see* darab
dedikáció: dedication, inscription
dedikációval: with dedication note
dedikált: dedicated, inscribed

dedikált példány: inscribed copy
defekt ív: faulty sheet
defektes: damaged, incomplete
dekoráció: decoration
dekoratív: decorative
diagr. *see* diagram
diagram(ok): diagram(s)
dicséretreméltó: praiseworthy
díj: charge, cost
díjazott: prizewinning
díjmentesen: without charge
díjnyertes: prizewinning
dimenzió: dimension
dióbarna: nut-brown
disszertáció: dissertation, thesis
dísz(ek): decoration(s), ornament(s)
díszbetű: ornamented letter
díszes bélés: doublure
díszítés: ornament
díszítésű: ornamented
díszített: decorated, ornamented
díszített címlap: decorated frontispiece
díszített címlap portré: frontispiece portrait
díszített kezdőbetű(k): decorated initial(s)
díszítmény(ek): decoration(s), ornament(s)
díszítő: decorative
díszítő anyag: ornament
díszítő burokráma: ornamental scroll
díszítő kezdőbetű(k): ornamental initial(s)
díszítő kötelék(ek): ornamental band(s)
díszítő vonaldísz(ek): ornamental fillet(s)
díszítővonalak: fillets
díszkiadás: deluxe edition
díszkötés: deluxe binding
diszkrét: discreet
díszléc(ek): decorative border(s)
disznóbőr: pigskin

doboz(ok): box(es), slipcase(s)
dokument: documentary
dokumentáció: documentation
dokumentum(ok): document(s)
dőlt betű: italics
domborít: emboss
domborítás: embossing
domborított: embossed
domborművű térkép: relief map
dombornyomás: stamping, embossing
dombornyomásos: stamped, embossed
dombornyomású: embossed, raised
domború kötelékek: raised bands
dörzsölés nyomai: trace of rubbing
doszkin: doeskin
drága: expensive, precious
dráma(k): drama(s)
dudorodás(ok): boss(es), knob(s)
dupla: double, twofold
dupla oszlopban: in double columns
duplikátum: duplicate
durva: coarse, rough
dúsan: profusely
dúslombú pergamentekercs: foliated scroll

é. *see* év
é.k.n. *see* év és kiadó nélkül
é.n. *see* év nélkül
e havi szám: this month's issue
e heti szám: this week's issue
eb. *see* egészbőrkötés
eddig: up to now
égés: burn
egész: all, complete, whole
egészbőr: full leather
egészbőrkötés: full-leather binding
egészében: in all
egészkötés: full-bound
egészlapos: full page
egészlapos ábra: full-page plate
egészmargók: full margins
egészoldalas: full-page

egészoldalas illusztráció: full-page
  illustration
egészvászon: full cloth
egészvászonkötés: cloth binding
egy. *see* egyetem
egy: one
egy kötetben: in one volume
egy oldalán nyomtatott: printed
  on one side only
egyben: in one
egybeolvadt: merged
egyenes: straight
egyenes szemcsésségű: straight-
  grained
egyéni: individual
egyenlő: equal
egyértelmű: explicit, unambiguous
egyes. *see* egyesület
egyes: separated, single
egyesek: some
egyesület: association, society
egyesült: merged, united
egyet. *see* egyetem
egyetem: university
egyetlen: only, unique
egyházi énekeskönyv: hymnal
egyidejűleg: simultaneously
egyik: either
egykorú: contemporary
egykorú kötés: contemporary
  binding
egykötetes kiadvány: single-
  volume work
egymásba fonódó dísz(ek): interlacings
egymást keresztező vonaldísz:
  interlaced fillets
egymást követő: consecutive
egyoldalas nyomtatvány: broadside
egységes: uniform
egyszer: once
egyszeri: one time, unique
egyszerű: simple, plain
egyszínű nyomás: monochrome
  print
együtt: joint, together

együtt kötött: bound together
egyúttal: simultaneously
együttműködés: collaboration,
  cooperation
ékszer: jewel
él(ek): edge(s)
eladás: sale
eladási ár: retail price
eladási feltételek: conditions of
  sale
eladva: sold
elárverezik: to be sold at auction
elavult: antiquated, obsolete
elbeszélés(ek): story(ies)
elbeszélő: narrative
elefántcsont: ivory
elefántcsontszínű: ivory color
elegáns: elegant, find
elégtelen: unsatisfactory
életlen: blurred
életr. *see* életrajz, életrajzi
életrajz(ok): biography(ies)
életrajzi: biographical
életrajzi jegyzet: biographical note
elfogyott: out-of-print, sold out
elfojtott: suppressed
elhalványult: faded, paled
elhasználódás: tear
elhasznált: worn-out
ellenőrzés: verification
elmosódott: blurred
előadás(ok): lecture(s)
előbbi: former, previous
élőfej: running title
előfizetés: subscription
előfizetési díj: subscription price
előfizető: subscriber
előhívott: developed
előirányzott ár: preset price
előkészületben: in preparation
elöl: at the front
előnyomás: proof
előrajzoló: tracer
előszó: foreword, preface
előszójegyzet: prefatory note
először: first time
elosztó: distributor

elött: before
előzék(ek): endpaper(s)
előzéklap(ok): endpaper(s),
  flyleaf(ves)
előzetes: preliminary
előzetes eladás: advance sale
előző: previous
előző számok: back numbers
előzőleg: previously
elpiszkolódtak: soiled
elsárgulnak: turning yellow
elsárgult: yellowed
első: first
első és hátsó tábla: front and
  back covers
első kiadás: first edition
első kinyomatás: first printing
első olvasókönyv: primer
első tábla: front cover
elszíntelenedett: discolored
elszíntelenedtek: discolored
eltérés(ek): variant(s)
elveszett: lost
elvesztek: lost
email: enamel
email kötés: enamel binding
embléma: emblem
emlékezések: memoirs
emlékirat(ok): memoir(s)
emlékkönyv: festschrift, memorial
  volume
emlékkötet: festschrift, memorial
  volume
említett: mentioned
enciklopédia: encyclopedia
eng. see engedély, engedélyezett
engedély: permission
engedélyezett: authorized
enyv-foltok: glue-spotted
enyves: glued
ép: intact, whole
epilógus: epilogue
er. see eredeti
érdesség: rough surface, graininess
eredet: provenance, origin
eredeti: original
eredeti fedél(ek): original cover(s)

eredeti kiadás: original edition
eredeti kötés: publisher's binding
eredeti margókkal: with full
  margins
eredeti szöveg: original text
érintetlen: intact, perfect
erős: strong
erősen: heavily, strongly
erősen sérült: badly damaged
erotika: erotica
ért. see értekezés
értek. see értekezés
érték: value
értékelt: appraised, valued
értékes: valuable
értekezés: dissertation, treatise
értéktelen: worthless
és: and
és a követezők: and the following
és a többi: et cetera
és így tovább: and so forth
és mások: and others
esetenként: occasionally
esszé(k): essay(s)
ésszerű: reasonable
eszpartópapír: esparto paper
észrevehető: noticeable
ev. see egészvászonkötés
év(ek): year(s)
év és hely nélkül: without date or
  place
év és kiadó nélkül: without date
  or publisher
év, kiadó és hely nélkül: without
  date, publisher, or place
év nélkül: without date
éves mutató: annual index
évf. see évfolyam
évfolyam: annual volume, year
évforduló: anniversary
évi: yearly
évk. see évkönyv
évkönyv(ek): annual(s), year-
  book(s)
évszám nélkül: without year
évszázad: century
ex-libris: bookplate

ex-libris a kötésen: super *ex libris*
extra finom: superfine
ezennel: hereby
ezer: thousand
ezüst: silver
ezüstnyomás: silver gilt
ezüstözött: silvered
ezúttal: this time
ezzel: herewith

f. *see* füzet
fa: wood
fa-fedél: wood boards
fabula(ák): fable(s)
fakó: fading
faks. *see* fakszimile
fakszimile: facsimile
fakszimile kiadás: facsimile edition
fakszimile reprodukció: facsimile
    reproduction
fakszimile újlenyomat: facsimile
    reprint
fakulás: fading
falcolások: guards
famentes: wood-free paper
fametszet(ek): woodcut(s)
fantáziadús: imaginative
faszcikulus(ok): fascicle(s)
faszén: charcoal
fatábla: wood board
fb. *see* félbőr
feddhetetlen: impeccable
fedél(ek): cover(s), board(s)
fedélborító vászna(k): side(s)
fedett: covered
fedőlap: wrapper
fehér: white
fehérítetlen vászon: unbleached
    cloth
fej. *see* fejezet
fej(ek): head(s), top(s)
fejezet(ek): chapter(s)
fejezetcím: chapter head, title
fejléc: head of page
fejrész: headpiece
fekete: black
fekete-fehér. black and white

fél: half
fel. *see* felelős
fel. szerk. *see* felelős szerkesztő
felavató disszertáció: inaugural
    dissertation
felbecsülhetetlen: invaluable
felbélyegzett: stamped, franked
félbeszakított: interrupted
félbőr: half leather
félbőrjúbőrkötés: half-calf binding
félbőrkötés: half-leather binding
felcserélés: transposition
felcserélt: transposed
feldolg. *see* feldolgozás, feldolgozta
feldolgozás: adaptation
feldolgozta: compiled by
felelős: responsible
felelős szerkesztő: managing editor
felemelt ár: increased price
felett: over
félévenkénti: half-yearly,
    semiannual
félévi: semiannual
felfeslett: unsewn
félhavonként: fortnightly
felhordott: laid in
felhorzsolt: scored
félig hajlékony: semiflexible
felirat: epigraph, superscription
feliratos szalag: lettered scroll
feljogosított: authorized
félkötet: half volume
félmargók: half margins
féloldal: half page
félpergamen: half-vellum
felragasztva: mounted, pasted on
félsagrén: half-shagreen
felső: upper
felső margó: top margin
felsőmetszés: top edge
felsőszél: top margin
félszatén: half-sateen
féltónus: halftone
felújítva: renewed
felül: above, on top
felvágatlan: uncut, unopened

felvágatlan példány: unopened
copy
felvágott: edges cut, opened
felvágva: cut with paper knife
félvászon: half-cloth
félvászonkötés: half-cloth binding
félvászönkötés vászonsarkokkal:
half binding with cloth corners
félvászonkötéses sarok: half-cloth
binding with corners
fém: metal
fémjelzés: stamping, hallmark
fémkapocs (fémkapcsok): metal
clasp(s)
fémsarok (fémsarkok): metal
corner(s)
fémveret(ek): boss(es), metal
clasp(s)
fényezett: polished, glazed
fényezett és préselt barkájú bőr:
embossed leather
fényezett metszés: burnished edges
fényk. *see* fénykép
fénykép: photograph
fényképnyomás: rotogravure
fényképnyomat: photoprint
fénylakk: glossy lacquer
fénymásolat: photocopy, photostat
fénynyomás: photoprinting,
photoengraving
fénypapír: glazed paper
ferdekötések: beveled boards
féregnyomok: traces of worms
féregrágás: wormhole
féregrágta: wormholed
festett: painted
fésült margó: combed edges
fig. *see* figura
figura(ák): figure(s)
finom: delicate, fine
finom fehér kartonpapír: bristol
board
finom fémmunka: filigree
finom kartonpapír: ivory paper
finom kiadás: fine edition
finom peldány: fine copy
fizetés: payment

fizetett: paid
flexikötés: flexible binding
flitter: spangles
főcím: main title
foglal magában: includes
fókabőr: sealskin
földrajz: geography
földrajzi: geographical
földrajzi lexikon: gazetteer
főleg: mainly
fólia: foil, leaf
foliáns: folio
fólió(k): folio(s)
fólió számozás: paging, numbering
fölös példány: duplicate
folt(ok): patch(es), speck(s)
foltmaratás: aquatint
foltos: spotted
foltozott: patched
folttalan: spotless
folyó: current
folyó ár: current price
folyó év: current year
folyóírás: cursive
folyóirat(ok): journal(s), maga-
zine(s), periodical(s)
folyószám: current issue
folyószámla: account
folyt. *see* folytatás
folytatás: continuation
folytatása következik: to be continued
folytatásos(ok): serial(s)
folytatásos mű: serial work
folytatólagos: continued,
continuous
folytonos paginálás: continuous
pagination
fonatos: lace-ribbon design
fonatos virágdísz: interlaced floral
ornament
fontos: important
ford. *see* fordítás, fordító
fordítás(ok): translation(s)
fordító: translator
fordított: translated
formátum: format, size

forradás(ok): scar(s)
forrás: source
főszerkesztő: editor in chief
fot. *see* fotográfia
fotó(k): photo(s)
fotográfia(ák): photograph(s)
fotogravűr: photogravure
fotokópia(ák): photocopy(ies)
fotolitográfia: photolithography
fototípia(ák): line etching(s)
fraktúra betű: Gothic type
francia: French
friss: fresh, new
frissen: as new
frisseség: freshness
fríz(ek): frieze(s)
függ. *see* függelék
függelék(ek): addendum,
    annex(es), appendix(es)
fül: flap, jacket flap
fülszöveg: blurb text
furcsaságok: curiosa
fuvar: freight
fűz: sew
fűz. *see* fűzet
fűzés: stitching, sewing
fűzésnélküli könyvkötés: unsewn
    binding, flexible binding
fűzet(ek): booklet(s), brochure(s)
fűzetekben megjelenő: published
    in parts
fűzetlen példány: copy in sheets
fűzők: laces
fűzött: stitched; paperbound
fűzött kiadású: in paper covers
fűzött könyv: paperback
fűzött kötésű: bound in paper
    covers
fűzővel: with laces
fűzve: stitched
fv. *see* félvászonkötés
fve. *see* fűzve

gazdag: rich
gazdagon: richly
gépelt: typewritten
gépírás: typescript

géppel írott: typewritten
gerinc: spine
gerinc és sarkok: back and corners
gerinccím: title on the spine
gerincen: on the spine
gesztenyeszínű: chestnut-colored
girland: garland
gond: care
gondosan: carefully
gondozásában: edited by
görbe vonalminta: curved-line
    patterns
gót betű: Gothic type
gótikus betűtípus: black letter,
    Gothic type
grafika: graphics, artworks
grafikon(ok): graph(s)
grafikus: graphic
grafikus ábrázolás(ok): graph(s)
gravírozott: etched, engraved
grízes nyomás: graininess
groteszk: grotesque
groteszk betűtípus: sans serif type,
    grotesque type
gumibélyegző: rubber stamp
gúnyirat: lampoon
gyakoriság: frequency
gyakran: often
gyapot: cotton
gyenge: weak
gyermekkönyv(ek): children's
    book(s)
gyöngyház: mother-of-pearl
gyűjt. *see* gyűjtemény
gyűjtemény: compilation,
    collection
gyűjteményes kötet: omnibus
    volume
gyűjtő: collector
gyűrődés(ek): wrinkle(s)
gyűrött: crumpled

h. *see* hasáb, hely
h.é.k.n. *see* hely, év és kiadó
    nélkül
h.é.n. *see* hely és év nélkül
h.k.n. *see* hely és kiadó nélkül

h.n. *see* hely nélkül
hagyaték: literary remains
hajlékony kötés: flexible binding
hajtás: fold
hajtogatás: folding
hajtogatott: folded
hajtogatott röpirat: folded leaflet
halvány: pale
halványkék: pale blue
hamarosan megjelenik: expected
to appear
hamis: false, simulated
hamis bordák: false bands
hamisítás: forgery
hamisított: spurious
hamisítvány: forgery
hangj. *see* hangjegy
hangjegy(ek): note(s)
har. *see* haránt
haránt: oblong
harántalak: oblong size
harmadik: third
hármas: triple
harminc: thirty
harmincadik: thirtieth
három: three
hártyakötés: bound in vellum
hártyapapír: Bible paper, parchment
hasáb(ok): column(s)
hasadt: torn
hasonmás kiadás: facsimile
használat nyomai: traces of wear
használatlan: unused
használt: used, worn
hasznos: useful
hat: six
hát: back
hátlap: verso
hatodik: sixth
hátoldal: verso
hátrahagyott: posthumous
hátsó: back
hátsó címlap: back cover
hátsó margó: back margin
hátsó tábla: back cover
hátul: at the back

hatvan: sixty
hatvanadik: sixtieth
havi szám: monthly issue
havilap: monthly publication
havonként: monthly
havonta: monthly
havonta kétszer megjelenő:
published semimonthly
házi: domestic
házinyomda: private press
hektografált: hectographed
hely: place, place of publication
hely és év nélkül: without place
and date of publication
hely és kiadó nélkül: without place
of publication and publisher
hely, év és kiadó nélkül: without
place of publication, date, and
publisher
hely nélkül: without place of
publication
hely vagy dátum nélkül: without
place or date
helyenként: here and there
helyesbítés(ek): correction(s)
helyettesít: substitute
helyi kiadás: local edition
helynév: place-name
helynévmutató: index of places
helyrajzi térkép(ek): topographical
map(s)
helységnévtár: gazetteer
heraldikai: heraldic
heraldikai címerpajzs: armorial
shield
hét: seven, week
hetedik: seventh
hetenként: weekly
hetente: weekly
heti: weekly
hetilap: weekly
hetven: seventy
hetvenedik: seventieth
hézag: blank, gap, lacuna
hiány(ok): defect(s), lack(s)
hiányos: incomplete
hiányos kópia: defective copy

hiánytalan: complete
hiányzanak: missing
hiányzik: missing, wanting
hiányzó: lacking, missing
hibaigazító: corrigendum
hibajegyzék: erratum
hibás: damaged, defective
hibátlan: intact, perfect
hidegtű: drypoint
hímzett: embroidered
híres: famous
hiteles: authentic
hiteles szöveg: definitive text
hivatalos: official
hivatalos használatra: for official
  use
hivatalos kiadvány: official
  publication
hó: month
hófehér: immaculately white
homályos: obscure, dark
homlokbetűk: small capitals
homloklap: recto, front side
hónap: month
hornyolt: fluted, grooved, notched
horzsolás(ok): abrasion(s), chafing
hossz: length
hosszú: long
hozzáadás(ok): addition(s)
hozzáadott: added, additional
hozzáfűzve: attached
hozzájárulás(ok): contribution(s)
hozzákötve: bound with
hozzávetőleg: approximately
hű: faithful
hullámos: wavy
húsz: twenty
huszadik: twentieth
húzásokkal: expurgated

id. *see* idézett
idegen betű: bastard type
ideiglenes: interim, temporary
ideiglenesen: temporarily
identikus: identical
idéz: quote
idézet: quotation

idézett: quoted, cited
idő: time
időrendi: chronological
időrendi táblázat: chronological
  table
időszaki: periodical
időszakos kiadvány: periodical
  publication
ifjúsági kiadás: juvenile edition
igen sok: very much
ill. *see* illusztrált
illetménykötet: gift volume, subscription volume
illumináció: illumination
illuminált: historiated
illuminált kézirat: illuminated
  manuscript
illusztr. *see* illusztrált
illusztráció(k): illustration(s)
illusztrációs papír: art paper
illusztrált: illustrated
illusztrátor: illustrator
imakönyv: prayer book
import: import
impresszum: imprint
impresszum nélkül: without
  imprint
incipit: incipit
ind. *see* index
index: index
indexlapok: index pages
individuális: individual
ingyen: free of charge, gratis
inic. *see* iniciálé
iniciálé(k): initial letter(s)
inkább: rather
inkunábulum(ok): incunabulum(a)
int. *see* intézet
interpretáló jegyzet(ek):
  explanatory note(s)
intézet: institution, institute
intézmény: institution
írás: works, writings
író: author, writer
irodalmi: history
irodalmi hagyaték: literary
  remains

irodalmi vezető: chief editor
irodalom: literature
irodalomjegyzék: bibliography
írói álnév: pen name, pseudonym
is: also
iskolakönyv(ek): textbook(s)
ism. *see* ismertetés, ismerteti
ismeretlen: unknown
ismertetés: review
ismerteti: review
ismételt kiadás: unchanged edition
ív(ek): sheet(s)
ívcsomóban: in fascicles
ívjelzőszám(ok): signature(s)
ívpéldány(ok): book(s) in sheets
ívrét: folio
ívrét alakú: folio
ívrét alakú könyv(ek): folio
   book(s)
ívrétű(k): folio(s)
ívszámozás: foliation, signature
   numbering
ízlés: taste
ízléses: tasteful

Jansen-kötés: jansenist binding
japánpapír: Japan paper
jav. *see* javítás, javított
javít. *see* javított
javít: repair
javítás(ok): correction(s), repair(s)
javított: revised, improved
javított kiadás: revised edition
javítva: repaired
jegyz. *see* jegyzet
jegyzék: index, list
jegyzés: indication
jegyzet(ek): note(s)
jegyzet oldal(ak): note page(s)
jegyzetekkel ellátott: annotated
jegyzettömb(ök): block book(s)
jegyzőkönyv: proceedings,
   transactions
jel(ek): mark(s), sign(s)
jelentékeny: considerable
jelentéktelen: insignificant, unimportant

jelentés(ek): report(s)
jelentősen: considerably
jelmondat: epigraph
jelölés(ek): notation(s), mark(s)
jó: good
jó állapotban: in good condition
jobb oldal: right-hand
jogosított: entitled
jogosított kiadás: authorized
   edition
jól konzervált: well preserved
jóváhagyás: imprimatur,
   permission
jóváhagyott: approved, authorized
jubiláris kiadvány: jubilee edition
jubileumi kötet: jubilee volume
jutalmazott: prizewinning
jutányos: inexpensive

k. *see* kötet
k.k. *see* könyvtári kötésben
k.n. *see* kiadó nélkül
kacskaringós: full of flourishes
kalligráfia: calligraphy
kalligráfikus: calligraphic
kalligráfus: calligrapher
kalózkiadás: pirated edition,
   unauthorized publication
kalózkiadvány: pirated edition
kámea: cameo
kámeakötés: cameo binding
kanavász: lightweight buckram
kand. ért. *see* kandidátusi értekezés
kandidátusi értekezés: dissertation,
   thesis
kapcsok: clasps
kapcsokkal: with clasps
kapható: available, in print
kapitális(ok): headband(s)
kapocs: clasp
kapocsmaradvány(ok): remnant(s)
   of clasps
káptalan minta: chapter-end
   design
kár: damage, loss
karbunkulus: carbuncle

karcnyomok: scraped spots,
   scratches
karcolat(ok): scratch(es)
karcolt: scraped
karikatúra(ák): caricature(s)
kartográfia: cartography
karton: cardboard
karton pappendekli: pasteboard
kartonált: board binding
kartonálva: bound in boards
kartonba kötött: bound in boards
kartonborítású: paperbound
kartonírozott: cartoned
kartonkötésben: bound in boards
kartonkötésű: bound in boards
kartonok: cardboard slipcase
kártus: cartouche
kártus díszítő: ornamental oval
   frame
kártya: card
katalógus: catalog
katalógusár: catalog price
kb. *see* körülbelül
kecskebör: goatskin, kidskin
kefe korrektúra: proof
kék: blue
kékre festett: blued
kelet: date
keletbélyegzés: dating
kelt: dated
keltezés(ek): date(s)
keltezett: dated
kemény: hard
keménykötés: case binding, hard
   cover
keménykötésű: bound in boards
kép(ek): picture(s), illustrations(s)
képanyag: illustrations
képes: illustrated
képes kiadás: illustrated edition
képeskönyv: picture book
képmelléklet(ek): plate(s)
képrészlet(ek): picture section(s)
képszöveg(ek): caption(s),
   legend(s)
kéregpapír: carton
kérem kérje: please request

kérem reklamáljon: please request
keresés: search
keresett: sought, in demand
kereskedelemben: in the trade
kereskedelmi: commercial
kereskedelmi forgalomban nem
   kapható: not for sale
kérésre: upon request
keressük: sought after
keresztnév: forename
keret: frame
keretbe foglalt: framed
keretdísz: border design
keretdísz szalag: border strips
keretezett: framed
keretlénia: ornamental border
keskeny: narrow
keskeny margó: narrow margins
késleltetett: delayed
kész: ready
készítés: preparation
készpénz: cash
készpénzár: cash price
készülék: device
készült: produced, printed
két: two
két kötet egyben: two volumes in
   one
kétéves: biennial
kéthasábos: double-columned
kéthetenként megjelenő folyóirat:
   biweekly
kéthetenkénti: fortnightly
kétkötetes: in two volumes
kétnyelvű: bilingual
kétrét hajtott papírív nagyságú:
   in folio
kétséges: doubtful
kétszínű: two-color
kettészakított: torn up
kettő: two
kettős: double
kettős borda: double-ribbing
kettős bordázatok: double bands
kettős előzéklapok: double endpapers
kettős könyvtok: double slipcase

kettős korona: double crown
kettős lap: double leaf
kettős oldal: double page
kézbesítés: delivery
kézbesített: delivered
kezdet: beginning
kezdőbetű(k): initial(s)
kezdőbetű(k) díszítő: ornamental
   initial(s)
kézi: manual
kézi aranyozás: hand gilding
kézi festésű: hand-colored
kézi szedésű: hand-set
kézikönyv(ek): handbook(s)
kézimunka: handwork
kézipéldány: personal copy
kézírás: handwriting
kézírásos: handwritten
kézirat(ok): manuscript(s)
kézirat díszes iniciáléi: illuminated
   initials
kézirat gyanánt: printed as
   manuscript
kéziratfestés: illumination
kéziratként: for private circulation
kéziratos(ok): manuscript(s)
kézzel gyártott: handmade
kézzel írott: manuscript, typescript
kézzel színezett: hand-colored
kiad. *see* kiadás, kiadó, kiadta
kiadás(ok): edition(s),
   publication(s)
kiadás alatt: in course of
   publication
kiadás dátuma: date of publication
kiadás helye: place of publication
kiadás helye nélkül: without place
   of publication
kiadásában: published by
kiadatlan: unpublished
kiadó: publisher, publishing house
kiadó emblémája: publisher's
   emblem
kiadó nélkül: without publisher
kiadó neve nélkül: without publisher
kiadó társulat: publishing firm

kiadói ár: publisher's price
kiadónál elfogyott: out-of-print
kiadósan: abundantly
kiadott: produced, published
kiadóvállalat: publisher, publishing
   house
kiadta: edited by, compiled by
kiadv. *see* kiadvány
kiadvány(ok): publication(s)
kicsi: small
kicsinyített: reduced
kidolg. *see* kidolgozta
kidolgozott: elaborated
kidolgozta: composed by
kidörzsölt: rubbed
kieg. *see* kiegészítés, kiegészítve
kiegészítés(ek): supplement(s)
kiegészítő: supplementary
kiegészítve: completed
kiemelések: extracts
kiemelkedő: outstanding
kiemelt: extracted
kifakít: discolor, fade
kifakult: discolored, faded
kifakultak: discolored, faded
kifogástalan: immaculate, perfect
kifogyott: out-of-print
kifogytak: out-of-print
kihajtható: foldout
kihúz: cross out
kijavítás: correction, mending
kijavítható: repairable
kijavított: corrected, mended
kiküszöbölt: eliminated
kilazult falcnyílások: loose in the
   joints
kilenc: nine
kilencedik: ninth
kilencven: ninety
kilencvenedik: ninetieth
kincseskáz: thesaurus
kinyomható: imprimatur
kinyomtatott: in sheets: printed
kirad. *see* kiradírozva
kiradírozott: erased
kiradírozva: erased
kirajzolás: drawing, design

királyi: royal
kis: slight, small
kis betűtípus: small print
kis lyukakkal: with small holes
kis szemcsésségű: small-grained
kis virágdísz(ek): floret(s)
kisbetű(k): lowercase letter(s),
small letter(s)
kisregény(ek): short novel(s)
kissé: slightly, a little
kissé foltos: slightly spotted
kissé rongált: lightly damaged
kiszakadt: torn out
kiszakított: torn out
kitörölve: blotted out
kitűnő: excellent, superior
kitűnő állapotban van: in perfect
condition, in excellent state
kiv. *see* kivonat
kiv. nélk. *see* kivétel nélkül
kivág: clip
kivágások: clippings
kivágott: cut out
kivágva: cut out, excised
kivakarva: erased with knife or
eraser
kiváló: outstanding
kiváló állapotban: in excellent
condition
kivánatra: on request
kivehető: loose-leaf
kivétel nélkül: without exception
kivételes: exceptional
kivéve: except
kivonat: abstract, résumé
kivonatol: abstract
kivonatos kiadás: abridged edition
kívül: outside, without
kizárólag: exclusively
kizárólagos: exclusive
kizárólagos terjesztés: exclusive
distribution
klasszikus: classic
klisé(k): block(s), plate(s)
klny. *see* különlenyomat,
különnyomat
kockás: checkered

kockás minta: checkered design
kockás papír: ruled paper
kód: key
kódex(ek): codex(ices)
kőírás: clock type
kollaborálás: collaboration
kollacionálás: collation
kollektív cím: collective title
kollektív munka: collective work
kollektor: collector
kollig. *see* kolligátum
kolligátum: work bound with
another
kollotípia: collotype
kolofon: colophon
kolorit: coloring
költemény(ek): poem(s)
költészet: poetry
költő: poet
költői művek: poetic works
költség(ek): cost(s)
kolumna(ák): column(s)
kommentár: commentary, notes
kommentátor: commentator
komoly: serious
kompendium: compendium
kompilátor: compiler
komplé: ensemble
konc: quire
kondíció: condition
konf. *see* konferencia
konferencia: conference
konfirmáció: confirmation
konfirmált: confirmed
konfiskált: confiscated
kongr. *see* kongresszus
kongresszus: congress
konkordancia: concordance
kőnyomással sokszorosított
példány: lithographed copy
kőnyomatos: lithographic print
könyv(ek): book(s)
könyvaranyozás: gilding
könyvbarát: booklover
könyvborító: book jacket
könyvcsere: book exchange
könyvdísz: book decoration

könyvdíszítés: book decoration
könyvecske(ék): booklet(s)
könyveladás: book sale
könyvész: bibliographer
könyvészeti: bibliographical
könyvgerinc: back, spine
könyvgerinc széle(i): joint(s)
könyvgyűjtő: book collector
könyvjegy: bookplate, *ex libris*
könyvkereskedelem: book trade
könyvkereskedés: bookstore
könyvkereskedő: bookseller
könyvkiadás: book publishing
könyvkiadó: printer, publisher
könyvklub: book club
könyvkötés: bookbinding
könyvkötészet: bookbindery
könyvkötő: bookbinder
könyvkötő cím: binder's title
könyvkötő karton: binder's boards
könyvkötőműhely: bookbindery
könyvkötővászon: calico
könyvmoly: bookworm
könyvnyomda: printing press
könyvnyomtatás: letterpress
  printing
könyvpiac: book market
könyvsiker: best-seller
könyvskatulya: book box
könyvt. *see* könyvtár
könyvtábla: book cover
könyvtábla-mező: book-cover
  panel
könyvtár(ak): library(ies)
könyvtár-bélyegző: library stamp
könyvtári bélyegző: library stamp
könyvtári kötés: library binding
könyvtári kötésben: in library
  binding
könyvtári példány: ex-library
  volume
könyvtárnok: librarian
könyvtáros: librarian
könyvtok: slipcover, slipcase
könyvvédő: dustcover
könyvzár(ak): clasp(s)
konzerválás: preservation

konzervált: preserved
kópia(ák): copy(ies)
kopott folt(ok): skinned spot(s)
kor: scope
korábban: earlier
korabeli: contemporary
korai: early
köralakú díszítés: circular design
kordobai: cordovan
korlátozott: limited
korona: crown
koros: aged
korrektúra(ák): correction(s)
kortársi: contemporary
körülbelül: approximately, circa
körülvágatlan: uncut
körülvágott: cropped
körvonalazott: outlined
köt. *see* kötet
kötelék(ek): cord(s)
kötelékkel: with bands
köteles példány: deposit copy
kötés: binding
kötés nélküli: unbound
kötéscím: binder's title
kötését vesztett: with binding gone
kötési költség: binding cost
kötésű: bound in
kötet(ek): volume(s)
kötetcédula: volume label
kötetenként: per volume
kötetlen: unbound
kötetszám: volume number
kötetszámozás: volume numbering
kötőszalagok: binding strips
kötött: bound
kötött írás: script
kötött példány(ok): bound
  volume(s)
kotta: musical score
kottamelléklet(ek): music supple-
  ment(s)
kötve: bound
köv. *see* következő
kövér betű: boldface
következő: following
közeg: medium

közel: around, near
közeljövőben megjelenik: about to
  be published
közepes: intermediate, mediocre
középkor: Middle Ages
középkori: medieval
közlemény: proceedings, transactions
közlés: notice
közlöny: gazette
közölt: announced, published
közös: common
között: between
közp. *see* központ
központ: center, central
közreadó: publisher
közreműködésével: with the
  collaboration of
közreműködött: with the
  collaboration of
közzététel: publication
kp. *see* készpénz
krémszínű: cream-colored
krétapapír: art paper
krétázott papír: coated paper
kreton: cretonne
kritikai kiadás: critical edition
kroki: sketch
kromatográfia: chromatography
kromotípia: chromotypography
kromotipográfia: color printing
krónika(ák): chronicle(s)
krúda: book in sheets
krúdában: copy in sheets
küld: send
külföldi: foreign
külön: extra, special
külön számozás: separate numbering
különálló: loose
különálló lap(ok): loose-leaf
  sheet(s)
különbözik: differs
különféle: different, various
különkiadás: special edition
különleges: special

különlenyomat(ok): offprint(s),
  reprint(s), separate(s)
különnyomat(ok): offprint(s), reprint(s)
különös: unusual, remarkable
különszám: special number
kulőr: color
külső: outside
külső cím: external title
külső margó: outer margin
külsőleg: externally
kumulált: cumulated
kurrens: current
kurzív: italics
kut. *see* kutatás
kutatás: research
kv. *see* könyv
kvart: quarto
kve. *see* kötve
kvtár. *see* könyvtár

l. *see* lap
lábjegyzet(ek): footnote(s)
láda(ák): box(es)
lajstrom: register
lakcím: address
lakk: enamel
lakkozott kötés: lacquered binding
láncos könyv: chained book
lap(ok): page(s), sheet(s)
lap szélére írt: written in the
  margins
lapalj: foot of the page
lapél(ek): edge(s) of a book
lapos kötelék: flat bands
lapszám(ok): page number(s)
lapszámmal ellátott: paginated
lapszámozás: paging, foliation
lapszámozva: paginated
lapszél: fore edge
lapszélfestészet: fore-edge painting
lapszéli: marginal
lapszéli jegyzetek: marginal notes
látszólag: apparently
lavírozott: washed
laza: loose
lazacszínű: salmon-colored

lebélyegzett: stamped, marked
with a stamp
legalacsonyabb ár: lowest price
legatúra: cover
legdrágább: most expensive
legenda: legend
legfinomabb: superfine
légiposta: airmail
legkiválóbb: foremost
legnagyobbrészt: mostly
legömbölyített: rounded
legrégibb: oldest
legszebb: finest
legújabb: newest, most recent
legújabb szám: current issue
legutolsó: last, latest
leheletszerűen vékony: ultrathin
lehetetlen megtalálni: impossible
to find
lehorzsolás(ok): abrasion(s)
lehorzsolodott: rubbed off,
scraped off, worn off
leírás: description
leíró: descriptive
lekapart: abraded
leláncolt kötés: chained binding
leláncolt példány: chained book
lemez(ek): plate(s)
lemezre ragasztott: mounted,
pasted on
lenvászon: linen
lenvászon damaszt: linen damask
lenyomat(ok): copy(ies), print(s)
leporello: foldout, folding album
leromlott: deteriorated
leszakadt: broken loose, torn off
leszakított: torn off
leszállított: reduced
leszállított áron: reduced in price
leszélezett: cut, trimmed
lev. *see* levél
levág: cut off
levágott: trimmed
levágva: cut away
leválasztott: detached
levált: detached
levél(ek): leaf(ves)

levéldísz: fleuron
levelenként számozva: foliated
leveles burokráma: leafy scroll
levelezés: correspondence
levélszám: foliation
levélszámozás: foliation
levéltár: archives
levendulaszínű: lavender
levett: removed
lexikális gyűjtemény: thesaurus
lexikon: encyclopedia
lexikon-alak: large octavo
lila: purple, violet
liliom(ok): fleur(s)-de-lys
liliom minta: lily design
liliomos: fleur-de-lys
linóleumdeszka: linoleum block
linóleummetszés: linoleum-block
print
lista(ák): list(s)
litogr. *see* litográfia
litografált: lithographed
litográfia(ák): lithograph(s),
lithography
litográfus: lithographer
litokromia: lithography
lombfűrészmunka: scrollwork
lovagregény: romantic novel
luxus: deluxe, fancy
luxus kiadás: deluxe publication
lyuk: hole
lyukas: with holes, wormholed
lyukasztott: punched out

m. *see* magyar, méret
magában foglaló: inclusive
magán: private
magángyűjtemény: private collection
magánkiadás: privately published
magánnyomás: privately printed
magasnyomtatás: relief printing
magasra maratás: relief etching
magasság: height
magy. *see* magyar
magyar: Hungarian
magyarázat: explanation

magyarázatokkal ellátott:
annotated
magyarázatos: annotated
magyarázó: explanatory
magyarázó jegyzet(ek): critical
note(s), annotation(s)
mai: contemporary
mai napig: up to now
makkok: acorns
makulátlan: immaculate, spotless
makulatúra: mackling
mappa(ák): portfolio(s)
mappában: in portfolio
maradék: remaining
maradék készlet(ek): remainder(s)
maratott: burnished, etched
marginália(k): note(s) in margins
margó(k): margin(s)
marhabőr: oxhide
marokén: morocco
marokkói kecskebőr: morocco
márványmetszés: marbling
márványos metszések: marbled
edges
márványozás: marbling, sprinkling
márványozott: marbled
márványozott papír: marbled
paper
márványpapír: marbled paper
más: different
más néven: otherwise
másik: other
másként: otherwise
második: second
másodlagos: secondary
másodlat: duplicated
másodpéldány: second copy
másolat(ok): copy(ies), duplicate(s)
másoló: tracer
matrica: mold
matt: dull, matte
mázolt: coated, painted
medalion: medallion
még: also, and, up to now, yet
még nem elérhető: not yet available
még nem jelent meg: not yet
published

még nem kapható: not yet
available
megaranyozott: gilt, tooled
megbarnulás: foxing
megbarnult: foxed
megbecsülhetetlen: inestimable,
invaluable
megbízás: commission
megbízható: reliable
megcsonkítás: mutilation
megcsonkított: mutilated
megcsonkítva: mutilated
megégetett: burned
megemlékező kötet: commemorative volume
megerősítés: strengthening
megerősített: strengthened
meghatározott ár: fixed price
megj. *see* megjegyzések, megjelenik
megjegyzések: comments, notes
megjelenés előtt: in press
megjelenés időpontja: date of
publication
megjelenési év: date of publication
megjelenik: appear, appears
megjelölt: marked
megkapható: may be obtained
megkapó: impressive
megkarcolás: scoring, scratching
megközelítőleg: approximately
meglazult kötéssel: with binding
loosened
meglevő: extant
megmaradó: remaining
megnyúlt: elongated
megperzselt: scorched
megrendelés: order
megrendelésre: on subscription
megrövidítés: abridgment
megsárgult: foxed, yellowed
megsemmisített: destroyed
megszámlalhatatlan: innumerable
megszűnt: ceased, no longer
published
megtisztított: cleaned, expurgated
megújít: renew
megújított: renewed

megváltozott: changed
megviselt: worn
mellékelt: enclosed
mellékelve: enclosed
melléklet(ek): annex(es), appendix(ces), supplement(s)
mellette: next to
mélynyomás: intaglio, photogravure
memoár(ok): memoir(s)
mennyiség: quantity
méret: size
merevített: reinforced
merített papír: handmade paper
merített szél(ek): deckle-edged, deckled edge(s)
mérsékelt: moderate
mérték: measure
mérvadó: authentic
mese(ék): tale(s)
mestermű: masterpiece
mesterséges: artificial
mesterséges sagrén: artificial shagreen
metsz. *see* metszés, metszet
metszés: tooling
metszet(ek): engraving(s)
metszett címlap: engraving on title page
mezzotinto(k): mezzotint(s)
mgy. *see* magángyűjtemény
mikrofilm: microfilm
mikrofilmkópia(ák): microcopy(ies)
mikromásolat: microcopy
min. *see* miniatúra
mindeddig: up to now
minden: all, each
minden jog fenntartva: all rights reserved
minden megjelentet: all published
minden oldalán: on all sides
mindkét: both
mindkét oldalán: on both sides
mindössze egy ismert: only one known
miniatűr kiadás: miniature edition
miniatúra(ák): miniature(s)

minimális: minimum
minőség: quality
mint az új: as good as new
minta(ák): design(s), pattern(s), sample(s)
mintapéldány: specimen volume
mintázott: figured
mintázott él: goffered edge
moáré: moiré
moáré selyem: watered silk
mocskos: dirty, smudged
modern: modern
mögött: behind
monda: legend, saga
monogr. *see* monográfia
monográfia(ák): monograph(s)
monogramm: monogram
mosható: washable
mosott: washed
most jelent meg: just issued, just published
mostanában: recently
mostanáig: up to now
motívum: design, pattern
mottó: motto
mozaik: mosaic
mozgatható: movable
mű: literary work, opus
műarany: imitation gilt
műbőr: artificial leather, leatherette
műfordítás: translation
műfordító: translator
műkedvelő: amateur
munka: work
munkatárs(ak): collaborator(s)
műnyomó papír: art paper
műsz. *see* műszaki
műszaki: technical
mutató(k): index(es)
műve: works
művek: miscellanea; miscellany
művészeti könyv: art book
művészi kiadás: art edition
művésznév: pen name
muzsika: music

nagy: big, large
nagy fóliáns: large folio
nagy margó(k): large margin(s)
nagy papír: large paper
nagyban: wholesale
nagybecsű: esteemed
nagybetű(k): capital(s), capital
    letter(s)
nagyformátumú: large-size edition
nagykereskedelmi ár: wholesale
    price
nagyon: very
nagyon értékes: extremely valuable
nagyon jó állapotban: in very
    good condition
nagyon kevés: very few
nagyon kicsit: very little
nagyon ritka: very rare
nagyon sok: very much
nagyrabecsült: highly esteemed
nap: daily
napilap: daily newspaper
napló(k): diary(ies)
narancssárga: orange color
narrátor: narrator
nedves folt(ok): damp spot(s)
nedves foltos: damp spotted
nedvesség: humidity, moisture
négy: four
negyedéves: quarterly
negyedévi: quarterly
negyedik: fourth
negyven: forty
negyvenedik: fortieth
négyzet: square
négyzetes: square
néha: occasionally
néhány: a few
nehéz: difficult, heavy
nem: not
nem a szövegben: not in the text
nem díszített: undecorated
nem eladó: not for sale
nem elérhető: not available
nem kapható: not available
nem kielégítő: unsatisfactory
nem közölt: unpublished

nem létező: nonexistent
nem összeillő: unmatched
nem teljes: incomplete
nem tiszta: soiled, dirty
nem új: shopworn
német: German
némileg: somewhat
nemrég jelent meg: recently
    published
nemsokára: soon
nemz. *see* nemzeti
nemzeti: national
nemzetk. *see* nemzetközi
nemzetközi: international
nettó: net
név: name
neves: famous, named
névt. *see* névtelen
névtelen: anonymous
névtelen mű: anonymous work
névtelenül: anonymously
nincs forgalomban: not in the trade
notesz(ek): notebook(s)
növekedés: increase
növekedett: increased
növel: augment
novella(ák): short story(ies)
ny. *see* nyomda
ny. n. *see* nyomda nélkül
nyár: Summer
nyelv: language
nyelvkönyv: reader
nyelvtan: grammar
nyers: raw
nyílt: open
nyitott hát: open back
nyolc: eight
nyolcadik: eighth
nyolcvan: eighty
nyolcvanadik: eightieth
nyom(ok): mark(s), print(s),
    trace(s)
nyomás: press, printing
nyomás alatt: in print, in the press
nyomat: impression
nyomda: printing office
nyomda nélkül: without printer

nyomdahiba: misprint
nyomdai: typographic
nyomdajegy: printer's mark
nyomdajel: printer's mark
nyomdász: printer
nyomóduc: woodblock
nyomóforma: woodblock
nyomógép: printing press
nyomott: printed
nyomtatás: printing
nyomtatás helye: place of printing
nyomtatásban megjelenik: appear
  in print
nyomtatott: printed
nyomtatott betű(k): block letter(s)
nyomtatott ív(ek): gathering(s),
  signature(s)
nyomtatott kiadás: printed edition
nyomtatvány: printed matter
nyomva: printed

o. *see* oldal
offszet: offset
offszetnyomás: offset printing
okker: ocher
oklevél: charter, diploma
oktáv: octavo
oktáv papírméret: octavo
oktávalak: octavo
olajbarna: olive green
olajfoltok: oil stains
olajzöld: olive green
olasz: Italian
olcsó: cheap, inexpensive
olcsó kiadás: popular edition
old. *see* oldal
oldal(ak): page(s), side(s)
oldalméret: page size
oldalszám: page number
olívaszínű: olive color
olvashatatlan: illegible
olvasható: legible
olvasókönyv: reader
önéletrajz: autobiography
organtin: book cloth
ornamentika(ák): ornament(s)
oromszalag(ok): headband(s)

orosz: Russian
orsz. *see* országos
országos: national
őrszó: catchword
ósdi: out-of-date
őskiadás: editio princeps, first
  edition
ősnyomtatvány: incunabulum
össz. *see* összes
összeállítás: compilation
összeállítva: compiled
összefirkált: scribbled on
összefoglalás: summary
összeg: amount
összegyűjtött: collected, gathered
összegyűjtött munkái: collected
  works
összegyűrődés: wrinkling
összehajtható: foldout
összehasonlít: compare
összehord: collate
összerongyolt: tattered
összes: all
összes művei: complete works
összevont: merged, summarized
összkiadás: entire edition
ősz: Fall
osztott: split
öt: five
ötödik: fifth
ötven: fifty
ötvenedik: fiftieth
ötvösmunka: filigree
őzbarna: fawn-colored
őzbőr: doeskin

p. *see* pagina
pagina: page
paginálás: pagination
palaszürke: slate gray
pálmalevél-motívum: palm-leaf
  design
pályamű: prizewinning publication
pamut: carton
papír: paper
papírkötés(ek): paper cover(s)

papírkötésben: paperbound, soft
cover
papírkötésű: paperback
paragrafus(ok): paragraph(s)
páratlan: odd
párhuzamos: parallel
párnázott kötés: padded binding
páros: even
partitúra: musical score
pasztell: pastel
pecsét(ek): seal(s), stain(s)
pecsétes: spotted, stained
pecsétnyomó: stamp
példány(ok): copy(ies),
specimen(s)
például: for example
penész: mildew
penészes: mildewed
penészesfolt(ok): damp stain(s),
mildew
penészfoltos: mildew spotted
perem: edge
perforálások: perforations
perforált: perforated
pergamen: parchment, vellum
pergamen-utánzat: imitation
parchment
pergamenkötés: parchment binding
pergamenpapír: parchment
pergamenpótló: imitation vellum
perkál: percale
pettyes: speckled
piaci ár: current price
pici: minute
piros: red
piszkos: dirty, soiled
piszkos foltok: dirty spots
piszokfoltok: soil marks
pl. *see* például
plágium: plagiarism
pld. *see* példány
politúrozatlan: unpolished
pont: point
pontozó bélyegző: dot stamping
pontozó metszés: stippling
pontozó technikával metszett:
stippled

pontozott: dotted
pontozott vonalak: dotted lines
ponyva hasáb: column
porfír: porphyry
poros: dusty
portré(k): portrait(s)
posta: mail
postaköltség: postage, mailing cost
poszthumusz: posthumous
pótfüzet: supplementary issue
pótlás(ok): addenda, supplement(s)
precíz: accurate, exact
préselt: crushed
préselt bőr: crushed leather
préselt díszítés: goffered, goffering
préselt marokén: crushed morocco
próbaminta: sample
próbanyomat: preprint
próbapéldány: examination copy
prospektus: prospectus
próza: prose
pszeudonim: pseudonym
publ. *see* publikáció
publikáció: publication
publikálás: publication
puha: soft
puhafedelű: flexible

quart-alak: quarto

r. *see* rész
rabatt: discount
radírozás: erasure
ragasztott: glued, pasted
rágcsált: gnawed
ragyogó: brilliant
rajz(ok): drawing(s)
rajzolás: drawing
rajzolt: drawn
raktáron: in stock
raktáron nem levő: out of stock
rámázott: framed
ráncos: wrinkled
ráncos röpirat: folded leaflet
ráragasztott: affixed
raritás: rarity
recenziós példány: review copy

recézett: dentelle
redaktor: editor
referátum: abstract
reg. *see* regiszter
régebben: formerly
regény(ek): novel(s)
regényíró: novelist
régi: old .
régi példányok: back numbers
régibb: older
régiségkereskedés: antiquarian
  shop
regiszter: index, register
rekesz: compartment
reklám(ok): advertisement(s)
reklámcédula: broadsheet
rekonstruálás(ok): restoration(s)
rektó: recto
relief: relief
remittenda: returns, remainders
rendbehozható: repairable
rendelés(ek): order(s)
rendelkezés: arrangement
rendelőlap: order blank, order form
rendes: common, ordinary
rendesen: neatly, normally
rendezett: arranged
rendkívül: unusually, unusual
rendkívül ritka: extremely rare
rendkívüli: exceptional, unusual
rendszeres: systematic
rendszerint: usually, usual
rendszertelenség: irregularity
rendszertelenül: irregularly
repedezett: cracked
reprodukció: reproduction
restaurált: restored
rész(ek): part(s)
részben: partly
részenként: in parts
részlet: extract, part
részletekben: in parts, in fascicles
részletes: detailed
részletesen: in detail
részletező: minute, small
retusált: retouched
revízió: revision

rézcsat(ok): brass clasp(s)
rézkapcsok: brass clasps
rézkapocs: brass clasp
rézkarc(ok): copperplate(s)
rézlemez: copperplate
rézmetszet(ek): copper
  engraving(s)
rézről: on copper
réztábla: copperplate
rezümé: résumé
riccelés: scratched
ritka: rare, scarce
ritka-könyvárus: rare book dealer
ritkán: rarely
ritkaság: rarity
rizspapír: rice paper
rögzített: attached
romantikus: romantic
rombusz: diamond, lozenge
rombusz alakú minto: diamond-
  shaped
rongálás(ok): defect(s)
rongált: damaged
rongált sarkokkal: with corners
  broken
rongypapír: rag paper
röpirat(ok): booklet(s),
  pamphlet(s)
röplap(ok): pamphlet(s), leaflet(s)
roskadozó: dilapidated
rossz: bad, defective
rossz állapotban: in poor condition
rossz helyre kötötték: misbound
rossz helyre kötve: misbound
röv. *see* rövidítés, röviditett
rovat(ok): column(s), rubric(s)
rovátkolás: hatching
rovátkolt: excised
rövid: short
rövid mű: opuscule
röviden: briefly, shortly
rövidesen: soon
rövidesen megjelenik: to be published soon
rövidítés(ek): abbreviation(s)
rövidítetlen: abridged
röviditett: abridged

rövidített kiadás: abridged edition
rozetta(ák): rosette(s)
rózsaszínű: pink
rozsda: rust
rozsdabarna: roan
rozsdafoltos: rust-stained
rubrika: heading, rubric
rubrikázott: rubricated
rugós: elastic
rusztikus: rustic

s.k. *see* saját kezű
sagrén: shagreen
sagrin: shagreen
saját kezű: autographed
saját kezű aláírás: autograph
saját kiadású: privately printed
sajátkezűleg írt: holograph
sajtó: press
sajtó alá rendezte: edited by
sajtó alatt: in press
sajtó nyomás alatt: in the press
sajtóhiba: misprint
sajtóhiba levél(ek): errata
  leaf(ves)
sajtóhibajegyzék: list of misprints
sajtótermék: print, publication
sakktáblaminta: checkered design
sapka bőrgerinc: headcap
sárga: yellow
sárga foltok: yellow spots, foxed
sárgaréz: brass
sárgásbarna színű: fawn-colored
sárgult: yellowed
sarok (sarkok): corner(s)
sarok desszén(ek): corner design(s)
sarokdíszítések: corner pieces
segédkönyv(ek): handbook(s)
sehol: no place
selyem: silk
selyemborítás: silk covering
selyempapír: silk paper
sem: neither
sematikus ábra: diagram
semmi cím: no title
semmi címlap: no title page
semmi dátum: no date

semmi év: no year
semmi rajz, semmi dátum: no
  place, no date
sértetlen: intact
sérült: damaged
sérült kópia: damaged copy
sillabusz: abstract, outline
sima: smooth
sima kötés: plain bound
sima metszések: smooth edges
skicc: sketch
soha: never
sok: many
soknyelvű: multilingual, polyglot
soksz. *see* sokszorosítás, sokszorosított
sokszínű: multicolored, varicolored
sokszorosítás(ok): reproduction(s)
sokszorosított: reproduced
sor. *see* sorozat
sor: line
sorközi: interlinear
sorok közé írott: between the lines
sorok száma: line numbers
sorozat: series
sorozatcím: series title
sorozati: serial
sorrend: order, sequence
sorszám: order number
sorszámozás: line numbering
sorvezetők: ink lines
sötét: dark
sötétpiros: dark red
spirálfűzés: spiral binding
spirálkötés: spiral binding
spriccelt: sprinkled
sraffírozás: hatching
sraffírozott: hatched
standard kiadás: standard edition
stb. *see* és a többi
stencil: stencil
stornirozva: canceled
sürgős: urgent
sűrűn: frequently
sz. *see* szám
szabad: free
szabadlapos: loose-leaf

szabálytalan: irregular
szabvány: standard
szaggatott: broken
szaggatott vonalak: broken lines
szakadás(ok): tear(s)
szakadt: torn, broken
szakértő: expert
szakítás(ok): break(s)
szakított: torn
szalag(ok): ribbon(s), tie(s)
szalagcím: running title
szalagfonatos: interlaced
szalagminta: strip pattern
szállítás: shipping
szállítási tartály: container
szállítmány: shipment
szám(ok): issue(s), number(s)
szamárfül: dog-ear
szamárfüles: dog-eared
számla: bill, invoice
számos: numerous
számos ábrával: with numerous
   illustrations
számoz. *see* számozott
számozás: numbering
számozatlan lap(ok): unnumbered
   leaf(ves)
számozott: numbered
számozott kiadás: bibliophile
   edition
számozott kópia(ák): numbered
   copy(ies)
számozott lap(ok): numbered
   leaf(ves)
számozott példányszámú kiadás:
   limited edition
számozva: numbered
számtalan: innumerable
szarvasbőr: buckskin
szarvasbőr kötés: suede binding
szatén: satin
szatinálás: calendering
szatinozott: calendered
szattyánbőr: morocco
száz: one hundred
század(ok): century(ies)
századik: one hundredth

százados: centennial
szedéstükör: layout
szegély(ek): border(s)
szegélydísz(ek): ornamental
   border(s)
szegélyezett: bordered
szegélyléc: border, frame
szegény: poor
szekvencia: sequence
szél(ek): edge(s), margin(s)
széles: wide
szélesség: width
széljegyzet(ek): marginal note(s)
szemben lévő: opposite
szemcsézés: graining
szemcsézett: pebbled
személyazonosság: identification
személyi példány: personal copy
szemle: review
szennycím: half title
szennycímlap: half-title page
szennylap: half-title page
szép: beautiful, handsome
szépia: sepia
szépirodalom: belles lettres
széria: series
szériacím: series title
szerint: according to
szerk. *see* szerkesztő
szerkesztés: editing
szerkesztő: editor
szerkesztőség: editorial office
szerző: author
szerző aláírásával: signed by the
   author, autographed
szerző neve nélkül: without
   author's name
szerzői jog: copyright
szerzői kézirat: author's manuscript
szerzői mutató: author index
szerzői példány: author's copy
szerzők névjegyzéke: author index
szerzőség: authorship
széteső: brittle
szétfeslett: unstitched
szétszakított: torn up

szétszedett: disjointed
szétválasztott: unglued
szignatúra: signature
szignet: printer's or publisher's
　device
szíj: leather tie
szín: color, tint
színes: colored
színes illusztráció(k): color illus-
　tration(s)
színes kép: color plate
színes litográfia(k): color litho-
　graph(s), lithography
színes margók: colored edges
színes nyomás: colored print
színes tábla(ák): color plate(s)
színezés: coloring
színezett: colored, tinted
színező: coloring
színnyomás: color printing
szinopszis: synopsis
szinoptikus: synoptic
színtelen: corner(s)
szöglet(ek): corner(s)
szójegyzék(ek): glossary(ies)
szóköztöltő(k): gap(s)
szólam(ok): part(s)
szőlőlevél: vine leaf
szóródás: scattering
szórólap: flyer
szórványszámok: single copies
szószedet(ek): glossary(ies)
szótár(ak): dictionary(ies), lexi-
　con(s)
szőtt: woven
szöveg: text
szöveg közti: in the text
szövegen belül: within the text
szöveggyűjtemény: anthology
szöveghely: text area
szöveghiány: loss of text
szövegközi ábra(ák): text illus-
　tration(s)
szövegközi illusztráció(k): figure(s)
　in text
szövegközi kép(ek): inset(s)
szövegközi térkép: inset map

szövegközti: in the text
szövegveszteség: loss of text
sztereotípia: stereotyping
szúette: worm-eaten
szükségessétett: indicated, required
szúrágás(ok): wormhole(s)
szürke: gray

t. see tábla
tábla(k): plate(s), cover(s)
táblázat(ok): table(s)
tag: member
tagság: membership
tájékoztatás: information
tankönyv(ek): textbook(s)
tanúk: witnesses
tanúkkal: with witnesses
tanulmány(ok): study(ies), essay(s)
tapéta: facing paper
tárgymutató: index, subject index
tárgyszó: keyword, subject
társ. see társaság
társadalom: society
társaság: association, company
társszerző: coauthor, joint author
tart. see tartalmaz, tartalom
tartalmaz: contains
tartalmazó: comprising
tartalmi kivonat: abstract, sum-
　mary
tartalmi összefoglalás: résumé,
　summary
tartalom: contents
tartalomjegyzék: table of contents
tartalommutató: index
tartályban: in container
tavasz: Spring
távolabbi: further
technikai: technical
téglalap alakú: oblong
téka: portfolio
tél: Winter
tele: full
teli: full
teljes: complete, full
teljes kiadás: complete edition

teljes szöveg: full text, unexpurgated text
teljesen: entirely
teljesen átdolgozott: entirely
revised
terjesztés: distribution
terjeszti: distributed by
térk. *see* térkép
térkép(ek): chart(s), map(s)
térképészet: cartography
térképvázlat(ok): sketch map(s)
természetes: natural
tétel(ek): item(s)
tetszés szerinti: optional
tévedés(ek): error(s), mistake(s)
textus: text
tezaurusz: thesaurus
tézis(ek): thesis(es)
tiltott: prohibited
tinta: ink
tintafolt(ok): ink stain(s)
tintafoltos: ink-stained
tipográfia: typography
tiszta: clean, spotless, blank
tisztarongypapír: pure rag paper
tisztátlan nyomás: mackle
tisztázat: fair copy
tiszteletpéldány: presentation copy,
review copy
titkos kiadás: clandestine publication
tíz: ten
tizedik: tenth
tizenegy: eleven
tizenegyedik: eleventh
tizenharmadik: thirteenth
tizenhárom: thirteen
tizenhat: sixteen
tizenhatodik: sixteenth
tizenhét: seventeen
tizenhetedik: seventeenth
tizenkettedik: twelfth
tizenkettedrét: duodecimo
tizenkettő: twelve
tizenkilenc: nineteen
tizenkilencedik: nineteenth
tizennégy: fourteen

tizennegyedik: fourteenth
tizennyolc: eighteen
tizennyolcadik: eighteenth
tizenöt: fifteen
tizenötödik: fifteenth
több: several
több kommentátor magyarázatával:
variorum
több mint: more than
több nem jelent meg: no more
published
többféle: several
többkötetes: multivolume
többnyelvű: multilingual
többnyire: mostly
többszínű: multicolored
többszörözés(ek): reproduction(s)
tok: box, case
tökéletesen: perfectly
tökéletlenség: imperfection
-tól, -től: from
toldalék(ok): appendix(es)
toll: pen
tollrajz(ok): pen and ink draw-
ing(s)
tönkrement: worn out
tópszínű: taupe
tördelt levonat: page proof
töredék(ek): fragment(s)
töredékes: fragmentary
töredezett: crumbled
törlés: erasure
töröl: efface
törölve: effaced
további: additional
továbbított: forwarded
tragédia: tragedy
traktátum: tract
transzlátor: translator
transzponál: transposed
transzponálás: transposition
trébelt: chased
tud. *see* tudományos
tudás: knowledge
tudományos: scientific
tudós társaság: learned society
tükrösítés: calendering

tulajdonbélyegző: property stamp
tulajdonos jele: ownership mark
tulajdonosított: attributed to
túlméret: oversize
tündérmese: fairy tale

ú.f. *see* új folyam
ügyes: skillful
ügyesen: ably, skillfully
új: new
új fedélbe köt: rebind, recase
új folyam: new series
új gerinccel ellátott: rebacked
új kiadás: new edition
új lenyomat: reissue, reprint
új megjelenés: new edition
új széria: new series
újabb: newer
újból megjelent: republished
újdonság: novelty
ujjnyomok: fingermarked
újonnan: as new
újonnan megjelent(ek): recent
   publication(s)
újra kinyomtat: reprint
újraenyvezett: reglued
újraköt: rebind, recase
újrakötött: rebound, recased
újranyomás: reimpression, reprint
újraöntés: recast
újság: gazette, newspaper
újságpapír: pulp
unciális(ok): uncial letter(s)
uniformizál: render uniform
unikum: unique item
ünnepi kiadvány: special issue,
   special number
üres lap(ok): blank leaf(ves)
üres oldal(ak): blank page(s)
üres tábla(k): blank cover(s)
után: after
utánnyomás: reissue, reprint
utánnyomás alatt: being reprinted
utánrendelés: reorder
utánzat: imitation
útikalaúz(ok): guidebook(s)
utóbbi: latter

utóhang: epilogue
utóirat: postscript
utolsó: last
utolsó előtti: next to last, penultimate
utószó: epilogue
ütött-kopott: bruised, injured
üzletkötés: bargain, deal

v. *see* vászon
v.ö. *see* vesd össze
vág: cut
vágatlan példány: untrimmed copy
vákát: blank
vaknyomás: blind stamping, tooling
vál. *see* válogatás, válogatott
-val, -vel: with
valódi: genuine
válogatás(ok): chrestomathy,
   selection(s)
válogatott: selected
válogatott művek: selected works
vált. *see* változat, változott
változat: version
változatlan: unchanged
változatos: variegated
változott: changed
változott cím: changed title
változtatás(ok): change(s)
változtatott: changed
valuta: foreign exchange
vámmentes: duty-free
variáns(ok): variant(s)
vásárlás: purchase
vastag: coarse, thick
vastag betű: boldface type
vastagság: thickness
vászon: cloth, linen
vászonkötés: cloth binding
vászonpapír: linen paper
vázlat(ok): sketch(es)
védőboríték: protective cover
védőborítékban: in covers
védőtok: box, case
végdarab: endpiece
vége: end

végén: at the end
végleges kiadás: definitive edition
végszó: postface
vegyes művek: miscellanies
vékony: thin
velinpapír: vellum paper
verdefényű: mint copy, in mint
  condition
veret(ek): joint(s)
versgyűjtemény: anthology of
  poems
verzál(ok): capital(s), uppercase
  letter(s)
verzó: verso
verzón: on the verso
vesd össze: see, compare
véset(ek): print(s), engraving(s)
vésett: engraved
vésnök(ok): engraver(s)
veszteség: loss
vétel: purchase
vételár: purchase price
vezérfonal: guidebook
vezérszó: keyword
vezetéknév: surname
vezető: guide
vígjáték(ok): comedy(ies)
vignetta(ák): vignette(s)
világos: clear, light, light colored
világoskék: light blue
virágdíszítmény: floral stamping
virágminta: floral ornament
virágos: flowered
visszamaradt példányok: remainders
vízfolt(ok): water stain(s)
vízfoltos: water-stained
vízjegy(ek): watermark(s)
vízjel(ek): watermark(s)
víznyomási vonalak: chain lines
volt-könyvtár példány: former
  library copy
vonal(ak): line(s)
vonalas: lined

vonalas ábra(ák): line drawing(s)
vonalas klisé(k): line engraving(s)
vonalas maratás: line etching
vonalas minta: line pattern
vonalazott: ruled
vonaldísz(ek): fillet(s)
vonalkázás: hatching
vonalkázott: hatched
vonalzott: lined, ruled
vonatkozólag: concerning
vörös: red
vörösesbarna: reddish brown
vörösréz: copper
vörössel kiemelt: rubricated

xerográfia: xerography

zárócím: colophon
záródísz: tailpiece
zárólap: endleaf
záróléc: cul-de-lampe
zárószó: epilogue
zárószöveg: colophon
záróvignetta: tailpiece
zárszó: epilog
zárt könyvtok: closed slipcase
zene: music
zeneszerző: composer
zergebőr: chamois skin
zöld: green
zöldes: greenish
zsanér(ok): hinge(s)
zseb: pocket
zsebatlasz: pocket atlas
zsebkiadás: pocket edition
zsebkönyv: pocketbook
zsebméretű: pocket-size
zsebszótár: pocket dictionary
zsineg(ek): tie(s)
zsineggel: with ties
zsírfolt(ok): grease spot(s)
zsírfoltos: grease-spotted
zsolozsmáskönyv: book of hours,
  breviary

Italian

a. *see* autore
a carico di: at the expense of
a colori: in colors
a contanti: cash
a cordoni: with bands
a cura di: edited by
a doppia col. *see* a doppia colonna
a doppia colonna: double column
a doppia facciata: double page
a doppia pagina: double page
a due colori: in two colors
a f. chiusi *see* a fogli chiusi
a fianco: alongside
a fogli chiusi: uncut
a fogli dispari: leaves of varying
  size
a fogli disuguali: on leaves of
  variable size
a fogli sciolti: loose leaves
a freddo: blind tooling
a fronte: opposite
a grana lunga: straight-grained
a grandi margini: with wide
  margins
a lapis: in pencil
a larga fascia: with wide bands
a lunga grana: long-grained
a mano: by hand
a matita: in pencil
a mezza pagina: half-page
a nervi: with raised bands
a nuovo: newly
a.p.pag. *see* a piena pagina
a penna: in pen
a piccoli ferri: tooled in small
  designs

a piena pagina: full-page
a pieni margini: with full margins
a richiesta: upon request
a secco: blind tooling
a specchio: mirror-finish
a spese dell'autore: at the author's
  expense
a spese dell'editore: at the
  publisher's expense
a spirale: spiral
a tergo: on the back
a tirat. limitata *see* a tiratura
  limitata
a tiratura limitata: in a limited
  edition
a tiratura ultimata: when the
  printing was completed, upon
  completion of publication
abb. *see* abbonamento
abbastanza: rather, sufficiently
abbinati: together
abbon. *see* abbonamento
abbonam. *see* abbonamento
abbonamento: subscription
abbonamento annuo: annual
  subscription
abbreviatura(e): abbreviation(s)
abbreviazione(i): abbreviation(s)
abbrunito: browned
abile: able, skillful
abilissimo: most skillful
abilmente: ably
abrasionato: abraded
abrasione(i): abrasion(s)
acc. *see* accresciuto
acciaio: steel

accomodato: mended, repaired
accresc. *see* accresciuto
accresciuto: enlarged
accuratezza: accuracy
accuratissima: most accurate
acquaforte: etching
acquatinta: aquatint
acquerellato: watercolored
acquerello: watercolor
adattato: adapted
aderenza(e): adhesion(s)
adorno: decorated, adorned
agg. *see* aggiunte
aggiorn. *see* aggiornato
aggiornato: brought up to date, modernized
aggiunte: additions, addenda
aggiunto: added
al costo: at cost
al principio: at the front
al retro: on the back
al risguardo: in the lining, on the flyleaf
alcune: a few
alcune pagine unite: a few pages combined, a few pages stuck together
all'inizio: at the front
alla fine: at the end, at the back
alleg. *see* allegato
allegati: attached items
allegato: attached
allungato: elongated
almanacco: almanac
alone: halo
alone d'umido: halos of dampness
alquanto: somewhat
alt. *see* altezza
altezza: height
altrimente: otherwise
altrove: elsewhere
amatore: amateur
ampiamente: profusely
ampiamente postillate: fully annotated
ampio: ample, extensive, numerous, profuse

ampl. *see* ampliato
ampliato: enlarged
anastatico: anastatic
ancora: still, yet
ang. *see* angolo
angolo(i): corner(s)
ann. *see* annata, anno
annali: annals
annata: year
annate arretrate: back years
annerita: darkened
annesso(i): annex(es)
anno: year
annot. *see* annotazione
annotato: annotated
annotaz. *see* annotazione
annotazione(i): annotation(s)
annuale: annual
annuario: yearbook
annunzio: announcement
annuo: annual
anonimo: anonymous
ant. *see* anteriore, antico
anter. *see* anteriore
anteriore: front, anterior
antico: old
antip. *see* antiporta
antiporta: frontispiece
antologia: anthology
append. *see* appendice
appendice: appendix
applicato: applied, fastened to
appressato: brought together
arabeschi: arabesques
arancio: orange, orange-colored
arancione: orange-colored
archivio: archives
argentate: silvered
argento: silver
armi: arms
arretrate: retrospective
arricchito: enriched
aross. *see* arrossato
arrossato: with reddish spots
arrossature: reddish spots
arrotondato: rounded
asport. *see* asportato, asportazione

asportato: removed, taken away, gone
asportaz. _see_ asportazione
asportazione: removal, extirpation
ass. _see_ assicelle
assai: rather
assai distinta: quite distinctive
assi: boards
assicelle: boards
assicelle di legno: wood boards
ast. _see_ astuccio
astuccio: slipcase, box
atl. _see_ atlante
atlante: atlas
attaccato: attached
atti: transactions
attraente: attractive
attualità: timeliness, quality of being up to date
aum. _see_ aumentato
aumentato: enlarged, increased
aut. _see_ autografo
autobiografia: autobiography
autogr. _see_ autografo
autografo: autograph
autore: author
autoritratto: self-portrait
autorizzato: authorized
avanzata: advanced
avaria: damage
avorio: ivory
avvertimento: notice
azz. _see_ azzurro
azzurrigno: bluish
azzurrina: bluish
azzurro: blue

b. _see_ bianco, brossura
balacronpelle: a patented book cloth
banda: band, strip
barbe: witnesses
basso: lower
bastardi: bastard type
baz. _see_ bazzana
bazzana: sheepskin
becca(che): dog-ear(s)

bellezza: beauty
belliss. _see_ bellissimo
bellissimo: most beautiful
ben conservate: well-preserved
ben tenuto: well-kept
bianco: white, blank
bianconero: black and white
bibliofilo: bibliophile
bibliografia: bibliography
bibliografico: bibliographical
bibliot. _see_ biblioteca
biblioteca: library
bibliotecario: librarian
bicol. _see_ bicolore
bicolore: bicolored
bicr. _see_ bicromia
bicromia: bichrome
bimestrale: bimonthly
bindakote: a patented book cloth
biografia: biography
bislungo: oblong
blasone: blazon
blocco _see_ in blocco
blu: blue
bod. _see_ bodoniana
bodon. _see_ bodoniana
bodoniana: in the style of Bodoni
bollettino: bulletin
borchie: bosses, knobs
bordo: edge
bordura: border
bozzetto(i): sketch(es)
br. _see_ brossura
bradel: bradel, a cased binding
brano(i): fragment(s)
broccato: brocaded
bross. _see_ brossura
brossura: stitched; paper-cover binding
brossurato: stitched; in paper covers
bruciato: burned
bruciature: burned spots
brunito: burnished
brunitura(e): burnishing(s)
brutto: coarse
bucherello: little hole

buchetti di tarme: motheaten
busta: box, case
busta editoriale: publisher's box,
   publisher's slipcase

c. *see* carta, coperta
c.b. *see* carta bianca
c.s. *see* come sopra
ca. *see* carta
cad. *see* cadauno
cadauno: each
calce *see* in calce
calcografia: brass engraving
calico: calico
calligrafato: calligraphed,
   elegantly handwritten
calligrafia: fine handwriting
calligraficamente: in fine
   handwriting
camicia(e): wrapper(s)
camicia cartoncino: thin board
   wrapper
cancellato: canceled, crossed out
cancellatura(e): canceled,
   crossed-out area(s), erasure(s)
canzoniere: songbook
capil. *see* capilettera
capilett. *see* capilettera
capilettera(e): initial letter(s)
capit. *see* capitolo
capitale(i): capital letter(s)
capitello: headband
capitolo(i): chapter(s)
capolavoro: masterpiece
car. *see* carattere
caratt. *see* carattere
carattere: letters, type
carattere corsivo: cursive type,
   italics
carattere grecia: Greek type
carattere rom. *see* carattere romano
carattere romano: roman type
carattere rotondo: roman type
carattere tondo: roman type
caric. *see* caricatura
caricatura(e): caricature(s)
cart. *see* cartonato, cartone

carta: paper, map
carta a mano: handmade paper
carta bianca: blank page
carta bibbia: Bible paper
carta forte: heavy paper
carta greve: coarse paper
carta india: India paper
carta lucida: glazed paper
carta patinata: coated paper
carta pesante: heavy paper
carta topografica: topographic map
carta uso-mano: handmade paper
carta vergata: laid paper
carte: pages
carte non numerate: unnumbered
   pages
carte vedute: pictorial illustrations
cartella: portfolio; label, cartouche
cartellino: label
cartiglio: small map
cartina: small map
cartografia: cartography
carton. *see* cartonato, cartonatura
carton. editor. *see* cartonatura
   editoriale
cartonnagio: board binding,
   boards
cartonato: bound in boards
cartonatura: board binding
cartonatura editoriale: publisher's
   board binding
cartonc. *see* cartoncino
cartoncino: thin cardboard
cartone: cardboard; bound in
   boards
cattivo: bad
cc. *see* carte
ccnn. *see* carte non numerate
celebre: celebrated, notable
cellofan: cellophane
censura: censorship
censurato: censored
centesimo: hundredth
centinaia: hundreds
cento: hundred
centro: center
cerchiette: circles

cerniera: joint, hinge
certam. *see* certamente
certamente: certainly
cesell. *see* cesellato
cesellato: chiseled, goffered
chiarezza: clarity, clearness
chiarissimo: very clear
chiaro: clear
chiaroscuro: chiaroscuro
chiave: key
chiodo: nail
chiosa: gloss
chiuso: closed, uncut
chiusura(e): catch(es), clasp(s)
ciasc. *see* ciascuno
ciascuno: each
ciclostilato: duplicated
cimelio: relic
cinquanta: fifty
cinquantesimo: fiftieth
cinque: five
circondato: surrounded by
cit. *see* citato
citato: cited
citazione(i): citation(s)
clandestino: clandestine
co-autore: coautor
codice: codex
coeva: coeval
coevo: contemporary
cofanetto: box, case, casket
col. *see* colore
collana: series
collaz. *see* collazione
collazione: collation
collez. *see* collezione
collezione: collection
colonna(e): column(s)
color. *see* colorato
color avana: Havana-brown
colorato: colored
colore: color
colorito: coloring, colored
coloritura: coloring
come nuovo: like new
come sopra: as above
comm. *see* commercio

commentato: commented
commercio: trade
committente: purchaser
compartimento(i): section(s), panel(s)
compendio: compendium
compilato: compiled
compilatore: compiler
compilazione: compilation
compiuto: complete, perfect
compl. *see* complessivo, completo
compless. *see* complessivo
complessivo: including, inclusive
complesso: set, group
completo: complete
composto a mano: set by hand
compr. *see* compreso
comprende: comprises, including
compreso: including
comune: ordinary
con: with
con barbe: with witnesses
con cord. *see* con cordoni
con cordoni: with bands
concordanza: concordance
cond. *see* condizione
condiz. *see* condizione
condizione: condition
confezione: makeup, production
connaturata: typical
conosciuto: known
cons. *see* conservato, conservazione
conserv. *see* conservazione
conservato: in good condition, well-preserved
conservaz. *see* conservazione
conservazione: state of preservation, condition
consunto: worn out, consumed
contemp. *see* contemporaneo
contemporaneo: contemporary
contenuto: contents
contin. *see* continuo
continuazione: continuation
continuo: continuous
conto: account
contornato: outlined, encircled

contorno: outline, frame
contraff. *see* contraffazione
contraffazione: pirated edition,
  counterfeit
cop. *see* coperta, copertina
cop. fitt. *see* coperta fittizia
cop. muta *see* coperta muta
cop. post. *see* coperta posticcia
coperchio: cover
copert. *see* copertina
coperta: covered, cover
coperta fittizia: an imitation book
  cover
coperta muta: plain cover
coperta posticcia: an imitation
  book cover
copertina: cover
copertina busta: envelope cover
copertina muta: blank cover
copia: copy
copia da prova: proof copy
copie numerate: numbered copies
copioso: copious
cord. *see* cordoni
cordonato: with bands
cordoncini: small, thin bands
cordoni: bands
corn. *see* cornice
cornice: border
corr. *see* corretto
corred. *see* corredato
corredato: furnished with
correttezza: correctness
corretto: corrected
correzzione(i): correction(s),
  amendment(s)
corros. *see* corrosione
corrosione(i): chafing
corrosioni d'umido: marks of
  dampness
corroso: eaten, corroded
cors. *see* corsivo
corsivo: cursive, italic
corso: course
corto: short
corto di margine: narrow margins
costa: side, edge

costola: spine
cp. *see* copertina
cremisi: crimson
crestomazia: anthology
crom. *see* cromolitografia
cromolitografia: chromo-
  lithography
cromolitografiche: chromo-
  lithographic
cromotipografia: chromo-
  typography
cronica(che): chronicle(s)
cros. *see* crostoso
crostoso: rough-grained
cuciti spostati: sewing irregular
cucitura: sewing, stitching
cuffia(e): rolled edge(s) at top or
  bottom of spine
cuoio: leather
cuoio di Russia: Russian leather
cupo: dark
cura *see* a cura di
curato: edited
curatore: editor
curioso: unusual
cust. *see* custodia
custod. *see* custodia
custodia: slipcase
custodia editoriale: publisher's
  slipcase

d. *see* dorso
da rilegare: needing binding
da riparare: needing repairs
da tempo: long since
danneggiato: damaged
danno: damage
data: date
dattilografato: typewritten
dattiloscritto: typewritten
debole: weak
dec. *see* decorazione
decimo: tenth
decor. *see* decorazione
decoratissimo: profusely decorated
decorato: decorated
decorazione: decoration

ded. *see* dedica
ded. aut. *see* dedica autografa
dedica: dedication, dedicatory note
dedica autografa: autograph, dedicatory note
definitivo: definitive
del rimanente: for the remainder
del tempo: of the time, contemporary
delizioso: delightful
dell'epoca: of the time
dentellature: lace patterns
dentelle: dentelle
descr. *see* descrizione
descritto: described
descrizione: description
destro: right-hand
deterior. *see* deteriorato
deteriorato: deteriorated
dettagliato: detailed
deturpato: stained, spoiled, damaged
di cui: of which
di gran lusso: very luxurious
di lusso: deluxe
di pregio: prized
di prossima pubblicazione: to be published soon
diagramma(i): diagram(s)
diario: diary; daily journal
diciannove: nineteen
diciannovesimo: nineteenth
diciasette: seventeen
diciasettesimo: seventeenth
diciottesimo: eighteenth
diciotto: eighteen
dicitura(e): wording
dieci: ten
difetto: defect
difettoso: defective
diffuse: scattered
dim. *see* dimensione, diminutivo
dimens. *see* dimensione
dimensione(i): dimension(s)
diminutivo: very small
dipinto: depicted, represented, painted

diritti d'autore: author's rights
dis. *see* disegnato, disegno
discreto: fair, moderate
disegnato: designed, drawn
disegno: design, drawing
dispari: disparate; odd, odd-numbered
dispensa: quire, part
disponibile: available
disponimo: we have available
dissertazione: dissertation
dist. *see* distinto
distinto: special, outstanding
diverso: varied
documentazione: documentation
documento(i): document(s)
dodicesimo: twelfth
dodici: twelve
domanda: demand, request
doppio: double
dor. *see* dorato
dorato: gilt
doratura(e): gilt design(s), gilding
dorso: back, spine
dovizia: abundance
due: two
duplice: double

ecc. *see* eccetera, eccezionale
eccess. *see* eccessivo
eccessivo: excessive
eccetera: et cetera
eccetto: except
eccezionale: exceptional
ed. *see* edito
ed. limit. *see* edizione limitata
ed. non ven. *see* edizione non venale
edit. *see* editore, editoriale
edito: edited, published
editor. *see* editoriale
editore: editor, publisher
editoriale: publisher's, editorial
ediz. *see* edizione
ediz. distinta *see* edizione distinta
ediz.f.c. *see* edizione fuori commercio

edizioncina: small edition
edizione: edition
edizione definitiva: definitive
 edition
edizione distinta: outstanding
 publication
edizione fuori commercio: private
 edition, not for sale
edizione limitata: limited edition
edizione non venale: edition not
 for sale
edizione principe: first edition,
 editio princeps
effige: effigy
eleganza: elegance
elenco: list
elettrofotolito: photolithographic
eliografiche: heliographic
eliogravure: photoengraving
eliotip. *see* eliotipia
eliotipia: phototype
emendato: amended, emended
entrambi: together, both
entro: in, within
ep. *see* epoca
epigrafe: epigraph
epoca: time, of the time
erroneam. *see* erroneamente
erroneamente: erroneously
errore: error
es. *see* esemplare
esattamente: exactly
esaur. *see* esaurito
esauriente: becoming scarce
esauritissimo: extremely hard to
 find
esaurito: exhausted, out of print
escluso: excluding, except for
escoriazione: excoriation
eseguito: executed, carried out
esemp. *see* esemplare
esempl. *see* esemplare
esemplare: copy
eserc. *see* esercizio
esercizio: exercise
esplicativo: explanatory
esposti: explanatory, expository

est. *see* esterno
esternamente: externally
esterno: externa, exterior
estero: foreign, abroad
estratto: extract, reprint;
 extracted
estremamente: extremely
etichetta: label
ex-libris: bookplate
ex possessore: former owner

f.c. *see* fuori commercio
f.c.o. *see* fuori commercio originale
f.comm. *see* fuori commercio
f.t. *see* fuori testo
facciata: page, face
facsim. *see* facsimile
facsimilato: done in facsimile
facsimile: facsimile
fallo: fault
fasc. *see* fascicolo
fascic. *see* fascicolo
fascicolo(i): fascicule(s), part(s)
fascio: fasces, a sheaf
fastosamente: ostentatiously,
 magnificently
faticato: worn, worked over
fattura: craftsmanship,
 workmanship
fcs. *see* facsimile
fedele: faithful
fedelissimo: extremely faithful
fenditura: break
fermagli: clasps, ties
ferro(i): tool(s)
fianco: side
fig. *see* figura, figurato
figg. *see* figure
figur. *see* figurato
figura: figure, illustration
figurato: decorated with designs
figure: figures, illustrations
fil. *see* filetto
filettatura(e): line pattern(s),
 border(s)
filetto(i): line(s), fillet(s)
fili: line patterns

filigrana: watermark
filigranato: watermarked
final. *see* finalino
finale: tailpiece
finaletto: tailpiece
finalino: tailpiece
finem. *see* finemente
finemente: beautifully
finora: hitherto, so far, up to now
finto: imitation
fior. *see* fioriture
fiordaliso: fleur-de-lys
fiorellini: small floral designs
fioretti: floral designs
fiorit. *see* fioriture
fiorito: flowered
fioriture: flowered designs
fioroni: large floral designs
firma: signature
firma di propr. *see* firma di
   proprietà
firma di proprietà: ownership,
   signature
firmato: signed
fitt. *see* fittizio
fittizio: artificial, fictitious
fless. *see* flessibile
flessibile: flexible
floreali: floral
foder. *see* foderato
fodera: lining, doublure
foderato: lined
foderato tela a cofanetto: covered,
   lined with cloth
fogli chiusi *see* a fogli chiusi
fogli di guardia: end papers
fogliame: scrollwork, resembling
   foliage
foglietto: small leaf, sheet
foglio: sheet, leaf
foglio volante: broadside
fondo: end, background
forature di tarlo: wormholes
forellini di tarlo: wormholes
fori di chiodo: nail holes
fori di tarlo: wormholes
form. *see* formato

formato: format
forse: perhaps, possibly
forte: strong
fossa: hole
fotocalcografia: photoengraving
fotogr. *see* fotografia, fotografico
fotografia: photograph,
   photography
fotografico: photographic
fotoincisione: photoengraving
fotolito: photolith
fotolitografia: photolithography
fotoriprod. *see* fotoriproduzione
fotoriproduzione: photorepro-
   duction
fototipia: phototype
fr. *see* fregi, frontispizio
frammento: fragment
franco: shipping costs paid,
   postpaid
franco di porto: shipping costs
   paid, postpaid
freddo *see* a freddo
fregi: ornaments, decorations
fregiato: decorated
freschezza: freshness
freschissimo: very fresh, clean
fresco: fresh, clean
front. *see* frontispizio
frontispizio: frontispiece
fulvo: fawn-colored, tawny
fuori comm. *see* fuori commercio
fuori commercio: not for sale
fuori commercio originale:
   originally not for sale
fuori numerazione: unnumbered
fuori testo: not in the text
fustagno: fustian, a coarse cloth

gazzetta: gazette
genuino: genuine
geogr. *see* geografico
geografico: geographic
gia: already
giallo: yellow
giallognolo: yellowish

giansenista: Jansenist, a plain
  binding
gioiello: jewel
giornale: daily
glossa: gloss
glossario: glossary
goffrato: goffered
gora(e) d'acqua: water stain(s)
gora(e) d'umido: damp stain(s)
got. *see* gotico
gotico: gothic
gr. *see* grande
graf. *see* grafico
graffi: scratches
graffiato: scratched
graffiatura(e): scratch(es)
graffio: scratch
grafico: graphic illustration, chart
grana: grain, texture
grana lunga: straight-grained
grana schiacciata: crushed grain
granato: grained
grande: large
grandezza: size
grasso: fat, thick
graz. *see* grazioso
graziosissimo: very pleasing
grazioso: pleasing, gracious
greve: serious, seriously
grezzo: raw
grigio: gray
grossis. *see* grossissimo
grossiss. *see* grossissimo
grossissimo: extremely large, thick
grosso: thick
grossolanamente: coarsely, roughly
guarnizione(i): decoration(s)
guasti: tears, damaged parts
guasti d'umido: water damage
guasto: torn, damaged
guazzo: gouache
gustosissimo: most highly pleasing

iconografia: iconography
ignorato: unknown
ignoto: unknown
ill. *see* illustrato, illustrazione

illegible: illegible
illustr. *see* illustrato, illustrazione
illustratissimo: profusely illustrated
illustrato: illustrated
illustratore: illustrator
illustrazione(i): illustration(s)
imballo: packing
imitlin: a patented book cloth
immacolato: immaculate
imminente: imminent
immune da: free of
imp. *see* impressioni
impag. *see* impaginazione
impaginazione: layout
impastato: pasted up, mounted
imperfezione: imperfection
impostazione: setup, arrangement
impr. *see* impressioni
imprecisato: undetermined
impress. *see* impressioni
impressioni: stamping, tooling
impressioni a freddo: blind tooling
impressioni in oro: gold tooling
impresso: blind-tooled
impreziosito: enhanced
in alto: at the top
in b.n. *see* in bianco e nero
in b.n. e a col. *see* in bianco nero
  e a colori
in bianco e nero: in black and
  white
in bianco nero e a colori: in black
  and white and in colors
in blocco: as a lot
in calce: at the foot of the page
in carta vergata: in laid paper
in certella: in portfolio
in ciclostile: duplicated
in corso di stampa: in press
in disordine: in disorder
in fine: at the end
in fogli: in sheets
in fogli sciolti: in loose sheets
in-Fol. *see* in-Folio
in-Folio: folio format, folio
in litografia: lithographed
in n. e col. *see* in nero e colori

in nero e colori: in black and colors
in oro zecchino: in pure gold
in parte: partly
in plano: in sheets
in pochissime copie: in very few
   copies
in preparazione: in preparation
in princ. *see* in principio
in principio: at the beginning
in regalo: as a gift
in ristampa: being reprinted
in rotocalco: in rotogravure
in sanguigna: in red
in scatola: in container
in sicofoil: in sicofoil, a patented
   book cloth
in simile pelle: in imitation leather
in tela: in cloth
in vendita: for sale
in viaggio: now on the way
inc. *see* incisione, inciso
incartonato: bound in boards
incatenato: chained
incc. *see* incisioni
inchiostro: ink
incis. *see* incisione, inciso
incisione: engraving
incisioni: engravings
inciso: engraved, cut in
incisore: engraver
incoll. *see* incollato
incollato: pasted in, mounted
incompiuto: incomplete, imperfect
incorn. *see* incorniciato
incornic. *see* incorniciato
incorniciare: to frame
incorniciato: framed
incunabulo(i): incunabulum(a)
indice: index, table of contents
indivisibili: not sold separately
ined. *see* inedito
inedito: unpublished
inesistente: nonexistent
inf. *see* inferiore
infer. *see* inferiore
inferiore: lower, bottom
ing. *see* ingiallito, ingialliture

ingiall. *see* ingiallito, ingialliture
ingiallimento: yellowing
ingiallito: yellowed, foxed
ingialliture: marks of foxing
iniz. *see* iniziale
iniziale(i): initial(s), initial letter(s)
inquadrato: framed, bordered
inquadratura: frame, border
ins. *see* insegna
inscrizione: inscription
insegna: mark
insegna del tipografo: printer's
   mark
insegna tipografica: printer's mark
insepar. *see* inseparabili
inseparabili: inseparable, not sold
   separately
inserito: inserted
inserti pubblicitari: advertising
   inserts
inservibile: unusable
insieme: together
insignif. *see* insignificante
insignificante: insignificant
int. *see* interno, intonso
intagliato: cut, carved, engraved
intaglio: engraving
intarsi: inlay, inlaid work
intarsio: inlay, marquetry
intatto: intact
integralmente: integrally
integro: integral
interamente: entirely, completely
interc. *see* intercalato
intercalato: intercalated, inserted
interess. *see* interessante
interessante: interesting
interfogliato: interleaved
interiore: inner, interior
internam. *see* internamente
internamente: internally
interno: internal
intonso: untrimmed, uncut
intrecci: interlacing
introd. *see* introduzione
introduttivo: introductory
introduzione: introduction

introvabile: impossible to find
invece: on the other hand
inversione: inversion
invertito: transposed
invio: forward
irregolarità: irregularity
iscr. *see* iscrizione
iscrizione: inscription
iscurito: darkened, obscured
istoriato: historiated, illuminated
ivi: joined
ivi accluso: enclosed
ivi incluso: included

laccato: lacquered
lacci: ties
lacer. *see* lacerazione
lacerato: torn
lacerazione(i): tear(s)
lacuna: lack, gap
lacunosa: full of gaps, with many
  gaps
lapis: pencil
largh. *see* larghezza
larghezza: width
larghiss. *see* larghissimo
larghissimo: very wide
largo: wide
lato: side
lavabile: washable
lavato: cleaned, washed
lavoraz. *see* lavorazione
lavorazione: craftsmanship
lavoro: work
leda: damage
ledente: damaging
ledibili: damaging
leg. *see* legato, legatura
leg. com. *see* legatura comune
leg. d'amatore *see* legatura
  d'amatore
legacci: fastenings, ties
legacci di chiusura: ties
legat. *see* legatura
legat. editoriale *see* legatura
  editoriale
legato: bound

legatore: binder
legatoria: bindery
legatura: binding
legatura a spirale: spiral binding
legatura comune: ordinary binding
legatura d'amatore: three-quarter
  binding
legatura editoriale: publisher's
  binding
legatura epoca: binding of the
  time, contemporary binding
legatura uniforme: uniform binding
legg. *see* leggero
leggenda: legend
leggerissimo: very light, very
  slight
leggerm. *see* leggermente
leggermente: slightly
leggero: light, frivolous, slight
leggiadro: graceful
leggibile: legible
leggiero: light, frivolous, slight
legni: woodcut blocks
legno: wood
lembo: bit, end
les. *see* lesione
lesi: damaged
lesionare: injuring, to injure
lesione: injury
lesione di t. *see* lesione di testo
lesione di testo: damaged part
  of text
leso: damaged
lessico: lexicon
lett. *see* lettera
lettera(e): letter(s)
letterale: literal
levigato: published
libello: lampoon, pamphlet
libraio: bookseller
libreria: bookstore
libretto: little book
libro: book
libro di festa: holiday book
libro d'ore: book of hours
liev. *see* lievemente
lieve: light

lievem. *see* lievemente
lievemente: lightly, slightly
lieviss. *see* lievissimamente
lievissimamente: very lightly, very
  slightly
lim. *see* limitato
limitato: limited
linea: line
lino: linen
liscio: smooth, flat
listello(i): fillet(s)
listino: list
lit. *see* litografato, litografia
litografato: lithographed
litografia: lithography
litografico: lithographic
logoro: worn
lunghezza: length
luogo: place
lusso: luxe, deluxe
lussuoso: luxurious, costly

m. *see* marocchino, mezzo
m.p. *see* mezza pelle
m.pl. *see* mezza pelle
m.pr. *see* mezza pergamena
m. zigrino *see* mezzo zigrino
macc. *see* macchia
macch. *see* macchia
macchia: stain
macchiato: stained, soiled
macchiato d'acqua: stained by
  water
macchiato di grasso: stained by
  grease
macchie d'inchiostro: inkstains
macchie d'olio: oil stains
macchie d'umidità: damp stains
macchie d'umido: stains of
  humidity
macchie d'uso: stains of use
macchie di terriccio: stains of mold
macchietta: small stain, spot
macchiettato: spotted
macchiolina(e): small stain(s)
maggior parte: the majority
magistralmente: masterfully

mai: never
maiuscola: capital letter
malamente: badly
malandata: in bad condition
malgrado: in spite of
man. *see* manovrato
manc. *see* mancante
manca: lacks
mancante: lacking
mancanza: lack
manoscritto: manuscript
manovrato: worked by hand,
  handmade
manuale: handbook
mappa: map
mar. *see* marocchino
marca: mark
marchio: mark
marezzato: marbled
marg. *see* marginoso
margin. *see* marginale
marginale: marginal
marginalmente: marginally
margine(i): margin(s)
margine esterno: outer margin
margine interno: inner margin
marginosissimo: with very wide
  margins
marginoso: with wide margins
marm. *see* marmorizzato
marmor. *see* marmorizzato
marmoreggiature: marbling
marmoriz. *see* marmorizzato
marmorizzato: marbled
marmorizzature: marbling
marocch. *see* marocchino
marocchino: morocco
marrone: chestnut-colored
martellato: hammered
mass. *see* massimo
massimo: largest
mat. *see* matita
matita: pencil
medagl. *see* medaglione
medaglione: medallion
medesimo: same
medio: medium, average

mediocre: mediocre
mende: reparations
mensile: monthly
meraviglioso: marvelous, wonderful
merlett. *see* merlettatura
merlettatura: dentelle design
merletto: dentelle
metà: half
metallico: metallic
mezza: half
mezza bazzana: half sheepskin
mezza pelle: half leather
mezza pergamena: half vellum
mezza tela: half cloth
mezzo: half
mezzo zigrino: half shagreen
migliaia: thousands
migliorato: improved
mille: thousand
millimetri: millimeters
milskin: a patented book cloth
miniato: illuminated, engraved
miniatura: miniature
minuscolo: diminutive
minutissimo: extremely minute
mirabilmente: admirably
mis. *see* misura
miscellanea: miscellany
misura: measure
mm. *see* millimetri
modesto: modest
molle: flexible, soft
molte: many
molti: many
moltiss. *see* moltissimo
moltissimo(i): a great deal, a great
    number
molto: much, very
molto raro: very rare
monocromo: single color,
    monochrome
monogr. *see* monogramma
monografia: monograph
monogramma: monogram
monotipia: monotype
montabile a parte: detachable
montato: mounted, pasted up

montone: ram's skin
mosaicato: decorated in mosaic
motivo: motif, design
motto: coat of arms
ms. *see* manoscritto
muffa: mildew
muta: blank
mutilato: mutilated
mutilaz. *see* mutilazione
mutilazione: mutilation
mutilo: mutilated, cut
mz. *see* mezza

n. *see* nero, numerato
n.n. *see* non numerato
n.t. *see* nel testo
n.t. e f.t. *see* nel testo e fuori testo
nastro: ribbon
nel bianco: in the white part
nel complesso: on the whole, for
    the most part
nel testo: in the text
nel testo e fuori testo: in the text
    and outside the text
nero: black
nervetti: ribs
nervi: cords, raised bands
nervi esposti: raised bands
nervi piatti: flat bands
netto: net
nitidamente: clearly, elegantly
nitidezza: clarity, elegance
nitido: clean-cut, clear
nn. *see* non numerato
nocciola: nut-brown
nome: name
non autorizzato: unauthorized
non comune: uncommon, unusual
non distribuito: not sold
non intoccano: do not damage
non numerato: unnumbered
non più pubblicato: no longer
    published
non tagliato: pages uncut,
    unopened
non tocca: does not affect
non venale: not for sale

nono: ninth
nota(e): note(s)
notaz. *see* notazione
notazione(i): notation(s)
notev. *see* notevole
notevole: notable
notissimo: known, renowned
novanta: ninety
novantesimo: ninetieth
nove: nine
novità: novelty
num. *see* numerato, numerazione,
    numero, numeroso
numer. *see* numerato, numerazione,
    numero, numeroso
numerate irregolarmente:
    numbered irregularly
numerato: numbered
numeraz. *see* numerazione
numerazione: numbering
numerazione continua: continuous
    numbering
numero: number
numerosiss. *see* numerosissimo
numerosissimo: extremely
    numerous
numeroso: numerous
nuovo: new
nuvolato: cloudy

o. *see* originale, oro
obl. *see* oblungo
oblun. *see* oblungo
oblungo: oblong
occasione: secondhand, bargain
occh. *see* occhiello, occhietto
occhiello: half-title page
occhietto: half-title page
offset: offset
ogni: every
ognuno: each, each one
oliva: oliva
olona *see* tela olona
oltre: over, beyond
ombra d'umido: damp-stained
ombreggiato: shaded, hatched

ombreggiatura omogenea: even
    shading
ombreggiature: shading
onciale: uncial
op. *see* opera
opera: work
opusc. *see* opuscolo
opuscolo: booklet, **pamphlet**
or. *see* originale
ordinato: put in order, arranged
ordine: order
orig. *see* originale
origin. *see* originale
originale: original
originario: original
ormai: now
orn. *see* ornamentale, ornato
ornamentale: ornamental
ornamento: ornament
ornato: decorated
oro: gold, gilt
ott. *see* ottimo
ottanta: eighty
ottantesimo: eightieth
ottavo: eighth
ottimo: excellent, the best
otto: eight
ottocentesca: of the 18th century

p. *see* pelle, pergamena, pieno
p.p. *see* piena pelle
p.pag. *see* piena pagina
pag. *see* pagina
pag.b. *see* pagina bianca
pagg. *see* pagine
pagina: page
pagina bianca: blank page
paginatura: pagination
pagine: pages
pagine pubblicitarie: advertising
    pages
paglierino: pale, straw-colored
pallido: pale
paraffato: initialed
paraffinato: waxed
paraffo: paraph
paragrafo: paragraph

parecchie: several
parodia: parody
parte(i): part(s)
particolare: particular, special;
  private
parziale: partial
pastello: pastel
patin. *see* patinato
patinato: coated, coated paper
patito: damaged
pegamoide: imitation leather,
  leatherette
pelle: leather
pelle di scrofa: pigskin
pelle zigrino: shagreen
penna: pen
per il resto: for the rest
percalle: book cloth
perdita del testo: loss of text
perfett. *see* perfettamente
perfettamente: perfectly
perfettissimo: most perfect
perfetto: perfect
perg. *see* pergamena
pergam. *see* pergamena
pergamena: vellum
pergamenato: made to resemble
  vellum, resembling vellum
pergamenoide: imitation parchment, vellum
periodico: periodical
pesante: heavy
pezzo(i): piece(s)
piacevolissimo: most pleasing
piani: sides
pianta(e): plan(s), map(s)
piantina(e): map(s), plan(s),
  small plan(s)
piatto(i): side(s)
piatto anteriore: front cover
piatto posteriore: back cover
picc. *see* piccolo
piccolo: small
piè di pagina: foot of the page
pieg. *see* piegatile, piegato
piega: fold
piegatile: folding

piegato: folded
piegatura dispari: uneven folds
pieghevole: folding
piena pagina: full page
piena pelle: full leather
pieno: full
pieno zigrino: full shagreen
più: several; plus
più volte: several times
placca: plaque, medallion
placchetta: booklet, small
  medallion
plancha(e): plate(s)
planche a colori: color plates
plasticota: plastic-coated
plastificata: plasticized
plastificata a specchio: plasticized
  to glossy finish
pochi: few
poco conosciuto: little-known
poco esperto: inexpert
poderoso: strong
policromia: polychrome
policromo: polychrome
polveroso: dusty
popolare: popular
portafoglio: portfolio
portatile: portable
porto: carriage, shipping costs
posposto: postponed
post. *see* posteriore
poster. *see* posteriore
posteriore: back
posticc. *see* posticcio
posticcio: artificial, imitation
postillato: with marginal notes
postille: marginal notes
postumo: posthumous
pp. *see* pagine
pre-tiratura: prepublication
prefaz. *see* prefazione
prefazione: preface
preg. *see* pregiato
pregev. *see* pregevole
pregevole: esteemed, of fine quality
pregevolissimo: highly esteemed,
  praiseworthy

pregiatissimo: highly esteemed
pregiato: esteemed
prel. *see* preliminare
prelim. *see* preliminare
preliminare: preliminary
premiato: prizewinning
prenotazione: reservation
preziosità: high value
prezzi fissi: fixed prices
prezzo: price
prezzo complessivo: complete price
prezzo di listino: list price
prezzo di vendita: list price
prima ed. *see* prima edizione
prima edizione: first edition
primissimo: the very first
primo: first
principio *see* al principio, in
   principio
priva di legatura: without binding
privilegio: privilege
privo di: without
propr. *see* proprietà, proprietario
propriet. *see* proprietario
proprietà: ownership, property
proprietà letteraria: copyright
proprietario: owner
proscritto: proscribed
prospetto: prospectus; view
prospetto editoriale: publisher's
   announcement
prossimo: near, imminent
protez. *see* protezione
protezione: protection
prova: proof
proveniente: coming from
provenienza: provenance, source
pseudonimo: pseudonym
pubbl. *see* pubblicato,
   pubblicazione
pubblic.f.c. *see* pubblicato fuori
   commercio
pubblicato: published
pubblicato fuori commercio: published privately, not for sale
pubblicazione: publication
pulito: clean

punta secca: drypoint
puntata: fascicle, part
puntato: etched
punte: corners
punte di tarli: wormholes
punteggiato: stippled
puntesecche: drypoint
pure: also
purgato: purged, censored

q. *see* qualche
qq. *see* qualche
quà e là: here and there
quaderno: quire
quadrante: cover
quadrato: square
quadratura: frame
quadrimestrale: quarterly
quadro: picture
qualche: a few
qualità: quality
quaranta: forty
quarantesimo: fortieth
quartino: four-page signature
quarto: fourth
quasi: almost, nearly
quattordicesimo: fourteenth
quattordici: fourteen
quattro: four
quindicesimo: fifteenth
quindici: fifteen
quindicinale: fortnightly
quinto: fifth
quotidiano: daily

racc. *see* raccolta
racchiuso: enclosed
raccoglitore: compiler
raccolta: compilation, collection
racconto: tale
raddoppiato: duplicated
raff. *see* raffigurante
raffigurante: showing
rafforzato: reinforced
ragionato: commented
rame(i): copper, copper engrav-
   ing(s), copperplate(s)

rappezzato: patched
rappezzo: patched place
rapporto: report
rarissimo: very rare
rarità: rarity
raro: rare
raschiato: erased, scraped
raschiature: erasures, scrapings
rattoppato: restored, patched
recente: recent
reclamistica: advertising
recto: recto
redatto: edited
redazione: editorship
regalo: gift
regolato: ruled, lined
rendiconti: transactions
reperibile: available, procurable;
   that can be found
repertorio: list, index
residuo(i): residue(s), remnant(s)
rest. *see* restaurato
restaur. *see* restaurato
restaurato: restored, repaired
restauri: restorations, repairs
retro: back, behind
ribasso: discount
ricamato: embroidered
ricamo: embroidery
ricc. *see* riccamente
riccam. *see* riccamente
riccamente: richly
riccamente annotato: copiously
   annotated
ricchiss. *see* ricchissimo
ricchissimo: very rich
ricercatissimo: in great demand
ricercato: in demand
richiesto: in demand
riconciato: mended
riconciatura(e): mended spot(s)
ricop. *see* ricoperto
ricoperto: recovered
ricordi: memoirs
ricorretto: corrected again
ridotto: reduced
riduzione: reduction

riedizione: republication
rielaborato: reworked, rewritten
rif. *see* rifatto
rifacimento: restoration, reworking
rifatto: reworked, rewritten
riferimenti: references
rifil. *see* rifilato
rifilato: trimmed
rifior. *see* rifioriture
rifioriture: foxing
rifioriture d'acqua: watermarks
riga: line
rigato: lined
righe: lines
rigida: stiff
riinciso: reengraved
ril. *see* rilegato, rilegatura
rilasciato: weakened, broken
rilegat. *see* rilegatura
rilegato: bound, rebound
rilegatura: binding
rilegatura d'amatore: three-quarter
   binding
rilegatura romantica: binding in
   the romantic style
rilevato: embellished
rilievi: reliefs
rimarginato: margins renewed
rimesso: recased
rimontato: remounted
rinf. *see* rinforzato
rinforz. *see* rinforzato
rinforzato: reinforced
rinforzi: reinforcings
rinforzo: reinforcement
rinnov. *see* rinnovato
rinnovato: renewed
rip. *see* ripiegato
ripar. *see* riparato
riparabile: repairable
riparato: repaired
riparaz. *see* riparazione
riparazione(i): repair(s)
ripet. *see* ripetuto
ripetuto: repeated
ripieg. *see* ripiegato
ripiegabile: folding

ripiegato: folded
ripr. *see* riproduzione
riprod. *see* riproduzione
riproduz. *see* riproduzione
riproduzione(i): reproduction(s)
ripubblicato: republished
riquadratura: frame
riquadro(i): border(s)
risguardi: cover linings, doublures
rist. *see* ristampa
ristampa: reprint, reimpression
ristampa anastatico: anastatic
    reprint
ristampato: reprinted
ristretto: limited
risvolti: linings
ritagliato: cut out
ritaglio: cutting, clipping
ritoccato: retouched, reviewed
ritr. *see* ritratto
ritratto(i): portrait(s)
riun. *see* riunito
riunito: combined
riv. *see* riveduto
rived. *see* riveduto
riveduto: revised
rivestito di: covered by, with
rivista: magazine
rlg. *see* rilegato
robusto: sturdy
romantico: in the romantic style
romanzo: novel
rossore: reddish hue
rotoc. *see* rotocalco
rotocalco: rotogravure
rotocalcografico: rotogravure
rotogravure: rotogravure
rotto: broken
rottura: break
rovescio: reverse
rovinato: damaged
rubrica: heading, rubric
rubricato: rubricated
rubricazione: rubrication
ruggine: rust
rugginoso: rust-colored
rust. *see* rustica
rustica: stitched; in paper covers

s. *see* senza
s.a. *see* senz'anno
s.d. *see* senza data
s.e. *see* senza editore
s.i.p. *see* senza il prezzo
s.l. *see* senza luogo
s.l. e d. *see* senza luogo e data
s.l.n.a. *see* senza luogo nè autore
s.l.n.d. *see* senza luogo nè data
s.l.n.stamp. *see* senza luogo nè
    stampatore
s.l. nè t. *see* senza luogo nè
    tipografo
s.tip. *see* senza tipografo
saggio: sample, specimen; essay
saltato: skipped
salvo: except
sanguigno: sanguine, red
sano: sound, in good condition
satinato: calendered
sbagliato: in error
sbaglio: error
sbiadito: discolored, faded
sbucciat. *see* sbucciatura
sbucciatura: peeling
scadente: inferior, poor
scarabocciato: scribbled on
scarabocchio: scribbling
scarso: narrow
scartellato: loose in its binding
scatola: box
scelta: selection
scelto: selected
schemi: schemes
schiacciato: crushed
schizzo(i): sketch(es)
sciolto: loose, unbound
sciup. *see* sciupato
sciupato: spoiled, worn
scollato: unglued
scolorito: discolored, colorless
scomp. *see* scomparti
scomparti: sections, panels
scompl. *see* scompleto
scompleto: incomplete
sconnessa: unknown
sconosciuto: unknown
sconto: discount

scorretto: faulty
scorticato: scratched
scorticatura: scratch
screpolato: split, cracked
screpolatura: split, crack
scrittura: writing
scrittura a stampatello: script-like type
scrittura bastarda: bastard type
scrittura gotica: gothic type
scrittura rotonda: round, roman type
scrofa: pigskin
scucito: unsewn, loose
scudo: armorial shield
scuro: dark
sdruc. *see* sdrucito
sdrucito: worn-out, torn
se si eccettua: except for
sec. *see* secolo, secondo
secolo: century
secondo: second
sedicesimo: sixteenth
sedici: sixteen
seg. *see* seguente
segg. *see* seguente
segn. *see* segnatura
segnacolo: bookmark
segnalibro: bookmark
segnalini: index marks
segnatura: signature
segni d'età: signs of age
segni d'uso: signs of wear
segni del tempo: contemporary marks
segni di lapis: pencil marks
segni di tarlo: marks of worms
segno: mark
seguente: following
sei: six
semestrale: half-yearly, semi-annual(ly)
semiannuale: semiannual
semintonso: partly trimmed
semplice: simple
sensibile: noticeable
senza: without

senz'anno: without year of publication
senza data: without date
senza editore: without publisher
senza il prezzo: without price
senza importanza: without importanza
senza legatura: without binding
senza luogo: without place of publication
senza luogo e data: without place or date
senza luogo nè autore: without place or author
senza luogo nè data: without place or date
senza luogo nè stampatore: without place or publisher
senza luogo nè tipografo: without place or printer
senza tipografo: without name of printer
separatamente: separately
seppia: sepia
serico: silken
serie: series
sessanta: sixty
sessantesimo: sixtieth
sesto: size, format; sixth
seta: silk
settanta: seventy
settantesimo: seventieth
sette: seven
settecentesca: of the 17th century
settimanale: weekly
settimo: seventh
sfarzoso: splendid, magnificent
sfasc. *see* sfasciato
sfasciato: loosened, weakened
sfasciocolato: fascicles undone
sfiora: barely touches
sfogl. *see* sfogliato
sfogliato: pages torn loose
sfondo: background
sfuggito: escaped
sgorbio: scribbling in ink
sgraffiato: scratched
sgualcito: rumpled, wrinkled

sguardia(e): flyleaf(ves)
si vende: sold
sicofoil: a patented book cloth
sigillo: seal
sigla: initial letter(s)
siglato: with initial letter(s)
silogr. *see* silografia
silograf. *see* silografia
silografia: wood-block print
similpelle: imitation leather
simpatico: appealing, attractive
singola annata: single year
singolarmente: singly
singolo: single
sinistro: left-hand
sinottico: synoptic
skivertex: a patented book cloth
sleg. *see* slegato
slegato: binding broken
smalto: enamel
smarg. *see* smarginato
smarginato: trimmed margin
smarginatura: trimming of margins
smussato: corners broken, dog-
  eared
smusso: broken-cornered
sobrio: sober, plain
soddisfacente: satisfying
solidam. *see* solidamente
solidamente: solidly
solitamente: generally, usually
solo pubblicato: the only one
  published
sommario: table of contents,
  résumé
sontuoso: sumptuous
soppresso: suppressed
sopra: above
soprac. *see* sopracoperta
sopracoperta: wrapper
soprascritta: superscription
sottolin. *see* sottolineature
sottolineato: underlined
sottolineature: underlining
sottoscrittore: subscriber
sottoscrizione: subscription
sottot. *see* sottotitolo

sottotit. *see* sottotitolo
sottotitolo: subtitle
sovr. cop. *see* sovracoperta
sovrac. *see* sovracoperta
sovracop. *see* sovracoperta
sovracoperta: wrapper
sovrapposto: superimposed
spaccato: split
sparse(i): scattered
spartito: separate
spazio: space
spedizione: forwarding, handling
spellat. *see* spellatura
spellatura: scratch
spelli. *see* spellicciata, spellicciatura
spellicciata(e): skinned spot(s)
spellicciatura(e): skinned spot(s)
spese di porto: shipping costs
spese postali: postal costs
spesso: often
spessore: thickness
spezzato: broken
spiegabile: folding
spieghevole: folding
sporca: dirtied, dirty, soiled
spostato: misplaced
spruzzato: sprinkled
stacc. *see* staccato
staccab. *see* staccabile
staccabile: detachable
staccato: detached
stamp. *see* stampato, stampatore
stampa: print
stampatello: scriptlike type
stampato: printed
stampatore: printer
stanco: worn
stato: condition
stato di conservazione: state of
  preservation
stato di nuovo: as new
stato perfetto: perfect condition
stazzonato: creased, crumpled
stemma: coat of arms
stemmato: with arms ·
stesso: same, itself
stile: style

stile monastico: monastic style
stima: esteem, value
stimatiss. *see* stimatissimo
stimatissimo: highly esteemed
stimato: esteemed
str. *see* stretto
stracciato: torn
stralcio: removal
straniero: foreign
strano: strange
straordinaria: extraordinary
strapp. *see* strappato
strappato: torn away, torn out
strappo: tear
stretto: narrow
striscia: strip, stripe
stupendo: very fine, wonderful
sul: on the
sunto: summary
sup. *see* superiore
superbo: superb, sumptuous
superexlibris: book stamp
superiore: upper, top
supplementare: supplementary
supplemento: supplement
svanito: missing
svariato: varied, speckled

t. *see* tela
t.p. *see* tutta pelle
t.pr. *see* tutta pergamina
t.t. *see* tutta tela
tab. *see* tabelle
tabelle: tables
tagli: cuts, edges
tagli cesellati: goffered edges
tagliato: cut, opened
taglio: edge, cut
taglio dolce: taille-douce, copper
   engraving
tagliuzzato: with very small cuts
tarda legatura: late binding
tariffa ridotta: reduced rate
tarlato: worm-eaten
tarlature: wormholes
tarle: wormholing
tarletti: wormholes

tarli: worms, wormholes
tartaruga: tortoise
tas. *see* tassello
tas. e tit. *see* tassello e titolo
tasc. *see* tascabile
tascabile: pocket-size
tascabilità: suitability for pocket
tass. *see* tassello
tassello: label
tassello e titolo: label and title
   piece
tav. *see* tavola
tavola: table
tavole: tables
tavv. *see* tavole
tela: cloth
tela bukram: buckram
tela canapa: hemp cloth
tela grezza: raw cloth
tela olona: sailcloth
tempera: watercolors
tenuto in pregio: valued
terzo: third
tesi: thesis
tessuto: woven, a woven material
testa di moro: black
testata: title, running head
testata di capitolo: chapter headpiece
testatine: headings, running titles,
   running heads
testimoni: witnesses, untrimmed
   edges
testo: text
testo lito: lithographed text
timbrato: stamped
timbretto: small stamp, mark
timbro: stamp, mark
timbro di biblioteca: library stamp,
   mark
tinto: tinted
tip. *see* tipografia, tipografo
tipogr. *see* tipografia, tipografo
tipografia: printing firm
tipografo: printer
tiraggio: print run, edition
tirat. *see* tiratura

tirato: printed
tiratura: edition, printing
tiratura limitata: limited edition
tit. *see* titolo
titolo: title, title page
tomo: volume
top. *see* topografico
topogr. *see* topografico
topografico: topographic
tr. *see* tradotto, traduzione
tracce: traces, marks
tracce di fermagli: traces of clasps, ties
tracce di penna: traces of pen
tracce di tarlo: traces of worms
tracce di tarme: traces of worms
tracce d'umidità: traces of moisture
tracce d'uso: traces of use
trad. *see* tradotto, traduzione
tradotto: translated
traduz. *see* traduzione
traduzione: translation
tras. *see* trascurabile
trasc. *see* trascurabile
trascrizione: transcription
trascurabile: negligible
trasposto: transposed
tratatto: treatise
tre: three
tredicesimo: thirteenth
tredici: thirteen
tremule: weak
trenta: thirty
trentesimo: thirtieth
tricr. *see* tricromia
tricromia: three-color illustration
trimestrale: quarterly
triplice: triple
tutta pelle: full leather
tutta pergamina: full vellum
tutta tela: full cloth
tutto: full, all
tutto il pubblicato: all published

ult. *see* ultimo
ultimissimo: most recent
ultimo: last

umid. *see* umidità
umidità: humidity
un po': a little
undicesimo: eleventh
undici: eleven
unghie: hooks
unico: single, unique, only
uniforme: uniform
unito: combined
unitovi: together with
uno: one
usato: worn
uscito: issued, published

vacchetta: calf
variamente: variously
variante: variant
variegato: variegated
vario: various
veduta(e): view(s)
vedutina: small view
vel. *see* velina
velatura d'acqua: shading by water
velina: vellum paper
velina di protezione: protective cover of vellum paper
velluto: velvet
venale *see* non venale
vendita: sale
venduto: sold
ventesimo: twentieth
venti: twenty
verde: green
vergato: ribbed
versione: version
verso: verso
veste: makeup, presentation
vignetta(e): vignette(s)
viola: violet
vitellino: yellow
vitello: calf
vivo: bright
voci: words, terms
vol. *see* volume
volante: loose-leaf
volantine: leaflet

voll. *see* volume
volume(i): volume(s)
volumetto: little volume

xilogr. *see* xilografico
xilografico: woodcut, wood-
  engraved
xyl. *see* xylografia
xylogr. *see* xylografico
xylografia: woodcut

xylografico: woodcut, wood-
  engraved

zecchino: pure, purest
zigrinato: made to resemble
  shagreen
zigrino: shagreen
zincografia: zinc engraving
zincografico: engraved on zinc

Polish

a trochę: a little
abonament: subscription
abonent: subscriber
abonować: to subscribe
abrewiacja: abbreviation
abstrakcyjny: abstract
adaptacja: adaptation
adnotacja: annotation,
   explanatory note
adnotowany: annotated
adres: address
adresat: addressee
agencja prasowa: press agency
akademia: academy
akademia nauk: academy of
   sciences
akademicki: academic
akademicki podręcznik: academic
   textbook
akta: records, archives
akwaforta: etching
akwarela: watercolor
akwatinta: aquatint
album(y): album(s)
album pamiątkowy: commemorative album
alfabetyczny: alphabetical
almanach: almanac
alternatywny: alternative
amator: amateur
analityczny: analytical
ang. *see* angielski
angielski: English
anonimowo: anonymously
anonimowy: anonymous
antologia: anthology

antydatowany: antedated
antykwa: roman type
antykwariat: antiquarian book
   shop
antykwariusz: antiquarian
   bookseller
antykwarnia: antiquarian
   book shop
anulowanie(a): cancellation(s)
apokryf: apocrypha
aprobata: approval
arabesk: arabesque
archiwalia: archival material
archiwum(wa): archive(s)
arcydzieło: masterpiece
ark. *see* arkusz
arkusz(e): sheet(s)
arkusz próbny: proof sheet
arkusz zamówień: order form
arkusze próbne: proof sheets
artykuł(y): article(s)
artystyczny: artistic
atlas(y): atlas(es)
atlas kieszonkowy: pocket atlas
atrakcyjny: attractive
atrament: ink
atramentowe plamy: ink spots
aukcja: auction
autentyczny: authentic, genuine
autobiografia: autobiography
autobiograficzny: autobiographical
autograf(y): autograph(s)
autor: author
autor broszur: pamphleteer
autorstwo: authorship
autorytatywny: authoritative

autoryzacja: authorization
autoryzowane wydanie: authorized
　edition
awiso: notice

b.m. *see* bez miejsca
b.m.r. *see* bez miejsca i roku
b.r. *see* bez roku
b.w. *see* bez wydawcy
badania porównawcze: compara-
　tive studies
badanie: research, investigation
bajeczny: fabulous
bajka(i): tale(s), fairy tale(s)
barania skóra: sheepskin
barchan: fustian
bardziej pożądany: preferable
bardzo: very
bardzo uszkodzony: badly
　damaged
barwn. *see* barwny
barwne ilustracje: colorful illustra-
　tions
barwny: colorful
beletrystyka: belles lettres, fiction
bez: without
bez blasku: lusterless
bez miejsca: without place
bez miejsca i roku: without place
　or date
bez okładek: without back cover
bez rabatu: no discount
bez roku: without date
bez skazy: flawless
bez wydawcy: without name of
　publisher
bezbarwny: uncolored
bezimienny: anonymous
bezpłatnie: gratis, free of charge
bezwartościowy: worthless
biały: white
bibliofil: bibliophile
bibliogr. *see* bibliografia
bibliograf: bibliographer
bibliografia: bibliography
biblioteka: library
bibliotekarz: librarian

bielizna: linen
bieżący: current
biograf: biographer
biografia: biography
biograficzny: biographical
błąd: error
błąd drukarski: misprint, printer's
　error
błąd druku: errata
blady: pale, paled
błędnie datowany: misdated
błędny: erroneous, faulty
blisko: nearly
blizna(y): scar(s)
błyskotka(i): spangle(s)
bogato ilustrowany: profusely
　illustrated
bogaty: rich
br. *see* broszura
brak: missing
brakujący: lacking
brakuje: lacking, missing
brązowy: bronze-colored
brewiarz: breviary
brokat: brocade
brokatowy: brocade
brosz. *see* broszura
broszura(y): paperbound
　book(s), pamphlet(s)
broszurowana: paperback
broszurowany: unbound
brudny: dirty
brunatny: brown
bryczka: break
brylant: brilliant
brystol: bristol board
brzeg(i): edge(s)
brzeg boczny: fore edge
brzeg dolny: lower edge
brzeg górny: top edge
brzegi złocone: gilt edges
bukram: buckram

c.d. *see* ciąg dalszy
całkowicie poprawiony: completely
　revised
całkowity: whole, complete

całokształt: ensemble
całość: all together, complete
całostronicowy: full-page
cały: full, whole
cecha: characteristic, typical
  feature
celofan: cellophane
cena: price
cena detaliczna: retail price
cena gotówkowa: cash price
cena kompletu: price of complete
  set
cena kupna: purchase price
cena poszczególnego egzemplarza:
  price per single copy
cena prenumeraty: subscription
  price
cena przybliżona: probable,
  likely price
cena stała: fixed price
cena zniżona: reduced price
cennik: price list
cenny: valuable
censurowany: censored
cenzura: censorship
cętkowany: mottled, speckled
charakterystyczny: characteristic
chrestomatia: chrestomathy
chromolitografia: chromolithograph
chronologiczny: chronological
chwalebny: praiseworthy
ciąg dalszy: sequel, continuation
ciągły: continuous
cielęca skóra: calfskin
ciemnobrunatny: bister
ciemnoszary: slate-colored
ciemny: dark, deep
cienki: thin
codzienny: daily
cudowny: admirable
cudzoziemski: foreign
cyfry arabskie: arabic numbers
cytat: quotation
cytrynowy: lemon-colored
cz. *see* czasopismo, część
czarno na białym: black and white
czarny: black

czasopismo(a): periodical(s),
  magazine(s)
czcionka(i): type, letter(s)
czerwonawy: reddish
czerwony: red
część: part
częściowo: partly
często: often
częstotliwość: frequency
częsty: frequent
członki: members
członkowstwo: membership
czołowa strona: obverse
czterdzieści: forty
czterdziesty: fortieth
czternaście: fourteen
czternasty: fourteenth
cztery: four
czwarty: fourth
czwórka: quarto
czysto: neatly
czystopis: clean copy
czystość: spotless
czysty: clean, neat, pure
czyszczony: cleaned
czyt. *see* czytelnik
czytelnik: reader
czytelny: legible

dalszy ciąg: sequel, continuation
dar: gift
data: date
data wydania: date of publication
datowany: dated
dawniejszy numer: back issue,
  back number
dedykacja: dedicatory note,
  inscription
defekt: defective copy
dekoracyjny: decorative,
  ornamental
delikatność: fineness
delikatny: delicate
deseń(nie): design(s)
deska: board
dewiza(y): device(s)
dezyderat: desiderata

diagram(y): diagram(s)
diariusz: diary
długi: long
długość: length
dnie: days
do nabycia: available
do naprawienia: repairable
do prania: washable
do przejrzenia: on approval, for
  review
dobry: fine, good
dobrze zakonserwowany: well-
  preserved
dod. *see* dodatek
dodany: appended
dodatek(tki): supplement(s),
  appendix(es)
dodatek źródłowy: appendix of
  sources
dodatkowy: added, additional
dokładna podobizna: facsimile
dokładność: accuracy
dokładny: exact
dokument(y): document(s)
dokumentacja: documentation
dokumentarny: documentary
doł strony: foot of a page
dolny brzeg: bottom edge
dopełnić: to supplement
doskonale: perfectly
doskonały: excellent, perfect
dosłowne tłumaczenie: literal
  translation
dostateczny: satisfactory, sufficient
dostawa: delivery
doświadczenie: experiment,
  experience
dowolny: optional
dramat: drama
drewniany: wooden
drobny: slight
drobny utwór: opuscule
drogi: expensive
drugi: other, second
druk(i): print(s), printing(s),
  printed matter
druk gruby: boldface type

druk tajny: clandestine publication
drukarnia: printing house
drukarz: printer
drukowany: printed
drzeworyt(y): woodcut(s)
dublura: doublure
duże litery drukowane: block
  letters
duży: large
dużymi literami: in capital letters
dwa: two
dwadzieścia: twenty
dwanaście: twelve
dwubarwny: bicolored
dwudziesty: twentieth
dwujęzyczny: bilingual
dwukolorowy: bicolored
dwum. *see* dwumiesięcznik
dwumiesięcznik: bimonthly
dwunastka: duodecimo
dwuroczny: biennial
dwustronny: two-sided
dwuszpaltowy: two-column
dwut. *see* dwutygodnik
dwutygodnik: biweekly
dwutygodniowy: fortnightly
dysertacja: dissertation
dyskretny: discreet
dystrybucja: distribution
dystyngowany: distinguished
dz. *see* dział, dziennik
dział(y): section(s)
dzieje: history, story
dzieła poetyckie: poetical works
dzieło(a): work(s)
dzieło anonimowe: anonymous
  work
dzieło podręczne: reference work
dzień: day
dzien. *see* dziennik
dziennik: daily, diary
dziesiąty: tenth
dziesięć: ten
dziewiąty: ninth
dziewięć: nine
dziewięćdziesiąt(y): ninety(ieth)
dziewiętnaście: nineteen

dziewiętnasty: nineteenth
dziura(y): hole(s)

efemeryczny: ephemeral
egz. *see* egzemplarz
egzekucja: execution
egzemplarz(e): copy(ies)
egzemplarz autorski: presentation
  copy
egzemplarz numerowany: numbered copy
egzemplarz okazowy: sample copy
egzemplarz osobisty: personal copy
egzemplarz przepisany na czysto:
  clean copy
egzemplarz recenzyjny: review
  copy
egzemplarz zastąpiony: replacement copy
ekslibris: bookplate, *ex libris*
ekspedycja: shipment
ekspert: expert
elegancki: elegant
elementarz: primer
emblemat(y): emblem(s)
encyklopedia: encyclopedia
epigraf(y): epigraph(s)
epika: epic
epilog: epilogue
epoka: epoch
europejski: European
ewaluacja: evaluation

facsimile: facsimile
faktura: invoice
fałdowanie: goffering
fałszerstwo: forgery
fałszowanie: fabrication
fantazje: fancy
fantazyjny: imaginative
fasc. *see* fascykuł
fascykuł(y): fascicle(s)
felieton(y): leaflet(s)
fig. *see* figura
figura(y): table(s), figure(s)
fikcyjny: fictitious
filigran: filigree

fioletowy: violet
fiołkoworóżowy: mauve
firma wydawnicza: publishing firm
folacja: foliation
foliał(y): large volume(s),
  folio(s)
foliant(y): large volume(s), folio(s)
folio wielkie: elephant folio
format: size
format bardzo duży: very large
  format
format kieszonkowy: pocket-size
fot. *see* fotografia
fotografia(e): photograph(s)
fotograficzny: photographic
fotograwiura: photogravure
fotooffs. *see* fotooffset
fotooffset: photo-offset
fotostat: photostat
fototypia: collotype
fragment(y): fragment(s)
fragmentaryczny: fragmentary
franco: postpaid
frontyspis: frontispiece
futerał: slipcase, box
futeralik: small slipcase

gazeta(y): newspaper(s)
gdzie indziej: elsewhere
geograficzny: geographic
girlanda: garland
gładki: smooth
gładziarka: calender
glansowany: glazed
glosariusz: glossary
głowny: principal
godło: motto
górny: top, upper
gotowy: ready
granulowany: pebbled
grawiura(y): cut(s), engraving(s)
groteska: grotesque
grubość: thickness
gruby: thick
grupa: group
gryzmoły: scribbling
grzbiet: spine, back of book

guz(y): boss(es), knob(s)
gwasz: gouache
gwiazdka: asterisk

haftka(i): clasp(s)
handlowy: commercial
hasło: catchword, heading
herb: coat of arms
herbarz: armorial design
hurtowy: wholesale

i: and
i inne: and others
i inni: and others
i tak dalej: and so on, et cetera
identyczny: identical
il. *see* ilustracja, ilustrowany
ilość: quantity
ilość stron: number of pages
iluminacja: illumination
iluminowany: illuminated
ilustr. *see* ilustracja
ilustracja(e): illustration(s)
ilustrator: illustrator
ilustrowany: illustrated
imię: forename
imitacja: imitation
imponujący: impressive
inaczej: otherwise
indeks: index
indeks ogólny: general index
indeks osób: index of names
indeks przedmiotowy: subject
    index
informacja bibliograficzna: bib-
    liographical information
informator: guide
inicjał(y): initial letter(s)
inicjał ozdobny: ornamental
    initial letter(s)
inkunabuł(y): incunabulum(a)
inni: others
instytut: institute
intaglio: intaglio
integralny: integral
interlinearny: interlinear
interpretacja: interpretation

introligator: bookbinder
introligatornia: bindery
introligatorstwo: bookbinding
ircha: chamois, doeskin
itd. *see* i tak dalej

jak następuje: as follows
jak nowy: like new
jak powyżej: as above
jakkolwiek: however
jakość: quality
jaskrawy: bright
jasno: clearly
jasny: light, clear
jeden: one
jedenaście: eleven
jedenasty: eleventh
jednostronny: one-sided
jedwab: silk
jedyny: only, unique
jesień: Autumn
jeszcze nie wydany: not yet
    published
jeszcze trochę: a few
język(i): language(s)

k. *see* karton
k.tyt. *see* karta tytułowa
kaligrafia: calligraphy
kamea: cameo
kanwa: canvas
kapitałka: headband
karta(y): leaf(ves), sheet(s)
karta nieliczbowana: unnumbered
    leaf
karta nienumerowana: unnumbered
    leaf
karta ochronna: endpaper
karta przedtytułowa: half-title
    page
karta pusta: blank page
karta tytułowa: title page
kartka(i): leaf(ves), sheet(s)
kartka(i) wstępna(e): preliminary
    leaf(ves)
kartografia: cartography
karton: pasteboard

kartusz: cartouche
karykatura(y): caricature(s)
kaseta: case
kasztanowaty: maroon
kasztanowy: chestnut
katalog(i): catalog(s)
katalog aukcyjny: auction catalog
katalog cen: priced catalog
katalog licytacyjny: auction
  catalog
katalogowany: listed
każdy: each
kierunek: direction
kieszeń: pocket
kilka: several, a few
klamra(y): clasp(s)
klasyczny: classic
klasyfikowany: classified
klasztorny: monastic
klej: glue
klejnot: jewel
klejony: pasted
klucz: key
kodeks: codex
kolacjonowany: collation
kolegium redakcyjne: editorial
  board
kolejny tom: successive volume
kolofon: colophon
kolor(y): color(s)
kolorowanie: coloring
kolorowany: colored
kolorowe ilustracje: colored
  illustrations
kolorowe ryciny: color plates
kolorowy: colored
kolorowy(e) druk(i): color print(s)
kolumna(y): column(s)
komedia: comedy
komentarz(e): commentary(ies)
komitet: committee
komitet redakcyjny: editorial
  committee
kompilacja: compilation
kompilator: compiler
komplet: complete set, complete
końcowy: final

konferencja: conference
koniec: end
konieczny: necessary
konserwacja: state of repair
konsp. *see* konspekt
konspekt: compendium, synopsis
kontynuacja: continuation
koperta: envelope
kopia: copy
kordyban: cordovan
korekta: proofreading
korespondencja: correspondence
koronka(i): lace(s)
kość słoniowa: ivory
koszt: cost
kosztowny: precious, costly
koszulka: jacket
koźla skóra: buckskin
krajowy: domestic
kratkowany: checkered
krawędź(ie): edge(s)
kremowy: cream-colored
kreton: cretonne
kronika(i): annals, chronicle(s)
kropkowana linia: dotted line
kropkowany: stippled
krótki: short
krótki zbiór: brief collection,
  compendium
krótkie streszczenie: short
  summary
kruchy: brittle
krytyczny: critical
krytyka(i): critique(s), review(s)
krzywy: crooked
książeczka: small book, booklet
książka(i): book(s)
książka dla dzieci: children's book
książka nieobcięta: uncut book
książka nieoprawna: unbound book
książka nierozcięta: unopened
  book
książka niezbroszurowana: book
  in sheets
książka obcięta: trimmed copy
książka obłożona: book in
  wrappers

książka podręczna: reference book
książka używana: secondhand
book
książka z notatkami: notebook
księga: book, volume
księga adresowa: directory
księga pamiątkowa: commemorative volume
księgarnia: book shop
księgarz: bookseller
którykolwiek: either
kurs: a course of lectures
kursywa: cursive, italic
kw. *see* kwadratowy, kwartał
kwadratowy: square, rectangular
kwarta: quarto
kwartał: quarter
kwartalnik: quarterly
kwiatek: fleuret
kwiaton: fleuron
kwiatowy: floral design
kwiecisty: ornate

łącznie: inclusive
łącznie z kosztem transportu:
carriage paid
łączny: inclusive
ładny: pretty
lakierowany: lacquered
lato: Summer
lawenda: lavender
ledwo: scarcely
legenda(y): legend(s)
lekko: slightly
lekko uszkodzony: slightly
damaged
leksykon: lexicon
lektura(y): lecture(s)
lepszy: better
lewa strona: left side
libra: quire
lichy: poor, shabby
licytacja: auction sale
liczba stron: number of pages
liczn. *see* liczny
liczny: numerous
lilia burbońska: fleur-de-lys

linia(e): line(s)
linia ozdobna: fillet
liryka(i): lyric(s)
list(y): letter(s)
lista cen: price list
literacki: literary
literalny: literal
literatura: literature
litograf: lithographer
litografia: lithography
litografowany: lithographed
lokalny: local
łososiowy: salmon
luka: lacuna
luksusowy: deluxe
luź.k. *see* luźne kartki
luźne kartki: loose leaves,
unstitched sheets
luźny: loose
luźnymi kartkami: loose-leaf

m.in. *see* między innymi
mądrze: ably
magazyn(y): magazine(s)
małe litery: lowercase
mało znany: little-known
malowany: painted
małoważny: unimportant
malowniczy: picturesque
mały: little, small
manuskrypt(y): manuscript(s)
mapa(y): map(s)
mapa konturowa: contour map
mapa plastyczna: relief map
margines(y): margin(s)
margines boczny: outside margin
margines dolny: lower margin,
bottom margin
margines górny: head margin,
top margin
margines grzbietowy: inner margin
marmurkowy: marbled
marokin: morocco
maszynopis: typescript copy
materiał archiwalny: archival
materials
materiały: sources, materials

matowy: dull, lusterless
medalion: medallion
metaliczny: metallic
mezzotinta(y): mezzotint(s)
mianowicie: namely
miedź: copper
miedzioryt(y): copper
  engraving(s), etching(s)
między: among, between
między innymi: among others
miejsce wydania: place of
  publication
miękka okładka: soft binding
miękki: soft
mies. *see* miesięcznie, miesięcznik
miesięcznie: monthly
miesięcznik: monthly
mieszany: mixed
miniatura: miniature
miniaturowy: miniature
miniejszym: hereby
minimalny: minimal
ministerstwo: ministry
mistrzostwo: craftsmanship
mniej: less
mniejszy: minor
mnóstwo: multitude
mocny: sturdy
modernizowany: modernized
modifikacja(e): modification(s)
mól książkowy: bookworm
monografia(e): monograph(s)
monumentalny: monumental
morowy: moiré
mosiądz: brass
motyw(y): motif(s)
mowa(y): speech(es)
mozaika: mosaic
możliwie: possibly
możliwy: possible
muślin: muslin
muzyka: music

na: on, upon
na górze: at the top
na końcu: at the back
na nowo pokryty: recovered
na odwrocie: verso, on the back

na prawach rękopisu: manuscript
  rights
na przykład: for example
na żądanie: on request, upon
  request
na zamówienie: on request
na zapotrzebowanie: on request
nabyć: to acquire, to purchase
nabywanie: acquisition
nacięty: notched
nadbitka: separate, offprint
nadmiar: excess
nadmierny: excessive
nadpis: superscription
nadzwyczajnie: extremely
nadzwyczajny: extraordinary
nagłówek(i): heading(s),
  headpiece(s)
najczęsciej: mostly
najlepszy: best
najnizsża cena: lowest price
najpiękniejszy: most beautiful
najprzedniejszy: superfine
nakł. *see* nakład
nakład: edition, impression
nakład i druk: published and
  printed by
nakład orgraniczony: limited
  edition
nakładem własnym: published by
  author
naklejka(i): label(s)
napis: inscription
napisać przedmowę: prefaced
napisany pod pseudonimen:
  pseudonymous
naprawa(y): repair(s)
naprawione kartki: patched leaves
naprawiony: mended, repaired
naprzeciwko tekstu: opposite,
  facing the text
narodowy: national
narożnik(i): corner(s)
następny: next, subsequent
następstwo: sequence
następujący: following,
  consecutive
naturalny: natural

nauka: science
naukowy: scientific
nazw. *see* nazwisko
nazwa: name
nazwisko: surname
nazwisko przybrane: pen name
netto: net
nie do nabycia: not available
nie istniejący: nonexistent
nie na sprzedaż: not for sale
nie posiada: lacks
nie sprzedany oddzielnie: not sold
    separately
nie ukazał się: did not appear
nie uszkodzony: undamaged
nie w tekście: not in the text
niebieski: blue
nieco: somewhat
nieczysty: unexpurgated
nieczytelny: illegible
niedatowany: undated
niedekorowany: plain
niedostateczny: insufficient
niedrogi: inexpensive
niekompletny: incomplete
niektóre: some
nielegalny: unauthorized
nieliczbowany: unpaged
niemoźliwy do znalezienia:
    impossible to find
nienaruszony: intact, untouched
nienumerowany: unnumbered
nieobcięty: untrimmed
nieoceniony: invaluable
nieokr. *see* nieokreślony
nieokreślony: indefinite
nieoprawny: unbound
nieopublikowany: unpublished
nieparzysty: odd-numbered
niepokalany: immaculate
nieponumerowany: unnumbered
nieporozcinany: pages uncut
nieprzezroczysty: opaque
nieregularność: irregularity
nieregularny: irregular
nierówny: rough
nierozłączny: inseparable
nieskazitelny: impeccable

nieskrócony: unabridged
niesłychanie: extremely
nietknięty: untouched
niewiele: not many, few
niezbędny: indispensable
niezgodny: divided
niezliczony: innumerable
niezmieniony: unchanged
niezmiernie: extremely, exceedingly
nieznaczny: insignificant
nieznany: unknown
niezrównany: unmatched
niezupełny: incomplete, imperfect
niezwykle: rarely
niezwykły: uncommon
nigdy: never
niski: low
niźej: below, lower
niższy: lower
nkł. *see* nakład
nlb. *see* nieliczbowany
nota bibliograficzna: bibliographi-
    cal note
notacja: notation
notatka wstępna: prefatory note
nowe wydanie: new edition
nowela(e): story(ies), novel(s)
nowelka(i): short story(ies),
    novella(s)
nowoczesny: up-to-date, modern
nowo-odkryty: newly discovered
nowość: novelty
nowożytny: modern
nowszy: newer
nowy: new
nr. *see* numer
numer: number, issue
numeracja: numeration
numeracja kartek: foliation
numerowanie: numbering
numerowanie stronic: pagination
numerowany: numbered
nuta(y): note(s); music score(s)

ob. *see* obacz
obacz: see
obaj: both
obcięty: trimmed

obcy: strange
obecny: recent
obejmować: to contain
obfitość: abundance
obfity: copious
objaśniający: explanatory
objaśnienie: explanation,
   explanatory notes
obliczenie: estimate
obramowanie: frame, border
obramowany: framed
obraz(y): picture(s)
obrazek: small picture
obrazki: small pictures
obszarpany: shabby
obszerny: ample
obw. *see* obwoluta
obwódka: border
obwoluta: wrapper, book jacket
oceniony: valued
oczyszczony: purged
odbitka z czasopisma: reprint
   from a periodical
oddzielny: separate
oderwany: torn away, torn off
odłożony: postponed
odmienny: diverse
odnośnie: concerning
odnośnik(i): footnote(s)
odnowiony: restored, renewed
odpowiedni: suitable
odpowiedzialny: responsible
odroczony: deferred
odwr. *see* na odwrocie
odwrotna strona: verso
odwrotność: reverse
oferta: offer
oficjalny: official
oficyna: workshop
ogł. *see* ogłoszony
ogłosić: to publish
ogłoszenie: advertisement,
   announcement
ogłoszony: published, announced
ograniczony: limited
okazja: opportunity
okł. *see* okładka

okładka(i): cover(s), wrapper(s)
okładka ochronna: dustcover
okładka ślepa: blank cover
okładka wydawnicza: original
   cover
okładzina przednia: front cover
okładzina tylna: back cover
około: about, approximately
okrojenie: mutilation
okrojony: mutilated
oktawo: octavo
oliwkowy: olive-colored
ołowek: pencil
opatrzył: supplied, provided
opis: description
opisany: described
opisowy: descriptive
opow. *see* opowiadanie
opowiadanie: story, short novel
opowieść(i): story(ies)
opr. *see* oprawa
opr.luks. *see* oprawa luksusowa
opr.skórk. *see* oprawa skórkowa
oprac. *see* opracowane
opracowane: prepared, produced
opracowanie(a): work(s)
oprawa: binding
oprawa luksusowa: deluxe binding
oprawa miękka: flexible binding
oprawa nakładowa: publisher's
   binding
oprawa ozdobna: decorative
   binding
oprawa pełna: full binding
oprawa pergaminowa: vellum
   binding
oprawa płócienna: cloth binding
oprawa półskórkowa: half-leather
   binding
oprawa skórkowa: leather binding
oprawa skórzana: leather binding
oprawa spiralna: spiral binding
oprawa trzy czwarte: three-quarter
   binding
oprawa w płótno: in cloth binding
oprawa w półskórek: quarter-
   binding

oprawa współczesna: contemporary
  binding
oprawione razem: bound together
oprawiony: bound
oprawiony na nowo: rebound
oprawiony z: bound with
opuszczenie(a): omission(s)
opuszczony: omitted
ornamentacja metalowa: metal
  ornaments
ornamentowany: ornamented
oryg. *see* oryginał
oryginał: original
oryginalny: original
orzechowy: nut-brown
osiem: eight
osiemdziesiąt(y): eighty(ieth)
osiemnaście: eighteen
osiemnasty: eighteenth
ośle uszy: dog-eared
ósmy: eighth
osobisty podpis: ownership mark
osobliwość(i): rarity(ies)
osobny: separate
ostateczne wydanie: definitive
  edition
ostatni tom: last volume
ostentacyjny: ostentatious
oszacowanie: appraisal
oszczerczy: libelous
otarcie: abrasion
otwarty: open, opened
ozdoba: ornament, decoration
ozdobiony: spangled
ozdobiony kwiatami: flowered
ozdobny: decorated, figured
oznaki: traces

p. *see* płótno
p.t. *see* pod tytułem
p.z. *see* praca zbiorowa
paginacja: pagination
paginacja ciągła: continuous
  paging
paginowany: paginated
pakowanie: packing

pamiątkowy: commemorative,
  memorial
państwo: state
papier: paper
papier bezdrzewny: wood-free
  paper
papier chiński: China paper
papier glansowany: glazed paper
papier kredowany: coated paper
papier pergaminowy: parchment
  paper
papier szmaciany: rag paper
papier welinowy: vellum
papier żeberkowany: laid paper
parafa: paraph
paragraf(y): paragraph(s)
parodia: parody
pasta: paste
paszkwil(e): lampoon(s), libel(s)
pełne wydanie: complete edition
perforacja(e): perforation(s)
perforowany: perforated
perg. *see* pergamin
pergamin: parchment
periodyczny: periodical, serial
periodyk: journal, periodical
  publication
perkalina: percaline
piąty: fifth
pięć: five
pięćdziesiąt(y): fifty(ieth)
pieczątka: rubber stamp
pieczęcie: seals
piękny: beautiful
pieniądze: money
pierwodruk: editio princeps
pierwotny: original
pierwsza obwoluta: original
  wrapper
pierwsze wydanie: first edition
pierwszy: foremost
piętnaście: fifteen
piętnasty: fifteenth
pilny: urgent
pisarz: writer
pisemko(a): pamphlet(s)

pismo tygodniowe: weekly
publication
pismo uncjalne: uncial letters
pł. *see* płótno
plagiat: plagiarism
plama(y): spot(s), stain(s)
plamy wodne: water spots
plan: plan, layout
plansza(e): plate(s)
płaski: flat
plastyczny: plastic
pleśń: mildew
pleśnialy: mildewed
płót: *see* płótno
płótno: cloth binding, cloth
płótno do oprawy: book cloth
płowozólty: buff-colored
płowy: fawn-colored
płyta: plaque
po słowie: postscript
pociągający: appealing
początek: beginning
poczet: list
poczta: mail
poczta lotnicza: airmail
poczytny: widely read
pod redakcją: edited by
pod tyt. *see* pod tytułem
pod tytułem: under the title,
entitled
podarty: torn
podkreślony ołówkiem: with pencil
underlining
podłużny: oblong
podobizna: likeness, photo
podobizna autografu: facsimile
autograph
podobny: similar
podpis: signature
podpisany: signed
podr. *see* podręcznik
podrapany: scratched
podręcznik(i): manual(s),
textbook(s)
podręcznik(i) uniwersytecki(e):
university textbook(s)
podrobiony: falsified, forged

podstawowy: basic
podszyć: lined
podtyt. *see* podtytuł
podtytuł: subtitle
pódwójna kopia: duplicate copy
pódwójna strona: double page
podwójny egzemplarz: duplicate
copy
podziały: divisions
poemat(y): poem(s)
poezja: poetry
pognieciony: crinkled
pogryziony: gnawed
pojedynczo: singly
pojedynczy: single
pokaz: exhibition
pokrowiec: case, container
pokryć rudymi plamami: foxing
pokryty rudymi plamami: foxed
połączony: combined
połączyć: merged with
polecona poczta: certified mail
półelastyczny: semiflexible
polerowanie: polishing
polityczny: political
półoprawa: half binding
półpergamin: half-vellum binding
półpłótno: half-cloth binding
półr. *see* półrocznik, półroczny
półrocznik: semiannual
półroczny: semiannual
półskórek: half-leather binding
półton: halftone
połyskujący: glossy
pomarańczowy: orange
pomyłka(i): mistake(s)
ponad: more than
ponowne wydanie: reprint, second
edition
poplamiony: smudged, spotted,
stained
poprawa(y): correction(s)
poprawione i uzupełnione: corrected and supplemented,
amended
poprawiony: corrected, revised
poprawka(i): correction(s)

popryskany: sprinkled
poprzedni: former
poprzednio: previously
poprzedzający: preceding
popularny: popular
poradnik: guidebook
porfir: porphyry
porównawczy: comparative
porto: postage
portr. *see* portret
portret(y): portrait(s)
porysowany: cracked
posiadacz: owner
pośmiertny: posthumous
postrzępiony: ragged
poświadczyć: authenticate
poświęcony: dedicated
poszczeg. *see* poszczególny
poszczególny: separate, individual
poszerzony: enlarged
poszukiwany: sought
potłuczony: bruised
potrzebny: needed
potwierdzenie: confirmation,
   approval
potwierdzony: confirmed
powiększony: enlarged, increased
powiel. *see* powielony
powielony: duplicated, reproduced
powieść(i): novel(s)
powieść detektywistyczna:
   detective story
powieściopisarz: novelist
powyżej: above
powyżej wzmiankowany: above-
   mentioned, above-cited
poz. *see* pozycja
poza tekstem: not in the text
pożądany: desired
pozłacane brzegi: gilt edges
później: later
późny: latest
pozostały: extant, remaining
pozwolenie: permission
pozycja(e): entry(ies), position(s)
ppł. *see* półpłótno
praca(e): work(s)

praca zbiorowa: collective work
prawie: almost
prawo przedruku: copyright
prawy: right-hand
prenumerata: subscription
prenumerata kwartalna: quarterly
   subscription
prenumerata roczna: annual
   subscription
prenumerować: to subscribe
próbka: sample
próbna kopia: specimen copy
próbny: tentative
próbny egzemplarz: specimen copy
prolog: prologue
prospekt: prospectus
prospekt wydawnictwa: publication
   prospectus
prosty: simple, straight
proweniencja: provenance
prywatna prasa: private press
prywatnie drukowany: privately
   printed
prywatnie wydane: privately
   published
przed: before
przed wydaniem: prepublication
przedmiot: subject
przedmowa: preface, introduction
przedostatni: penultimate
przedpłata: payment in advance
przedr. *see* przedruk
przedruk(i): reprint(s)
przedrukowany: being reprinted;
   reprinted
przedtytuł: flyleaf
przedwojenny: prewar
przedwstępny: preliminary
przegląd(y): review(s)
przejrzane: revised
przekł. *see* przekład
przekład: translation
przemieniony: rearranged
przenośny: portable
przepłacony: prepaid
przepleść: interlacing
przerobiony: revised

przeróbka: recast
przerwany: discontinued
przerwy: gaps
przestarzały: obsolete, outdated
przeważnie: largely
przewodnik(i): guide(s),
    directory(ies)
przód: front
przyczynek: contribution
przygotować: to prepare
przygotowanie: preparation
przyjemny: pleasing
przykład(y): example(s)
przyklejony: glued, pasted on
przypadkowo: occasionally
przypalony: scorched
przypis(y): annotation(s),
    remark(s)
przypisek(ki): footnote(s)
przywiązany: prized
pseudonim: pseudonym
publikacja(e): publication(s)
publikacja oficjalna: official
    publication
purpura: purple
pusty: blank
pytanie: question

r. *see* rok
rabat: discount
rama: frame
raport(y): report(s)
raz na trzy lata: triennial
rdza: rust
rdzawy: rust-colored
recenzja(e): review(s)
recenzowany: reviewed
recto: recto
ręcznie: by hand
ręcznie malowany: hand-painted
red. *see* redagowany, redakcja
redagowany: edited
redakcja: editorship, editorial
    office
redaktor: editor
redaktor naczelny: editor in chief
redaktorski: editorial

redaktorstwo: editorship
redukcja: reduction
referat(y): lecture(s)
regularny: regular
rejestr(y): index(es), register(s)
rękopis(y): manuscript(s)
relacja: report, version
remanentów ksiązek: remainder
reorganizowany: reorganized
reparacja: mending
reportaż: press report
reprodukcja: reproduction
restoracja: restore, renew
restoracja(e): restoration(s)
retrospekcyjny: retrospective
retuszowany: retouched
rewidowany: searched
rewizja: revision
rezerwa: reserve
roczne księgi: annual volumes
rocznica: anniversary
rocznie: annually
rocznik: yearbook, annual register
roczniki: annals
roczny: yearly
rodz. *see* rodzaj
rodzaj: type
rok: year
rok bieżący: current year
rok wydania: year of publication
romans: romance
romb: lozenge
ros. *see* rosyjski
rosyjski: Russian
rotograwiura: rotogravure
również: also
równocześnie: simultaneously
równoległy tekst: parallel text
równy: equal
rozdział(y): chapter(s), section(s)
rozdzielony: separately
rozetka: rosette
rozkaz: order
rozmieszczenie: arrangement
różnić się: differs from
różny: different
różowy: pink

rozprawa(y): treatise(s)
rozprawa naukowa: dissertation,
   scholarly work
rozprawka(i): essay(s)
rozprawy: proceedings
rozsprzedany: sold out
rozszerzony: enlarged
rubryka: rubric
rubrykować: rubricate
rubrykowany: rubricated
ruchomy: movable
ryc. *see* rycina
rycina(y): engraving(s),
   illustration(s)
rynek: market
rys. *see* rysunek
rysunek: drawing, sketch
rysunki: drawings, sketches
rysunki kreskowe: line drawings
rysunki ołówkami: pencil drawings
rytowany: engraved
rzadki: rare, scarce
rzadkość: rarity

s. *see* seria, strona, stronica
safian: crushed morocco
sam: only
satyna: sateen
ściąć: cut off
ścięgno: bands
sekcja: section
ser. *see* seria
seria: series
setny: hundredth
sfałszowanie: counterfeit
siedem: seven
siedemdziesiąt(y): seventy(ieth)
siedemnaście: seventeen
siedemnasty: seventeenth
silny: strong
siódmy: seventh
skasowany: deleted
składany: folding
sklep antykwaryczny: antiquarian
   book shop
skolacjonowany: collated
skonfiskowany: confiscated

skóra: leather
skóra barania: roan
skóra cielęca: calfskin
skóra koźla: kidskin
skóra marokańska: morocco
skóra szagrynowa: shagreen
skóra wołowa: oxhide
skorowidz: index, table
skrócenie: abbreviation,
   abridgment
skrócone: abridged
skromny: modest
skrót: digest
skrót(y): abbreviation(s),
   abridgment(s)
skumulowany: cumulated
słaby: weak
sławny: famous
śliczny: lovely
słomkowy: straw-colored
słowniczek: small dictionary
słownik: dictionary
słownik kieszonkowy: pocket
   dictionary
solidny: solid
spacjowany: spaced
spalić: burn
spalony: burned
specialny: special
śpiewnik: songbook
spis: list, catalog; index
spis przedmiotowy: subject list
spis rycin: list of illustrations
spis rzeczy: table of contents
spłowiały: faded
spółdzielnia wydawnicza: cooperative publishing house
sprawozdania: proceedings
sprawozdanie: report, account
sprostowanie: emendations
spryskane brzegi: sprinkled edges
srebro: silver
średni: mediocre
średniowieczny: medieval
staloryt: steel engraving
staranny: elaborate
starodruk: early printed book

starszy: older
stary: old
statystyczny: statistical
stempel: stamp
stemplowany: stamped
sto: hundred
stosowany: applied
str. *see* strona
streszcz. *see* streszczenie
streszczenie: summary
strona(y): page(s)
strona tytułowa: title page
stronica(e): page(s)
strzępiony: deckled
stulecie: century
stuletnie: centennial
styl romantyczny: romantic style
sucha igła: drypoint
surowo: severely
surowy: crude, raw
światlocień: chiaroscuro
światłodruk: photoprint
świeży: fresh
świńska skóra: pigskin
sygnet drukarski: printer's mark
symulowany: simulated, spurious
szacunek: esteem
szagryn: shagreen
szanowany: esteemed
szary: gray
szeroki margines: wide margin(s)
szerokość: width
sześć: six
sześćdziesiąt(y): sixty(ieth)
szesnaście: sixteen
szesnasty: sixteenth
szkic(e): sketch(es)
szlak(i): frieze(s)
szósty: sixth
szp. *see* szpalta
szpalta(y): column(s)
sztych: engraving
sztych kreskowany(e): line
    engraving(s)
sztycharz: engraver
sztywny: stiff
szycie: sewing, stitching

t. *see* tom
tab. *see* tabela
tabela(e): table(s), index(es)
tabl. *see* tablica
tablica(e): table(s), plate(s)
tablica barwna: table in colors
tani: cheap
tarcie: rubbing
tarcza herbowa: blazon
targi księgarskie: book fairs
techniczny: technical
teczka(i): small portfolio(s)
teka(i): portfolio(s)
tekst: text
tekstowy: textual
tekstura: black letter
temat(y): theme(s)
teraz: now
teza(y): thesis(es)
tłok: stamp, tool
tłum. *see* tłumaczenie
tłumacz: translator
tłumaczenie(a): translation(s)
tłumaczenie autoryzowane:
    authorized translation
tłumaczenie dosłowne: literal
    translation
tłumaczył: translated
tłuste plamy: grease spots
tłusty druk: boldface type
tom(y): volume(s)
tom bieżący: current volume
tom dodatkowy: additional volume
tom różnych utworów: omnibus
    volume
tomik(i): small volume(s)
towarzystwo naukowe: learned
    society
traktat(y): treatise(s)
transliteracja: transliteration
tranzakcje: transactions
treść: contents
trochę uszkodzony: slightly
    damaged
troska: care
troskliwy: careful
trudny: difficult

trylogia: trilogy
trzeci: third
trzy: three
trzydzieści: thirty
trzydziesty: thirtieth
trzynaście: thirteen
trzynasty: thirteenth
tyg. *see* tygodnik
tygodnik: weekly
tygodniowy: weekly
tylko: only
tylko dla prenumeratorów: for
  subscribers only
tymczasowy: preliminary,
  temporary
tynta: tint
typ: type
tysiąc: thousand
tyt. *see* tytuł
tytuł: title
tytuł grzbietowy: title on spine
tytuł nadrzędny: collective title
tytuł okładkowy: cover title
tytuł oryginału: original title
tytuł wstępny: half title

uderzający: striking
ukazało się drukiem: just published
ukaze się niebawem: to be
  published soon
ukazywać: appear
układ: arrangement, makeup
układ alfabetyczny: alphabetical
  order
ulepszony: improved
ulotka: broadside
umiarkowany: moderate
umiejętność: knowledge
umieścić: laid in
umieszczać wstawki: interpolate
unikat: unique copy
uniwersytet: university
upiększony: embellished
uprawniony: authorized
uproszczony: simplified
urzędowy: official
ustępliwy: flexible

uszkodzenie: damage, injury
uszkodzony: damaged, defective
utwór(y): work(s)
uwagi marginesowe: marginal notes
uwydatniony: enhanced
uzupełnienie: supplement
uzupełnione: supplemented
używany: used, secondhand

w: in, into
w. *see* wiek
w dobrym stanie: in good condition
w doskonałym stanie: in an
  excellent state of preservation;
  in excellent condition
w druku: in press
w niektórych miejscach: in some
  places
w prenumeracie: by subscription
w przygotowaniu: in preparation
w rękopisie: in manuscript
w rkpsie. *see* w rękopisie
w sprzedaży: in the book trade
w tekście: in the text
wada: defect
wadliwość: imperfection
Warszawa: Warsaw
wartość: value, worth
wartościowy: valuable
warunki prenumeraty: conditions
  of subscription
warunki sprzedaży: conditions
  of sale
wąski: narrow
wątpliwy: doubtful
ważny: important
wcześnie: early
według: according to
welin: vellum
wersja: version
wewnątrz: inside
wewnętrzny: inner
wg. *see* według
widoczny: noticeable
wiecej nie wyszło: no more
  published
wiek: century, age

większość: most, majority
większy: larger
wielce: greatly
wielobarwny: many-colored
wielojęzyczny: polyglot
wielojęzykowa: multilingual
wielotomowy: voluminous
wielu: many
wierzch: top
wierzchni: upper
wilgoć: moisture
wilgotne plamy: damp spots
winieta(y): vignette(s)
winieta końcowa: tailpiece
winieta tytułowa: headpiece
wiosna: Spring
wkl. *see* wklejka
wkładka(i): insert(s)
wklejka(i): insert(s)
wklejone kartki: interleaved
wkrótce: shortly
włącznie: inclusive, including
własnoręczna dedykacja: auto-
    graphed dedication
własnoręcznie podpisany: auto-
    graphed
wolny od opłaty celnej: duty-free
wprawadzony: intercalated
wspaniały: splendid, magnificent
współautor(zy): coauthor(s)
współczesny: contemporary
współdziałanie: cooperation
współpraca: collaboration
współtwórcy(a): contributor(s)
współudział: participation
wspomnienia: memoirs
wstęp: preface, introduction
wstępna notatka: introductory
    note
wszechstronny: comprehensive
wszelkie prawa zastrzeżone: all
    rights reserved
wszystek: all
wszystkie prawa zastrzeżone: all
    rights reserved
Wwa. *see* Warszawa
wybierany: excerpted

wybitny: outstanding
wybór: selection
wybór pism: selected works
wybrane prace: selected works
wyciąć: cut out
wycięcie: excision
wycięty: excised
wycinki: clippings
wycisk: tooling, embossing
wycisk ślepy: blind tooling
wycisk złocony: gold tooling
wycofać: suppress
wycyzelowany: chiseled
wyczerpany: out-of-print
wyczerpujący: exhaustive
wyd. *see* wydanie, wydawnictwo
wydać dzieło: to publish
wydane, opublikowane: all
    published
wydanie(a): edition(s), printing(s),
    publication(s)
wydanie bezprawne: pirated
    edition
wydanie bibliofilskie: bibliophile
    edition
wydanie jubileuszowe: jubilee
    edition
wydanie kieszonkowe: pocket
    edition
wydanie masowe: popular edition
wydanie miniaturowe: miniature
    edition
wydanie nowe: new edition
wydanie ocenzurowane: expurgated
    edition
wydanie ostateczne: definitive
    edition
wydanie poprawione: revised
    edition
wydanie popularne: popular
    edition
wydanie wstępne: preliminary
    edition
wydanie wyczerpane: out-of-print
wydany z: issued with
wydawca: editor, publisher of
    a book

wydawnictwo(a): publishing
house(s); publication(s)
wydawnictwo ciągłe: serial
publication
wydawnictwo periodyczne:
periodical
wydawnictwo zawieszone: sus-
pended publication
wydawnictwo zeszytowe: book
published in parts
wydawnictwo(a) zwarte: mono-
graph(s)
wydawniczy: publishing
wydłużony: elongated
wyeliminowany: eliminated
wyhaftowany: embroidered
wyjaśmiony: clarifying
wyjątkowy: exceptional
wykaz: list
wykaz alfabetyczny: alphabetical
list
wykład: lecture, reading
wykłady akademickie: series of
academic lectures
wyklejka: endpapers
wykonanie: workmanship
wykr. see wykres
wykres(y): diagram(s), graph(s)
wykreślony: crossed out
wyłącznie: solely
wyłączny: exclusive
wyłączone ze sprzedaży: not for
sale
wyłączony: excluded
wymazany: erased
wymiana: exchange
wymiar: size
wynosić: amount
wypisy: extracts
wypłowiały: discolored
wypolerowany: polished
wypracowany: elaborated
wypukły: embossed
wyrwany: torn out
wysoko poważany: highly
esteemed
wysortowany: assorted

wysprzedany: sold out
wysprzedaż: sale
wystawa: display, exhibit
wyszukany: extremely elaborate
wytączny: sole
wywołany: roughened
wzmocniony: reinforced,
strengthened
wznowić wydanie: republish
wznowione: renewed
wzór(y): design(s)

z: with
z. see zbiór, zeszyt
z oślimi uszami: dog-eared
za duży: oversize
za granicą: abroad
za lata: covering the period
za wyjątkiem: except for
zabrudzony: soiled
zachowany: preservation
żądanie: demand
żądany: requested
zadedykowany: inscribed
zagadnienia: problems
zagraniczny: foreign
zajmujący: interesting
zakazany: banned
zakład: establishment, institution
zakończenie: conclusion
zakonserwowany: preserved
zakrętas: flourish
zakurzony: dusty
zał. see załącznik
załącznik: enclosure, annex
załączony: annexed
zaliczka: prepayment, advance
payment
zamsz: suede
zaopatrzył: supplied by
zapiski: short notes
zapłata: payment
zapoczątkować: originate
zapowiedzi wydawnicze: publisher's announcements
zareprodukować: reproduce
zarezerwowany: reserved

zarówno: alike
zarys(y): outline(s), sketch(es)
zarys monograficzny: monographic
   study
zasadniczy: fundamental
zasięg: scope
zastąpić: replace
zastępca: substitute
zatwierdzono do druku: approved
   for printing
zawartość: contents
zawarty: comprising
zawiera: contains
zawierający: inclusive
zbieracz: collector
zbiór(y): collection(s)
zbiorowe dzieła: collected works
zbliżony: approximate
zbroszurowany: stitched in paper
   covers
zdobnictwo: ornamentation
zdolny: able
zdrobniały: diminutive
zepsuty: spoiled, damaged
zestawienie: compilation
zestawił: compiled
zeszyt(y): fascicle(s), part(s),
   issue(s)
zeszyty: stitched
zewnętrzny: exterior, external
zgnieciony: crushed
zgubiony tekst: loss of text
zielonkawy: greenish
zielony: green
zima: Winter
zjawienie: appearance
złamany: broken
złocenie: gilt, gilding
złoto: gold
złożony: composed; folded
zmatowiały: dulled

zmazany: effaced, rubbed off
zmieniona numeracja: renumbered
zmieniony: altered, changed
zmieniony tytuł: changed title
zmięty: crumpled
zmniejszenie: decrease
znaczący: significant
znacznie rozszerzony: considerably
   enlarged
znak(i): mark(s)
znak drukarski: printer's mark
znak firmowy: imprint
znak firmowy drukarni: printer's
   mark
znak(i) wodny(e): watermark(s)
znak wyd. *see* znak wydawnictwa
znak wydawnictwa: publisher's
   mark (trademark)
znakomity: notable
znaleziony: found
znany: known
znawca: expert
znikomy: minute, insignificant
zniszczony: damaged, destroyed
zniszczony korozją: corroded
znowu: anew
żółtawy: yellowish
żółte plamy: yellow stains
żółty: yellow
zręczny: skillful
źródło: source
zsumowanie: summary
zt. *see* zeszyt
zupełnie: altogether, entire
zupełny: entirely
zwięzły: concise
zwitek: scroll
zwykły: ordinary, usual
życzenie: request
żywa pagina: running title,
   running head

Portuguese

a buril: by graver
à cabeça: at the head
a côres: in colors
à direcção de: under the direction of
a douração: gilt
a duas colunas: in two-column format
a ferros secos: blind tooling
à frente: opposite, facing
a grande maioria: the majority
a licença: with permission
a maneira de: in the manner of
à mão: by hand
a melhor: the best
a negro: in black
a ofertas: subject to offers
à parte: apart, separately
à pena: by pen
a sêco: blind tooling
a sepia: in sepia
a tinta: in ink
à venda: for sale
a vermelho: in red
aberta a buril: worked by tool
aberto: engraved, open
acabado: finished, completed
acabar de sair: just published
acamurçado: buffed
acêrca de: concerning
acetinado: calendered
acima: above
aço: steel
acompanha: accompanies
acondicionado: packaged
acontecimento(s): event(s)

acrescentado: enlarged
actualizado: brought up to date, modernized
adapt. see adaptação
adaptação: adaptation
adequado: suitable
adiado: postponed
adiantamente: in advance
adiante: before
adornado: adorned, ornate
adôrno: ornament
afastado: removed
afectar: affect, affecting
afetando: simulating
afora: excluding, except
agora: now
agradável: attractive, nice
agua-forte(s): etching(s)
agua-tinta(s): aquatint(s)
aguarela(s): watercolor(s)
aguarelado: colored with watercolors
ainda: still, yet
alcance: scope
alegórico: allegorical
além de: in addition to, beyond
alg. see algumas
algodão: cotton
algumas: some
alguns: several
aliás: otherwise
alongado: elongated
alto: high, height, tall
amador see encadernação amador
amarelado: yellowed
amarelo: yellow

ambas as pastas: both covers
ambos os lados: both sides
amostra: sample
amp. *see* ampliação
ampliação: enlargement
ampliado: enlarged
anais: annals, chronicles
anexo: attached
anexo(s): annex(es), supplement(s)
ângulo(s): corner(s)
ano: year
anônimo: anonymous
anotação(ões): annotation(s)
anotado: annotated
ante-rosto: frontispiece; half-title
    page
anterior: front, former
antigo: old, antique
antigos compradores: former
    purchasers
antiguidades: antiquities
antiquado: out-of-date
antiquário: antiquarian
antologia: anthology
anual: annual, yearly
anualmente: annually
anuário: yearbook
apagado: obliterated
aparado: trimmed
aparar *see* por aparar
aparatoso: magnificent, ornate
aparte: not in the text
apelido: surname
apenas: scarcely, only
apêndice(s): appendix(es)
apenso: added, appended
aperfeiçoado: perfected
apesar de: notwithstanding
apontado: pointed out
apostilha(s): marginal note(s)
apreciado: prized, valued
aprêço *see* de aprêço
apresentação: presentation,
    appearance
aproximadamente: approximately
arabêsco(s): arabesque(s),
    flourish(es)

argênteo: silver
armoreado: decorated with coats
    of arms
arrancado: torn out
artigo(s): article(s)
artístico: artistic
aspecto: aspect, condition
ass. *see* assinado
assaz: very
asseado: clean
assetinado: with satin finish
assim: even so
assim por diante: and so forth
assin. *see* assinatura
assinado: signed
assinante(s): subscriber(s)
assinat. *see* assinatura
assinatura: signature; subscription
assunto: subject
até: until
até agora: so far
atinge: touches, affects
atingido: lightly damaged
atribuido: attributed
atribuindo: attributing
atual. *see* atualizado
atualizado: brought up to date
aum. *see* aumentado
aumentado: enlarged, increased
aumento: increase
ausente: missing
autenticar: to authenticate
autêntico: authentic, genuine
auto-retrato: self-portrait
autografado: autographed
autógrafo: autograph; autographic
autor: author
autoria: authorship
autorizado: authorized
avaria: damage
avariado: damaged
avermelhado: reddish
avulso: separate, loose
azul: blue

b. *see* bom, brochura
baixo: bottom, lower

baixo-relêvo: bas-relief
banido: banished
barato: cheap
barbado: deckle-edged
bast. *see* bastante
bastante: rather, sufficiently
belamente: beautifully
beleza: beauty
belíssimo: most beautifully
belo: beautiful, lovely
bem acabado: well-finished
bem conservado: well-preserved
bem cuidado: well-kept
bem tratado: well-kept
bibl. *see* biblioteca
bibliofilo(s): bibliophile(s)
bibliografia: bibliography
bibliográfico: bibliographic
biblioteca: library
bibliotecário: librarian
bich. *see* bichado
bichado: wormholed
bicho(s): worm(s)
bicolor: in two colors
bienal: biennial
bilingüe: bilingual
bimestral: bimonthly
bissemanal: semi-weekly
bistre: bistre
boa: good
bol. *see* boletim
boletim: bulletin
bôlso: pocket
bom: good
bonito: pretty
borda(s): border(s)
bordado: embroidered
borrado: erased, smudged
br. *see* brochado, brochura
branco: blank, white
brasão(ões): coat(s) of arms
brocado: brocade
broch. *see* brochado, brochura
brochado: stitched in paper covers
brochura: pamphlet, paperback
   binding
brunido: burnished

buril: graver
busca: search
buscado: sought, wanted

cabeça: head
cabeçal: vignette at top of page
cabeçalho: title page; heading
cabeção(ões): headpiece(s),
   vignette(s)
cabeceira(s): headband(s)
cada: each
caderninho(s): small copybook(s)
caderno(s): quire(s), signature(s);
   notebook(s)
caixa: case, box
caixa de amador: collector's box,
   case
caixa de proteção: protective box
caixa protectora: protective box
caligrafia: handwriting
camageu: cameo
camurça: chamois
camurçado: buffed, soft leather
cansado: worn-out
canto(s): corner(s)
capa(s): cover(s)
capa(s) de brochura: binding
   cover(s)
capa de resguardo: protective
   cover
capital(ães): capital letter(s)
capitular(es): initial letter(s) of
   chapter(s)
capítulo(s): chapter(s)
caracteres góticos: Gothic letters
característico: typical
carecendo: lacking
carecente: lacking
caricatura: caricature
caricaturista: caricaturist
carimbo: rubber stamp, seal
carn. *see* carneira
carneira: sheepskin
cart. *see* cartonado
cartilha(s): hornbook(s)
cartolina: bristol board, pasteboard

cartonado: bound in boards
cartonador: bookbinder
cartonagem: cardboard box, carton; binding
cartonagem do editor: publisher's binding
casa editôra: publishing house
castanho: chestnut-colored
cat. *see* catálogo
catálogo: catalog
catorze: fourteen
célebre: famous, renowned
cem: hundred
censura: censorship
centena(s): hundred(s)
centésimo: hundredth
centímetros: centimeters
centro: center
cerca de: near, about
cercadura(s): panel(s)
cetim: satin
cetinata: sateen
chagrém: shagreen
chamuscado: scorched
chapa: plate
chapa de aço: steel engraved plate
chapa de cobre: copper engraved plate
chapa de metal: metal engraved plate
charneira: joint
cheia: excess, abundance
cientifico: scientific
cinco: five
cinzento: gray
circundado: encircled
citação: citation, quotation
citado: cited
clandestino: clandestine
claro: clear
claro-escuro: chiaroscuro
clássico: classic
clicheria: engraving shop
cm. *see* centímetros
co-author: joint author
cobre: copper
códice: codex

coetâneo: contemporary
coevo: contemporary
coiro: leather
col. *see* coleção, colorido
colaboração: collaboration
colação: collation
colado: glued
colchete: fastenings
coleção(ões): series, set(s)
coleção de livros: set of books
colecionador: collector
coletado: collected
coletânea: collection, complete works
coligido: compiled, collected
colocado: placed
colofão: colophon
colorado: reddish color
colorido: color, colored
cols. *see* colunas
coluna(s): column(s)
com cantos: with corners
com falta de: lacking
com nervuras: ribbed
começando: beginning
comemorativo: commemorative
comentário(s): commentary(ies)
como novo: as new
comp. *see* compilado
compendiado: abridged
compêndio: compendium
compilação: compilation
compilado: compiled
compilador: compiler
completo: complete
completo de margens: with full margins, untrimmed
composto: composed, made
compra: purchase
compre(h)endido: included
comum: common
comumente: generally, usually
concluído: concluded
concordância: concordance
condição: condition
condicionado: prepared for
confeccionado: executed, compiled

confiscado: seized
conhecido: known
conhecimento: knowledge
conjunto com: together with
consertado: mended
conserva: retains
conservação: conservation
conservado: preserved, retained
conservando: conserving,
  preserving
consta de: consists of
constituido: constituted
conta: account
contemporâneo: contemporary
conteúdo: contents
continuação: continuation, sequel
continuo: continuous
contra: against
contracapa(s): endpaper(s)
contrafação: forgery, imitation
cooperação: cooperation
cópia: copy, imitation
cópia figurada: facsimile copy
copiador: copying machine
copiosamente: copiously
copioso: copious
côr(es): color(s)
côr cinza-azulada: slate-colored
côr de corça: fawn-colored
côr de laranja: orange-colored
côr ruiva: russet
cordovês: cordovan
corôa: garland
corôado: awarded a prize;
  completed
correcção(ões): correction(s)
correição(ões): correction(s)
corrente: current
correto: correct
corrigido: corrected
cortado: cut, trimmed
corte: cut, incision
cortes: edges
cortes de traça: cuts by bookworm,
  silverfish
cosedura: stitching
cotação: quotation

cotado: quoted, priced
couché: coated, glazed
couro: leather
couro de bezerra: calfskin
creme: cream-colored
crítico: critical, in bad state
crônica: chronicle
crônicas: annals
cuidado: careful, considered
cuidadosamente: carefully
curioso: curious, rare
cursivo: cursive

da autoria de: by authorship of
da frente: front, of the front
dactilografado: typewritten
danificado: damaged
data: date
de: from
de aprêço: valuable
de consulta: for research
de grande estimação: highly
  esteemed
de grande formato: in large
  format
de reserva: in reserve
décimo: tenth
décimo nono: nineteenth
décimo oitavo: eighteenth
décimo primeiro: eleventh
décimo quarto: fourteenth
décimo quinto: fifteenth
décimo setimo: seventeenth
décimo sexto: sixteenth
décimo terceiro: thirteenth
decorado: decorated
decorativo: decorative
ded. *see* dedicatória
dedic. *see* dedicação
dedic. aut. *see* dedicação autógrafa
dedicação: dedication
dedicação autógrafa: autographed
  dedication
dedicado: inscribed
dedicatória: dedication note
def. *see* defeito
defectivo: defective

defeit. *see* defeito
defeito(s): defect(s)
defeituoso: blemished, defective
defendido: protected; prohibited
deficiente: insufficient
definitivo: definitive
delgado: thin
demais: besides
demanda(s): request(s)
demasia: excess, too much
demasiadamente: excessively
dentro: within
des. *see* desdobrável, desenho
desbotado: faded
descolorido: faded
desconhecido: unknown
desconjuntado: unstitched,
  loosened
descontinuado: discontinued
desconto: discount
descosido: unstitched
descrição: description
descripção: description
descritivo: descriptive
desd. *see* desdobrável
desde: from
desdobr. *see* desdobrável
desdobrando: unfolding
desdobrar: to unfold
desdobrável: unfolding
desencad. *see* desencadernado
desencadernado: unstitched, covers
  gone
desenhado: designed
desenho(s): sketch(es), design(s)
desgastado: chafed, worn
desgastes: abrasions
desgasto: abraded
desigual: disparate
deslustrado: dulled, tarnished
despesas de transporte: costs of
  carriage
destacado: detached
destruido: broken, destroyed
deteriorado: deteriorated
detrás: in back, behind
deveras: truly

dez: ten
dezena(s): ten(s)
dezenove: nineteen
dezesseis: sixteen
dezessete: seventeen
dezoito: eighteen
diário: daily
dicionário: dictionary
dicionário geográfico: gazetteer
difícil: difficult
difícil de obter: difficult to find
dificílima: very difficult
difícilmente: with difficulty
dimensões: dimensions
direção: direction, supervision
direito: right-hand
direitos autorais: copyright
dirigido: directed
disperso: scattered
disponível: available, ready
dissertação(ões): dissertation(s)
distribuído: distributed
dobrado: folded
dobrável: folding, folded
dobro: double
documentado: documented
documento(s): document(s)
dois: two
dour. *see* douração, dourado
douração: gilding, gold decoration
dourado: gilt, decorated with gold
dourado por fôlhas: gilt edges
dourados: gold designs
doze: twelve
duas: two
duodécimo: twelfth
dupla página: double page
duvidoso: doubtful, dubious

e. *see* encadernação, encadernado
ed. *see* edição
ediç. *see* edição
edição(ões): edition(s)
edição comum: ordinary, popular
  edition
edição esgotada: out of print
edição limitada: limited edition

edição pirateado: pirated edition
edição príncipe: first edition
edição provisória: temporary
edition
edição romântica: edition in
romantic format
edição vulgar: ordinary edition
editado: published
editor: publisher
editôra: publishing house
elegante: elegant, tasteful
elevado: high
em: in, into
em anexo: herewith
em breve: soon
em carneira: in sheepskin
em chagrém: in shagreen
em contrapartida: in offset
em data próxima: at an early date
em demasia: excessive
em diante: forward, following
em enteira: full
em enteira de pele: in full leather
em extra-texto: not in the text
em grande papel: on large paper
em lona: in canvas
em madeira: in wood
em mau estado: in poor condition
em metal: in metal
em página enteira: in full page
em papel: in sheets
em parte: partly
em perfeito estado: in perfect
condition
em perfeito estado de conservação:
in perfect state of conservation
em pergaminho: in vellum
em policromia: in many colors
em preto e branco: in black and
white
em relevo: raised
em separado: not in the text
em tôda a volta: on all sides, all
around
em tôda parte: throughout
em urgência: rush
embalagem: packing

emblema: emblem
embora: though, even
embutido: inlaid, inlay; mosaic
emenda(s): emendation(s)
emendado: emended
em(m)oldurado: framed, bordered
empastado: bound in boards
empregado: used
enc. *see* encadernação, encadernado
enc. antiga *see* encadernação
antiga
enc. da época *see* encadernação
da época
enc. de amador *see* encadernação
de amador
enc. edit. *see* encadernação de
editor
enc. editor *see* encadernação de
editor
encad. *see* encadernação,
encadernado
encadernação(ões): binding
encadernação amador: three-
quarter binding
encadernação antiga: old binding
encadernação característica: usual
binding, characteristic binding
encadernação da época: contemporary binding
encadernação de amador: three-
quarter binding
encadernação de editor: publisher's
binding
encadernação do tempo: contemporary binding
encadernação vulgar: common
binding
encadernado: bound
encadernador: binder
encantador: charming
encerra: includes
encimado: above, surmounted by
encorpado: thick, heavy; solid
enegrecido: darkened
enfeite(s): ornaments
enquadrado: framed
enriquecido: enriched, adorned

enrugado: wrinkled
ensaio: essay
entre: between
entre o texto: within the text
entrelação: interlacing
entretela: buckram
enumerado: enumerated,
 enumerative
envernizado: glossy, coated
enxovalhado: dirty, soiled
epígrafe: inscription
epílogo: epilogue, postface
época: time period, epoch
errado: erroneous
êrro(s): mistake(s)
erudição: erudition
erudito: scholarly
esboçado: outlined
esbôço: draft, rough outline
escasso: scarce
esclarecimento(s): explanation(s),
 explanatory note(s)
escolhido: selected
escrito(s): writing(s)
escritor(es): writer(s)
esculpido: sculptured
escurecido: obscured
escuro: dark
esfarrapedo: tattered
esfolado: abraded, scratched
esfoladura(s): abraded spot(s)
esgotado: exhausted, out of print
esmaltado: embellished; enameled
esmalte: enamel
esmeradamente: perfectly
esmerado: perfect
espalhado: scattered, scattering
especial: special
especialidade: specialty
espécimen: sample
espelhado: polished, smooth
espessura: thickness
espiral: spiral
esplendido: splendid
esquadria: right angle
esquerdo: left-hand
est. *see* estampa

estado: condition, state
estado de novo: as new
estalado: split
estampa: print, engraving
estilo: style
estimação: esteem, value
estimado: valuable
estôjo: box, case
estôjo de luxo: deluxe box
estragado: deteriorated, damaged
estrangeiro: foreign
estreito: narrow
estropiado: mutilated
estudo(s): study(ies)
etiquêta: label
ex. *see* exemplar
ex-libris: *ex libris*
exausto: exhausted
excepcional: uncommon
excluido: excluded
excluindo: excluding
exclusivamente: exclusively
exclusivo: exclusive
execução: execution, workmanship
executado: executed
exemplar(es): copy(ies)
existente: existing
expedição: shipment
expl. *see* exemplar
expungido: expunged, deleted
expurgado: expurgated, purged
ext. *see* externo
externo: external
extra-grande: oversize
extra-texto *see* em extra-texto
extraído: extracted
extrememente: extremely
extremo: extreme

f. *see* fôlha
fabrikoid: imitation leather
fac-símile(s): facsimile(s)
facs. *see* fac-símile
facsimilado: reproduced in
 facsimile
factício: artificial, imitation
facultativo: optional

faixa(s): ribbon(s)
faixa(s) decorativo(s): headband(s)
faixa(s) ornamental(es): head-
  band(s)
falha: break, split; defect
falsamente: falsely
falso: fake
falta: defect; lacks
fasc. *see* fascículo
fascículo: fascícule, part
fatura: invoice
fecho(s): clasp(s)
feio: ugly
feito à mão: handmade
ferro(s): tooled design(s)
ferros do romantismo: tooling in
  the romantic style
ferros secos *see* à ferros secos
ff. *see* fôlhas
ffls. *see* fôlhas
ficção: fiction
figura(s): chart(s); figure(s)
figurinha(s): small chart(s),
  figure(s)
filetado: tooled
filete(s): fillet(s)
filigrana: watermark
filigranada: watermarked
fim: end
final(aes): tailpiece(s)
finalizado: completed
fino: fine, thin
fixo: fixed
fl. *see* fôlha
flexível: flexible
flht. *see* folheto
flor-de-lis: fleur-de-lys
florão(ões): floral design(s)
fol. *see* fôlha
fôlha(s): leaf(ves), sheet(s)
fôlha dupla: double page
folhado: foliated
folhas sôltas: loose-leaf
folheação: foliation
folheto(s): pamphlet(s)
fólio: folio
fonte(s): source(s)

fora de dúvida: without doubt
fora de texto: not in the text
fora do comércio: not for sale
fora do mercado: not for general
  sale, privately printed
forma: form
formato: format
formidável: striking
formosíssimo: very beautiful
formoso: beautiful
fornecido: provided
forte: strong
fôsco: mat, opaque
foto(s): photograph(s)
fotocópia: photocopy
fotografia(s): photograph(s)
fotogravura(s): photoengraving(s)
fotolito(s): photolithograph(s)
fotóstato: photostat
fototipia: phototype
fotozincogravura: photo-
  zincography
frágil: brittle
fragmento(s): fragment(s)
frente a: facing
freqüente: frequent
fresco: fresh
frescura: freshness
friso: frieze
front. *see* frontispício
frontisp. *see* frontispício
frontispício: frontispiece
fulvo: tawny
fundido: molded
fundo: background
furo(s): hole(s)
furo(s) de traça: wormhole(s)
furos de bicho: wormholes
fustão: fustian

g. *see* grande
galante: gallant
gasto: worn-out
gazeta: gazette
género antigo: of the old style
geográfico: geographic
geral: general

glosa(s): gloss(es), note(s)
glosado: commented
glossário: glossary
gofrado: embossed
gôsto: taste
Gótico: Gothic
gr. *see* grande
gracioso: gracious
gráf. *see* gráfico
gráfico: graphic
granadino: maroon
grande: large
granido: stippled
granulado: pebbled
gratuito: free
grav. *see* gravado, gravura
gravação a fris: drypoint engraving
gravação(ões) em aço: steel engraving(s)
gravação(ões) em cobre: copper engraving(s)
gravado: engraved
gravador: engraver
gravamente: severely
gravs. em aço *see* gravação em aço
gravs. em cobre *see* gravação em cobre
gravura(s): engraving(s)
gravura(s) a água forte: etching(s)
gravura a maneira negra: mezzo-tint
gravura(s) em madeira: woodcut(s)
gravurinha(s): small engraving(s)
grosseiramente: grossly, coarsely
grosseiro: coarse
grosso: thick, voluminous
grossura: thickness
grotesco: grotesque
grupo: lot
guache: gouache
guarda(s): endpaper(s), flyleaf(ves)
guarda(s) de seda: silk lining(s)

hàbilmente: ably
heliográfico: engraved
heliogravura(s): engraving(s)

heliótipo: heliotype, photoengraving
hológrafo: holograph

idêntico: identical
ignorado: unknown
igual: equal, similar
il. *see* ilustrado, ilustrador
ilegível: illegible
iluminado: illuminated
iluminura(s): illumination, illuminated page(s)
ilustr. *see* ilustração, ilustrado
ilustração(ões): illustration(s)
ilustrado: illustrated
ilustrador: illustrator
imaculado: immaculate, spotless
imitação: imitation, copy
imitando: imitating
imp. *see* impresso
impecável: impeccable
imperfeição(ões): blemish(es)
importação: import
impr. *see* impresso
imprensa: press, printing plant
imprescindível: indispensable
impressão(ões): printing(s)
impressionante: impressive
impresso: printed; pamphlet
impressor: printer
impressos: printed matter
inacabado: unfinished
inadequado: unsatisfactory
inalterado: unchanged
inalteravel: unchangeable
incluído: included
inclusivo: inclusive
incontestável: incontestable
incrustação: inlay
incrustado: inlaid
incunábulo(s): incunabulum(a)
ind. *see* indicação
indene: undamaged
indicação: indication
índice(s): index(es)
índice de unha: thumb index
índice geral: general index

indispensável: indispensable
inédito: unpublished
inexpurgado: unexpurgated
in-F. *see* in-fólio
inferior: lower
in-fólio: in folio format, folio
informação: information
inicial(aes): initial letter(s)
in-octavo: octavo
inscrição: subscription
inscripção: inscription
inseparável: inseparable
inserção: insertion, inset
inserto: inserted
int. *see* inteiro, interno
int. de pele *see* inteira de pele
intacto: intact, undamaged
intacto de margens: with full
    margins
integral: complete, unabridged
íntegro: intact
inteira de pele: full leather
inteira de pele de carneira: full
    sheepskin
inteira de pelica inglesa: full kid
    leather
inteira de pergaminho: full vellum
inteira de vitela: full calf
inteiramente: entirely, quite
inteiro: full, whole
intercalado: intercalated
interessante: interesting, attractive
interessantíssimo: most interesting,
    most attractive
interfoliado: interleaved
ínterim: interim
interior: inner, interior
interiormente: internally
interno: internal
interpretação: interpretation
intitulado: entitled
intrínseco: intrinsic
introdutório: introductory
inum. *see* inumerado
inumerado(s): unnumbered
inumerável: innumerable
inúmero: innumerable

inums. *see* inumerados
inverno: Winter
isoladamente: singly
isolado: detached, isolated
itálico: italics

já: now, already
já anunciado: just announced,
    just out
jansenista: Jansenist binding
jóia: jewel
jornal: newspaper
juntamente: together
junto: together
junto com: together with

l. *see* lugar
lacre: sealing wax
lado: side
lado a lado: parallel
lápis: pencil
laqueado: lacquered
largamente: largely, generously
largura: width
lavado: cleaned
lavanda: lavender
lavável: washable
ldo. *see* limitado
letra(s): letter(s), type
letra(s) capitular(es): chapter-
    heading letter(s)
letra(s) de forma: block letter(s)
letra gótica: Gothic type
letra(s) inicial(aes): initial letter(s)
letra(s) maiúscula(s): capital
    letter(s)
letra(s) minúscula(s): lowercase
    letter(s)
letra(s) uncial(es): uncial letter(s)
leve: slight, light
levemente: slightly
léxico: lexicon, dictionary
libelo infamatório: lampoon
licença(s): authorization(s),
    license(s)
ligeir. *see* ligeiramente
ligeiramente: slightly

ligeiro: light, slight
liminar: preliminary
limitado: limited
limpado: cleaned
limpo: neat, clear
lindo: attractive
lingua(s): language(s)
linho: linen
liso: plain, smooth
lista: list
lito(s): lithograph(s)
litografado: lithographed
litografia(s): lithograph(s),
   lithography
litográfico: lithographic
liv. *see* livraria
livraria: book shop
livreiro: bookseller
livreto: small book
livrinho: small book
livro: book
livro de bôlso: pocketbook
livro de consulta: reference book
livro escolar: textbook
local: place
local de impressão: place of
   printing
lombada: back of a book, spine
lona: canvas, sailcloth
losango: lozenge
lote: lot
louvável: praiseworthy
lug. *see* lugar
lugar: place
lugar de impressão: place of
   printing
lustrado: glazed, polished
lustroso: polished
luxuosamente: luxuriously
luxuosíssima: most luxurious
luxuoso: deluxe, luxurious

má: bad
maculado: spotted
madeira: wood
madrepérola: mother-of-pearl
magnífico: magnificent

maior formato: large format
maioria: majority
mais: and, besides, more, plus
mais despesas de cobrança: plus
   costs of collection
mais encorpado: thicker
mais tarde: later
maiúsculo(s): capital letter(s)
mal: badly
maleável: flexible
manancial: source
mancha: spot, stain
mancha(s) de agua: water stain(s)
mancha(s) de umidade: moisture
   stain(s)
manchado: spotted, stained
manchado de umidade: damp-
   stained
manuscrito: manuscript
mapa: map
mapa em relêvo: relief map
mar. *see* marroquim
maravilhoso: marvelous
marca(s): mark(s)
marca de impressor: printer's mark
marca de propriedade: ownership
   stamp
marcado a lápis: pencilled
marfím: ivory
margem(ens): margin(s), border(s)
marmoreado: marbled
marmorização: marbling
marrom: brown
marroquim: morocco
mas: but
material sintético: synthetic
   material
mau: bad
máx. *see* máxima
máxima: very large
medalhão: medallion
mediano: mediocre
médio: medium
medíocre: mediocre
meio: half
meio de chagrin: half-morocco
   binding

melh. *see* melhorado
melhor: better
melhorado: improved
melhoramento(s): improvement(s)
membro(s): member(s)
memórias: memoirs
mensal: monthly
mercado: market, trade
merecimento: merit, worth
mesmo: same
microfilme: microfilm
mil: thousand
míldio: mildew
milhar(es): thousand(s)
mimeógrafado: mimeographed
miniatura: miniature
mínimo: minimum
minuciosamente: minutely
minucioso: minute
miscelânea: miscellany
misto: mixed
modernizado: modernized
moderno: modern
modesta: plain
modificação: modification
moldura: frame, molding
môle: soft
monástico: monastic
monografia: monograph
monográfico: monographic
monograma: monogram
monumental: monumental
mosaico: mosaic
mosqueado: mottled
motivo: motif
móvel: movable
ms. *see* manuscrito
mto. *see* muito
muitas vezes: often
muitíssimo: very much
muito(s): much, numerous, very
muito curioso: very unusual
muito estimada: highly esteemed
muito ilustrada: profusely
   illustrated
muito pouco vulgar: very
   uncommon

muito procura: eagerly sought
multicolor: varicolored
mus. *see* música
música: music
musselina: muslin
mutilação: mutilation
mutilado: mutilated

na caixa protectora: in protective
   case
nada frecuente: seldom found
nada vulgar: not common
não: never
não cortado: uncut, unopened
não numerado: unnumbered
não vulgar: not common
narrativo: narrative
negro: black
nem: nor
nenhum: any, neither, none
nervos: (raised) bands
nítidamente: neatly, clearly
nítido: neat, clear
no final: at the end
no inicial do: at the beginning
no mercado: in the trade,
   available
no prelo: in press
no texto: in the text
nome: name
nonagésimo: ninetieth
nono: ninth
notação: notation
notas: notes
notas marginais: marginal notes
notável: notable
notàvelmente: notably
notícias: news, announcement
novamente: anew, newly, again
nove: nine
novela(s): novel(s), novelette(s)
novidade: news, novelty
nôvo: new
núm. *see* número
numeração: numbering
numerado(s): numbered
número(s): number(s)

numerosíssimos: in great numbers
numeroso(s): numerous
numes. *see* numerados
nums. *see* numerados
nunca: never

o melhor: the best
o ótimo: the very best
oblongo: oblong
obra(s): work(s)
obra espúria: spurious work
obra(s) poética(s): poetic work(s)
obra-prima: masterpiece
observações: observations
óbvio: obvious
ocre: ochre
octagésimo: eightieth
of. *see* oficina
oferta(s): offer(s)
ofic. *see* oficina
oficial: official
oficialmente: officially
oficina: shop, print shop
oitavo: eighth
oito: eight
omissão: omission
ondeado: moiré
onomastico: onomastic
onze: eleven
op. *see* opúsculo
oportunidade: occasion
oposto: opposite
ops. *see* opúsculos
óptimo: the best, the finest
óptimo exemplar: superb copy
opúsculo(s): small work(s)
ordinario: usual
org. *see* organizado
organizado: organized
origem: origin
original: original
orla: border, edge
orlado: bordered
ornado: decorated, adorned
ornamentação: decoration
ornamentado: decorated
ornato: decorated, adorned

ótimo: the best, the finest
ouro: gold
outono: Fall, Autumn
outro(s): other(s), otherwise

p. *see* página
padrão(ões): pattern(s)
pag. *see* página
pagamento: payment
pagamento adiantado: advance
    payment, prepayment
página(s): page(s)
página de rôsto: title page
página(s) numerada(s): numbered
    page(s)
paginação: pagination
paginação seguida: continuous
    paging
págs. *see* páginas
pálido: colorless
panfleto: pamphlet
pano: cloth, panel
papel: paper
papel assetinado: glazed paper
papel avergoado: laid paper
papel azul: blue paper
papel comum: common paper
papel couché: coated paper, art
    paper
papel de algodão: rag paper
papel de arroz: rice paper
papel de linho: linen paper
papel de pergaminho: parchment
    paper
papel extra: extra-quality paper
papel Japão: Japan paper
papel pergaminho: parchment
    paper
papel velino: vellum paper,
    parchment
para cima de: more than
para restaurar: needing repairs
parágrafo: paragraph
paralela: parallel
parcialmente: partially
paródia: parody
parte(s): part(s)

pé: foot, bottom
peça(s): piece(s), part(s)
pedaço(s): piece(s)
pedido(s): order(s)
pele: skin, leather
pele de bezerro: calfskin
pele de cabra: goatskin
pele de porco: pigskin
pelica: kid leather
pen(n)a: pen
penúltimo: next to last
peq. *see* pequeno
pequeno: small
perc. *see* percalina
percal: percale
percalina: percaline
perceptivél: noticeable
perda: loss
perda de têxto: loss of text
perfeito: perfect
perfuração: perforation
perfurado: holed
perg. *see* pergaminho
pergaminho: parchment
pergaminho vegetal: parchment
  paper
pergaminho velino: vellum
perícia: craftsmanship
periódico: periodical
perito: expert
permissão: permission
pesado: heavy
picado: wormholed, perforated
pico(s) de traça: wormhole(s)
pintado: colored, painted
pirateado: pirated
placa: plaque
plágio: plagiarism
plano: flat
plasticizado: plasticized
plastico: plastic
pleno: full
pobre: poor
poema(s): poem(s)
poesia: poetry
polêmica: polemic
policromia: polychrome

poliglota: polyglot
polvoroso: dusty
ponta-sêca: drypoint
pontilhado: dotted, stippled
ponto: point
popular: popular
popularissimo: most popular
por abrir: pages uncut
por aparar: pages uncut
por fôlhas: in sheets
porém: still, yet, however
pórfirio: porphyry
pormenorizadamente: in detail
porta-fólio: portfolio
porte: postage
porte page: postpaid
possível: possible
possívelmente: possibly
possue: has, having
posta a venda: offered for sale
posterior: later, subsequent
póstumo: posthumous
pouco: little
pouco comum: uncommon
pouco frequente: rare
pouco vulgar: uncommon
poucos: few
pouquíssimo: very few
pp. *see* páginas
prancha(s): plate(s)
prazenteiro: pleasing
prec. *see* preciso
precedente: preceding
preciosidade: preciousness
precioso: precious, costly
preciso: necessary; exact, distinct
preço: price
preço de assinatura: subscription
  price
pref. *see* prefação
prefação: preface
prefaciado: prefaced
prefaciador: writer of preface
prefácio: preface, foreword
preferível: preferable
prega: fold
prejudicado: damaged, injured

prejuízo: damage, injury
prel. *see* preliminar
preliminar(es): preliminary page(s)
prelo: printing press
prels. *see* preliminares
premiado: prize-winning
preparação: preparation
preservação: preservation
prêto: black
prèviamente: previously
prévio: previous
prezado: prized, esteemed
primeira edição: first edition
primeiro: first
primitivo: original
primoroso: first-class, excellent
princípio: beginning, front
privilégio: permission
processo: process
procura: sought, in demand
procurado: sought, searched for
profusamente: profusely
proibido: forbidden
prólogo: prologue
prontamente: soon
próprio: own; personal
prospeto: prospectus
prova: proof
provisório: temporary
pseud. *see* pseudônimo
pseudônimo: pseudonym,
    pseudonymous
publicação(ões): publication(s)
publicado: published
púrpura: purple

quadrado: square
quadriculado: checkered
quadro: picture
qualidade: quality
quanto possível: as much as
    possible
quarentesimo: fortieth
quarto: fourth; quarto
quase: almost
quase não: almost never, scarcely
quatro: four

quebrado: split
queimadura: burn
quinquagesimo: fiftieth
quinto: fifth
quinze: fifteen
quinzenário: biweekly, fortnightly

rabisco: scribbling
raramente encontrado: seldom
    found
rareando: becoming rare
raridade: rarity
raríssimo: very rare
raro: rare
rascadura: scratch, abrasion
rascunho: draft, outline
rasgado: torn, ripped
rasgadura(s): tear(s)
rasgão(ões): tear(s)
raspado: scratched, erased
raspadura(s): scraped spot(s)
rasurado: scraped
ratado: gnawed
razoável: reasonable
reajustado: rearranged
realçado: enhanced
realização: presentation, format
recente: recent
recentemente: recently
recolhido: collected
reconhecido: recognized
recopilação: abridgment,
    compilation
recortado: cut out
redação: editing
redator: editor
redução: reduction
reduzido: reduced
reedição: reediting, reprinted
reeditado: reedited, reprinted
ref. *see* refundido
reforçado: reinforced
reforço: reinforced
refundido: recast
registo: index, register
registro: index, register
reimpressão: reprint

relação(ões): story(ies),
  report(s), list(s)
relacionado: related
relevado: embossed
rematado: finished off
remate: finishing, final touch
remendado: mended, patched
remendo: mend, mending
renovado: renewed
renovar: renew
renumerado: renumbered
reparação: restoration
repertorio: repertory
repetido: repeated
repleto: replete
reprodução(ões): reproduction(s)
reproduzindo: reproducing
reservado: reserved
resguardo: protective cover
restante: remainder
restauração: repair
restauro: restoration
restituido: restored
restrito: limited
resumo: abstract, summary
ret. *see* retrato
reto: recto
retocado: improved; retouched
retrato: portrait
retrospectivo: retrospective
rev. *see* revisão, revista
reverso: reverse
revestido: provided with
revisado: revised
revisão(ões): revision(s)
revista: review, journal
revisto: reviewed, revised
rica: rich
ricamente: richly
rigorosamente: rigorously
roçado: rubbed, worn away
romano: roman type
rompimento: break
roseta(s): rosette(s)
rôsto: title page, frontispiece
rôto: torn
rotogravura: rotogravure

rótulo: label, inscription
roxo: purple
ruão: roan
rúbrica: rubric, flourish
rubricado: rubricated
rústico: rustic

s. *see* sem
s.d. *see* sem data
s.d. de impressão *see* sem data de
  impressão
s.ed. *see* sem editôra
s.l. *see* sem lugar
s.l.n.d. *see* sem lugar nem data
s. lugar *see* sem lugar
s.n. *see* sem numeração
saído: appeared
saliente: outstanding
salmão: salmon
salpicado: dotted, sprinkled
sanguíneo: blood-colored
sátira: satire, lampoon
seção, se(c)ção: section
sêco *see* a sêco
século dezessete: seventeenth
  century
sêda: silk
seguidamente: in succession
seguido de: followed by
seguinte(s): following, next
segundo: according to; second
seis: six
seleção(ões), selecção(ões):
  selection(s)
sêlo: seal, stamp
sem: without
sem afetar o texto: without
  affecting the text
sem autorização: without
  permission
sem data: without date
sem data de impressão: without
  date of publication
sem data nem local: without date
  or place
sem editôra: without publisher

sem ferir o texto: without damaging the text
sem local nem data: without place or date
sem lugar: without place
sem lugar nem data: without place or date
sem lustre: lusterless
sem mancha: spotless
sem numeração: unnumbered
sem o nome do autor: without the author's name
sem ofenso ao texto: without harm to the text
sem pecado: without a fault, immaculate
sem preço: priceless
sem prejuício: without damage
sem prejuízo do texto: without damaging the text
sem valor: without value, worthless
semanal: weekly
semelhante: resembling, similar
semestral: semiannual
semi-anual: semiannual
sep. *see* separata
separadamente: separately
separata: separate, reprint
separável: detachable
sépia: sepia
septuagésimo: seventieth
seqüência: sequence
sér. *see* série
sèriamente: seriously
série: series
serifa: serif
sete: seven
sétimo: seventh
sexagésimo: sixtieth
sexto: sixth
simili-gravura: halftone engraving
simplificado: simplified
simpósio: symposium
sinête: signet
sintético: artificial, synthetic
só: sole, only

sob: under
soberbo: superb
sôbre: on, upon
sobrecapa: book jacket
sobreposto: superimposed
sobrescrito: superscription
sóbrio: modest, discreet
sofrido: suffered
sofrivel: fair
solicitado: requested
sòlidamente: solidly
solteiro: single
sôlto: loose, unbound
sombreado: shaded
sòmente: only
sortido(s): assorted
sucessivo: successive
sujado: soiled
sujo: dirty
sumamente apreciado: highly esteemed
sumário: summary
suntuoso: costly, sumptuous
super-libros: ownership stamp
superior: upper; better
suplementar: additional
suplementar(es): supplementary
suplemento: supplement
suposto: imaginary, supposed
supresso: suppressed
suprimido: suppressed

t. *see* tomo
tabela: table, index
tábua(s): table(s)
talão de encomenda: order form
talhe doce: taille douce, copper engraving, copperplate
talvez: perhaps
tamanho: size
também: also, otherwise
tarja: black border design; ornamental painted border
tarjado: bordered in black; with ornamental border
tecido: cloth
tecnico: technical

tela: cloth
tela alemã: German cloth
terceiro: third
tesouro: thesaurus
texto: text
tip. *see* tipografia
tipo: type, typeface
tipo graúdo: huge type
tipocromia: color printing
tipografia: typography
tipográfico: typographic
tiragem: edition, printing
tiragem especial: special edition
tiragem limitada: limited edition
tiragem reducida: limited edition
tiragem restrita: limited edition
tiragem vulgar: ordinary edition
título: title, title page
título de página: running head
tôda a volta: all edges
todas as margens: full margins
todos os lugares: everywhere
tomo: tome
tôpo: top
trabalhado: tooled, worked
trabalho: work
traça(s): worm(s)
traçado: wormholed
trad. *see* tradução, tradutor
tradução: translation
tradutor: translator
traduzido: translated
transações: proceedings,
   transactions
transposto: transposed
tratado: treated, treatise
três: three
treze: thirteen
tricromia: three-color printing
trigésimo: thirtieth
trimestral: quarterly, every three
   months
trocado: exchanged, out of place;
   replaced by
truncado: truncated
tudo: everything, all

tudo quanto se publicou: all
   published until now

último: last
um: one
um pouco: a little, somewhat
um pouco cansada: a little weak
um pouco esfolada: a little
   abraded, scratched
uma: one
umidade: humidity, moisture
undécimo: eleventh
únicamente: solely
único: unique, sole
unido: combined
usado: worn, secondhand
uso: wear
útil: useful
utilidade: utility
utilizado: utilized

v. *see* volume
valiosíssimo: extremely valuable
valioso: important, rich, valuable
valor: value
valorisado: enhanced in value
variadíssimo: extremely varied
variante: variant
várias: various, several
vastíssimo: very vast
velho: old
velino: vellum
veludo: velvet
venda: sale
venda por atacado: wholesale
vendido: sold
verão: Summer
verdadeiramente: truly
verdadeiro: true, truly
verde: green
verde-escuro: dark green
verde-olive: olive green
verdoso: greenish
verificado: verified
vermelhão: vermilion
vermelho: red
versão: version, translation

verso: verso, back side
vestígio(s): trace(s)
via aérea: airmail
vigésimo: twentieth
vinheta: tailpiece, vignette
vinte: twenty
violeta: violet
vista: view, panorama
vitelo: calf

vocábulo(s): word(s)
vol. *see* volume
volante: broadsheet
volume: volume
voluta(s): scroll(s)
vulgar: common, ordinary

xilogravs. *see* xilogravuras
xilogravura(s): woodcut(s)

Romanian

abecedar: hornbook, primer, reader
abonament: subscription
abonat: borrower, subscriber
abreviaţie(i): abbreviation(s)
abreviere(i): abbreviation(s)
abstracţie: abstract
abundent: abundant, abundantly
academic: academic
academie: academy
achiziţie: acquisition
acoperit: coated, covered
acoperit cu pete roşcate: foxed
acuarelă(e): aquatint(s), water-
  color(s)
acumulat: cumulated
adaos: addition, insertion
adaptare: adaptation
adaptat: adapted
adendă: addenda, appendix
adeseori: frequently
adînc: deep
adiţional: additional, supplementary
adnota: annotate
adnotare(ări): annotation(s),
  comment(s)
adnotat: annotated
adresare: address
adunare: assembly
afişat: pasted
agrafă(e): clasp(s)
ajutător: accessory, additional
al cincilea: fifth
al cincisprezecelea: fifteenth
al cincizecilea: fiftieth
al doilea: second

al doisprezecelea: twelfth
al douăzecilea: twentieth
al nouăsprezecelea: nineteenth
al nouăzecilea: ninetieth
al noulea: ninth
al optsprezecelea: eighteenth
al optulea: eighth
al optzecilea: eightieth
al paisprezecelea: fourteenth
al patrulea: fourth
al patruzecilea: fortieth
al şaisprezecelea: sixteenth
al şaizecilea: sixtieth
al şaptelea: seventh
al şaptesprezecelea: seventeenth
al şaptezecilea: seventieth
al şaselea: sixth
al sutălea: one hundredth
al treilea: third
al treisprezecelea: thirteenth
al treizecilea: thirtieth
al unsprezecelea: eleventh
al zecelea: tenth
alamă: brass
alăturat: enclosed, herewith
alb: blank, white
albastru: blue
album(e): album(s)
alcătui: compile, compose
aldin: black face
alfabetic: alphabetical
algrafie: aluminography
almanah(uri): almanac(s)
alt: other
alternativ: alternative
altfel: differently, otherwise

alungit: elongated, oblong
amănunt: detail
amănunţit: detailed
ambalaj: packing, wrapper
an(ii): year(s)
anale: annals
analitic: analytical
anastatic: anastatic
anexă(e): annex(es), appendix(es)
anexă detaşată: insert
angros: wholesale
anonim: anonymous, anonymously
anotaţie marginală: marginal note
ansamblu: ensemble
anterior: former
antetitlu: data before the title
antic: old
anticar: antiquarian, secondhand
  bookseller
anticariat: antiquarian book shop
antologie: anthology
anual: annual, yearly
anuar(e): yearbook(s)
anul apariţiei: year of publication
anul curent: current year
anunţ(uri): advertisement(s),
  announcement(s), notice(s)
apă tare: aqua fortis, nitric acid
apare: appear, published
apare in curînd: soon to appear
apărea: appear, publish
apărut: recent
apendice(i): appendix(es),
  supplement(s)
apreciat: prized, valuable
aproape de: near, next to
aprobat: approved
aproximativ: approximately
arabesc: arabesque
aramă: copper
aranjament: arrangement
aranjare: arrangement
aranjat: arranged
arde: burn
argint: silver
arhivă(e): archive(s)
arhivistică: archival science

ars: burned, scorched
arsură: burn
articol(e): article(s), item(s)
artificial: artificial
artistic: artistic
asociaţie: association
asterisc: asterisk
asupra: on, over, upon; about,
  concerning
ataşat: attached
atlas: atlas
atlas de buzunar: pocket atlas
atribuit: attributed
aur: gold
auri: gild
aurire de mînă: hand gilding
aurit: gilded
autentic: authentic
autobiografie(i): autobiography(ies)
autograf(e): autograph(s)
autografiat: autographed
autor: author
autor colectiv: corporate author
autoriza: authorize
autorizat: authorized
avariat: damaged
avariat superficial: lightly damaged
avarie: damage
aviz: note, notice
avizul dreptului de autor: copyright notice
azuriu: azured

balama(le): hinge(s), joint(s)
bandă: band, tape
bandă de cap: headband
bandă dublă: double bands
banderolă numerotată: foliated
  scroll
banderolă ornamentală: ornamental
  scroll(s)
bani: cash, money
bătrîn: aged, ancient, old
benzi: bands, tapes
benzi decorative: ornamental bands
benzi false: false bands
benzi falsificate: imitation bands

benzi ridicate: raised bands
benzi turtite: flat bands
bianual: semiannual
bibliofil: bibliophile, book collector
bibliograf: bibliographer
bibliografic: bibliographic
bibliografie: bibliography
bibliografie internă: internal
  bibliography
bibliotecă: library
bibliotecar: librarian
bienal: biennial
bifat: checked, lined through
bilingv: bilingual
bilunar: bimonthly, fortnightly,
  twice a month
bine: well
bine conservat: well-preserved
biografic: biographical
biografie(i): biography(ies)
bisăptămînal: biweekly
blazon: blazon, coat of arms
bloc de lemn: woodblock
bloc de linoleum: linoleum block
bogat: rich, richly
bordura(i) decorativă(e): ornamental border(s)
briliant: brilliant
brocart: brocade
brodat: embroidered
bronz: bronze
bronzat: browned
broşat: in paper covers, sewed
broşate: paperbound
brosură(i): booklet(s), brochure(s),
  pamphlet(s); preprint(s)
brosură pliantă: folded leaflet
brun: brown
buletin: bulletin
bun: good
bun de tipar: final proof
buton(i): knob(s)
buzunar: pocket

ca şi nou: as new
cadou: gift
cafeniu: coffee-colored

caligrafie: handwriting
caligrafor: calligrapher
calitate de autor: authorship
cam: nearly; rather, somewhat
camee: cameo
cap. *see* capitol
cap: head
cap de pagină: head of page
capitol(e): chapter(s)
capodoperă: masterpiece
căptuşit: lined
caracter de tipar: typeface
caracter gotic: black letter
caractere cursive: italics
caractere latine: Roman type
caractere romane: antiqua
caricatură(i): caricature(s)
carnet: notebook
carte(cărţi): book(s), manual(s)
carte aurită: gilt book
carte cadou: gift book
carte de artă: art book
carte de buzunar: pocketbook
carte de cîntece: songbook
carte de rugăciuni: prayer book
carte încătuşată: chained book
carte pentru copii: children's book
carte rară: rare book
cărticele: booklets
cărticică: booklet
cartografie: cartography
carton: cardboard, pasteboard
cartonat: bound in boards
cartuş: scroll
cartuş ornamental: cartouche,
  ornamental oval frame
casetă dublă: double slipcase
castaniu: chestnut-colored, maroon
catalog: catalog
catalog de licitaţie: auction catalog
catifea: velvet
celofan: cellophane
centimetru(i): centimeter(s)
centru: center
cenzurare: censorship
cenzurat: censored
cercetare: research

cerneală: ink
cheie: key
cheltueli: costs
cicatrice(i): scar(s)
cinci: five
cincisprezece: fifteen
cinizeci: fifty
cîrpă pură: pure rag
cîrpit: mended
ciselat: chiseled
citat: quotation
cîteva: some, a few
cititor: reader
ciuntit: mutilated
clar: clear, light colored
clişeu: plate
coadă: tail
coală: sheet
coală de tipar: quire
coase: sew, stitch
coautor: coauthor, joint author
codex(ice): codex(ices)
colabora: collaborate
colaborare: collaboration
colaborator: collaborator
colaţiona: collate
colaţionare: collation
colator: collator
colecţie: collection
colecţiune: collection
colectiv: collective, joint
colector: collector
colectorul bibliotecilor: book
    jobber for libraries
coli: sheets
coloană(e): column(s)
coloană dublă: double-columned
colofoniu: colophon
colontitlu: running title
colorant: coloring
colorat: colored, stained
colţ(i): corner(s)
colţi rupţi: with corners broken
comandă: commission, order
comanda fermă: firm order
comedie(i): comedy(ies)

comemorativ: commemorative,
    memorial
comentarii: comments, glosses
comentat: commented
comentator: commentator
comercial: commercial
comerţ: trade
comerţ angros: wholesale trade
comerţ cu amănuntul: retail trade
comerţ de cărţi: book trade
comitet: committee
compendiu: compendium
compilare: compilation
compilat: compiled
compilator: compiler
complet: complete
completa: complete
completat: completed
compus de: composed
compus din: composed
comun: common
concis: brief, concise
concluzie: conclusion
concordanţă: concordance
condei: pen
condensat: condensed
condiţie: condition, state
condiţii de vînzare: conditions of
    sale
conferinţă: conference, lecture
confirmare: confirmation
confirmat: confirmed
confiscat: confiscated
consecutiv: consecutive
conservare: preservation
conservat: preserved
considerabil: considerably
consistent: consisting
consolidat: reinforced
conspect: abstract, conspectus,
    summary
constă: consists of
cont: account
contemporan: contemporary
conţine: contains
continuare: continuation
conţinut: contents

contrafacere: forgery
contrafăcut: forged, spurious
contrapagină: verso
contratitlu: series title
contribuţie(i): contribution(s)
cooperaţie: cooperation
copertă(e): binding(s), cover(s)
copertă absentă: with binding gone
copertă cîrpită: mended cover
copertă colectivă: collective bind-
     ing
copertă de editor: publisher's
     binding
copertă de email: enamel binding
copertă de titlu: title leaf
copertă desfăcută: with binding
     loosened
copertă flexibilă: flexible binding
copertă interioară: title page
copertă Jansenistă: Jansenist
     binding
copertă protectoare: protective
     cover
copertă spirală: spiral binding
copertă suplă: limp binding
coperte de lemn: wood boards
coperte orginale: original covers
copie(i): copy(ies)
copie autografiată: autographed
     copy
copie de recenzie: review copy
copie(i) numerotată(e): numbered
     copy(ies)
copie pentru recenzie: review copy
copie unică: single copy
copios: copious
cordovan: cordovan
corectare(ări): correction(s)
corectat: corrected
corectură: proof
corespondenţă: correspondence
coroană: crown
coroană dublă: double crown
corp de literă: type size
cost: cost
costisitor: expensive
cotidian: daily

creion: pencil
crestătură: cut, notch, score
crestomaţie: chrestomathy
cromolitografie: chromolithography
cronică(i): chronicle(s)
cu: including, with
cu agrafe: with clasps
cu autograf: autographed
cu bandă: with bands
cu colţurile îndoite: dog-eared
cu foi detaşabile: loose-leaf
cu găuri mici: with small holes
cu grijă: carefully
cu îndemînare: ably, skillfully
cu margine amplă: with full
     margins
cu muchie in aur: with gilt edges
cu notă de dedicaţie: with
     dedicatory note
cu şireturi: with laces, with ties
cu totul: entirely
cu urechi de măgar: dog-eared
culegere: collection; typesetting
culoare: color
culoare de măslină: olive
culoare de portocală: orange
culoare de somon: salmon-colored
culori: colors
cumulativ: cumulative
cunoscut: known, renowned
cunoştinţă: knowledge
cuprinde: comprise
cuprins: content
cuprinzînd: comprising
cupru: copper
curat: clean, cleanly; neat, neatly
curînd: shortly, soon
curiozitate: curiosity
cursiv: cursive, italic
cusut: stitched
cutie: case, box
cuvertură: cover
cuvînt: word
cuvînt înainte: foreword
cuvînt-titlu: catchword
cuvînte cheie: key words
cvarto: quarto

dactilografie: typewriting
damasc: linen damask
dantelă: dentelle, lacework
dată: date
data apariţiei: date of issue
data bunului de tipar: imprimatur date
data ediţiei: publication date
datat: dated
datînd: dating
de exemplu: for example
de la: from
de lux: deluxe
de mînă: by hand
de mîna a două: secondhand
de prim rang: foremost
de proastă calitate: coarse
de serie: serial
de tipografie: typographic
de vreme ce: since
deasemenea: also
deasupra: over
decolorat: discolored, drab, faded
decorat: decorated
decorat cu aur: decorated with gold
decoraţie(i): decoration(s)
decoraţie marginală: border design
decupa: clip
decupări: clippings
decupat: clipped
dedicaţie autografată: autographed dedication
defect(e): defect(s)
defectuos: defective
deferi: refer, submit
definitiv: definitive
depozit de cărţi: book depository
deschis: open
deschizătură: gap, opening
descriere: description
descriptiv: descriptive
descris: described
desen(uri): design(s), drawing(s), sketch(es)
desen cadru: frame, design forming a frame
desen circular: circular design

desen de colţ: corner design
desen de linie curbată: curved line pattern
desen de margine: border design
desen de ramuri şi flori: branch and flower design
desen decorativ: decorative design
desen heraldic: armorial design
desen în colţ: corner design
desen în creion: pencil drawing
desen în crin: lily design
desen încrustat: encrusted design
desen liniar: line drawing
desen pentru colţuri: corner design
desen ramură de palmier: palm-leaf design
desen romboidal: diamond-shaped pattern
desen simil-dantelă: lace-like pattern
desen spirală: spiral design
desen viţă de vie: leafy vine design
desena: illustrate
desenare(ări): drawing(s)
desenat: drawn, figured
desfăcut: detached, open, untied
desfăcut in balamale: loosened joints
despre: about, concerning
detaşat: detached, loose
deteriora: deteriorate
deteriorat: deteriorated
developat: developed
deviză: device, motto
dezarticulat: disjointed
deziderat: desideratum
dezlegat: unbound
diagramă(e): diagram(s)
dibaci: skillful
dicţionar: dictionary
dicţionar bilingv: bilingual dictionary
dicţionar enciclopedic: encyclopedic dictionary
dicţionar poliglot: multilingual dictionary

diferit: different
dimensiune: size
din: from
din scorţă în scoarţă: cover-to-cover
dinainte: before
disertaţie: dissertation
disertatie inaugurală: inaugural dissertation
disponibil: available
dispozitiv: device
distribuţie: distribution
distrus: destroyed
divers: various
document: document
documentar: documentary
documentare: documentation
doi, două: two
doisprezece: twelve
dorit: desired, wanted
dos: back, reverse
dos scobit: hollow back
dosul paginei: back of page
două: two
douăzeci: twenty
dramă: drama
drept de autor: copyright
dubios: dubious, questionable
dublat: duplicated
dublet: duplicate
dublu: double, twofold
dublură(i): doublure(s)
după: after, behind
duplicat: duplicate
durabil: strong

edita: editing
editare: publishing
editat: edited, printed
editat de: edited by
ediţie(i): edition(s)
ediţie autorizată: authorized edition
ediţie comandată: ordered edition
ediţie comemorativă: commemorative or memorial volume
ediţie completată: enlarged edition

ediţie corectată: revised edition
ediţie de artă: art edition
ediţie de bibliotecă: library edition
ediţie de buzunar: pocket edition
ediţie de lux: deluxe edition
ediţie definitivă: definitive edition
ediţie epuizată: out-of-print edition
ediţie excelentă: fine edition
ediţie facsimil: facsimile edition
ediţie liliput: miniature edition
ediţie locală: local edition
ediţie minusculă: miniature edition
ediţie neautorizată: pirated edition
ediţie nouă: new edition
ediţie omagială: festschrift
ediţie originală: original edition
ediţie populară: popular edition
ediţie prescurtată: abridged edition
ediţie princeps: first edition
ediţie revăzută: revised edition
editor: publisher
editură: publishing firm
egal: equal, identical
elabora: elaborate
elegant: elegant
eliberat: delivered
eliminat: eliminated
emblema editurii: publisher's mark
enciclopedie: encyclopedia
englez: English
epigraf(e): epigraph(s)
epilog: epilogue
epuizat: out of stock
erată: errata
eroare: error
erori: errors
erotică: erotica
eseu(ri): essay(s)
etichetă(e): label(s)
etichetă de titlu: title label
etichetă de volum: volume label
evaluare: appraisal
ex. *see* exemplar
exact: exact
excelent: excellent, splendid
excepţional: exceptional

exclus: excluded
exclusiv: exclusive
executat: executed
exemplar(e): copy(ies)
exemplar anticipat: advance copy
exemplar avariat: damaged copy
exemplar de autor: author's copy
exemplar de bibliotecă: ex-library
  copy
exemplar de control: specimen copy
exemplar dedicat: inscribed copy
exemplar defect: defective copy
exemplar imperfect: defective copy
exemplar obligatoriu: legal deposit
  copy
exemplar oferit ca omagiu:
  presentation copy
exemplar perfect: fine copy
exemplar răzleț: odd copy
existent: extant
expediat: forwarded, sent
explicare: explanation
explicaţie: key
expurgat: expurgated
extirpat: eradicated, removed
extras(e): excerpt(s), offprint(s),
  reprint(s)
extras pentru autor: author's
  offprint
extrem de rar: extremely rare

fabulă(e): fable(s), legend
facsimil(i): facsimile(s)
factură(i): invoice(s), bill(s)
făcut de mînă: handmade
fals: forged, counterfeit
falsificat: spurious
fantezist: fancy
fără: without
fără an: without year
fără conţinut lemnos: wood-free
fără copertă: without cover
fără dată: without date
fără editor: without publisher
fără lemn: wood-free
fără loc de publicaţie: without
  place of publication

fără loc, fără dată: without place,
  without date
fără loc si dată: without place or
  date
fără luciu: mat, matte
fără pagină titlu: without title page
fără pată: spotless
fără preţ: without price
fără titlu: without title
fasciculă(e): brochure(s),
  number(s), part(s)
faţă: face
ficţiune: fiction
fiecare: each, every
figură(i): figure(s)
filă(e): leaf(ves), page(s)
fildeş: ivory
filigran: filigree
fin: fine
final: final
fişă: slip
flexibil: flexible
floricică(cele): fleuret(s),
  floret(s)
foaie: leaf, page, sheet
foaie albă intercalată: interleaved
foaie de erată: errata leaf
foaie de probă: proof sheet
foaie detaşabilă: loose-leaf sheet
foaie inserată: unnumbered leaf
foaie nenumerotată: unnumbered
  leaf
foaie numerotată: numbered leaf
foaie titlu: title leaf
foaie volantă: flyleaf
foarte apreciat: much appreciated
foarte mic: very small
foarte stimat: highly esteemed
foi: leaves, pages, sheets
foiţă: foil, thin paper
foiţă de aur: gold leaf
folio mare: large folio
fond: stock
fond de cărţi: bookstock
fond de rezervă: reserve stock
format: format
format de buzunar: pocket-size

format larg: oversize
fotocopie: photocopy
fotografie(i): photograph(s)
fotogramă: photocopy
fotogravura(i): photoengraving(s)
fragment(ţi): fragment(s),
    passage(s)
fragmentar: fragmentary
francat: postpaid
francez: French
franco: postpaid
frecare: chafing, rubbing
frecat: rubbed
frecvenţa: frequency
friză(e): frieze(s)
frontispiciu: frontispiece
frumos: beautiful, handsome
funcţie de redactor: editorship
funie: cord

galben: yellow
garnitură: set
gata: ready
gaură: hole
gaură de vierme: wormhole
găuri: holes
găurit: holed, full of holes
gazetă: gazette
gazetar: gazetteer
general: general
geografic: geographical
german: German
ghid: guidebook
ghindă(e): acorn(s)
ghirlandă(e): garland(s)
glosar(e): glossary(ies)
gofrare: goffering
gofrat: goffered
gotic: Gothic type
grabă: rush
grafic(i): graph(s)
gramatică: grammar
granulat mic: small-grained
gratuit: free, free of charge
grăunte: grain
grăunţos: grainy
gravare(ări): etching(s)

gravat: engraved, etched
gravor: engraver
gravură(i): engraving(s), etching(s)
gravură colorată: color engraving
gravură(i) în cupru: copper
    engraving(s)
gravură(i) în lemn: woodcut(s)
gravură(i) în otel: steel engrav-
    ing(s)
gravură(i) placa de arama: copper-
    plate engraving(s)
greşeală: defect, mistake
greşeală de tipar: misprint
greşeli: defects
greşi: err, make a mistake
greu de găsit: scarce
grijă: care
grijuliu: careful
gris: gray
gros: thick
grosime: thickness
grosolan: coarse, rough
grotesc: bizarre, grotesque, odd

hartă: chart, map
hartă astronomică: astronomical
    chart
hartă in relief: relief map
hartă inserată: inset map
hartă schiţă: sketch map
hartă topografică: topographical
    map
hărţi: medallions, insets; maps
haşurat: hatched, shaded
hîrtie: paper, sheet
hîrtie acoperită: coated paper
hîrtie colorată: colored paper
hîrtie cu luciu: glazed paper
hîrtie de Biblie: Bible paper
hîrtie de cîrpă: rag paper
hîrtie de India: India paper
hîrtie de Japonia: Japan paper
hîrtie de mătase: silk paper
hîrtie de orez: rice paper
hîrtie esparto: esparto paper
hîrtie imprimată pe o singură
    parte: broadsheet

hîrtie largă: large paper
hîrtie lucioasă: glossy paper
hîrtie marmurată: marbled paper
hîrtie pergament: parchment paper
hîrtie velină: vellum paper

iarnă: Winter
identic: identical
identificare: identification
ilustra: illustrate
ilustrat: illustrated
ilustraţie(i): illustration(s)
ilustraţie colorată: color illustration
ilustraţii în culori: illustrations
   in color
ilustraţii în text: illustrations in
   the text
ilustrator: illustrator
imaculat: immaculate
imaginativ: imaginative
îmbinare: gathering, joining
îmbinat: merged
îmbrăcăminte: wrapper preserved
imitat: counterfeit, imitated
imitaţie: imitation, forgery
imitaţie de marmoră: marbling
imitaţie de piele: leatherette
impachetare: packing
impecabil: impeccable
import: import
imposibil de găsit: impossible to
   find
impresionant: impressive
împreună: together
imprima: print
imprimare(ări): imprint(s),
   printing(s)
imprimat privat: privately printed
împrumut: loan
în: in
în abonament: on subscription
în bună stare: in good condition
în cerere: in demand
în condiţie perfectă: in perfect
   condition
în condiţie proastă: in poor condition

în coperţi: in covers
în culori: in color(s)
în curs: current
în curs de apariţie: about to be
   published
în curs de retipărire: being reprinted
în cutie: in container
în depozit: in stock
în facsimil: in facsimile
în fascicule: in fascicles
în foaie: in sheets
în-folio: folio, in folio
în frunte: at the front
în litere mici: in small print
în loc de: instead of
în mapă: in portfolio
în mare parte: mainly
în-octavo: octavo
în ordine alfabetică: in alphabetical order
în parte: partly
în presă: in press
în privinţă: of, with respect to
în spate: at the back
în stare perfectă: in excellent condition
în subsolul unei pagini: foot of the
   page
în text: in the text
înafară de comerţ: not in the trade
înainte: before
înalt: high
înălţime: height
înapoiere: return
încă ne disponibil: not yet published
încă ne valabil: not yet available
încă nepublicat: not yet published
încadrat: framed
început de capitol: chapter head
înceta: cease
încheiere: ending, conclusion
închis: closed
încleiat: glued
inclusiv: inclusive
incluzînd: including
incomparabil: unmatched

incomplet: defective, fragmentary,
  incomplete
inconsiderabil: unimportant
încrețit: crumpled, wrinkled
încrețitură: wrinkles, wrinkling
incunabul(e): incunabulum(a)
index: index
indicat: indicated
indice(i): index(es)
indice alfabetic: alphabetic index
indice clasificat: classified index
indice de autor: author index
indigen: domestic
individual: individual
inedit: unpublished
inferior: bottom, lower
infloritură a scrisului: flourish
informație: information
ingălbenit: yellowed
ingriji: edit
ingrijit: careful, correct, trim
inițială(e): initial(s)
inițială decorată: decorated initial
inițială ornamentală: ornamental
  initial
inițiale ornamentale: ornamental
  initials
înregistra: calender
înregistrare: recording
inscripție(i): inscription(s)
însemnare(ări): note(s)
insera: insert
inserare: insertion
instituție: institution
intercala: intercalate
intercalat: intercalated
interimat: interim
interior: inner, inside, interior
interlinie: interlinear
întîi: first
întîia ediție: first edition
întîrziat: delayed
intitulat: entitled
intocmi: compile, draw up
intocmit de: prepared by
intrare(ări): entry(ies)
între: between

întreprindere: enterprise
întrerupt: cut off
întrețesut: interlacings
întroducere: introduction
introductiv: introductory
învechit: antiquated, obsolete,
  out of date
înveliș: cover
învelitoare: dust jacket
inversat: inverted
istoric: historic
istorie: history
istorisit: historiated
izvor: source

jansenist: Jansenist
josul paginei: foot of the page
jumătate: half
jurnal(e): journal(s)
justificat: authorized

la cerere: on request
la sfîrșit: at the end
lacună: blank, gap
lambriu: panel
lambriuri: panels
lanț: chain
larg: vast, wide
lărgime: width
lărgit: enlarged
latură(i): side(s)
lega: bind
lega cu: bind with
legat: bound
legat de: bound in
legat impreună: bound together
legat în întregime: full bound
legat în pînză: bound in cloth
legător: binder
legător de cărti: bookbinder
legătorie: bindery
legatul cărților: bookbinding
legătură(i): binding(s)
legătură contemporană: contemporary binding
legătura de amator: amateur
  binding

legătura de catifea: velvet binding
legătura de trei sferturi: three-quarter binding
legătură heraldică: armorial binding
legătură în pînză: cloth binding
legătură încătuşată: chained binding
legătură piele de viţel: calfskin binding
legături: ties
legendă(e): legend(s)
lemn: wood
lemnos: wooden
levănţică: lavender
lexic: lexicon
lexicon: thesaurus
librar: bookseller
librărie: bookstore
licitaţie: auction sale
limbă: language
limbaj: language
limitat: limited
liniat: ruled
linie(i): line(s)
linie de cerneală: ink line
linie de gravură: line engraving
linie intreţesută: interlaced fillet
linie ornamentală: ornamental fillet
linie punctată: dotted line
lipi: glue
lipsit: lacking, wanting
listă: catalog, list
listă de preţ: price list
literă(e): character(s), letter(s)
literă mare: uppercase letter
literă mică: lowercase letter
literatură: literature
litograf: lithographer
litografie(i): lithograph(s); lithography
litografie în culori: color lithography
lizibil: legible
loc: place

locul publicării: place of publication
locul tipăririi: place of printing
lucios: moiré
lucra: emboss
lucrare: transaction, work
lucrat: embossed, worked
lucrat în relief: embossed
lună: month
lunar: monthly
lung: long
lungime: length
lustrui: burnish
lustruit: polished, rubbed

machetă: layout
maghiar: Hungarian
mai ales: mostly
maj. *see* majusculă
majusculă(e): capital(s)
manual(e): handbook(s), manual(s), textbook(s)
mănunchi(uri): fascicle(s)
manuscris: manuscript
manuscris dactilografiat: typescript
manuscris de autor: author's manuscript
marcă(i): mark(s), sign(s)
marcă de creion: pencil mark
marcă de proprietate: ownership mark
marcă de tipar: printer's mark
mare: large, tall
marginal: marginal
margine(i): border(s), edge(s), margin(s)
margine extremă: outer margin
margine inferioară: bottom margin
margine interioară: inner margin
margine largă: full margins
margine scurtată: cut edges
margine strîmtă: narrow margins
margine superioară: top margin
mărire: enlargement
mărit: enlarged
marmorat: grained

marochin: morocco
martori: witnesses
mastic: mastic
mat: dull
mătase: silk
materie de faţă: front matter
medalion: medallion
mediocru: mediocre
mediu: average
memoriu: memoirs
metal: metal
mic: small, little
microcopie: microcopy
microfilm: microfilm
microfişă: microfiche
mie: thousand
mijloace: media, means
mîncat de viermi: worm-eaten
miniatura(i): miniature(s)
mînjit: dirty, soiled
minunat: charming, splendid
minuscul: minute
mîzgălit: smudged, soiled
moale: smooth, soft
mobil: movable
modern: modern
molie(i) de carţi: bookworm(s)
monahal: monastic
monocrom: monochrome
monografie(i): monograph(s)
monogramă(e): monogram(s)
montat: mounted
mostră: sample
mototolit: crushed
mozaic: mosaic
mucegai: mildew, mold
muchie(i): edge(s)
muchie inferioară: bottom edge
muchie superioară: top edge
muchii aurită: gilt edges
muchii colorate: colored edges
muchii gofrate: goffered edges
muchii marmurate: marbled edges
muchii moi: smooth edges
muchii neingrijite: untrimmed
  edges
muchii pieptănate: combed edges

mult, mulţi: many
multicolorat: variegated
multilingv: multilingual
murdar: dirty
murdărit: soiled
murg: roan
muşama: buckram
muzică: music

narativ: narrative
narator: narrator
neciteţ: illegible
necitibil: illegible
nedătat: undated
nedecorat: undecorated
nedeschis: unopened
neexpurgat: unexpurgated
negru: black, dark
neînsemnat: insignificant
nelegat: unbound
nelipit: unglued
nenumerotat: unnumbered
neobişnuit: uncommon, unusual
nepătat: spotless
nepublicat: unpublished
neregulat: irregular
nescris: blank
nescurtat: uncut
neştirbit: intact, untouched
nevalabil: not valid
nevandabil: unsalable
nici: neither
niciodată: never
notă(e): note(s), annotation(s)
notă de dedicaţie: dedicatory note
notă de subsol: footnote
notă explicativă: explanatory note
notă introductivă: prefatory note
notaţie: notation
note explicative: explanatory notes
nou: fresh, new
nouă: nine
nouăsprezece: nineteen
nouăzeci: ninety
noutate: freshness
nu de vanzăre: not for sale
nu în text: not in the text

nu în vânzare: not in the trade
nu pentru vînzare: not for sale
nuanţă(e): shade(s)
nuanţat: tinted
număr: number
număr arab: arabic number
număr curent: current issue
număr de linie: line number
număr de pagini: number of pages
număr de volum: volume numbering
număr de volume: number of
  volumes
număr impar: odd number
număr par: even number
număr vechi: back number
numărare de foi: foliation
numărat: numbered
numărătoarea paginilor: pagination
numărul de ordine al ediţiei:
  number of edition
nume: name
numeros: numerous
numerotare: numbering
numerotat: foliated, numbered
nuvelă(e): novelette(s), short
  story(ies)

oblic: beveled
oblong: oblong
ocazional: occasional
ocru: ocher
oferire: presentation
ofertă: offer
oficial: official
oficiu: office
ofset: offset
olograf: holograph
omisiune: omission
omnibus: omnibus
ondulat: wavy
operă(e): work(s)
operă colectivă: collective work
operă mică: small work
opere alese: selected works
opere anonime: anonymous works
opere complete: collected works

opt: eight
optsprezece: eighteen
optzeci: eighty
opus: opposite
opuscul: opuscule, small work
ordine: sequence
oricare: either
original: original
ornament: ornament
ornament floral: floral ornament
ornamentat: ornamented

pag. *see* pagină
pagină(i): page(s)
pagină de gardă: flyleaf
pagină de titlu: title page
pagină dublă: double page
pagină goală: blank page
pagină întreagă: full page
pagină nenumerotată: unnumbered page
paginare: pagination
paginaţie: pagination
paginaţie continuă: continuous
  pagination
pagini de notă: pages of notes
pagini faţă în faţă: double-page
  spread
pagini preliminare: preliminary
  pages
paietă(e): spangle(s)
paisprezece: fourteen
palid: pale
pamflet: pamphlet(s)
parafă: flourish, paraph, scroll
parafă de litere: lettered scroll
parafă frunzoasă: leafy scroll
paragraf(e): paragraph(s)
paralel: parallel
parte: part
parţial: partly
partitură: musical score
pasaj: extract
pastă: paste
pastă de lemn: wood pulp
pastel: pastel
pată: spot, stain

pată de murdărie: dirty spots
pată de ulei: oil spot
pată de umiditate: damp spots, damp stains
pată frecată: scraped spot
pătat: speckled, spotted
pătat de apă: water-stained
pătat de grăsime: grease-spotted
pătat de ulei: oil-stained
pătat de umezeală: stained by dampness
pătat de umiditate: damp-spotted
pătrat: square
patru: four
patruzeci: forty
pe: on, upon
pe abonament: on subscription
pe aprobare: on approval
pe cupru: on copper
pe lemn: on wood
pe lîngă: besides
pe muchie: on the edge
pensulă: brush
pentru: for
pentru uz oficial: for official use
perfecta: perfect
perforare(i): perforation(s)
perforat: holed
pergament: parchment, sheepskin, vellum
pergament veritabil: genuine parchment
perimat: antiquated
periodic(e): periodical(s)
permisiune: permission
pete: spots, stains
pete de umezeală: mildew
petic: patch, scrap
pictat: painted
pictură(i): picture(s)
piele: full leather, leather
piele artificială: artificial leather
piele de capră: goatskin
piele de caprioară: doeskin, buckskin
piele de ied: kidskin
piele de oaie: sheepskin

piele de porc: pigskin
piele de rechin: sharkskin
piele de vițel: calf
piele moale: chamois skin
piele rusească: Russian leather
piele satinată: glazed leather
pierdere de texte: loss of text
pierdut: lost, missing
piesă(e): piece(s)
pînză: cloth, linen
pînză de in: flaxen cloth
pînză nealbită: unbleached cloth
placă de aramă: copperplate
plagiat: plagiarism
plan: plan
planșă(e): pasted inset(s), plate(s)
planșetă(e): board(s)
plătit dînainte: prepaid
pliant: folding
plic: jacket, wrapper
plic preservat: wrapper preserved
plin: full
poem(e): poem(s)
poet: poet
poezie: poetry
policrom: polychrome
poliglot: multilingual
poligrafic: multifaceted
porfir: porphyry
portret(e): portrait(s)
portret frontispiciu: frontispiece portrait
portrivit: laid in
poștă: mail
postfață: epilogue, postface
postscriptum: postscript
postum: posthumous
poveste(ști): story(ies)
povestire(i): tale(s)
prăda: spoil
prăfuit: dusty
precorectură: editing
precuvîntare: foreword
prefață: foreword, preface, introduction
prefață și note: preface and notes
preliminar: preliminary

prelucrare: processing
premiant: prizewinning
prenume: forename
preparat: preparation
presă: press
presă privată: private press
presărat: spangled
prescurta: shorten, abridge
prescurtare: abridgment
preţ: list price, price
preţ curent: current price
preţ de catalog: catalog price
preţ de vînzare: cash price
preţ evaluat: estimated price
preţ sporit: increased price
preţios: valued
prezentare grafică: graphic layout
prim: first
prima ediţie: first edition
prima pagină: front page
primăvară: Spring
primul tiraj: first printing
prin abonare: on subscription
prin aprobare: on approval
prin solicitare: on request
privilegiu: privilege
probă: pattern, proof
proces-verbal: minutes, proceedings
produs: produced
prolog: prologue
prospect: prospectus
prost: common, ordinary
provenienţă: provenance, provenience
proză: prose
pseudonim: pseudonym
publica: publish
publicare(ări): issue(s)
publicat: published
publicat in fascicule: in parts
publicaţie(i): edition(s), publication(s)
publicaţie anonimă: anonymous publication, anonymous work
publicaţie bilunară: bimonthly publication

publicaţie bimensuală: bimonthly publication
publicaţie clandestină: clandestine publication
publicaţie datată: dated publication
publicaţie de lux: deluxe publication
publicaţie de reclamă: advertising publication
publicaţie oficială: official publication
publicaţie periodică: periodical
publicaţie specială: special publication
publicaţie trimestrială: quarterly
punct: point
punctat: dotted
pur: fine

rabat: discount
rade: efface, erase
rafinat: fine
ramă: chase, frame
ramă albă: page margin
rămăşiţă: remainder
raport: report
rar: rare
răspunzător: responsible
rău: bad, worthless
răzleţ: separated
rearanjat: rearranged
recenzie: review
recipient: container
recto: recto
redacta: compile, edit
redactare: editing
redacţie: editing
redactor: editor
redus: reduced
reeditare: reissue
refăcut: remade
refasonat: recast
referat: review
registru: register
regulat: ordinary
reimprimare: reprint

reînnoit: renew, renewed
relipit: reglued
remania: rework
renumit: famous
reorganizat: reorganized
reparabil: repairable
reparaţie: mending, repairs
repertoriu(i): directory(ies)
reprezenta: represent
reproducere: reproduction
reproducţie(i): reproduction(s)
reproducţie facsimili: facsimile
  reproduction
reprografie: reprography
restaurare(ări): restoration(s)
restaurat: restored
retipărire: reissue, reprint
retipărit: reprinted
retuşat: retouched
revăzut: revised
revistă(e): magazine(s), review(s)
revizui: revise
revizuit: revised
rezervă: reserve
rezumat: abstract, résumé, summary; outlined
ridicat: raised
rînd: line
roade: abrade; rub off
roadere(i): abrasion(s), abrasure(s)
roman(e): novel(s)
român: Romanian
roman cavaleresc: romance
romancier: novelist
romb: lozenge (pattern)
ros: gnawed
roşu: red
rotogravură: rotogravure
rozetă(e): rosette(s)
rubin inchis: carbuncle
rubrică: rubric
rubricat: rubricated
rugină: rust
ruinat: dilapidated
ruptură: break
rustic: rustic

şagrin: shagreen
şagrin artificial: artificial shagreen
şaisprezece: sixteen
şaizeci: sixty
săptămînal: weekly
şapte: seven
şaptesprezece: seventeen
şaptezeci: seventy
şase: six
satin: sateen
satinată: glazed
satiră: lampoon
schimb: exchange
schimbat: changed
schiţă(e): drawing(s), sketch(es)
scoarţa de faţă: front cover
scobit: hollowed
scop: scope
scriere: writing
scriitor: author, writer
scris: written
scrisoare: letter
scrisoare autografă: autograph
  letter
sculă: instrument, tool
scurt: brief, short
scurtat: cropped
scut: escutcheon, shield
scutit: exempt
scutit de taxe: duty free
secol(e): century(ies)
secventa: sequence
selecţionat: selected
selecţiune(i): selection(s)
semestrial: semiannual
semi: half
semi copertă: half binding
semi copertă cu colţi: half binding
  with corners
semi flexibil: semiflexible
semi margine: half margins
semi pagină: half page
semi pergament: half-vellum
semi piele: half-leather
semi pînză: half-cloth, half-linen
semi şagrin: half-shagreen
semi viţel: half-calf

semianual: semiannual
semn: signal, sign
semn de carte: bookmark
semnat de autor: signed by the
  author
semnătură(i): signature(s)
semne de corectură: proofreader's
  marks
separat: separate
serie: series
serie nouă: new series
serios: serious
servietă(e): portfolio(s)
sfîrşit de capitol: chapter end
sfîşiat: torn
sgâriat: scratched
şi: and, both
şi alte: and others, et cetera
şi aşa mai departe: and so forth
sigiliu(i): seal(s), signet(s)
simile piele: imitation leather
simpoziu: symposium
simulat: simulated
singur: alone, only
sinoptic: synoptic
sintetic: artificial, synthetic
sinteză: synthesis
sîrb: Serbian
şiret(uri): cord(s), lace(s), string(s)
sistematizat: systematic
slab: weak
şliţ: groove, slot
smalţ: enamel
smulge: tear out
smuls: torn out
şoarece de bibliotecă: bookworm
societate: society
societate savantă: learned society
somptuos: rich, sumptuous
spălăcit: dull, pale
spălat: washed
spart: broken
spărtură: split
spate: back
special: special
specificaţie editorială: publisher's
  specification

specimen: specimen
spin: spine
spinare deschisă: open back
sporit: enhanced, increased
spre: to, toward
stambă: calico
stampă(e): print(s)
stampare: stamping
stampat în aur: gold-stamped
ştampilă: stamp
ştampilă bibliotecii: library stamp
ştampilă proprietarului: owner's
  stamp
ştampilat: stamped
ştampilat în aur: gold-stamped
stare: indentation; state
stereotip: stereotype
şterge: abrade; wipe out, erase
ştergere: erasure
ştiinţă: science
ştiinţific: scientific
stilou: pen
stimă: esteem
stimat: esteemed
stoc: stock
străin: foreign
stropit: sprinkled
studiu introductiv: introductory
  study
sub: under
subliniat: underlined
subliniere: underlining
subţire: thin
subtitlu: subtitle
succes de librărie: best-seller
sumă: amount
sumar: summary
superficial: slight, superficial
superfin: superfine
superior: upper
supliment: addendum, supplement
supliment: supplementary
suplimentar: extra
supracopertă(e): wrapper(s)
supracopertă conservată: wrapper
  preserved

supracopertă cu șireturi: wrapper
  with ties
suprafață: outside
suprimat: suppressed
supusă aprobarii: as approved
surogat: substitute
sursă: source
sursă primară: original source
sus: above
suspendat: deferred
sută: one hundred

tabelă: table
tabelă cronologică: chronological
  table
tabelă sinoptică: synoptic table
tablă(e): plate(s)
tablă de materii: table of contents
tăiat: cut out, excised
tăietură: clipping, cutting
tărcat: mottled
tare: hard, strong
teacă: case, sheath
tehnic: technical
tehnoredactor: technical editor
temporar: temporarily, temporary
termen: term
tern: dull
text: text
text original: original text
teză: thesis
teză de doctorat: doctoral thesis
tezaur: thesaurus
tipar: printing; stencil
tipar adînc: intaglio printing
tipar cu racletă: rotogravure
tipar în relief: relief printing
tipar matriță: stencil printing
tipar metalografic: copperplate
  printing
tipărire: printing, typography
tipărire pe ascuns: pirated edition
tipărit: printed
tipograf: printer
tipografie: printing firm, printshop
tipografie in culoare: color
  printing

tiraj: print run
tîrg: bargain
titlu(ri): heading(s), title(s)
titlu alternativ: alternative title
titlu colectiv: collective title
titlu de copertă: cover title
titlu de serie: series title
titlu frontispiciu: title frontispiece
titlu nelegitim: bastard title
titlu prescurtat: short title
titlu principal: main title
titlu schimbat: changed title
titlu tipărit pe două pagini:
  double title page, two-page title
titlul autorului: author's title
toamnă: Fall
tocmai publicat: just issued, just
  published
tom: tome
tot: all
total: thoroughly
total publicat: all published
traducător(i): translator(s)
traduce: translate
traducere(i): translation(s)
traducere cuvînt cu cuvînt: literal
  translation
tradus: translated
tragedie(i): tragedy(ies)
tragere separată: offprint
transcrie: rewrite, transcribe
transcriere: transcription
transport: freight
transpoziție: transposition
transpune: transpose
tranzacții: transactions
trasat: tracing
tratat(e): treatise(s)
trei: three
treisprezece: thirteen
treizeci: thirty
trimestrial: quarterly
triplu: triple

ucrainean: Ukrainian
ultim: last, latest
umbrire: shading

umbrit: shaded
umezeală: moisture
umiditate: dampness, humidity
unciale(i): uncial letter(s)
unic: unique
uniform: even, uniform; uniformly
universitate: university
unsprezece: eleven
urgent: urgent
urmărit: sought
următor: following
urme: traces
urme de uz: traces of wear
uzat: used, worn

valoare: value
valoros: precious
vară: Summer
varianta(e): variant(s)
veche: old, ancient
vechiu: old
verde: green
verificare: testing

verificaţie: verification
versiune: version
verso: verso
verzui: greenish
viermănos: worm-eaten
vignetă: vignette
vigneta copertei: design on cover
vîndut: sold
vînzare: sale
vînzare în avans: advance sale
vocabular: lexicon, vocabulary
volum(e): volume(s)
volum anual: annual volume
volum comemorativ: festschrift
volum specimen: specimen volume
vreo, vreun: some

zdrenţuit: frayed, tattered
zece: ten
zgîriat: bruised, scratched
zi: day
ziar: newspaper
zincografie: zincography

Russian

RUSSIAN ALPHABET											
				И и		О о		Ф ф		Ъ ъ	
				Й й		П п		Х х		Ы ы	
А а		Д д		К к		Р р		Ц ц		Ь ь	
Б б		Е е		Л л		С с		Ч ч		Э э	
В в		Ж ж		М м		Т т		Ш ш		Ю ю	
Г г		З з		Н н		У у		Щ щ		Я я	

А.Н. *see* Академия наук

абзац(ы): paragraph(s), indent(s), break(s)

абон. *see* абонент

абонемент: subscription; loan (libraries)

абонент(ы): subscriber(s); borrower(s)

авиапочта: airmail

авт. *see* автор

авт. не указан *see* автор не указан

автобиог. *see* автобиографический

автобиографический: autobiographical

автобиография: autobiography

автограф(ы): autograph(s)

автографированный: autographed

автор(а): author(s)

автор настоящего труда: author of this book

автор не указан: no author, author not indicated

автореферат: author's abstract

авториз. *see* авторизованный

авторизованный: authorized

авторизованный перевод: authorized translation

авторитетный: authoritative

авторский лист: a signature for book production

авторский указатель: author index

авторское право: copyright

авторство: authorship

автотипия: autotype, halftone engraving

адаптированный: adapted

адрес: address

азбука: alphabet

азбучный: alphabetical

Ак.Н. *see* Академия наук

Акад., акад. *see* академия

Акад. наук *see* Академия наук

академический: academic

академия(и): academy(ies)

Академия наук: academy of sciences

акварель: watercolor
акватинта: aquatint
алфавитный каталог: alphabetic
  catalog
алфавитный порядок: alphabetical
  order
алфавитный список: alphabetic
  list, register
алфавитный указатель: alphabetic
  index
альб. *see* альбом
альбом(ы): album(s)
альбом иллюстраций: album of
  illustrations
альбомный формат: oblong format
альманах: almanac, calendar
амер. *see* американский
американский: American
анализ: analysis
аналитич. *see* аналитический
аналитический: analytical
анг. *see* английский
английский: English
анкета: blank form
анналы: annals, chronicles
аннот. *see* аннотация,
  аннотированный
аннотация(и): annotation(s),
  note(s), commentary(ies)
аннотированный: annotated
анонимные произведения:
  anonymous works
анонимный: anonymous
антиква: antiqua, antique (type)
антикварный: secondhand,
  antiquarian
антикварный рынок: antiquarian
  market
античный: ancient, antique
антология(и): anthology(ies)
аппретированный холст: buckram
арабеска: arabesque
арабские цифры: Arabic numerals
архив(ы): archive(s)
астериск: asterisk
атлас(ы): atlas(es)

аукцион(ы): auction(s), sale(s)
аукционный каталог: auction
  catalog
аутентичный: authentic

б. *see* без, большой, брошюра,
  буква
б–ва *see* буква
б.г. *see* без года
б.г.п. *see* без года печатания, без
  года публикации
б. загл. листа *see* без заглавного
  листа
б–ка *see* библиотека
б.л. *see* большие листы
Б.м. и г.п. *see* без места и года
  публикации
Б.о.м. и г.п. *see* без обозначения
  места и года публикации
Б.у.м. и г.п. *see* без указания
  места и года публикации
б.ф. *see* большой формат
б–фия *see* библиография
б.ц. *see* без цены
б–чка *see* библиотечка
баранья кожа: sheepskin
бархатный: velvet
без: without
без года: no date
без года печатания: without date
  of printing
без года публикации: no
  publishing date
без заглавного листа: without
  title page
без задатка: without deposit, no
  advance payment
без места: without place (of
  publication)
без места и года публикации: no
  place or date of publication
без обозначения места и года
  публикации: without
  indication of place or date of
  publication
без пер. *see* без переплета
без переплета: unbound

без стоимости пересылки: shipping charge not included, without shipping charge

без тит.л. и обл. *see* без титульного листа и обложки

без титульного листа и обложки: without title page and cover

без указания места и года публикации: no place or date of publication

без цены: no price, price not indicated, unpriced

беллетристика: belles lettres, fiction

бескрасочное тиснение: blind tooling

беспл. *see* бесплатно

бесплатная доставка: free delivery

бесплатно: free of charge, gratis

бесплатный экземпляр: free copy

бесценный: priceless, invaluable

библ. *see* библиографический, библиотечный

библ. очерк *see* библиографический очерк

библ. указатель *see* библиографический указатель

библ. штемп. на загл. *see* библиотечный штемпель на заглавии

библиогр. *see* библиограф, библиографический

библиограф(ы): bibliographer(s)

библиограф. *see* библиографический

библиографическая(ие) редкость(и): bibliographical rarity(ies)

библиографический: bibliographical

библиографический(ие) очерк(и): bibliographic survey(s)

библиографический(ие) указатель(и): bibliographical index(es)

библиография(и): bibliography(ies)

библиотека(и): library(ies)

библиотекарь(и): librarian(s)

библиотечка(и): small library(ies), small series

библиотечная марка: bookplate, *ex libris*

библиотечная скидка: library discount

библиотечный: of or pertaining to the library

библиотечный знак: bookplate, *ex libris*

библиотечный переплет: library binding

библиотечный штемпель на титульном листе: library stamp on the title page

библиофил(ы): bibliophile(s), booklover(s), amateur collector(s)

библьдрук: Bible paper

бинт(ы): raised band(s)

биог. *see* биографический

биографический: biographical

биография(и): biography(ies)

блокнот(ы): notebook(s)

богато иллюстр. *see* богато иллюстрированный

богато иллюстрированный: richly illustrated

более не выходило: no more published

более не издано: no more published, no more issued

большие листы: large leaves, pages, sheets

большой: big, large

большой формат: large size, "folio"

бордюр(ы): border(s), ornamental border(s), edge(s)

брайлевская печать: Braille

бронзированный: bronzed

брошюра(ы): brochure(s), pamphlet(s), opuscule(s)

брошюрованный: sewn, stitched

буква(ы): letter(s)

буквально: literally

букварь: ABC book, primer

букинист: second-hand book
  dealer
букинистическая книга: secondhand book
букинистический: out-of-print,
  antiquarian, second-hand
бум. л. *see* бумажный лист
бумага: paper
бумага из льняного тряпья: linen
  paper
бумага ручной выделки: handmade paper
бумажная обложка: paper cover
бумажный(ые) лист(ы): sheet(s),
  signature(s)
бумажный переплет: paperback
  binding, soft-cover binding
бюлл. *see* бюллетень
бюллетень(и): bulletin(s)

в: in, into
в. *see* век; выпуск
в алфавитном порядке: in
  alphabetical order
в вып. дан. *see* в выпускных
  данных
в выпускных данных: in imprint;
  in publishing data
в дальнейшем: in the future
в красках: in color
в мягкой обложке: in soft covers
в мягком переплете: in soft covers
в начале: at the beginning
в некоторых местах: in some places
в о.б.л. *see* в очень больших
  листах
в обложке: bound
в общем: generally, as a whole
в одн. пер. *see* в одном переплете
в одн. т. *see* в одном томе
в одном переплете: bound together
в одном томе: in one volume
в основном: generally, principally
в отличной сохранности: excellently preserved
в отличном состоянии: in excellent
  condition

в оч. б.л. *see* в очень больших
  листах
в очень больших листах: in very
  large leaves
в папке: in pasteboard case
в пер. *see* в переплете
в перепл. *see* в переплете
в переплете: bound
в печати: in press, at the printer's
в плохом состоянии: in poor condition
в полном виде: complete set, edition
в портфолио: in portfolio
в прекрасной сохранности: in
  excellent condition
в продаже: available at bookstores,
  available for sale
в прошлом: in the past
в прошлом году: in the last year
в пятнах: stained
в случае: in case of
в столбцах: in columns
в т.ч. *see* в том числе
в твердом переплете: in hard covers
в том числе: including, inclusively
в ———— томах: in ———— volumes
в употреблении: in use
в хорошем состоянии: in good
  condition
в честь: in honor of
валюта: currency
валюта по курсу дня: currency at
  the current rate of exchange
вариант текста: textual variant
вв. *see* века
введение: introduction, preface,
  foreword
вводная статья: introductory
  article
вводный: introductory
век(а): century(ies)
велен. *see* веленевый
веленевый: vellum
великолепно сохранено: in
  excellent condition
вероятная цена: approximate price
верхнее поле: upper margin

верхний: upper, top
верхняя обложка: front cover
весна: Spring
вестник: review
весь: all, entire
весьма: extremely
виньетка: vignette
вкл. *see* вкладка, включая,
  включительно
вкладка: supplementary sheet,
  insertion
вкладной(ые) лист(ы): loose
  supplementary leaf(ves), sheet(s)
вклееная иллюстрация: tipped-in
  illustration
вклееный: pasted in, glued in
включ. *see* включая,
  включительно
включая: including, inclusively
включенный(ые) лист(ы): intercalated leaf(ves)
включительно: inclusively
влияние: influence, effect
влияющий: affecting
влож. *see* вложение
вложение: enclosure
внешний: outside; foreign
внешняя книжная торговля:
  foreign book trade
внимание: attention; NB
внутр. *see* внутрений
внутреннее поле: inner margin
внутренний: inner, inside
водян. знак *see* водяной знак
водяное пятно: moisture stain,
  water stain
водяной(ые) знак(и): water-
  mark(s)
возврат книг не допускается: no
  book returns allowed
воздушная почта: airmail
вообще: generally, totally
восемнадцатый: eighteenth
восемнадцать: eighteen
восемь: eight
восемьдесят: eighty
восемьдесятый: eightieth

воспоминания: memoirs
восьмой: eighth
временный: temporary
время: time
все: all, entire
все изд. *see* все издание
все издание: whole edition,
  complete set
все права сохранены: all rights
  reserved
все, что вышло до с.п. *see* все, что
  вышло до сих пор
все, что вышло до сих пор: all
  published so far
все, что издано: all published
всего: in all, total
всерос. *see* всероссийский
всероссийский: all-Russian
всесоюз. *see* всесоюзный
всесоюзный: all-union
вспомогательный указатель:
  auxiliary index, supplementary
  index
вставка: insertion
встречается: occurs, is encountered
вступ. *see* вступительный
вступительная статья: introductory article, essay
вступительный: preliminary,
  introductory
вступление: foreword, introduction
вся: all, entire
второй: second
выбор: selection
вывод: conclusion
выдающийся: outstanding
выйдет из печати: will be
  published, to be published
выноска: footnote
вып. *see* выпуск
вып. дан. *see* выпускные данные
выполнение заказа: fulfillment
  of order
выпуск: issue, number, part,
  fascicle; edition
выпуск серии: series
выпускные данные: imprint

выпустить в свет книгу: publish
a book

вырванный: torn out

вырез. *see* вырезанный

вырезанный: engraved, carved;
cut out

вырезка(и): clipping(s); cut(s),
engraving(s)

выставка: exhibition, show

выход в свет: appearance,
publication

выходит ежемесячно: published
monthly

выходной лист: title page

выходные данные: imprint

выходные сведения: imprint

вычеркивание: expurgation

вычеркивать: score out, cancel

вышеуказанный адрес: above
indicated address

вышитый: embroidered

вышло из печати: just published

вязь: an elaborate Russian
decorative writing or type

г. *see* год

газ. *see* газета

газета(ы): newspaper(s)

гг. *see* годы

гелиогравюра(ы): heliogravure(s)

герб(ы): coat(s) of arms

гербовый: heraldic

гибкий: flexible

гл. *see* глава, главный

глав. *see* главный

глава(ы): chapter(s)

главная редакция: main
editorial office

главный: main, chief, principal

главный редактор: editor in chief

главным образом: chiefly, mainly

глаголица: Glagolitic alphabet

гладкий: smooth, crushed (leather)

глазированный: glazed, coated
calendered

год(ы): year(s)

год издания: imprint date, year of
publication

годовой: annual, yearly

годовщина: anniversary

Гос. *see* Государственный

Гос. издат-во *see* Государственное
издательство

Госиздат. *see* Государственное
издательство

Государственное издательство:
State publishing house

Государственный: (pertaining to
the) State

готический шрифт: Gothic type

готовится к печати: in
preparation

готовить к печати: prepare for
publication, make ready for
the press

гр. *see* графа

грав. *see* гравированный,
гравюра

гравер: engraver

гравир. *see* гравированный

гравирование: engraving, etching

гравированный: engraved

гравюра(ы): engraving(s), cut(s),
print(s), plate(s)

гравюра на дереве: wood
engraving, woodcut

гравюра на меди: copper engraving

гравюра на стали: steel engraving

гравюра сухой иглой: drypoint
etching

гравюры исполнены пунктиром:
stippled engravings

гражданский шрифт: standard (as
contrasted with Church Slavic)
type

граммофонная пластинка: phonorecord

гранки: proofs, galleys

графа(ы): column(s)

графика: drawing, graphics

гриф: signature stamp

гротесковый шрифт: block-letter
type

грубо раскраш. *see* грубо
раскрашенный
грубо раскрашенный: crudely
colored, painted
грубый: crude
грязный: soiled, dirty

д. *see* доллар
давно: long since
даритель: donor
даром: gratis, free
дарственная надпись: presentation
inscription
дарственный экземпляр: presentation copy
дата закрепления авторского
права: copyright date
дата издания: date of publication
датир. *see* датированный
датированный: dated
датированный неверно: misdated
два: two
двадцатый: twentieth
двадцать: twenty
две: two
двенадцатый: twelfth
двенадцать: twelve
двойной: double
двухлетний: biennial
двухмесячный: bimonthly
двухтомник: two-volume edition
двуязычный: bilingual
девиз: motto, device
девяносто: ninety
девяностый: ninetieth
девятнадцатый: nineteenth
девятнадцать: nineteen
девятый: ninth
девять: nine
дезидераты: desiderata
действительная цена: firm price
действительный выход: actual
date of publication
деление: division
деревянная печатная форма: block
деревянный переплет: wood covers
десятый: tenth

десять: ten
деф: *see* дефектный
дефектный: defective, imperfect
дешевое издание: inexpensive
edition, cheap edition
дешевый: cheap, inexpensive
диагр. *see* диаграмма
диаграмма(ы): diagram(s),
drawing(s), chart(s)
диапозитив: photographic slide,
transparency
дисконт: discount
дисконтировать: discount
дисс. *see* диссертация
диссертация(и): dissertation(s),
thesis(es)
дл. *see* длина
длина: length
для широкого круга читателей:
for wide readership
до с.п. *see* до сих пор
до сих пор: until now
добавл. *see* добавление
добавление: appendix, supplement
дозволено цензурой: passed by the
censor
докл. *see* доклад
доклад(ы): report(s)
документ(ы): document(s)
дол. *see* доллар
доллар(ы): dollar(s)
доп. *see* дополнение,
дополнительный
допеч. *see* допечатка
допечатка(и): additional, supplementary print(s)
допол. *see* дополнение,
дополнительный
дополнение: addition, supplement,
addenda
дополненное издание: enlarged
edition
дополнительный: supplementary,
extra
допущ. к печати *see* допущенный
к печати

допущенный к печати: approved
for printing

допущено к печатанию: approved
for printing; privileged

дорев. *see* дореволюционный

дореволюционный: prerevolu-
tionary

дорогой: costly

дорогостоящая книга: costly,
expensive book

доска(и): board(s), cover(s) (of a
book); wooden board(s)

дослов. *see* дословный

дословный: literal, textual

дословный перевод: literal
translation

доставка: delivery

достоверность: authenticity,
validity

достойный особого внимания:
worthy of special attention

доступный только специалистам:
esoteric

др. *see* другие

драма: drama

древний: antique, ancient

другие: others

дубликат(ы): duplicate(s),
duplicate copy(ies)

дырка(и), проделанная личинкой:
wormhole(s)

европ. *see* европейский

европейский: European

единица: unit

единообразный: uniform

единств. *see* единственно,
единственный

единственно: only, solely

единственный: only, sole, unique

ежегод. *see* ежегодник, ежегодный

ежегодник: annual, yearbook;
almanac

ежегодный: yearly

ежедневн. *see* ежедневный

ежедневная газета: daily paper

ежедневный: daily

ежеквартальник: quarterly

ежеквартальный: quarterly

ежемесячн. *see* ежемесячный

ежемесячный: monthly

еженедельн. *see* еженедельник,
еженедельный

еженедельник: weekly

еженедельный: weekly

еще не вышло: not yet published,
net yet printed

ж. *see* журнал

желанный: desired, sought

желаемый: in demand

желтый: yellow

жёсткий: stiff

живописный: picturesque, pictorial

жирный шрифт: boldface

жур. *see* журнал

журн. *see* журнал

журнал(ы): journal(s),
magazine(s); review(s)

за: for, at

за (весь) комплект: for the
(entire) set

за исключ. *see* за исключением

за исключением: except for

за наличные: for cash

за счет: at the expense of

заг. лист *see* заглавный лист

загл. *see* заглавие

заглавие: title

заглавие на обложке: cover title

заглавного листа нет: no title page

заглавный лист: title page, title leaf

загнутый угол страницы: dog-
eared

заголовок(и): heading(s),
rubric(s), caption title(s)

заграничная книжная торговля:
foreign book trade

заграничный: foreign

загрязненный: soiled, dirty

задняя часть обложки: back cover

заказ(ы): order(s)

заказное письмо: registered letter

заказчик: customer

заказы направлять: order from

заключение: conclusion

законченный: completed, finished

зам. редактора *see* заместитель редактора

заменительный экземпляр: substitute copy

заменять: replace

заместитель редактора: assistant editor

заметка(и): note(s), paragraph(s), notice(s)

заметки на полях: marginal notes

замечательного происхождения: of notable provenance

замечательный: remarkable

записная книжка: notebook

заплесневелый: moldy

запрещенное издание: forbidden edition, suppressed edition

запрос: inquiry, request

заруб. печать *see* зарубежная печать

зарубежная печать: foreign press

зарубежное издание: foreign edition, foreign publication

зарубежный: foreign

заставка(и): headpiece(s)

застежка(и): clasp(s)

застежки утрачены: clasps lost

звездочка: asterisk

зел. *see* зелёный

зелёный: green

зима: Winter

знак(и): mark(s), sign(s), trace(s)

знак пользования: trace, mark of use

знак сноски: reference mark

знак тома: volume number

золот. *see* золотой

золото: gold

золотое тиснение: gold tooling

золотой: gilt, gilded

золотые обрезы: gilded edges

и. *see* иллюстрация

и др. *see* и другие

и другие: and others

и мн. др. *see* и многие другие

и многие другие: and many others

и проч. *see* и прочее

и прочее: and so on, etc.

и т.д. *see* и так далее

и т.п. *see* и тому подобное

и так далее: etc., and so on

и тому подобное: likewise, and so on

идеальный: ideal, perfect

идентичный: identical

избр. *see* избранный

пзбран. *see* избранный

избранные произведения: selected works

избранные сочинения: selected works

избранные труды: selected works

избранный: selected

изв. *see* известия, извлечение

известия: news, information

извещение: announcement

извещенный: announced

извлечение: extract, excerpt

изд. *see* издание, издатель

издат. *see* издатель

издавать: publish

издается: in course of publication; published by

издание: edition, publication

издание некоммерческой типографии: privately printed edition

издание неофиц. *see* издание неофициальное

издание неофициальное: unofficial edition

издание прекратилось: publication discontinued, ceased

издание с лимитированным тиражом: limited edition

издат. *see* издатель, издательство

издатель(и): publisher(s)

издательская марка: publisher's device

издательский лист: publisher's signature

издательское дело: publishing

издательское объявление: pre-publication announcement

издательство: publishing house; published by

издать: publish

изд-во *see* издательство

изм. *see* изменение, измененный

изменение: correction, revision

измененный: corrected, revised

изношенный: worn-out

изображ. *see* изображение

изображение: picture, portrait

изрезанный: with cuts

изящная литература: fiction; belles lettres

изящный: refined, deluxe

илл. *see* иллюстрация

иллюстр. *see* иллюстратор, иллюстрированный

иллюстратор(ы): illustrator(s)

иллюстрация(и): illustration(s), plate(s)

иллюстрированный: illustrated

им. *see* имени

имеется в наличии: available

имеется в ограниченном количестве: available in limited quantity

имени: named, in the name of

имени (e.g., Библиотека имени Ленина): named for (e.g., The Lenin Library)

именной указатель: author index

имеются в продаже (книги): (books) available for sale

индийская бумага: India paper

инициал(ы): initial(s)

инкрустированный: mosaic, inlaid

инкунабула(ы): incunable(s), incunabulum(a)

иностр. *see* иностранный

иностранный: foreign

инст. *see* институт

институт: institute

ин-т *see* институт

интерпретация: interpretation

искаженный: mutilated

искать: to search for

исключительной красоты: of exceptional beauty

исключительный: exceptional

искусственный: artificial, imitation

искусство: art

испачканный: soiled, stained, dirty

использованная литература: literature consulted, sources

использование: usage

испорченный: spoiled

испр. *see* исправленный

исправление(я): correction(s)

исправленное издание: corrected edition

исправленный: corrected, revised

иссл. *see* исследование

исследование: research, investigation

исторический: historical

источенный личинками: worm-holed

источник: source

истрепанная книга: frayed book, torn book

истрепанный: worn-out

исчерпано: out-of-print, exhausted

исчерпывающий: exhaustive, comprehensive

итог: sum, total, result

к: to, for

к. *see* копейка

к (пятидесяти)летию: on the (50th) anniversary

какой-либо: some, any

какой-нибудь: some, any

каллиграф. *see* каллиграфический

каллиграфический: calligraphic

кант(ы): edge(s)

капиталь(и): headband(s), turn-in

капитальный труд: major work, magnum opus

карандашные пометки: annotations in pencil

карикатура(ы): caricature(s), cartoon(s)

карманное издание: pocket edition

карманный: pocket

карманный размер: pocket-size

карманный словарь: pocket dictionary

карманный формат: pocket-size

карт. *see* картина

карта(ы): map(s), chart(s)

картина(ы): picture(s), illustration(s)

картогр. *see* картограмма

картограмма(ы): cartogram(s)

картографический: cartographical

картон: binding board, pasteboard

картонаж: pasteboard case, portfolio

карточка: card

картушь: cartouche

кат. *see* каталог

каталог(и): catalog(s)

качество: quality

квадратный формат: square format

квартал: quarter

квартальный: quarterly

кварто: quarto

кириллица: Cyrillic alphabet

китайская бумага: China paper

к.–л. *see* какой-либо

классификация: classification, arrangement

классифицированный: classified, systematic

клеенка: buckram

клеенчатый переплет: buckram binding

клей: glue

клише: block

к.–н. *see* какой-нибудь

кн. *see* книга

кн–во *see* книгоиздательство

книга(и): book(s)

книги большего формата: large-size books, folios

книги для детей: children's books

книги для юношества: books for youth, young adults

книги малого формата: small-size books, booklets

книги по искусству: art books

книги разного содержания: miscellanea

книгоиздатель: book publisher

книгоиздательство: publishing house

книголюб: bibliophile

книгообмен: book exchange

книгопечатание: book-printing

книгопродавец(вцы): bookseller(s)

книготорговец(вцы): bookseller(s)

книготорговля: book trade

книготоргующая организация: book-selling organization

книгохранилище: book repository

книжка(и): booklet(s), notebook(s), small book(s)

книжная закладка: bookmark, ribbon

книжная лавка: bookstore

книжная торговля: book trade

книжный базар: book fair

книжный знак: bookplate

книжный магазин: bookstore, book shop

книжный переплет: bookbinding, book cover

книжный червь: bookworm

кож. пер. *see* кожаный переплет

кожа: leather

кожа, покрытая тисненными квадратиками: diced leather

кожаный переплет: leather binding

козлиная кожа: morocco

кол. *see* коллекция

коленкор: calico, buckram

коленкор. пер. *see* коленкоровый переплет

коленкоровый переплет: buckram binding

колич. *see* количество

количество: quantity, amount, number
коллация: collation
коллектив авторов: joint authors
коллектив редакторов: editorial staff
коллективный: collective
коллективный труд: work of joint or corporate authorship
коллектор: book-supply agency
коллекция(и): collection(s)
колонка(и): column(s)
колонтитул: running title
колофон: colophon
ком. *see* комиссия, комитет
комиссия(и): commission(s), committee(s)
комитет(ы): committee(s)
коммент. *see* комментарий
комментарий: commentary
компенд. *see* компендиум
компендиум: compendium, digest
компилятивный труд: compilation
компилятор(ы): compiler(s)
компиляция: compilation, compiling
комплект(ы): set(s), complete set(s)
комплектование: acquisition
ком–т *see* комитет
конверт: envelope
конец: end
конкорданция: concordance
конспект(ы): compendium(ia), synopsis(es)
конфискованный: seized, forbidden
концовка(и): tailpiece(s)
коп. *see* копейка
копейка(и): kopeck(s)
копия(и): copy(ies), duplicate(s), transcription(s)
корешковое заглавие: spine title
корешок: spine of a book
корректура: proofreading
краеведение: area studies, regional studies
краеведческий: area studies, regional studies

краешек: narrow edge
край(я): edge(s)
крайне: extremely
крайняя цена: lowest price
крапчатый обрез: sprinkled edge
красивый: beautiful
краска(и): color(s), dye(s)
красочный: colorful
крат. *see* краткий
краткий: short, concise
краткий словарь: concise dictionary
краткое заглавие: short title
краткое изложение: summary
критика: criticism, reviews
критицизм: criticism
критические замечания: critical notes
кромка: edge
крупный: large, big
крышка переплета: case, book jacket
ксилографическая книга: block book
ксилография: xylography
к–т *see* комитет
курсив: italics
курсивный шрифт: italic type
кьяроскуро: chiaroscuro

Л. *see* Ленинград
л. *see* лист
лакуна: lacuna
латин. *see* латинский
латиница: roman alphabet
латинский: Latin
латинский алфавит: roman alphabet
лауреат: laureate, prizewinner
Л–д. *see* Ленинград
лекция(и): lecture(s)
Ленинград: Leningrad
лента(ы): ribbon(s), bookmarker(s)
лет: years
–летие (пятидесяти-): the (50th) anniversary
лето: Summer

летопись(и): chronicle(s), annal(s)

летучее издание: fugitive publication

линейка: ruling, rule

линия(и): line(s)

линованный: lined, ruled

лирика: lyric poetry

лист(ы): leaf(ves), sheet(s), signature(s)

листки вступительной части: preliminary pages

листовка(и): small pamphlet(s)

листок: slip; leaflet

листы подклеенные: patched leaves

лит. *see* литература, литературный

литература: literature

литературный: literary

литогр. *see* литография

литограф. *see* литографированный, литографический, литография

литографированный: lithographed

литографический: lithographic

литография: lithography

лит-ра *see* литература

лишь: only, limited to

лишь в одном экземпляре: single copy

лл. *see* листы

Лнгр. *see* Ленинград

ложн. *see* ложный

ложный: false, fictitious

лозунг: catchword

льняной: (of) linen

любительский: amateur

любительский переплет: amateur binding

любопытное издание: curio

М. *see* Москва

м. *see* масштаб

м.с. *see* малая серия

м.ф. *see* малый формат

м. форм. *see* малый формат

магазин: store, shop

магазин антикварных книг: antiquarian bookstore

магазин букинистических книг: antiquarian bookstore

малая серия: small series

мало: little, few

малоизвестный: little known

малотиражный: small, limited edition

малоупотребительный: rarely used

малоценный: of little value

малочисленный: not numerous

малый: small, little

малый формат: small size

манускрипт(ы): manuscript(s)

маргиналии: marginal notes, marginalia

марокен: morocco

масса: many, numerous

массовое издание: mass publication

масштаб: scale

материалы: materials

медальон(ы): medallion(s)

межбиблиотечный абонемент: interlibrary loan

междустрочный: interlinear

мелкая печать: small print, small type

меловая бумага: art paper, enameled paper

мемориальный экземпляр: association copy

мемуары: memoirs

местный: local

место издания: place of publication

месяц(ы): month(s)

месячный: monthly

металлическое украшение: boss

метод. *see* методический

методический: instructional, methodological

меццотинто: mezzotint

микрофильм(ы): microfilm(s)

миллиметр(ы): millimeter(s)

мимеографирование: mimeographing

миниатюра(ы): miniature(s)

миниатюрный: tiny, miniature

минимальный: minimum

мм. *see* миллиметр

мн. *see* многие, множество

многие: many

много: much

многовековый: centuries-old, ancient

многокрасочный: multicolored, polychromatic

многотиражный: large edition

многотомное издание: multivolume edition

многочисленный: numerous

множество: many, the majority

множит. аппар. *see* множительным аппаратом

множительным аппаратом: mimeographed

модель(и): pattern(s)

может быть: possibly

мозаичный: mosaic

монография(и): monograph(s)

монотип: monotype

монументальный: monumental

Москва: Moscow

мрам. *see* мраморный

мраморн. обл. *see* мраморная обложка

мраморная обложка: marbled cover

мраморный: marbled

мраморный обрез: marbled edge

муаровый: moire, watered silk

музейная редкость: museum piece

мягк. обл. *see* мягкая обложка

мягкая обложка: soft cover

мягкий: soft

н. *see* номер

н.э. *see* нашей эры

на: on

на машинке: by typewriter

на обороте: verso, on the back

на обороте заглавного листа: on verso of the title page

на полях: at edges, in margins

на правах рукописи: all rights reserved

на просмотр: on approval

на складе: in stock

набавка в цене: additional charge, surcharge

набор: typesetting, (type) composition

набранный: composed, set up

надбавка в цене: additional charge, surcharge

надпись(и): inscription(s), epigraph(s), heading(s)

назв. *see* название

название: title, name

название главы: chapter heading

накл. *see* наклеенный, наклейка

накладная: invoice

накладные расходы: additional charges

наклеен. *see* наклеенный

наклеенный: pasted on, mounted

наклейка(и): label(s), patch(es)

накрашенный: painted

наличные деньги: cash

наново: anew, again

напеч. *see* напечатано

напечатано: printed

написано: written

написано от руки: handwritten

напоминание: reminder, notice

напр. *see* например

например: for example, e.g.

нар. *see* народный

народный: national

наружное поле: outer margin

науч. *see* научный

научн. *see* научный

научный: scientific, scholarly

находится: is found

находится в печати: at the printer's, being printed, in press

находится в производстве: in process of printing, being printed, in press

нац. *see* национальный

национальный: national

нач. *see* начальный

начало: beginning

началось печататься: printing
started

начальный: first, original

начиная с каталога N°.____:
beginning with catalog no.____

начитанный: scholarly

нашей эры: A.D.

не для общей продажи: not for
general sale

не для продажи: not for sale

не допускается: is not permitted

не первой свежести: not in good
condition

недельно: weekly, every week

неделя(и): week(s)

недорогой: inexpensive

недостает: lacking, missing

недостаточный: insufficient, scanty

недостающие страницы (части . . .):
lacking pages (parts . . .)

незаконная перепечатка: pirated
reprint

незаконное издание: pirated edition

незаконченный: incomplete

незначительный: insignificant,
slight

неизвестный: unknown

неизданный: unpublished

неисправный: defective, faulty

некролог(и): obituary(ies)

нельзя: impossible

нем. *see* немецкий

нем. обл. *see* немая обложка

немая обложка: blank cover

немецкий: German

немного: slightly, little

немногочисленный: not numerous

немножко: slightly, little

немножко поврежден: slightly
damaged

ненаходимый: impossible to find

ненумер: *see* ненумерованный

ненумерованный: not paginated,
unnumbered

необрезанный: untrimmed

неоконч. *see* неоконченный

неоконченный: unfinished, not
completed

неопубликованный: unpublished;
unpublicized

неофициальный: unofficial

непериодический: irregular serial
publication

неподписанный: unsigned

неполный: incomplete

непоступивший в продажу: not for
sale

непрерывный: uninterrupted,
continuous

непригодный: unsuitable

неразрезанный: uncut, unopened

нерегулярный: irregular

несколько: several; few

несокращенный: unabridged

нетто: net

неудовлетворительный: unsatisfactory

нечетная страница: right-hand
page, recto page

нигде: nowhere

ниже: lower, below

нижнее поле: bottom margin,
foot of page

новинки: new items

новое издание: new edition

новый: new

номер(а): number(s), issue(s)

номинальная цена: list price

нотификация: notification

ноты: sheet music

нр. *see* номер

нуждается в ремонте: needs repair

нумер. *see* нумерование,
нумерованный

нумерация: numbering, pagination

нумерование: numbering,
pagination

нумерованное издание: numbered
edition, limited edition

нумерованный: numbered,
paginated

о: about, of

о. *see* очень

оба: both

об–во *see* общество

обгорелый: burned, scorched

обесцвеченный: faded

обертка(и): portfolio(s); case(s) for a pamphlet set

обзор: survey, review

обл. *see* областной; обложка

областной: regional

обложка(и): cover(s), jacket(s), binding

обмен: exchange

обозначение: designation, symbol

обозр. *see* обозрение

обозрение(я): review(s)

оборван. *see* оборванный

оборванный: ragged, torn

оборот заглавия: verso of title

оборотная сторона: verso

оборотное заглавие: title on verso

оборотный: verso, back

обр. *see* обрез, обрезанный

обраб. *see* обработанный

обработанный: edited

образец(зцы): pattern(s), specimen(s)

обрамленный: framed

обратная почта: return post

обрез(ы): edge(s)

обрез книги с рисунком: painted edge

обрезанный: trimmed

обрезанный край: trimmed edge, cut edge

общ. *see* общий

общ. тит. л. *see* общий титульный лист

общая нумерация: consecutive numbering

общ–во *see* общество

общее заглавие: collective title

общество: society, association, company

общий: common, general

общий титульный лист: common title page, general title page

объедин. изд. *see* объединенное издание

объединение: association, society

объединенное издание: combined edition

объем: size

объявл. *see* объявление

объявление(я): announcement(s), advertisement(s), notice(s)

объявленный: announced, advertised

объясн. *see* объяснение, объяснительный

объяснение(я): explanation(s)

объяснительный: explanatory

обыкновенный: ordinary

обязательный: compulsory

обязательный экземпляр: legal deposit copy

о–во *see* общество

огл. *see* оглавление

оглавление: table of contents

огласка: publicity

огранич. колич. экз. *see* ограниченное количество экземпляров

ограниченное количество экземпляров: limited number of copies

ограниченный: limited

ограниченный тираж: limited printing

один: one

одиннадцатый: eleventh

одиннадцать: eleven

одна: one

одно: one

однотомник: single-volume edition

одобр. *see* одобренный

одобрение: approval

одобренный: approved

означение: meaning, significance, indication

ок. *see* около

окаймленный: bordered, edged

окаймлены золотым бордюром: gilded borders, gilded edges

около: approximately

окрашенный обрез: combed, colored edge

окружен бордюром: bordered, edged

октаво: octavo

оленья кожа: buckskin

опечатка(и): misprint(s), printing error(s), corrigendum(a)

описание: description

оплата: payment

оплаченный вперед: prepaid

оплаченный заранее: prepaid

определение: definition

определенный: certain, definite

оптовая книжная торговля: wholesale book trade

оптовый: wholesale

опублик. *see* опубликовано

опубликованные труды: published works

опубликованный в печати: printed, published in press

опубликовано: announced, advertised, published

опущ. *see* опущенный

опущенный: omitted

организация: organization

ориг. *see* оригинальный

оригинал(ы): original(s)

оригинальный: original

ориентировочная цена: approximate price

орнамент(ы): ornament(s)

орнаментированный(ые) инициал(ы): ornamental initial(s)

осень: Autumn, Fall

основной: main, principal

особый: special

остальной: remaining, other

от: from, because

от руки: by hand

отбор: selection

отв. ред. *see* ответственный редактор

ответ: answer, reply

ответственность за: responsibility for

ответственный редактор: editor in chief, editor in charge

отд. *see* отдел, отделение, отдельный

отдел: division, section, department

отделение(я): part(s), section(s)

отдельной почтой: under separate cover

отдельный: separate

отдельный оттиск журнала: journal offprint

отд–ние *see* отделение

отзыв: comment, review; reference

отличный: excellent, perfect

отметка(и): annotation(s), note(s), mark(s)

относительно: relatively

относящийся: relevant, pertinent to

отпеч. множит. аппар. *see* отпечатано множительным аппаратом

отпечатанный: printed

отпечатано множительным аппаратом: mimeographed

отпечатать весь тираж книги: print the whole edition of the book

отпечаток: imprint, impress

отсутствует: missing, lacking, absent

отт. *see* оттиск

оттиск(и): impression(s), print(s); reprint(s)

отчет(ы): report(s), account(s)

отчетливый шрифт: distinct print, clear type

отчетный доклад: report

офиц. *see* официальный

официальный: official

оформление: design, makeup

офорт(ы): etching(s)

офсет: offset

оценка: appraisal

оч. *see* очень, очерк

оч.б.л. *see* очень большие листы

очень: very

очень большие листы: very large
  sheets, very large leaves

очень редкий: very rare

очерк(и): sketch(es), essay(s)

ошибка: error, mistake

ошибочный: erroneous

П. *see* Петербург, Петроград

п. *see* портрет

Пб. *see* Петербург

Пг. *see* Петроград

п.л. *see* печатный лист

п.с.с. *see* полное собрание
  сочинений

паг. *see* пагинация

пагинация: pagination

пакет: package, parcel

памфлет(ы): pamphlet(s),
  brochure(s); lampoon(s)

памятная книга: memorial book

папка(и): portfolio(s), pasteboard
  case(s)

параграф(ы): paragraph(s)

паралл. *see* параллельно

параллельно: in parallel,
  simultaneously

параллельный текст: parallel text

парчевый: brocaded

пер. *see* перевод, переплет

первоначальный: original

первый: first

перг. *see* пергамент

пергам. *see* пергамент

пергамент: parchment

перев. *see* перевод

перевод(ы): translation(s),
  translated by

переводчик(и): translator(s)

перед заглавием: at the head of title

переделка(и): adaptation(s)

передний: first, front

передний обрез: fore edge

передняя доска: front cover

передняя часть обложки: front
  cover

перезаказывать: reorder

переизд. *see* переизданный

переизданный: republished,
  reprinted

переклеенный: reglued

перенумерованный от руки: renumbered by hand

переп. *see* переплет

перепечатанный: reprinted

перепечатка(и): reprint(s), another
  printing

перепечатка воспрещается: copyright reserved

переписка: correspondence,
  collected letters

переплет(ы): binding(s)

переплет из телячьей кожи: calf
  binding

переплетенный: bound

переплетная крышка: case

переплетная ткань: book cloth

переплетное заглавие: binder's title

переплетчик: bookbinder

перераб. *see* переработанный

переработанный: revised

пересм. *see* пересмотренный

пересмотренное издание: revised
  edition

пересмотренный: revised, checked

переставленный: transposed

переставший выходить: ceased
  publication

пересылка: postage, shipping costs

пересылка включена: postpaid,
  post-free

перечень: listing

перечислять: to enumerate

период. *see* периодический

периодический: periodic, serial

периодическое издание: serial,
  periodical publication

песенник(и): songbook(s)

Петербург: St. Petersburg

Петроград: Petrograd,
  St. Petersburg

печ. *see* печатный

печ. л. *see* печатный лист

печатается: in press, being printed
печатание: printing
печатная(ые): буква(ы): block
letter(s)
печатный: printed
печатный лист: signature (of a
book); printer's sheet, quire
печать: press; impression, printing;
stamp, seal
печать для слепых: Braille
писатель(и): author(s), writer(s)
письмо(а): letter(s)
пишущая машинка: typewriter
план(ы): plan(s), map(s)
пластинка: phonodisc, phonorecord
платить по частям: to be paid by
installments
плесень: mildew
плотная бумага: heavy paper
плохо связанный: loose in binding
плохое состояние: poor condition
по: according to
по алфавиту: alphabetically
по ошибке напечатано: printer's
error
по повышенной цене: at increased
price
по подписке: on subscription
по случаю (50-летн.) юбилея: on
occasion of the (50th) anniversary
по сниженной цене: at reduced price
по требованию: on request, on
demand
по этому адресу: to this address
поблекнувший: faded
повесть(и): story(ies)
по-видимому: apparently
поврежден: damaged, mutilated
поврежден в корешке: back
damaged, spine damaged
повреждение: damage
повышенная цена: increased price
повышенной прочности: reinforced (binding)
погрешность: error, mistake
под заглавием: under the title,
under the heading; headed, entitled

под ред. *see* под редакцией
под редакцией: edited by
подарочное издание: gift edition
подбитый: lined
подготовлено к печати: readied for
publication, readied for printing
подготовляется к печати: in
process of preparation for printing
подделка(и): counterfeit(s), falsifi-
cation(s), forgery(ies)
подержанный экземпляр: used or
secondhand copy
подзаголовок: subtitle, subheading
подклейка(и): pasted patch(es),
pasting(s)
подлиннык: original text
подлинный: authentic
подмочен. *see* подмоченный
подмоченный: damaged by
moisture
подносный экземпляр: compli-
mentary copy
подобно: similarly, in like manner
подп. к печати *see* подписано к
печати
подписанный: signed
подписано к печати: officially
approved for publication
подписка: subscription
подписка продолжается: subscription time extended, subscription
still active
подписная цена: subscription price
подписное издание: subscription
edition
подписной лист: subscription list
подпись(и): personal signature(s)
подпись автора: autograph
подпись иллюстрации: legend
подразделение: subdivision,
subsection
подробный: detailed
подстроч. *see* подстрочный
подстрочное примечание: footnote
подстрочный: interlinear
подстрочный перевод: interlinear
translation

подчеркнутый: underlined, underscored
подчистка: erasure
пожелтелый: yellowed, browned
поиск: search
покрытый бурымй пятнами: foxed
покрытый плесенью: mildew-spotted
покрытый пятнами: spotted
покупатель: customer
пол. *see* половина
поле(я): margin(s), edge(s)
полигр. *see* полиграфический, полиграфия
полиграфический: typographical
полиграфия: typography
полированный: burnished
полит. *see* политический
политипаж: polytype
политический: political
полное издание: complete edition
полное собрание сочинений: complete works
полностью разошлось: completely sold out
полный: full, complete
полный комплект: full set
половина: half
полоска орнамента: fillet, ornamental line
полосная(ые) иллюстрация(и): full-page illustration(s)
полотн. *see* полотняный
полотняная бумага: linen paper
полотняный: of linen
полугодовой: semiannual
полукож. с угл. пер. *see* полукожаный с углами переплет
полукожаный с углами переплет: three-quarter binding
полумесячный: semimonthly
полупереплет: half binding
полусафьян: half-morocco
полутом(а): half volume(s)
получать: to receive
получение: receipt

полушагр. *see* полушагреневый
полушагреневый: half-shagreen
пометка(и): mark(s)
пометки в тексте карандашом: pencil marks in text
пометки в тексте чернилами: ink marks in text
попорчен сыростью: damaged by moisture
поправка(и): correction(s)
попул. *see* популярный
популярный: popular
порванный: torn
портр. *see* портрет
портрет(ы): portrait(s)
порядок: order, sequence, arrangement
посвящен: dedicated
посвящение: dedication
посеребренный: silvered (edge)
последний: last
послесловие: epilogue
посмертное издание: posthumous edition, posthumous work
пособие(я): textbook(s)
постоянный: regular
постоянный заказ: standing order
поступило в продажу: on the market, on sale
потертый: shabby
потеря: loss
потрепанный: tattered
почерк: handwriting
починенный: repaired
почти: almost, nearly
почтовые расходы: postage charges
появиться в печати: to come out, to be published
появление в свет: publication
пояснительный: explanatory
практический: practical
превосходный: excellent, perfect
предварительное объявление: advance announcement
предварительный: preliminary, advance
предисл. *see* предисловие

предисловие: preface, introduction

предполагаемая цена: probable price

предполагаемый автор: presumed author

предмет: subject, topic

предметный: topical

предметный указатель: subject index

представитель: representative

предстоящий выпуск издания: to be published shortly

предыдущий: previous, preceding

прекрасно сохранившийся: well preserved

прекрасный: beautiful, fine, excellent

прекратилось: discontinued

прекратилось изданием в (1915 г.): last edition in (1915), no more published since (1915)

премированная книга: award-winning book

при заказах: when ordering

при ответе: when answering

приб. *see* прибавление

прибавл. *see* прибавление

прибавление(я): supplement(s), appendix(es)

прибл. *see* приблизительно

приблизительно: approximately

привлекательный: attractive

прил. *see* приложение

прилож. *see* приложение

приложение(я): enclosure(s); appendix(es), supplement(s), annex(es), addendum(a)

прим. *see* примечание

применение: application

примечание(я): annotation(s), note(s)

принимается: accepted

приобретение книг: acquisition of books

приписываемый: attributed to

пробный номер: sample copy

пробный экземпляр: specimen, sample copy

проверять: to verify

прод. *see* продолжение

продаваться: to be on (for) sale

продажа: sale

продано: sold

продолг. *see* продолговатый

продолговатый: elongated

продолж. *see* продолжение

продолжающие издаваться: in progress

продолжающиеся издания: serial publications

продолжение: continuation

продолжение следует: to be continued

проза: prose

произведение(я): work(s)

прокладный(ые) лист(ы): inter-leaf(ves)

прописная(ые) буква(ы): capital letter(s)

пропуск(и): omission(s)

просим: we request, please

просм. *see* просмотренный

просмотренный: revised

просмотрено цензурой: censored

проспект(ы): prospectus(es)

простой переплет: ordinary binding

протерто: perforated by erasure

против текста: opposite, facing the text

процесс: process

пряжка(и): clasp(s)

прямой корешок: flat band

прямой шрифт: roman type

псевд. *see* псевдоним

псевдоним(ы): pseudonym(s), pen name(s)

публикация: publication; publishing

пунктир: dotted line

пунктирная манера: dotted print

пунктирный: stippled

путеводитель(и): guidebook(s)

пыльный: dusty

пятнадцатый: fifteenth
пятнадцать: fifteen
пятна от времени: spotted by age;
    foxing
пятно(а): stain(s), spot(s)
пятый: fifth
пять: five
пятьдесят: fifty
пятьдесятый: fiftieth

р. *see* рубль
разброшюрованный: unstitched
разд. *see* раздел
раздел(ы): division(s), section(s)
раздельный: detached, separated
размер: size
разное: miscellanea
разнообразные литературные
    произведения: miscellaneous
    pieces, works
разноцветный: many-colored
разночтение: variant reading
разный: various, different
разорванный: torn
разошлись: sold out
разошлись полностью: completely
    sold out
разработка: elaboration,
    treatment
разрезанный: cut, opened
разрозненные тома: odd volumes
разукрашенный: painted, colored
разъяснение: explanation,
    interpretation
разъяснительный: explanatory
разыскивается: being sought,
    in demand
рамка(и): border(s), frame(s)
ранее: earlier, previously
раньше: earlier, previously
раскр. от руки *see* раскрашенный
    от руки
раскраска(и): coloring(s),
    illumination(s)
раскрашенная рукопись: illumi-
    nated manuscript
раскрашенный: colored, illuminated

раскрашенный от руки: hand-
    colored
расписка в получении: receipt
располагается: arranged, placed
расположение: arrangement
распоряжение(я): order(s),
    direction(s)
распродажа: sale, clearance sale
распродано: sold out, out of print
распространение: distribution
рассказ(ы): story(ies)
рассмотренный: revised; reviewed
расставленный: spaced
растительный орнамент: floral
    design, ornament
расходы: expenses, charges
расчет(ы): account(s)
расширенный: enlarged
регулярный: regular
ред. *see* редактор
редактирование: editing,
    editorship
редактор(ы): editor(s)
редакц. *see* редакционный
редакционная коллегия: editorial
    board
редакционный: editorial
редакционный коллектив: edi-
    torial board
редкие издания: rare editions
редкий: rare
редко встречается: rarely found
редко попадается: hard to find
редкость: rarity
редчайшее издание: rarest edition
рез. на дереве *see* резанный на
    дереве
резан. *see* резанный
резан. на меди *see* резанный на
    меди
резанный: carved, engraved
резанный на дереве: woodcut
резанный на меди: copper-
    engraved
резюме: summary, résumé
реклама: advertisement
репр. *see* репродукция

репрография: reprography
репродукция(и): reproduction(s), facsimile(s)
реставр. *see* реставрированный
реставрация: restoration
реставрированный: restored, mended
ретроспективный: retrospective
ретуш. *see* ретушированный
ретушированный: retouched
реферат(ы): abstract(s)
реферативный журнал: abstracting journal
рец. *see* рецензия
рецензия(и): review(s)
римские цифры: roman numerals
рис. *see* рисунок
рисунок(нки): drawing(s), illustration(s), design(s)
розничная продажа книг: retail bookselling, book trade
розничная цена: retail price
роман(ы): novel(s)
роскошн. *see* роскошный
роскошное издание: deluxe edition, luxury edition
роскошный: deluxe, magnificent
росс. *see* российский
российский: Russian
ротапринт: mimeograph copy
руб. *see* рубль
рубль, рубля, рублей: ruble(s)
рубрика(и): rubric(s), topical heading(s)
рубчик(и) переплёта: joint(s) (of the binding)
руководство: manual, handbook, treatise
рукописный: manuscript
рукопись(и): manuscript(s)
русск. *see* русский
русский: Russian
ручной выделки: handmade

с: with
с. *see* серия, страница
с автографом: autographed

с.г. *see* сего года
с инициалами: rubricated, with initials
с оттенком: tinted
с пересылкой: postpaid, shipping charge included
с подписью: signed
с примечанием: with annotation
с проложенными чистыми листами: interleaved
с тиснением: tooled
с.ф. *see* средний формат
самая редкая книга: most rare book
самостоятельный: independent
самый выдающийся: most distinguished
самый популярный: most popular
самый точный: most accurate
Санкт-Петербург: Saint Petersburg
сантиметр(ы): centimeter(s)
сафьяновый: morocco
сб. *see* сборник
сбереженный хорошо: in good condition
сборник: collection
сборник статей: collection of essays
сборный лист: preliminary pages, front matter
сведния: information
сверенный: verified, collated
сверху: from the top
свиная кожа: pigskin
сводный выпуск: cumulation
свыше: more than
сгиб(ы): fold(s)
сдано в набор: set in type
сего года: this year
седьмой: seventh
семидесятый: seventieth
семнадцатый: seventeenth
семнадцать: seventeen
семь: seven
семьдесят: seventy
сер. *see* серия
серия: series
сигнатура(ы): signature(s)

сильно поврежденный: badly damaged

систем. указ. *see* систематический указатель

систематический: classified, arranged by subject

систематический указатель: classified index

сказка(и): tale(s), story(ies)

скидка: discount

скл. *see* складной

склад: warehouse, stock

складной: folded, folding

скоро: soon, quickly

скоро выйдет в свет: soon to be published

слабые водяные пятна: slight moisture spots

славянский шрифт: Old Slavic type, Old Slavic print

слегка: slightly

слегка поврежден: slightly damaged

слегка подмочен: slightly damaged by moisture

след. *see* следующий

след. обр. *see* следующим образом

следующий: following, next

следующим образом: as follows

слепой шрифт: blind type

словарь(и): dictionary(ies), lexicon(s)

слоновая бумага: elephant folio

случайный: occasional

см. *see* сантиметр, смотри

см. также *see* смотри также

смотри: see

смотри также: see also

снабженный: provided, supplied with

снабженный примечаниями: annotated

снабжено: provided, furnished

сниженная цена: reduced price

снизу: from the bottom

снимк. *see* снимок

снимок(мки): photograph(s)

снова: again, anew

сноска(и): footnote(s), note(s)

сноски на полях: marginal notes

соавтор(ы): coauthor(s), joint author(s)

собиратель(и): collector(s)

собр. *see* собрание

собр. сочинений *see* собрание сочинений

собрание(я): collection(s)

собрание сочинений: collected works

собственноручно подписанный автором: autographed by the author

сов. *see* совет, советский

совет: Soviet, council

советский: Soviet

совместно с: along with

совр. *see* современный

соврем. *see* современный

современный: contemporary

согласно: according to

содерж. *see* содержание

содержание: table of contents

сокр. *see* сокращение, сокращенный

сокращ. *see* сокращение, сокращенный

сокращение(я): abbreviation(s), abridgment(s)

сокращенное издание: abridged edition

сокращенное заглавие: catchword title

сокращенный: abbreviated, abridged

сомнительный: dubious, doubtful

сообщение(я): proceeding(s), report(s); information

сопроводительный текст: accompanying text

сопровожденный: accompanied by

сорок: forty

сороковой: fortieth

сост. *see* составитель

составитель(и): compiler(s)

составление(я): compilation(s), composition(s)

составленный: compiled

составной переплет: half-cloth binding

состояние: condition

сотрудник(и): contributor(s), collaborator(s)

сотый: one hundredth

сохран. *see* сохранённый

сохраненный: preserved

сохранность великолепная: very good condition

сохранность превосходная: excellent condition

сохранность средняя: fair condition

сочинение(я): work(s)

СПб. *see* Санкт-Петербург

спец. *see* специальный

специализированный: specialized

специальный: special, specific

спиральный орнамент: lettered scroll

список(ски): list(s)

список дезидератов: want list

список опечаток: errata list

сплетенный орнамент: interlacing

сплошная нумерация: consecutive numbering

справочная книга: reference book

справочник(и): reference book(s)

ср. *see* сравни

сравни: compare

среди: among

сред. форм. *see* средний формат

средневековый: medieval

средний формат: medium size

срок: period, length of time

срочный заказ: rush order

ссылка: citation, reference

ст. *see* статья, столбец

стандарт: standard

старинная рукопись: codex

старинный: ancient

стат. *see* статистический, статья

статистический: statistical

статья(и): article(s), paper(s)

стереотип. *see* стереотипный

стереотип: stereotype

стереотипный: stereotype

стержень(жни): guard(s)

стертый: effaced, faded

стихи: verses

стихотворение: poem

стлб. *see* столбец

сто: one hundred

стоимость: value, cost

стоимость пересылки: mailing charges, shipping charges

столб. *see* столбец

столбец(бцы): column(s)

столетие(я): century(ies)

сторона(ы): side(s)

стр. *see* страница

страница(ы): page(s)

страницы пожелтели: pages yellowed

строчная(ые) буква(ы): small letter(s), lowercase letter(s)

сумма: sum

суперобложка(и): book jacket(s), dustcover(s), wrapper(s)

сфальцованная иллюстрация: folding plate

сфальцованный: folded

схема(ы): diagram(s), chart(s)

схематич. *see* схематический

схематический: schematic, outlined

счет(ы): account(s), expense(s)

сшитый: sewed, stitched

сырость: dampness

т. *see* том

т.е. *see* то есть

т.к. *see* так как

т.н. *see* так называемый

табл. *see* таблица

таблица(ы): table(s), plate(s), chart(s)

таблица в красках: color plate

так как: as, since

так называемый: so-called

также: also

таким образом: thus
твердый переплет: hardcover
т–во *see* товарищество
тезис: thesis
текст(ы): text(s)
телячья кожа: calf leather
тем. пл. *see* тематический план
тематический план: thematic plan,
  topical plan
темнозел. *see* темнозеленый
темнозеленый: dark green
темносн. *see* темносиний
темносиний: dark blue
тесьма(ы): tie(s)
тетрадь(ы): section(s), fascicle(s)
техн. *see* технический
технический: technical
тип. *see* типографский,
  типография
типогр. зн. *see* типографский
  знак
типограф. *see* типографский,
  типография
типограф. знак *see* типографский знак
типография: printing house
типографская марка: printer's
  device, mark
типографская ошибка: printer's
  error
типографский: typographic
типографский знак: printer's
  mark
типографский шрифт: typeface
типолит. *see* типолитографический, типолитография
типолитогр. *see* типолитографический, типолитография
типолитографический: typo-
  lithographic
типолитография: typolithography
тираж: pressrun, size of edition
тисн. *see* тиснение, тисненый
тиснение: stamping, tooling,
  embossing
тисненый: tooled, stamped,
  embossed

тит. *see* титул
тит.л. *see* титульный лист
титул(ы): title(s)
титульный лист: title page
тифдрук: mezzotint
тканьевый: cloth
то есть: that is., i.e.
товарищество(а): company(ies),
  society(ies)
того времени: contemporary
тоже: also
толкование: interpretation,
  commentary
толстая бумага: heavy, thick
  paper
толстый: thick, fat
только: only
только для подписчиков: for
  subscribers only
только–что: just recently
только–что вышло из печати: just
  published
том(ы,а): volume(s)
том разрозненного комплекта:
  odd volume
тонкий: fine, thin
торшонированный обрез: goffered
  edge
точный: exact
трактат(ы): treatise(s)
транскрипция: transcription
транслитер. *see* транслитерация,
  транслитерированный
транслитерация: transliteration
транслитерированный: trans-
  literated
третий: third
трехлетний: triennial
трехмесячный: quarterly
трехтомник: three-volume edition
три: three
тридцатый: thirtieth
тридцать: thirty
тринадцатый: thirteenth
тринадцать: thirteen
трудно находимый: hard to find
труды: scientific works

труды научного общества: transactions of a scientific society

тт. *see* томы

тщательно: thoroughly

тыс. *see* тысяча

тысяча: thousand

убористая печать: close-set type

увеличенный: enlarged, increased

увеличивается: is increased

угол(глы): corner(s), angle(s)

удлинен. *see* удлиненный

удлиненный: oblong, elongated

удовлетворительный: satisfactory

узкий: narrow

ук. *see* указатель

указ. *see* указание, указатель

указание: indication, direction

указанный: indicated

указатель(и): index(es)

укомплектов. *see* укомплектованный

укомплектованный: full,
complete set

украш. *see* украшение,
украшенный

украшение(я): decoration(s),
ornament(s), illumination(s)

украшенный: ornamented,
decorated, illuminated

укрепленный: reinforced

улучш. *see* улучшенный

улучшен. *see* улучшенный

улучшенный: improved, revised,
amended

уменьшенный: reduced

умнож. *see* умноженный

умноженный: enlarged

унив. *see* университет

университет(ы): university(ies)

уникум: unique

ун–т *see* университет

унциальная(ые) бука(ы): uncial
letter(s)

упаковка: packing, wrapping

уполномоч. *see* уполномоченный

уполномоченный: commissioned,
authorized

упоминается: is mentioned

употребление: use, usage

упущение(я): omission(s)

урез. *see* урезанный

урезанный: cut off

условно: on condition

усовершенствованный: perfected,
improved

уст. *see* устарелый

устар. *see* устаревший, устарелый

устаревший: obsolete, outdated

устарелый: obsolete, archaic

утв. *see* утверждение, утвержденный

утверждение: confirmation,
affirmation, approval

утвержденный: confirmed,
affirmed, approved

утеря: loss

утрачен. *see* утраченный

утраченный: lost, missing

уцелевший: intact, untouched

уч. зап. *see* ученые записки

учеб. *see* учебник

учебник(и): textbook(s), manual(s)

учебное пособие: study aid,
textbook

ученые записки: transactions,
proceedings

ученый: learned, scientific

факс. *see* факсимиле

факсимиле: facsimile

фактура: invoice

факультативный: optional

фальсификация(и): forgery(ies),
falsification(s)

фальсифицированный: forged

фальц(ы): fold(s)

фантастический: fantastic

фантастичный: fabulous

фиг. *see* фигура

фигура(ы): figure(s), diagram(s)

фиктивный год издания: fictitious
date of publication

филигрань: watermark
фолио: folio
фонд: stock, holdings
форзац: flyleaf; lining paper
форм. *see* формат
формальный: formal
формат: size, format
фот. *see* фотография
фотогелиотипический: photohelio-
  typed
фотограв. *see* фотогравюра
фотогравюра(ы): photogravure(s),
  photoengraving(s)
фотография(и): photograph(s)
фотокопия: photocopy
фотолит. *see* фотолитографический
фотолитогр. *see* фотолитографический
фотолитографический: photolithographic
фотомех. *see* фотомеханический
фотомеханический: photo-
  mechanical
фотоофсет: photo-offset
фотостат. *see* фотостатический
фотостатический: photostatic
фототип. *see* фототипический
фототипич. *see* фототипический
фототипический: phototype
фр. *see* французский
фрагментарный: fragmentary
фрактура: black-letter type
франкированный: prepaid
франц. *see* французский
французский: French
фрахт: freight
фронт. *see* фронтиспис
фронтиспис: frontispiece
фундаментальный: fundamental
фундаментальный труд: basic
  work
футляр(ы): container(s),
  portfolio(s)

ходкая книга: best-seller
холст: canvas, cloth

холщ. пер. *see* холщевый переплет
холщевый переплет: canvas
  binding
хор. *see* хороший, хорошо
хорош. *see* хороший
хороший: good
хорошо: well
хрестоматия: reader
хромолит. *see* хромолитографированный, хромолитография
хромолитографированный:
  chromolithographed
хромолитография: chromolithograph, chromolithography
хромотипография: chromotypo-
  graph, chromotypography
хроника(и): chronicle(s), annal(s)
хронолог. *see* хронологический
хронологический: chronological
худое состояние: poor condition
худож. *see* художественный
художественная литература:
  fiction, belles lettres
художественное издание: artistic
  edition
художественное произведенние:
  work of art
художественный: artistic
художественный редактор: design
  editor

ц. *see* цена
цв. *see* цветной
цвет: color
цветн. *see* цветной
цветная бумага: colored paper
цветная гравюра: colored print,
  colored engraving
цветная обложка: colored cover
цветная продукция: color printing,
  printed in colors
цветная фотография: color
  photograph
цветной: colored, in colors
цветные иллюстрации: colored
  illustrations
целиком: entirely

целый: full, whole

цена: price

цена без пересылки: mailing charges not included

цена без упаковки: packing charges not included

цена включая пересылку: price including mailing charges

цена за том по подписке: subscription price per volume

цена каждой части отдельно: price for each separate part

цена комплекта в обертке: price for set in portfolio

цена нетто: net price

цена повысилась: price increased

цена с пересылкой: price postpaid

цензура: censorship

ценность: value

ценный: valuable

центр. *see* центральный

центральный: central

церковнославянский: Old Church Slavonic

церковнославянский шрифт: Old Church Slavonic type

церковный шрифт: ecclesiastical type

церк.-слав. *see* церковнославянский

цинкограф. *see* цинкографический

цинкографический: zincographic

цитата(ы): quotation(s)

цифра(ы): numeral(s), figure(s)

ч. *see* часть; число

частично: partially

часто: frequently, often

частый: frequent

часть(и): part(s)

частью: partly

чернилы: ink

черный: black

черт. *see* чертеж

черта(ы): scoring, line(s)

чертеж(и): drawing(s), sketch(es), chart(s)

четверть: quarter

четвертый: fourth

четная(ые) страница(ы): left-hand page(s), verso(s)

четыре: four

четырехтомник: four-volume edition

четырнадцатый: fourteenth

четырнадцать: fourteen

число: date, number

чистая обложка: blank wrapper, plain cover

чистописание: calligraphy, penmanship

чистый: clean, blank, plain

читатель(и): reader(s)

член(ы): member(s)

чрезвычайный: extraordinary, extreme

чудесный: wonderful

чч. *see* части

шаблон(ы): stencil(s), pattern(s)

шагр. *see* шагреневый

шагреневый: shagreen

шагрень: shagreen

шарж(и): cartoon(s), caricature(s)

шедевр(ы): masterpiece(s)

шелковый: silk

шестидесятый: sixtieth

шестнадцатый: sixteenth

шестнадцать: sixteen

шестой: sixth

шесть: six

шестьдесят: sixty

ширинта: width

широкий: broad, wide

шифр: pressmark

шмуцтит. *see* шмуцтитул

шмуцтитул: half title, bastard title

шнур(ы): raised band(s)

шрифт: print, type

штамп(ы): stamp(s), seal(s)

штемп. *see* штемпель

штемпель(я): stamp(s)

штриховка: hatching

штриховой рисунок: line drawing

эквивалент. *see* эквивалентный
эквивалентный: equivalent
экз. *see* экземпляр
экземпляр(ы): copy(ies), issue(s)
экслибрис: bookplate, *ex libris*
экспериментальный: experimental
экспертный: expert
экспортная торговля: export trade
экстракт(ы): extract(s)
экстраординарный: extraordinary, unusual
элегант. *see* элегантный
элегантный: elegant
эмблема(ы): emblem(s), device(s)
энцикл. *see* энциклопедия
энциклопедический словарь: encyclopedic dictionary
энциклопедия: encyclopedia
эпиграф(ы): epigraph(s)
эпика: epic(s)
эпилог(и): epilogue(s)
эпический: epic
эпоха(и): epoch(s)

эра(ы): era(s)
эскиз(ы): sketch(es), outline(s)
эстамп(ы): print(s), plate(s)
этот, эта, это: this
этюд(ы): study(ies), sketch(es)

юбил. *see* юбилей
юбилей: anniversary, jubilee
юбилейное издание: anniversary edition, jubilee publication, festschrift
юмористич. *see* юмористический
юмористический: humorous, comic
юридич. *see* юридический
юридический: legal, juridical
юфть: Russian leather

явный: evident, obvious
яз. *see* язык
язык(и): language(s)
японская бумага: Japan paper
ясный: clear, lucid

Spanish

a. *see* año
a colores: in colors
a continuación: following
a doble folio: double folio
a doble página: two-page
a doble plana: two full pages
a doble texto: parallel text
a dos columnas: in two columns
a dos tintas: in two colors
a fines de: at the end of
a frío: blind-tooled
a grandes márgenes: with wide
   margins
a la bandeja: like a tray
a la rom. *see* a la romántica
a la romántica: in the style of the
   romantic period
a la rústica: paper binding
a la venta: on sale
a mano: by hand
a página entera: full page
a pesar de: in spite of
a plana: full page
a plena página: full page
a reeditar: to be republished
a seco: blind-tooled
a toda pág. *see* a toda página
a toda página: full page
a toda plana: full page
a todo color: in full color
a todo lujo: deluxe
a tres tintas: in three colors
a varias tintas: in various colors
abigarrado: variegated
abreviación: abridgment
abreviatura(s): abbreviation(s)

acaba de: just, has just
acabado de publicar: just published
acanelado: cinnamon-colored
acero: steel
aclaratorio: clarifying
aconsejado: advised
acotación(es): annotation(s),
   footnote(s)
acta: proceedings
actualmente: at present
acuarela(s): watercolor(s)
acuarelado: watercolored
acuatinta(s): aquatint(s)
adentro: inside, within
adicional: additional
adiciones: addenda
adolecido: defective, damaged
adornado: decorated
adorno(s): ornament(s)
afectando: affecting
aficionado(s): amateur(s)
afuera: outside
agot. *see* agotado
agotadísimo: scarce
agotado: out-of-print
agregado(s): addition(s), added
aguafuerte(s): etching(s)
agujereado: wormholed
agujero(s): wormhole(s)
ahuesado: bone color, off-white
al acero: in steel
al aguafuerte: etched
al cobre: in copper
al comienzo: at the front
al cromo: in colors

al día: up to date
al fin: at the end
al final: at the end
al margen: in the margin
al mercado: to market, for sale
al parecer: apparently
al pie de página: at the bottom of
   the page
al respaldo: on the back
alargado: long, elongated
álbum: album
aldino: Aldine
algo deficiente: slightly defective
algo deslucido: slightly off-color,
   dulled
algo deteriorado: slightly
   deteriorated
algo estropeado: slightly damaged
algo rozado: slightly scuffed
algunas: some, a few
alisado: smooth, matte
almanaque: almanac
alrededor de: around
alterado: altered
alto: high, tall
alto costo: high price
altura: height
amarilleado: yellowed
amarillento: yellowed
amarilleo: yellowing
amarillo: yellow
ambos: both
amenidad: amenity
ampliado: enlarged
amplio: ample
amplitud: amplitude, fullness
anales: annals
análisis: abstract
anaranjado: orange-colored
anastatico: anastatic
ancho: wide
anchura: width
anchuroso: very wide
anejo(s): annex(es), supplement(s)
anexo: annexed, attached
ángulo: corner, angle
año: year

anónimo: anonymous
anotación(es): note(s),
   annotation(s)
anotaciones al pie de páginas:
   annotations at the foot of pages
anotaciones marginales: marginal
   notes
anotado: annotated
anotado y glosado: annotated and
   provided with a gloss
ant. see antiguo
antaño: in olden times
anteado: buff
antep. see anteportada
anteportada: half-title page
anteportadilla: small half title
anticuado: out-of-date
antiguo: old, former
antiguo poseedor: former owner
antología(s): anthology(ies)
anual: annual
anual. see anualmente
anualmente: annually
anuario(s): yearbook(s), annual(s)
anverso: recto, front side
apais. see apaisado
apaisado: oblong
aparatoso: sumptuous
aparecido: appeared
aparición: appearance, publication
aparición irregular: irregular
   publication
aparición reciente: recently
   published
aparte: separately
aparte texto: separate from the
   text
apenas: scarcely
apéndice(s): appendix(es)
apéndice documental: documentary
   appendix
aplic. see aplicaciones
aplicaciones: appliqués
apolillado: perforated by worms,
   worm-eaten
aprec. see apreciado
apreciable: valuable

apreciado: esteemed, valued
aproximadamente: approximately
aproximado: approximate
apuntes: notes
arabesco(s): arabesque(s)
archivo: archives
armas: arms
arpillera: coarse cloth
arrancado: torn out
arreglos: repairs
arreglos hechos por el autor:
    revisions made by the author
arreglos hechos por el compilador:
    revisions made by the compiler
arreglos hechos por el editor:
    revisions made by the publisher
arrugado: wrinkled
artístico: artistic
atacado: attacked; damaged
aterciopelado: made to resemble
    velvet
atlas: atlas
atrasado: out-of-date, delayed
aum. *see* aumentado
aumentado: enlarged
autobiografía(s): auto-
    biography(ies)
autocromía(s): color print(s)
autografiado: autographed
autógrafo(s): autograph(s)
autor(es): author(s)
autor desconocido: author un-
    known
autor privado: privately published
autores extranjeros: foreign
    authors
autorizado: authorized
autorretrato: self-portrait
avellana: nut-colored
aviso: notice
azul: blue
azulado: bluish
azurado: azured, azure blue

badana: sheepskin
badana chagrinada: grained sheep-
    skin

badana valenciana: marbled sheep-
    skin
bajo costo: low price
bajo-relieve: bas-relief
bajorrelieve: bas-relief
Balboas: Panamanian monetary
    units
Bals. *see* Balboas
banda(s): border(s), strip(s)
bandera: foldout
barbas: witnesses, uncut edges
barnizado: varnished, polished
barroco: baroque
básica: basic
bastante: rather, somewhat
bastarda: bastard type
bastardilla: italic type
becerro: calfskin
bellamente: beautifully
bermellón: vermilion
bibliófilo: bibliophile
bibliografía: bibliography
bibliográfico: bibliographical
biblioteca: library, series,
    collection
biblioteca particular: private,
    personal library
bibliotecario(s): librarian(s)
bicromía: two-color print
bimen. *see* bimensual
bimensual: semimonthly
bimestral: bimonthly
biografía: biography
biográfico: biographic
bisagra(s): hinge(s)
bisemanal: semiweekly, twice a
    week
bistre: bister
bitono: two-tone
bl. *see* blanco
blanco: white, blank
blanco y negro: black and white
blasón: armorial bearing
Bls. *see* Bolivares
bocacé: buckram
boj(es): woodcut(s)
boletín: bulletin

boletín de información: news
   bulletin
boletín de novedades: new title list
Bolivares: Venezuelan monetary
   units
bolsillo: pocket
bonito: pretty
bordado: embroidered
borde(s): border(s), edge(s)
borde(s) estropeado(s): dog-eared
borrado: erased
botón(es): boss(es)
bradel: bradel, a cased binding
breve: short
brin: sailcloth, canvas
brocado: brocaded
broche(s) de metal: metal clasp(s)
broche(s) de plata: silver clasp(s)
broche(s) metálico(s): metal
   clasp(s)
bronce: bronze
bronceado: bronzed, bronze-
   colored
bruñido: crushed, burnished
Bs. *see* Bolivares
btca. *see* biblioteca
bucarán: buckram
buen: good
bullones: bosses
burlería(s): fairy tale(s)
buscado: in great demand, sought
búsqueda: search

c. *see* centímetros, columna, con,
   corte
cabecera(s): headpiece(s)
cabeza: top
cabezada(s): headband(s)
cada: each
caja: box, case
caja-estuche: slipcase
calandrado: calendered
calcografía: art of engraving
calderón(es): paragraph sign(s)
calidad: quality
caligrafía: calligraphy
calígrafo: scribe

cambio: change
camisa: book jacket, wrapper
cancelación: cancellation
cancelado: canceled
cancionero(s): songbook(s)
cant. *see* canto
canto(s): edge(s)
cantonera(s): corner piece(s)
cantonera esquinero: corner reinforcement
cantos y planos: edges and sides
cap. *see* capítulo
capa-estuche: slipcase
capitulares: chapter headings
capítulo(s): chapter(s)
caps. *see* capítulo
caracteres: letters, type
caracteres arábigos: Arabic letters,
   type
caracteres griegos: Greek letters,
   type
caracteres romanos: roman letters,
   type
carátula: title page
carcomido: worm-eaten
carecer *see* por carecer de
carente: lacking
caricatura(s): caricature(s)
carpeta: slipcase, portfolio
cart. *see* cartón, cartulina
cartilla: primer, hornbook
cartografía: cartography
cartón: cardboard
cartón cuero: imitation leather
cartón flexible: flexible cardboard
cartón forrado: lined board
cartoné: boards, bound in boards
cartoné plastificado: plasticized
   boards
cartulina: bristol board, thin cardboard
cartulina gamuzada: yellowed
   board
cartulina plastizada: plastic-coated
   board
cartulina satinada: coated board
castizo: pure

catorce: fourteen
celebérrimo: most celebrated, famous
célebre: celebrated
celofán: cellophane
cenefa(s): border(s)
censura: censorship
censurado: censored
centenar(es): hundred(s)
centésimo: hundredth
centímetros: centimeters
centralice sus pedidos: orders may be combined for various publishers
centro: center
cerdo: pigskin
chagrín: shagreen
chamuscado: scorched, singed
chaqueta: book jacket
charnela(s): hinge(s)
cien: one hundred
ciento: one hundred
cierres: clasps
cierres de cintas: ribbon ties
cierres de cuero: leather clasps
cierres metálicos: metal clasps
cincelado: goffered, goffering
cinco: five
cincuenta: fifty
cinta(s): tie(s)
círculos: circular designs, circles
citado: cited
citrón: lemon-colored
clandestina: clandestine, underground
claroscuro: chiaroscuro
clave: key
clavo(s): nail(s), peg(s)
clisé(s): cut(s), plate(s)
cms. *see* centímetros
coautor: coauthor
cobre: copper
códice: codex
codiciable: highly desirable
codiciado: desired, coveted
coetáneo: contemporary

col. *see* colaboración, colección, colorado, coloreado
colaboración: collaboration
colación: collation
colección: collection, series
colección privada: personal collection
coleccionado: collected
coletivo: collective
colocación: placement
colofón: colophon
colones: Costa Rican monetary units
colorado: colored
coloreado: colored
colorido: colored, coloring
cols. *see* colones
colum. *see* columna
columna(s): column(s)
com. *see* comentario
comentario: commentary
como nuevo: as new
comp. *see* compartimientos, compilación, compilador
compart. *see* compartimientos
compartimientos: line design used in decorating bindings in square or oblong panels
compendiado: organized into a compendium
compilación: compilation
compilado: compiled
compilador: compiler
complemento: complement
completado: completed
completo: complete
compuesto: composed
con: with
con adornos: with decorative motifs
con estuche: with slipcase
con firma auténtica: with genuine signature
con grandes márgenes: with large margins
con sus márgenes: with original margins

concordancia: concordance
conjunto: together, the group
conmemorativo: commemorative
conservación: conservation
conservado: well-preserved
contemporáneo: contemporary,
    contemporaneous
contenido: contents
contexto: context
contiene: contains
continuación: continuation
contracanto(s): lacework tooling
    inside edges of covers
contracubierta: back cover
contraguarda(s): doublure(s),
    lining(s) of a book cover
contrahecho: counterfeited
contraportada: page opposite the
    title page, frontispiece
contratapa(s): lining(s),
    doublure(s)
coop. *see* cooperativo
cooperativo: cooperative
copia(s): copy(ies)
corcho: cork
cordobán: cordovan
corr. *see* corregido
corrección(es): correction(s)
corregido: corrected
correo certificado: certified mail
corriente: common, current
cort. *see* corte
cortado: opened, trimmed
corte(s): edge(s)
corte de cabeza: head, top edge
corte de pie: bottom edge
corte delantera: fore edge
corte desbarbado: trimmed edge
corte(s) dorado(s): gilt edge(s)
corte gofrado: goffered edge
corte(s) labrado(s): chiseled edge(s)
cortesía(s): endpaper(s), fly-
    leaf(ves)
corto: short
corto de márgenes: narrow margins
cosido: sewing, stitching
costeado: paid for

costo: price, cost
costo equitativo: fair price
costo neto: net price
cotidiano: daily
cotización: price, evaluation
couché: laid
crédito: credit
crédito aceptado: credit approved
crédito aumentado: credit
    increased
crédito suspendido: credit sus-
    pended
crestomatía: anthology
cribado: dotted
crisografía: gold lettering
cromo(s): color(s), colored
    illustration(s)
cromo. *see* cromolitografía
cromolitografía: chromolithography
cromotipia: chromotypography
crónica(s): chronicle(s)
croquis: sketch
cruceiros: Brazilian monetary
    units
cuadernillo: a small pamphlet,
    unit of five folded sheets
cuaderno(s): notebook(s), pam-
    phlet(s); quire(s)
cuadrado: square
cuadrados: pattern of squares
cuadragésimo: fortieth
cuadro(s): picture(s); border(s)
cuajado: highly decorated
cuarenta: forty
cuarterones: quarters
cuarto: fourth
cuatricromías: four-color prints
cuatro: four
cubierta(s): cover(s)
cubierta de celofán: cellophane
    cover
cubierta en blanco: blank wrapper
cubierta ornamentada: decorated
    cover
cubierta plástica: plastic-coated
    cover

cubierta protectora: protective cover
cubiertas de tela: cloth covers
cubiertas dobladas: folded wrapper
cubretapas: book jacket, wrapper
cuenta: account
cuenta corriente: on account
cuenta saldada: account closed
cuento(s): tale(s)
cuerina: imitation leather
cuero: leather
cuero artificial: imitation leather
cuero de avestruz: ostrich leather
cuero de cerdo: pigskin
cuero de la época: contemporary leather
cuero de Rusia: Russian leather
cuero labrado: tooled leather
cuero repujado: embossed leather
cuidado: care; carefully done
culo de lámpara: tailpiece(s)
curioso: curious
cursiva: italics
curvado: curved

d.c. *see* doble columna
dañado: damaged
dañando: damaging
daño(s): damage(s)
data: date
datos bibliográficos: bibliographic data
datos equívocados: wrong data
de época: contemporary
de gran estima: highly valued
de gran rareza: very rare
de insigne rareza: of the highest rarity
de la época: contemporary
de lujo: deluxe
de márgenes estrechos: with narrow margins
de mucha estima: very highly esteemed
de mucha venta: in great demand
de mucho aprecio: highly valued

de poca importancia: of little importance
de próxima aparición: to be published very soon
de próxima publicación: to be published soon
de suma rareza: of the utmost rarity
débil: weak
debilitado: weakened
décimo: tenth
décimocuarto: fourteenth
décimonono: nineteenth
décimooctavo: eighteenth
décimoquinto: fifteenth
décimoséptimo: seventeenth
décimosexto: sixteenth
décimotercero: thirteenth
decoración(es): decoration(s)
decoraciones restauradas: decorations restored
decorado(s): decoration(s), decorated
ded. *see* dedicado, dedicatoria
dedicación: dedication
dedicado: dedicated, inscribed
dedicatoria: dedication
defecto(s): defect(s)
defectuoso: defective
definitivo: definitive
delante: front side of a book
delantero: top margin
delgado: thin
dentellado: ornamented with dentelle patterns
dentelle: dentelle
dentro del texto: within the text
depurado: cleaned up
derecho: right
derechos de autor: author's rights, copyright
derechos reservados: rights reserved
desbarbado: trimmed, smoothed
descolorido: discolored, faded
desconocido: unknown

descosido: unsewn, stitching broken
descripción: description
descuento: discount
descuidado: careless
desencolado: unglued
desencuadernado: binding loose or gone
desgarro(s): tear(s)
desgastado: worn away
desgraciadamente: unfortunately
deslustrado: without luster
desmerecer: to decrease in value
desordenado: in disorder
desperfecto: imperfection
desplegable(s): folded insert(s)
desplegable: folded, folding
desprendido: loosened, separated
destacado: detached
destinado: destined
deteriorado: damaged, deteriorated
diagr. *see* diagrama
diagrama(s): diagram(s)
diario: daily publication, daily
dib. *see* dibujo
dibujado: drawn, sketched
dibujo(s): drawing(s), sketch(es)
dibujo(s) a lápiz: pencil sketch(es)
diecinueve: nineteen
dieciocho: eighteen
dieciséis: sixteen
diecisiete: seventeen
diez: ten
difícil: difficult
digítales: thumb index
diminutivo: diminutive
dirección: address
dirigido: directed
discontinuado: no longer published
diseño(s): design(s)
disertación: dissertation
disminuido: reduced, diminished
disponible: available
distribución exclusiva: exclusive distribution

distribuciones oficiales: official distribution
distribuidor encargado: authorized distributor
distribuidor exclusivo: exclusive distributor
distribuidor único: sole distributor
dividida: divided
doblado: folded
doble: double
doble columna: double column
doble hilo: double thread, line
doble texto: parallel text, two-column page format
doce: twelve
docum. *see* documento
documentado: documented
documento(s): document(s)
documentos fotografiados: photo-copied documents
dollares: dollars
dolls. *see* dollares
donativo(s): gift(s)
dor. *see* dorado
dorado(s): gilding, gilt, gold decoration(s)
dorado de cabeza: gilt top
dos: two
duodécimo: twelfth

ed. *see* edición(es), editor
edic. *see* edición
edición(es): edition(s)
edición abreviada: abridged edition
edición aum. *see* edición aumentada
edición aumentada: enlarged edition
edición aumentada y corregida: enlarged and corrected edition
edición autorizada: authorized edition
edición autorizada por el autor: edition authorized by the author
edición autorizada por el gobierno: edition authorized by the government
edición censurada: censored edition

edición clandestina: clandestine, underground edition
edición compendiada: abridged edition
edición confiscada: confiscated edition
edición conmemorativa: commemorative edition
edición corregida: corrected edition
edición corta: limited edition
edición crítica: critical edition
edición de bibliófilo: bibliophile edition
edición de bolsillo: pocket edition
edición de lujo: deluxe edition
edición definitiva: definitive edition
edición en rama: edition in sheets
edición esmerada: finely worked edition
edición especial: special edition
edición espurgada: expurgated edition
edición facsimilar: facsimile edition
edición furtiva: clandestine edition
edición limitada: limited edition
edición mutilada: mutilated edition
edición para estudiantes: textbook
edición políglota: polylingual edition
edición póst. *see* edición póstuma
edición póstuma: posthumous edition
edición príncipe: editio princeps, first edition
edición privada: private edition
edición reducida: abridged edition
edición sintetizada: edition of minimal text
edición supervisada: official edition, approved edition
edición trunca: abridged edition
edit. *see* editorial
editar: to print, to publish
editor: publisher
editora: of the publisher

editorial: of the publisher
editorial desconocida: publisher not known
efímero: ephemeral
ej. *see* ejemplar
ejecutado: executed
ejecutoria: execution
ejem. *see* ejemplar
ejemp(s). *see* ejemplar
ejemplar(es): copy(ies)
ejemplar apolillado: wormholed copy
ejemplar en rama: copy in sheets
ejemplar manuscrito: manuscript copy
elenco(s): list(s)
embalaje: packing
empastado: bound in boards
empastadura: board binding
en acero: steel
en blanco: blank, white
en boga: popular, the vogue
en breve: shortly
en buen estado: in good condition
en cartoné: in boards
en cartulina: in thin cardboard
en colores: in colors
en conjunto: all together
en curso de publicación: in course of publication
en de lujo: deluxe
en el mercado: in the market, for sale
en el texto: in the text
en gran folio: large folio
en gran papel: on large paper
en huecograbado: in mezzotint
en letra cursiva: in italics
en letra microscópica: in very small print
en madera: wood
en mal estado: in poor condition
en oro: in gold
en papel corriente: on common paper
en pasta española: in marbled leather

en pasta valenciana: in color-
marbled leather
en perfecto estado: in perfect
condition
en pliegos: in folded sheets
en prensa: in press
en preparación: in preparation
en rama: in sheets
en reimpresión: being reprinted
en relieve: in relief
en rústica: paperback, paperbound
en saco: in a case
en seco: drypoint
en venta: on sale
enc. *see* encuadernación,
encuadernado
enc. lujo *see* encuadernación de
lujo
enc. plastificada *see* encuadernación
plastificada
encabezamiento: heading, subject
heading
encadenado: chained
encaj. *see* encaje
encaje: inlay
encarnado: flesh-colored
encarte(s): insert(s), tip-in(s)
encartonado: bound in boards
encolado: pasted up, mounted
encontrar: to find
encuad. *see* encuadernación,
encuadernado
encuader. *see* encuadernación,
encuadernado
encuadernación: binding
encuadernación arpillera: heavy
cloth binding
encuadernación barata: cheap
binding
encuadernación coetánea: contemporary binding
encuadernación de edición: edition
binding
encuadernación de lujo: deluxe
binding
encuadernación en cartón: cased
boards

encuadernación en cuero: leather
binding
encuadernación de tela: cloth
binding
encuadernación nominal: usual
binding
encuadernación nueva: new binding
encuadernación original: original
binding
encuadernación plastificada: plastic
impregnated on coated binding
encuadernación provisional: temporary binding
encuadernación romántica: bound
in romantic style
encuadernación sin cosido: perfect
binding
encuadernación sin costura: perfect binding
encuadernado: bound
encuadernado en pergamino:
bound in parchment
encuadernador: binder
encuadernados juntos: bound
together
encuadernar: to bind
encuadrado: framed, bordered
encuadre: line pattern forming a
frame
enmarcado: marked
enmendado: emended
enmienda(s): emendation(s)
ennegrecido: darkened, blackened
enriquecido: enriched, embellished
ensayo: essay; trial
ensuciado: dirtied
entelado: cloth-covered, cloth-
backed
enteramente: entirely
entero: entire
entre el texto: within the text
entre texto: within the text
entredós: strip
entrega(s): part(s), installment(s)
entrega especial: special delivery
entrel. *see* entrelazados
entrelazados: interlaced fillets

entrelazamientos: interlacings
entrenervios: space between
  raised bands
envío aéreo: airmail shipment
envío marítimo: by sea, surface
  shipment
envueltos en celofán: cellophane
  wrapped
epígrafe: epigraph, inscription
epílogo: epilogue
epístola: epistle
época: epoch, of the time
equivoca *see* se equivoca
errata: misprints, errata
erróneo: erroneous
esbozo(s): sketch(es)
escaso: rare
escogido: selected
escolios: critical notes
escribano: scribe
escs. *see* escudos
escudo(s): shield(s)
escudo(s) de armas: coat(s) of
  arms
escudo(s) heraldico(s): heraldic
  shield(s)
escudos: Chilean monetary units
esmeradamente: carefully
esmerado: careful
especial: special
espécimen: specimen, sample
espléndido: splendid
espurgado: expurgated
esquema(s): plan(s), outline(s)
esquina(s): corner(s)
esquinas dobladas: dog-eared
esquinas rasgadas: corners torn
est. *see* estampado
estado: condition, state
estado de conservación: condition,
  state of preservation
estado de cuenta: statement of
  account
estamp. *see* estampado
estampa(s): print(s), engraving(s)
estampación: tooling
estampación(es): tooled design(s)

estampación(es) a fuego: hot-iron
  stamping(s)
estampado: tooled
estampado en oro: tooled in gold
estampadura: tooling
estilo: style
estilo corriente: contemporary
  style
estilo romántico: romantic style
estima: esteem, value
estimado: esteemed, valued
estimado apróximado: estimated
  value
estrecho: narrow
estrecho-apaisado: narrow and
  elongated
estropeado: mutilated, torn
estuche: slipcase
estuche de cartón: board slipcase
estuche de cuero: leather slipcase
estuche de madera: wooden slipcase
estuche de metal: metal slipcase
estuche de terciopelo: velvet slipcase
estupendo: stupendous
etiqueta: label
ex-libris: ownership plate or mark
excelente: excellent
excelentemente: excellently
exito del año: best-seller of the year
exclusivo: exclusive
exornado: embellished
explicativo: explanatory
expurgato: expurgated
extracto: extract
extranjero: foreign
extremado: extreme

f. *see* fecha
fabricado: manufactured, made
facsím. *see* facsímil
facsímil(es): facsimile(s)
facsimilar: in facsimile
facsímile: facsimile
facticio: artificial, factitious
factura: invoice, bill

factura cancelada: invoice canceled

factura pagada: invoice paid

falsa portada: half-title page

falta: lacking

falto de: lacking, for lack of

fantasía: fancy

fascículo(s): fascicle(s), part(s)

fasciculos coleccionables: parts of a volume

fatigado: worn

fé de errata: errata slip

fecha(s): date(s)

fechado: dated

fg. *see* figura

fgs. *see* figura

fielmente: faithfully

figura(s): illustration(s)

fil. *see* filete

filete(s): fillet(s)

filete de lineas: design of lines

fileteado: adorned with fillets

filetes dorados: gold fillets

filiforme: filiform, threadlike

filigrana: filigree, watermark

fils. *see* filete

fin: end

finales: end

fino: fine, thin

finura: fineness, perfection

firma: signature

firma apócrifa: apocryphal signature

firma auténtica: authentic signature

firmado: signed

firmado y fechado: signed and dated

flete: freight

flete pagado: freight paid

flete pagado por el cliente: freight paid by the customer

flete pagado por el comprador: freight paid by the buyer

flete por nuestra cuenta: freight at our expense

flor de lis: fleur-de-lys

floral: floral

floreado: flowered

florones: large floral designs used in tooled bindings

fol. *see* foliación, folio

foliación: foliation

foliado: foliated

foliar: foliate, foliating

foliatura: foliation

folio: a folio, folio-size

folio atlántico: atlas folio

folio mayor: large folio

folio menor: small folio

follajes: scroll design

folletín: leaflet, small pamphlet

folleto(s): pamphlet(s)

fondo: background

forrado: lined

forro(s): jacket(s), lining(s); cover(s)

foto(s): photograph(s)

fotocopia(s): photocopy(ies)

fotograbado(s): photoengraving(s)

fotograbs. *see* fotograbado

fotografía(s): photograph(s)

fotográfico: photographic

fotolitográfico: photolithographic

fototipia: phototype

fototípico: phototype

fototipográfico: phototypographic

fragmento: fragment

franco: postpaid

franco de paga: free of charge

franco de porte: postpaid, prepaid

frecuente: frequent

frescura: freshness

frío: *see* a frío

front. *see* frontispicio

frontis: frontispiece

frontis. *see* frontispicio

frontis-retrato: portrait frontispiece

frontispicio: frontispiece

frotado: rubbed

fuera de circulación: out of circulation

fuera de comercio: not for sale

fuera de texto: not in the text
fuerte: serious, strong
funda(s): case(s)

gaceta: gazette, journal
gaceta oficial: official gazette
gacetilla: news sheet, section of a
  newspaper
gamuzado: yellowed
garabateado: with scribblings
garabato(s): pothooks, poorly
  formed characters
garrapatos: scribblings
gastado: worn, soiled, spoiled
gastos de envío: costs of shipping
glosa(s): gloss(es)
glosado: provided with a gloss
glosario: glossary
gofrado: blind stamping, goffered,
  goffering
gofreado: goffered
gótico: in Gothic type
gr. *see* grano
grab. *see* grabado
grabadito(s): small engraving(s)
grabado(s): illustration(s),
  engraving(s)
grabado: engraved
grabado al aguafuerte: etched
grabado al boj: woodcut
grabado antiguo: old engraving
grabado en acero: steel engraving
grabado en cobre: copper engraving
grabado(s) en madera: woodcut(s)
grabador(es): engraver(s)
gráf. *see* gráfico
gráfico(s): illustration(s)
gran: large
gran folio: double folio
gran papel: large paper
grande: large
graneado: grained, stippled
grano: grain
grano bruñido: crushed, polished
  surface
grano grueso: heavy, thick grain
grano largo: straight-grained

grasa: grease
grbs. *see* grabado
greca(s): ornamental design(s)
grisáceo: gray, grayish
grueso: thick, heavy; thickness
guaflex: a plastic type of binding
guaraníes: Paraguayan monetary
  units
guarda(s): endpaper(s)
guardapolvo: dustcover, wrapper
guardas cortadas: endpapers cut
guardas sin cortar: endpapers
  uncut
guía: guide
gusto: taste

h. *see* hoja
h. en b. *see* hoja(s) en blanco
hábil: able
hábilmente: ably
hacia: about
hecho: made
heliograbado: helioengraving
heliotypia: heliotype
hermoso: beautiful
hierro(s): tooled design(s)
hierro(s) en seco: blind-tooled
  design(s)
hilo(s): thread(s), line(s)
historiado: highly decorated,
  ornamented
hoj. *see* hoja
hoja(s): leaf(ves)
hoja(s) añadida(s): added leaf(ves),
  cancel(s)
hoja(s) arrancada(s): leaf(ves)
  torn out
hoja(s) desprendida(s): leaf(ves)
  loosened
hoja(s) doble(s): double leaf(ves)
hoja(s) en blanco: blank leaf(ves)
hoja volante: broadside
hol. *see* holandesa
holand. *see* holandesa
holandesa: half-leather binding
holandesa chagrín: half-shagreen
  binding

holandesa piel: half-leather binding
hueco(s): mezzotint(s)
huella(s): trace(s)
hule: oilcloth
humedad: dampness
humedades: spots caused by dampness

ilegible: illegible
iluminación: illumination
iluminado: illuminated
ilus. *see* ilustración
ilust. *see* ilustración, ilustrado
ilustración(es): illustration(s)
ilustrado: illustrated
ilustrador: illustrator
imitación: imitation
imitado: imitated, artificial
imp. *see* imprenta
impecable: impeccable
imprenta: imprint, press
imprentario: printer
imprentero: printer
inprescindible: indispensable
impresión: printing, edition
impresión aparte: reprint, separate
impresión imperfecta: imperfect
  edition, imperfect printing
impresión offset: offset printing
impresionante: impressive
impreso(s): printed matter,
  printed piece(s)
impresor: printer
inasequible: out of reach,
  unattainable
incisión(es): cut(s), scratch(es)
incl. *see* inclusive, incluyendo
incluido: included, including
inclusive: inclusive
incluso: including
incluyendo: including
incompleto: incomplete
incrustación: embossing
incrustado: embossed
incunable: incunabulum
ind. *see* índice
índice(s): index(es)

índice alfabético: alphabetic index
índice analítico: analytic index
índice cronológico: chronological
  index
índice de autores: index of authors
índice de materias: subject index
índice de títulos: title index
índice geográfico: geographic index
índice onomástico: index of names
indispensable: indispensable
inédito: unpublished
inferior: lower
infinidad: a great number
informe(s): report(s)
inicial(es): initial letter(s)
inicial historiada: profusely
  ornamented initial
inicial orlada: decorated initial
inmaculado: immaculate
inmediato: imminent
inscripción: inscription
inserto: inserted, laid in
insigne: famous
insignificante: insignificant
int. *see* interior
íntegramente: completely, wholly
íntegro: complete, whole
interc. *see* intercalado
intercal. *see* intercalado
intercalado: intercalated
interesa a: affects
interesando: affecting, touching
interfoliado: interleaved
interior: inside, inner
interlineado: interlinear
intitulado: entitled
intonso: uncut, untrimmed
intransparente: opaque
intro. *see* introducción
introd. *see* introducción
introducción: introduction
inverso: inverse; obverse
izquierdo: left

jaquelado: square checkerboard
  pattern
jaqueta del libro: book jacket

jasp. *see* jaspeado
jaspead. *see* jaspeado
jaspeado: marbled
jaspeadura: marbling
joya bibliográfica: bibliographic gem
juego de filetes: pattern of lines
juntos: together

keratol: Keratol, a book cloth

l. *see* letra, lugar
labrado: polished, worked
ladillo(s): marginal note(s)
lám. *see* lámina
lámina(s): plate(s)
lámina(s) desgarrada(s): plate(s) torn out
lámina(s) desprendida(s): loose plate(s)
lámina(s) en colores: color plate(s)
lámina(s) firmada(s): signed plate(s)
lámina(s) fuera de texto: plate(s) not in the text
lámina(s) incluida(s) en bolsillo: plate(s) included in pocket
lámina(s) restaurada(s): plate(s) restored
lámina(s) rota(s): plate(s) broken
lámina(s) suelta(s): loose plate(s)
lamparone(s): large grease spot(s)
láms. *see* láminas
larg. *see* largo
largo: large, long, wide
lastimado: damaged
lateral: lateral
laureado: prize-winning
lavado: washed
lazos: ties, laces
legajo: packet
legible: legible
lejos de: far from
let. *see* letra
letra: letter, typeface
letra abastonada: Gothic type
letra bastarda: bastard type

letra bastardilla: bastard type
letra borrosa: illegible type
letra(s) capital(es): capital letter(s)
letra(s) capitular(es): chapter letter(s)
letra cursiva: italics, cursive type
letra de imprenta: block letters
letra de plano: block letters
letra gótica: Gothic type
letra(s) inicial(es): initial letter(s)
letra italica: italic type
letra(s) mayúscula(s): uppercase letter(s)
letra(s) minúscula(s): lowercase letter(s)
letra redonda: roman type
letra romana: roman-letter type
levantado: raised
leve: light, slight
levemente: lightly, slightly
léxico(s): lexicon(s)
libre de cargo: free of charge
libre de pago: free of charge
librería: bookstore, book shop
librería de viejo: secondhand bookstore
librero: bookseller, bookstore
libreto(s): libretto(s)
librito(s): little book(s)
libro(s): book(s)
libro(s) de mayor venta: best-selling book(s)
ligeramente: lightly
ligeramente amarillento: slightly yellowed
ligeramente apolillado: slightly wormholed
ligeramente deteriorado: slightly damaged
ligerísimo: very light
ligero: light, slight
limitado: limited
limón: lemon-colored
limpio: clean
limpísimo: very clean
lindo: pretty
lista(s): list(s)

lit. *see* litografía
literal: literal
literalmente: literally
litografía(s): lithographic print(s)
litografiado: lithographed
lom. *see* lomera, lomo
lomera: back strip
lomera valenciana: Valencian
  leather back strip
lomo: back
lomo con nervios: back with
  raised bands
lomo de piel: leather back
lomo jaspeado: marbled back
lomo liso: flat back, smooth back
lomo listo: flat back, smooth back
lomo roto: back broken
lomo y puntas: back and corners
lugar: place
lugar de publicación: place of
  publication
lujo: deluxe, highest quality
lujosa presentación: elaborate
  production
lujosamente: sumptuously
lujosísima: most elaborate
lujoso: elaborate, luxurious

m. *see* marroquí, medio
m.n. *see* moneda nacional
m.o. *see* moneda oficial
m.s. *see* manuscrito
macula(s): blemish(es), stain(s)
madera: wood
maderas: woodcuts
magníficamente: magnificently
magnífico: magnificent
mal: bad
mal cosido: badly sewn
mal foliado: badly foliated
mal paginado: badly paged
maltratado: badly treated
mancha(s): spot(s), stain(s)
manchado: spotted, stained
manchas de agua: water stains
manchas de humedad: damp stains,
  foxing

manchas de moho: damp stains,
  foxing
manchas de tinta: ink stains
manchas del tiempo: stains of time
manuable: portable
manual(es): manual(s)
manus. *see* manuscrito
manuscrito: handwritten, manuscript
map(s). *see* mapa
map(s). col(s). *see* mapa(s)
  coloreado(s)
map. pleg. *see* mapa(s) plegable(s)
mapa(s): map(s)
mapa(s) coloreado(s): colored
  map(s)
mapa(s) doblado(s): folded map(s)
mapa(s) plegable(s): folding map(s)
mapamundi: world map
mapa-ruta: route map
maps. pleg. *see* mapa(s) plegable(s)
marbete(s): label(s)
marca: device, mark
marca de agua: watermark
marca del impresor: printer's mark
marcado: marked
márfil: ivory
margen(es): margin(s)
margen de cabeceras: top margin
margen de cabeza: top margin
margen de cosido: inner margin
margen de fondo: inner margin
margen de pie: bottom margin
margen del lomo: inside margin
margen exterior: outside margin
margen inferior: bottom margin
margen interior: inner margin
margen superior: top margin
márgenes anchos: wide margins
márgenes anotados: notes on
  margins
márgenes cortados: cropped
  margins
márgenes estrechos: narrow
  margins
márgenes manchados: stained
  margins

marginal: marginal
mármoleado: marbled
marr. *see* marroquí
marrón: chestnut color
marroquí: morocco
más: more, plus
material(es): material(s)
mayor: large
mayoría: majority
mayúscula(s): capital letter(s)
mecanografiado: typewritten
medallón(es): medallion(s)
media badana: half-sheepskin
media basana: half-sheepskin
media pasta: half-leather
media piel: half-leather
media tela: half-cloth
media tinta: mezzotint
mediados: about half
medio: half, center
medio cuero: half-leather
medio pergamino: half-parchment
mediocre: mediocre
mejorado: improved
memorias: memoirs
menor: small
mensual: monthly
meritísimo: very praiseworthy
metálico: metallic
micro-ficha: microfiche
micro-película: microfilm
microscópico: microscopic, very
  small
miniado: colored, illuminated
miniatura(s): miniature(s)
miniaturado: painted in miniature
minuciosamente: minutely
minucioso: minute
minúsculas: lowercase letters
miscelánea: miscellany
mismo: same
mitad: half
moaré: moiré, watered
modernizado: brought up to date
moderno: modern
modificado: changed

moneda nacional: money of the
  country
moneda oficial: official money
monografía(s): monograph(s)
monograma(s): monogram(s)
montado: mounted
morado: violet
mordedura: bite
mordido: gnawed
mosaico(s): mosaic design(s)
mota(s): defect(s)
moteado: with small defects
motivo(s): motif(s)
movible: movable
ms. *see* manuscrito
muestra(s): sample(s), example(s)
muestra gratis: free sample copy
muestra sin costo: free sample copy
multicolor: many-colored
multitud: a great number
mutilación: mutilation
mutilado: mutilated
mutilado por la censura: mutilated
  by the censor
muy: very
muy agotada: completely out of
  print
muy apreciada: highly thought of,
  esteemed
muy buscada: in great demand
muy escasa: very scarce
muy rara: very rare

nácar: mother-of-pearl
nacarado: decorated with mother-
  of-pearl
nada frecuente: seldom found
naranja: orange-colored
nervios: raised bands
neto: net
nítido: clean, clear
no(s). *see* número
no es frecuente: infrequent, seldom
  found
no venal: not for sale
nombre: name
nominado: named

nominal: nominal
nonagésimo: ninetieth
nota(s): note(s)
nota bibliográfica: bibliographic note
nota del autor: author's note
nota del compilador: compiler's note
nota del editor: publisher's note
nota editorial: publisher's note
nota(s) marginal(es): marginal note(s)
notabilísimo: outstanding
noticia: piece of information
novedades: new announcements
novela(s): novel(s)
noveno: ninth
noventa: ninety
nro. *see* número
nueve: nine
nuevo: new
num. *see* numerado, numerar, número
numeración: numbering
numeración consecutiva: continuous numbering
numeración equivocada: erroneous numbering
numeración saltada: irregular numbering
numerado: numbered
numerar: numbering
número(s): number(s)
número agotado: out-of-print issue
número(s) atrasado(s): previous, retrospective issue(s)
número clausurado: forbidden issue
número corriente: current issue
número(s) retrospectivo(s): retrospective issue(s)
número suspendido: postponed issue
numeroso: numerous
nunca: never
nutrido: abundant, full, dense

ob. *see* obra
ob. póst. *see* obra póstuma
oblongo: oblong
obra(s): work(s)
obra agotada: out-of-print work
obra censurada: censored work
obra clandestina: clandestine work
obra dedicada por el autor: work dedicated by the author
obra definitiva: definitive work
obra en colaboración: work done as a collaboration
obra póstuma: posthumous work
obrita: small work
obs. *see* obra
ochenta: eighty
ocho: eight
octagésimo: eightieth
octavo: eighth
oferta especial: special offer
offset: offset
once: eleven
opúsculo: short or small work
orden de compra: purchase order
orden temático: in subject order
ordenado: arranged, put in order
ordenado alfabéticamente: arranged in alphabetical order
ordenado cronológicamente: arranged in chronological order
ordenado por materia: arranged in subject order
ordenado por títulos: arranged in order by title
orejas de burro: dog-eared
original: original
orilla(s): border(s), edge(s)
orilla barbada: deckle edge(s)
orla(s): border(s)
orla(s) ornamental(es): ornamental border(s), scroll(s)
orlado: ornamented with a decorative border
ornado: ornamented
ornam. *see* ornamento
ornamentación: ornamentation
ornamentado: decorated

ornamento(s): decoration(s)
oscurecido: darkened, obscured
oscuro: dark

p. *see* página
p.e. *see* pasta española
pág. *see* página
página(s): page(s)
página(s) ilegible(s): illegible page(s)
página(s) orlada(s): bordered page(s)
página(s) preliminar(es): preliminary page(s), front matter
página(s) restaurada(s): page(s) restored
paginación: pagination
pagos a noventa días: payment in ninety days
pagos al contado: payment in cash
pagos al recibio de ordenes: payment on receipt of orders
págs. *see* página
págs. prelims. *see* páginas preliminares
palidecido: faded
pamfleto(s): pamphlet(s)
papel: paper
papel acanillado: laid paper
papel agarbanzado: yellowed paper
papel ahuesado: ivory-colored paper
papel alfa: esparto paper
papel avitelado: vellum paper
papel biblia: Bible paper
papel calandrado: calendered paper
papel cebolla: onionskin paper
papel corriente: ordinary paper
papel couché: laid paper
papel de arroz: rice paper
papel de corcho: cork paper
papel de estraza: brown, coarse paper
papel de forro: endpapers
papel de hilo: rag paper
papel de Japón: Japan paper
papel en hilo: rag paper
papel fantasía: fancy paper

papel francés: French paper
papel fuerte: heavy paper
papel gaceta *see* papel legal
papel holanda: Dutch paper
papel hueso: off-white, bone-colored paper
papel Japón: Japan paper
papel jaspeado: marbled paper
papel legal: legal, register paper
papel medio-satinado: dull-coated paper
papel offset: offset paper
papel picado: stippled paper
papel pluma: fine paper
papel recio: coarse paper
papel registro: register paper
papel satinado: glazed paper, calendered paper
papel satiné: glazed paper
papel verjurado: laid paper
papel vitela: vellum paper
párrafo(s): paragraph(s)
párrafo francés: indented paragraph
parte: part
partida(s): part(s)
pasta: leather binding
pasta de la época: contemporary leather binding
pasta época: contemporary leather binding
pasta español: leather-covered board binding
pasta holandesa: half-leather binding
pastoril: pastoral
paulatinamente: little by little, slowly
pauta: line, lines
pautado: lined
pecarí: peccary
pedacito: a little piece
pedazo: a piece
pedido: order
pegado: glued, pasted
pegamoide: imitation leather
penúltimo: next to last
peq. *see* pequeño

pequeñísimo: very small
pequeño: small
percal: calico
percalina: book cloth, muslin, percaline
pérdida de texto: loss of text
perfecto: perfect
perfil: outline
perforación(es): perforation(s)
perg. *see* pergamino
pergamino: parchment
pergamino a la romana: parchment in roman style
pergamino editorial: publisher's parchment
pergamino época: contemporary parchment
pergamoide: imitation parchment
pericia: craftsmanship
periódicamente: periodically
periódico: newspaper, periodical
perjudicado: damaged
peseta(s): Spanish monetary units
pesos arg. *see* pesos argentinos
pesos argentinos: Argentine monetary units
pesos col. *see* pesos colombianos
pesos colombianos: Colombian monetary units
pesos mex. *see* pesos mexicanos
pesos mexicanos: Mexican monetary units
pesos urug. *see* pesos uruguayos
pesos uruguayos: Uruguayan monetary unit
pgs. *see* página
picado: wormholed
picado de polilla: perforated by worms
picadura: wormholing
picadura de polilla: wormholing
pico(s): corner(s)
pie de imprenta: imprint
pie de página: foot of the page
piel: leather
piel becerrillo: calfskin
piel chagrín: sheepskin

piel corriente: standard leather
piel de cerdo: pigskin
piel de la época: contemporary leather
piel de Levante: Levant leather
piel fina: fine leather
piel flexible: flexible leather
piel jaspeada: marbled leather
piel labrada: carved leather
piel lisa: smooth leather
piel repujada: embossed leather
piel sintética: synthetic leather
piel valenciana: colored marbled leather
pieza(s): piece(s)
pintado: painted, colored
piroflex: a modern patented publisher's binding
pl. *see* plano
placa: plaque
plancha(s): board(s)
plancha(s) de madera: wood board(s)
plancha(s) de metal: metal side(s)
planchas secas: sides decorated with drypoint
plano(s): design(s), plan(s)
planos: sides (of a book)
plást. *see* plástico
plástico: plastic
plastificado: plasticized, coated or impregnated with plastic
plata: silver
plateado: plated
pleg. *see* plegable, plegado
plegable: folding
plegadizo: folding
plegado: folded
plena piel: full leather
pleno: full
pliego(s): sheet(s)
pliego doblado inserto: folded sheet inserted
pliego(s) suelto(s): loose sheet(s)
pliegue: fold, crease
pls. *see* plano
pluricolor: multicolor

poco frecuente: infrequent
pocos márgenes: narrow margins
policromo: polychrome
poligloto: multilingual
polilla *see* picadura de polilla
polvoriento: dusty
popular: popular
por: by
por ambas caras: on both sides
por carecer de: for lack of
por carga aérea: by air shipment
por carga marítima: by sea, surface shipment
por correo aéreo: by air mail
por correo ordinario: by regular mail
por error: by error, mistake
por lo demás: for the remainder
por vía marítima certificada: by insured sea shipment
pórfido: porphyry (color)
port. *see* portada
portada: title page
portada grabada: engraved title page
portadilla: half title
portaf. *see* portafolio
portafolio(s): portfolio(s)
porte pagado: cost of carriage paid
post. *see* posterior
posterior: back, later
postizo: stuck on, artificial
póstumo: posthumous
pp. *see* página
precedente: preceding
precedido: preceded
precio: price
precio alterado: changed price
precio estimado: estimated price
precio fijo: fixed price
precio fuerte: firm price
precio modificado: changed price
precio reducido: reduced price
precioso: precious
prefacio: preface, foreword
prel. *see* preliminar
preliminar(es): preliminary(ies)

premiado: prize-winning
prensa: press
prensa censurada: censored press
prensa clandestina: clandestine, underground press
prestigiado: highly esteemed
prestigio: prestige, esteem
prestigioso: very highly esteemed
primera tirada: first printing
primero: first
primorosamente: elegantly
primoroso: elegant, handsome
principio: beginning
priv. *see* privilegio
privado: private
privilegio: privilege, permit to publish
prof. *see* profusión
profus. *see* profusamente, profusión
profusamente: profusely
profusión: profusion
pról. *see* prólogo
prologado: prefaced
prólogo(s): preface(s)
prólogo aumentado: enlarged preface
prólogo corregido: corrected preface
prólogo revisado: revised preface
prolongado: elongated, long
prols. *see* prólogo
promedio: average number
propio: suitable
próximamente: soon
próximo: imminent
próximo a publicarse: to be published soon
prueba: proof
ps. *see* página
pta. *see* peseta
ptas. *see* peseta
publicación: publication
publicación censurada: censored publication
publicación confiscada: confiscated publication

publicación en prensa: publication in press
publicación mensual: monthly publication
publicación original: original publication
publicado: published
puesto al día: brought out
puesto en venta: offered for sale
pulcritud: cleanliness, neatness
pulcro: clean, neat
pulido: polished
pulimentado: polished, smooth
punt. *see* punta, puntera
punta(s): corner(s)
punta seca: drypoint
puntas rotas: with broken corners
punteado: stippled
puntera(s): corner(s)
puntera(s) de metal: metal corner piece(s)
puntera(s) de plata: silver corner piece(s)
puntillado: stippled

quebradura: break, crack
quemado: burned
quemadura: burn, burning
quince: fifteen
quincenal: fortnightly
quinquagésimo: fiftieth
quinto: fifth

r. *see* rústica
raído: chafed, worn
rama(s): sheet(s)
rara vez: rarely
rareza: rarity
raridad: rarity
rarísimo: very rare
raro: rare
raro en comercio: rarely offered for sale
rascado: scraped, scratched
rascadura: scraped spot, scratch
rasgado: rubbed, torn
rasgadura(s): tear(s)

rasguño(s): scratch(es)
raso: satin
rayado: decorated with a line pattern
razonado: commented
rca. *see* rústica
real: royal
realizado: completed
rebajado: reduced
rebajo: discount, reduction
recién: recently
recién publicado: recently published
recientísimo: very recent
recio: thick
reclamado: in great demand
reclamo(s): catchword(s)
recobrado: recovered
recogido: collected again
recop. *see* recopilado
recopilación: compilation
recopilado: compiled
recopilador: compiler
recortado: trimmed; cut off
recorte: cutting, clipping
recto: recto
recuadrado: laid out in square or oblong line patterns
recuadro(s): square or oblong line patterns
recubierto: covered
redacción: editing; editorial staff
redactado: edited, arranged
redactor: editor
redecorado: redecorated
redondeado: rounded
redondilla: roman type
redondo: round
reducido: reduced
reedición: republication
reeditado: reprinted, republished
reemplazado: replaced
reencuadernado: rebound
reforzado: reinforced
refuerzo: reinforcing
refundición: adaptation
refundido: reworked, reedited

regalo: gift, present
regiamente: royally
regio ejemplar: magnificent copy
registro: register
registro de autor: copyright
registro de propiedad: copyright
reglado: ruled, lined
regocijante: pleasing, very amusing
rehecho: renovated, restored
reimpresión: reprint
reimpresión autorizada: authorized
    reprint
reimpreso: reprinted
rejilla: grid, textured material
relato(s): story(ies)
relieve: relief
remarg. *see* remarginado
remarginado: margins reworked,
    improved
remendado: mended
renglón: line
renombrado: renowned
renovado: renewed
reparación: repair
reparado: repaired
reparado parcialmente: partly
    repaired
repartido: divided, separated
repertorio: list, index, reference
    tool
repetido: repeated
representantes y distribuidores:
    representatives and distributors
reproducción(es): reproduction(s)
reproducción facsimilar: facsimile
    reproduction
reproducido: reproduced
repujado: embossed, repoussé work
reserva(s): reservation(s)
reserva(s) aceptada(s): reserva-
    tion(s) accepted
reservar: to reserve
respaldo: back
respectivamente: respectively
restante: remainder, remaining
restaurado: restored
resto: remainder

resumén: résumé, synopsis
retocado: retouched
retrato(s): portrait(s)
reunir: to bring together, collect
reverso: verso
revisado: revised
revisión: review
revista(s): journal(s), review(s)
ricamente: richly
rodado: encircled, surrounded
rodeado: encircled, surrounded
roido: gnawed, eaten
rojizo: reddish
romano: roman
romántico: in the style of the
    romantic period
rombal: rhombic
rombo: lozenge- or diamond-shaped
rompimiento: break, tear
rotaprint: printed by rotary press
roto: damaged, broken
rótulo(s): label(s)
rotura(s): break(s)
rozado: rubbed, scuffed
rstca. *see* rústica
rtca. *see* rústica
rúbrica(s): rubric(s)
rúbrica apócrifa: apocryphal
    flourish
rúbrica auténtica: authentic
    flourish
rúbrica ilegible: illegible flourish
rúbrica legible: legible flourish
rubricado: rubricated
rueda: circular design
rueda greca: lace pattern
ruedas de cadenas: chain design
rúst. *see* rústica
rústica: sewed, unbound;
    paperbound

s. *see* siglo, sin
s.a. *see* sin año
s.f. *see* sin fecha, sin foliar
s.i.t. *see* sin indicaciones tipo-
    gráficas
s.l. *see* sin lugar

s.l.i.ni a. _see_ sin lugar de impresión ni año
s.l.n.a. _see_ sin lugar ni año
s.l.ni a. _see_ sin lugar ni año
s.l.y a. _see_ sin lugar y año
s.n. _see_ sin numerar
s.n.d.p. _see_ sin nota de precio
s.p.d.i. _see_ sin pie de imprenta
s.p.i. _see_ sin pie de imprenta
salpicado: sprinkling on edges
salta: skips, jumps
salvado: preserved
satinado: calendered, coated
se equivoca: errs, is mistaken
sección(es): section(s), passage(s)
seco: blind tooling
seda: silk
según: according
segundo: second
seis: six
sellado: bearing a seal
sello(s): seal(s), stamp(s)
sello de biblioteca: library stamp
sello de la institución: institutional stamp
sello seco: dry stamp
semanal: weekly
semes. _see_ semestral
semestral: semiannual(ly)
semintonso: half cut, trimmed
seña(s): mark(s)
señalando: indicating
señales de sellos: stamp mark(s)
señas: address
separadamente: separately
separado: separated
separata: reprint, separate
séptimo: seventh
septuagésimo: seventieth
serie: series
serocopia: xerox copy
sesenta: sixty
sesentésimo: sixtieth
setenta: seventy
setentésimo: seventieth
seud. _see_ seudónimo
seudónimo: pseudonym

sexagésimo: sixtieth
sexto: sixth
siete: seven
sig. _see_ signatura
sigla: pressmark, acronym
siglo(s): century(ies)
signatura(s): signature(s)
sigue: there follows
siguiente: following
silografía: woodblock print
símil-cuero: imitation leather
símil piel: imitation leather
similicuero: imitation leather
similpergamino: imitation parchment
sin: without
sin abreviar: unabridged
sin abrir: unopened
sin afectar el texto: without affecting the text
sin año: without date, year
sin año ni pie de imprenta: without date or imprint
sin bordes abiertos: without edges cut, untrimmed
sin bordes cortados: without edges cut
sin cargo: without charge
sin censura: without censor
sin cobrar: without paying
sin cortar: untrimmed, unopened
sin coser: unsewn
sin costo adicional: without extra cost
sin cotización: without price
sin dañar: without damaging
sin enc. _see_ sin encuadernar
sin encuadernar: without binding
sin expurgar: unexpurgated
sin facturar: without invoicing
sin fecha: without date
sin foliación: without foliation
sin foliar: without foliation
sin i.t. _see_ sin indicaciones tipográficas
sin importancia: unimportant

sin indicaciones tipográficas:
    without name of publisher
sin interesar: without affecting,
    without touching
sin las tapas: without its covers
sin lugar: without place
sin lugar de impresión: without
    place of publication
sin lugar de impresión ni año:
    without place of publication or
    year
sin lugar ni año: without place or
    year
sin lugar y año: without place or
    year
sin nota de precio: without indica-
    tion of price
sin notificar: without advance
    notice
sin numerar: without numbering
sin orden(es): without order(s)
sin pagar: without payment
sin paginación: without pagination
sin pie de imprenta: without
    imprint
sin precio: without price
sin previo aviso: without previous
    notice
sin recortar: untrimmed
sin signar: unsigned
sin signatura: without signature
sin tapas: without covers
sin tasación: without price
sinóptico: synoptic
sobado: shopworn, mauled
soberbio: superb, splendid
sobre: envelope; on, upon
sobrecubierta: book jacket
sobrecubierta de plástico: plastic
    wrapper
sobrescrito(s): superscription(s)
sobretapas: book jacket, wrapper
sobretiro: reprint, separate
sobrio: sober
solapa: inner fold of a book jacket
solapa descriptiva: descriptive
    wrapper

solapa impresa: printed wrapper
solapa informativa: informational
    wrapper
soles: Peruvian monetary units
solicite catálogos: request catalogs
sólidamente: solidly
sólido: firm, solid
sombreado: shaded by cross-
    hatching
ss. *see* siguiente
subrayado: underlined
subscribir: to subscribe
subscripción: subscription
subscriptor(es): subscriber(s)
subtitulo: subtitle
sucio: dirty
suelto: odd, single
sueltos: loose, detached
sujeto a cambio de moneda:
    subject to change in value of
    money
sumamente: extremely
sumamente agotada: totally out
    of print
sumario: summary
suntuoso: sumptuous
sup. *see* superior
superior: top, upper
suplemento(s): supplement(s)
suplido: supplied, made up
suprimido: suppressed, censored
suscripción *see* subscripción
symposium: symposium

t. *see* taller, tomo
tabla: table, table of contents;
    board
tabla de contenido: table of con-
    tents
tabla de materias: table of con-
    tents
tabla de precios: price list
tabla(s) estadística(s): statistical
    table(s)
tachado: crossed out
tafilete: morocco
taladrado: with holes

taladro(s): hole(s)
taladro(s) de polilla: wormhole(s)
tall. *see* taller
talla dulce: taille-douce, copper engraving
taller: shop
taller de imprenta: printshop
tamaño: size, format
tapa(s): side(s) of a book
tapa(s) de cartón: board(s), cased binding
tapa(s) de madera: wood side(s)
tapa(s) de metal: metal side(s)
tapa inferior: back cover
tapa(s) suelta(s): loose board(s)
tapa superior: front cover
tapado: covered
tarifa(s): price(s)
tarifa(s) fija(s): established price(s)
tasación: appraisal, price
tejuelo: book label
tela: cloth
tela chagrín: morocco cloth, cloth grained to imitate shagreen
tela editorial: publisher's cloth
teñido: stained, tinted
tercero: third
terciopelo: velvet
tésis: thesis, dissertation
texto: text
texto amarillento: yellowed text
texto aparte: separate from the text
texto apocrifo: apocryphal text
texto apolillado: worm-eaten text
texto borrado: text eliminated
texto censurado: censored text
texto incompleto: incomplete text
texto manchado: stained text
texto mutilado: mutilated text
texto revisado: revised text
tinta: color, tint; ink
tip. *see* tipografía
tipo: type, font
tipo gótico: Gothic type
tipografía: printing house
tipográfico: typographical

tirada: edition, printing
tirada aparte: offprint, separate
tirada autorizada por la censura: printing authorized by the censor
tirada corriente: ordinary edition
tirada corta: limited edition
tirada de lujo: deluxe printing
tirada del autor: published by the author
tirada limitada: limited edition
tirada nominal: ordinary edition
tirada numerada: numbered edition
tirada reducida: small edition
tirada única: sole printing
tirado: printed
tiraje: printing
tít. *see* título
título: title
título aclaratorio: explanatory title
título alterado: changed title
título cambiado: changed title
título colectivo: collective title
título ilegible: illegible title
título modificado: changed title
tocado: touched
toda tela: full cloth
todo lo publicado: all published
tomito: small volume
tomo(s): volume(s)
tomo: color, hue
trabajado: worked
trabajo(s): work(s)
trad. *see* traducción, traducido, traductor
traducción: translation
traducido: translated
traductor: translator
transcripción: transcription
transparente: transparent
transpuesto: transposed
tratado: treated; treatise
trece: thirteen
treinta: thirty
tres: three
tres cuartos cuero: three-quarter leather binding
tricolor: three-color

tricromía: three-color print
trigésimo: thirtieth
trim. *see* trimestral
trimestral: quarterly
trocito: small piece
trozo(s): bit(s), piece(s)
ts. *see* tomos

últimas ventas anunciadas: last
  items offered
últimas ventas conocidas: last
  known sales
último: last, latest
un: one
un millar: one thousand
uncial: uncial
undécimo: eleventh
única cotización: fixed price
únicamente: solely
único: sole, unique
único publicado: only one
  published
uniforme: uniform
usado: worn, soiled, used
uso: wear
utilizado: used

v. *see* verso
v. en b. *see* verso en blanco
v. imp. *see* verso impreso
valenciana: colored, marbled
  leather
valioso: worthy, valuable
vaqueta: calfskin
variante(s): variant(s)
varios: some, a number of
veinte: twenty
velín: vellum paper

venal: for sale
vendido: sold, sold out
venta: sale
venta al contado: cash sale
verde: green
verde olivo: olive green
verjurado: bone-colored
versión: version
versión autorizada por el autor:
  version approved by the author
versión castellana: Spanish version
versión revisada: revised version
verso: back side, verso
verso autográfiado: signed on back
verso en blanco: verso blank
verso impreso: printed back side
veteado: grained, marbled
viejo: old
vigésimo: twentieth
viñeta(s): vignette(s), border(s)
vinil: vinyl
vista(s): view(s)
vistoso: beautiful, colorful
vit. *see* vitela
vitela: parchment, vellum
volante: fugitive
volumen(es): volume(s)
volumen suelto: single, odd volume
voluminoso: voluminous

xilografía: woodblock print,
  engraving
xilográfico: xylographic, pertaining
  to wood engraving
xirocopia: xerographic copy

zangala: buckram

Swedish

å: on, upon
a.a. *see* akademisk avhandling
a.s.u. *see* allt som utkommit
a.u. *see* allt som utkommit
ABC-bok(böcker): hornbook(s),
  primer(s)
abonnemang: subscription
abstrakt: abstract
accidenstryck: job printing
ackvisition: acquisition
aderton: eighteen
adertonde: eighteenth
ägarestämpel: owner's stamp
ägo: possession
akad. *see* akademisk
akad.avh. *see* akademisk
  avhandling
akademisk: academic
akademisk(a) avhandling(ar):
  thesis(es), dissertation(s)
akvarell(er): watercolor(s)
akvatint: aquatint
album: album(s)
äldre: older
aldrig: never
allt som utkommit: all published
alltför hårt skuren: cropped
almanack(or): almanac(s)
alternativ titel: alternative title
amatörband: three-quarter binding
anastatisk: anastatic
andra(e): second, other
anfang: initial letter
ang. *see* angående
angående: concerning
anmärkning(ar): comment(s),
  note(s)

annan: other
annars: otherwise, besides
annat: other
annons(er): advertisement(s)
annotation(er): annotation(s),
  note(s)
anonym: anonymous
ansv. *see* ansvarig
ansvarig: responsible
ant.-bl. *see* anteckningsblad
antages: presumably
antal: number, amount
anteckn. *see* anteckning
anteckning(ar): note(s)
anteckningsblad: note page(s)
anteckningsbok(böcker): note-
  book(s)
antikva: roman type
antikvariatbokhandlare: antiquarian bookseller
antikvarisk: used, secondhand
antologi: anthology
appendix: appendix
appreterad: calendered
år: year(s)
arabesk: arabesque
arb. *see* arbete
arbete: work, item
årg. *see* årgång
årgång: year, annual volume
ark: signature(s), sheet(s) of paper
arkiv: archives
årlig: annual
arrangerad: arranged
års-: annual
årsbok(böcker): yearbook(s)
årtal: year, date

arton: eighteen
artonde: eighteenth
atlas(er): atlas(es)
åtta: eight
åttio: eighty
åttionde: eightieth
åttonde: eighth
audiovisuell: audiovisual
auktion: auction sale
auktoriserad: authorized
autograf(er): autograph(s)
autotypi: halftone
avbeställa: cancel
avbildn. *see* avbildning
avbildning(ar): illustration(s)
avd. *see* avdelning
avdelning(ar): part(s), section(s)
även: also
avgiven: delivered
avh. *see* avhandling
avhandling(ar): dissertation(s), thesis(es)
avkortning: truncation
avlång: elongated, oblong
avriven: torn off, torn out
avskrapning(ar): scratch(es)
avskrift: copy
avsnitt: section, paragraph
avtrubbad: dulled
avtryck: copy(ies), impression(s)
avvikande: differing

båda: both, either
bägge: both, either
bakpärm: back (of) cover
bakre: back, rear
baksida: verso
band: binding; volume(s)
banderoll: banderole, tassel
barnbok(böcker): children's book(s)
bastardtyper: bastard type
bd. *see* band
bearb. *see* bearbetad, bearbetning
bearbetad: revised
bearbetning: adaptation
begränsad: limited
beh. *see* behandla

behandla(r): deal(s) with
bemyndigad: authorized
berättare: narrator
berättelse(r): narrative(s), transaction(s)
beskrivning: description
beslag: metal ornaments, clasps
bestå(r): consist(s)
bestående: consisting
beställning: order
beteckning: designation
beträffande: concerning
betydelsefull: significant
bev. *see* bevarad
bevarad: preserved
bibl.-uppl. *see* bibliofilupplaga
bibliofil: bibliophile
bibliofilband: book collector's fine binding
bibliofilupplaga: book collector's edition
bibliogr. *see* bibliografisk
bibliografi: bibliography
bibliografisk: bibliographic
bibliotek: library
bibliotekarie: librarian
biblioteksstämpel: library stamp
bidrag: contribution(s)
bifogad: attached
bihang: appendix
bilaga(or): appendix(es), supplement(s)
bilageband: appendix volume
bilagsband: supplement(s)
bild(er): illustration(s), picture(s)
billighetsupplaga: popular edition
bind: raised band
bind. *see* bindning
binderi: bindery
bindning: binding
biogr. *see* biografi, biografisk
biografi: biography
biografisk: biographical
bl. *see* blad
bl.a. *see* bland annat
blå: blue
bläcklinjer: ink lines

bläckteckning(ar): pen and ink
  drawing(s)
blad: leaf(ves), sheet(s)
bladornament: floral scrollwork
bland annat: among other things
blank: blank, glossy
blek: faded, pale
blindpressning(ar): blind tooling
blindstämpel(stämplar): blind
  stamp(s)
blockband: rubber back binding
blockbok(böcker): block book(s)
blomstringstid: golden age
blott: only
blyertsstreckad: pencil-marked
böcker: books
bok: book
bokband: cover, binding
bokbestånd: book stock
bokbindare: bookbinder
bokbinderi: bindery
bokförteckning: books in print
bokh. *see* bokhandel
bokhandel: bookstore
bokhandlare: bookdealer
bokhist. *see* bokhistoria
bokhistoria: history of books
boknummer: book number
bokpärm: book cover
bokrealisation: book sale
bokrygg: spine
boksamlare: book collector
bokstav(stäver): letter(s), charac-
  ter(s)
boktr. *see* boktryckeri
boktryckarmärke: printer's mark
boktryckeri: printing firm
bomärke: flourish, paraph
bordyr: ornamental border
början: beginning
borta: missing
bortraderad: erased
bortskärning: clipping, excision
bortskuren: cut off, trimmed
bortskurits: been cut off
brändes: destroyed by fire
brandrök: smoke

brandskada: fire damage
brandskadad: damaged by fire
bransch: branch
bredd: width
breddformat: broad format
bredrand. *see* bredrandig
bredrandig: with wide margins
brist(er): defect(s)
broderad: embroidered
brokig: varicolored
bronserad: reddish-brown
broschyr: booklet, pamphlet
broschyromsl. *see* broschyromslag
broschyromslag: stitched wrappers
brott: break
brottskada: break
brunfl. *see* brunfläckad
brunfläckad: foxed
bunden: bound
bundna: bound
byggnad: plant

ca. *see* cirka
censur: censorship
censurerad: censored, suppressed
chagrin: shagreen
chagrinband: bound in shagreen
cirka: approximately
ciselerad: chiseled
clairobscur: chiaroscuro
clot *see* klot

d. *see* del
då: since, when, then
dammig: dusty
därtill: in addition to this
daterad: dated
dåtida: of that period
ded. *see* dedikation
dedikation: dedication
dedikationsexemplar: presentation
  copy
definitiv: definite, definitive
dek. *see* dekoration, dekorerad
dekor. *see* dekorerad
dekoration: decoration, ornamentation

dekorerad: decorated
del(ar): part(s)
delbeteckning(ar): designation(s)
   of parts
delvis: partly
denna(e): this, the latter
denteller: dentelle tooling
dessutom: besides, in addition
devis: device, motto
diagram: diagram, graph
diagramblad: diagram leaf
differerad: differing
differerande: differing
dikt(er): poem(s)
dimension: dimension
dir. *see* direkt
direkt: direct
disponibel: available
dissertation(er): dissertation(s)
dittills: up to that date,
   previously
djuptryck: photogravure
dlr. *see* delar
dokument: document
dokumentnamn: document name
dubbel: couple, double
duplett(er): duplicate(s)
duplic. *see* duplicerad
duplicerad: duplicated, mimeographed
dygn: day

edition: edition
efter: after, according to, from
efterfrågad: in demand, sought
   after
efterlämnad: posthumous
efterskrift: postscript
eftersökt: sought after
eftertryck: reprint
egentlig: real, actual
eget förlag: published by the
   author
ej heller: neither
ej i bokhandeln: not in the trade,
   privately printed
eleg. *see* elegant

elegant: elegant, elegantly
elfte: eleventh
eljest: otherwise
elva: eleven
elvte: eleventh
emaljband: enamel binding
en: one
end. *see* endast
enda: unique
endast: only
engelskt band: limp binding
enkel: simple
enl. *see* enligt
enligt: according to
enstaka exemplar: odd copy
ersatt(s) med: replaced by
etikett: label
etsn. *see* etsning
etsning(ar): etching(s)
ett: one
ett par: a few
ettbandsverk: single volume
   publication
ettbladstryck: broadside
ex. *see* exemplar
exemplar: copy(ies)
exlibris: *ex libris*
exlibrisstämplar: marks of ownership
expl. *see* exemplar

f.ö. *see* för övrigt
faksimil: facsimile(s)
faksimilupplaga: facsimile edition
fals(ar): joint(s)
falsad: folded
falsarium: forgery
falsk: wrong, false
fält: panel(s)
färg(er): color(s)
färglagd: colored
färglitografi: color lithography
färglitografi(er): color lithograph(s)
färgplansch(er): color plate(s)
färgtryck: color printing, color
   prints
färgtryckspl. *see* färgtrycksplansch

färgtrycksplansch(er): color plate(s)
fårskinn: sheepskin
fast order: standing order
fäste(n): tie(s)
fastlimmad: glued, reglued
fåtal: few
felaktig: erroneous, incomplete
felaktigt årtal: false date
feltryckt: misprinted
fem: five
femte: fifth
femtio: fifty
femtionde: fiftieth
femton: fifteen
femtonde: fifteenth
festskrift: festschrift, commemorative volume
ficka: pocket
ficklexikon: pocket dictionary
fig. *see* figur
figur: figure, illustration
filet: fillet
fin: fine, delicate
fjärde: fourth
fjorton: fourteen
fjortonde: fourteenth
fl. *see* fläckad, flera
fläck: spot
fläck. *see* fläckad
fläckad: spotted, stained
fläckfri: spotless
flera: several
flerbandsverk: multivolume publication
flerfärgstryck: multicolor printing
flerspråkig utgåva: polyglot edition
flertal: most, majority
flock: group(s), section(s)
flygblad: flyleaf; leaflet
foder: lining, doublure
fodral: case, slipcase
föga: little
foliant: folio
folierad: foliated
foliering: foliation
folio: foolscap (size)
följd(er): series

följdskrift: serial work
följesedel: packing slip
folkupplaga: popular edition
för medlemmar: for members
för övrigt: otherwise, in addition
förbjuden: forbidden, banned
före: before, in front of
föreg. *see* föregående
föregående: preceding
föregiven: fictitious
förekomma: occur
föreläsning(ar): lecture(s)
föreligga: be present
föreliggande: present
föreligger: is (are) present
företal: preface
förf. *see* författar
förfalskad: forged
författar(e): author(s)
författarkollektiv: team of authors, joint authors
författarrätt: copyright
förgylld: gilt
förhållandevis: relatively
förhandlingar: proceedings
förklaring(ar): explanation(s), notice(s)
förkortad: abbreviated, short
förkortning(ar): abbreviation(s)
förl. *see* förlag
förlag: publishing firm
förlaga: original
förläggare: publisher(s)
förlagsort: place of publication
förlagsreklam: publisher's advertising, blurb
förlagsstämpel: publisher's stamp
format: format, size
formering: square
förminskad: reduced
förnyad: renewed
förord: preface
försäljning: sale
försäljningspris: retail price
försättsblad: endpaper, endsheet
försättspapper: endpaper
försedd: furnished
förskuren: trimmed

första(e): first
första upplaga: first edition
första utgåva: first edition
förstärkt: reinforced
förteckn. *see* förteckning
förteckning: list
förtextsidor: front matter
förtitel: half title
förtitelblad: half-title page
fortsättning(ar): continuation(s)
förut: previously
fotnot: footnote
fotografi(er): photograph(s)
fotografisk: photographic
fotogravyr(er): photogravure(s)
fotokopia: photocopy
fotolitografi: photolithograph,
    photolithography
fotostatkopi(or): photostatic
    copy(ies)
fototypi: phototype
fr. *see* främre, från, fräsch
fraktur: black letter
främmande: different, strange
frampärm(ar): front cover(s)
främre: front
främre omslag: front wrappers
främre snitt: fore edge
framsida: recto
från: from
frånsett: apart from, except
franskt band: leather binding, calf
    binding
fräsch: clean
fris(er): heading(s), headpiece(s)
frontespis: frontispiece(s)
frsp. *see* frontespis
fuktfl. *see* fuktfläckad
fuktfläck(ar): damp stain(s)
fuktfläckad: damp-stained
fullständig: complete
fyra: four
fyrtio: forty
fyrtionde: fortieth

gammal: old
gång(er): time(s)
ganska: quite, rather

gått upp i limningen: loose in
    binding
gedigen: well made, strong
gemena bokstäver: lowercase
gemensam titel: collective title
genom: through
genomgående: all through, con-
    tinuous
genomsedd: revised
genomskinlig: transparent
ggr. *see* gånger
glättad: calendered, burnished
glättad marokäng: crushed
    morocco
gldsn. *see* guldsnitt
gotisk: Gothic
gott: good
granskad: revised
gråpappersomsl. *see* gråpappers-
    omslag
gråpappersomslag: plain wrapper(s)
grav. *see* graverad
graverad: engraved
gravör: engraver
gravyr(er): print(s), etching(s)
grön: green
groteska typer: block letters
grundlinje: basic line
grundritning: outline
grupptitel: group title, collective
    title
gul: yellow
gulbrun: fawn-colored
guld: gold
gulddekor: gold ornamentation
guldorn. *see* guldornerad
guldornerad: decorated in gold
guldpress. *see* guldpressad
guldpressad: gilt-stamped
guldsnitt: gilt edge(s)
gulnad: yellowed

h. *see* häfte
häftad: stitched; paperbound,
    paperback
häfte(n): issue(s), part(s)
häfteomsl. *see* häfteomslag
häfteomslag: issue cover(s)

häftning: sewing, stitching
hål: hole(s)
halvår: half-year, semiannual
  volume
halvband: half binding
halvfr. *see* halvfranskt
halvfranskt: half-leather, half-calf
halvfranskt band: half-calf binding
halvfrbd. *see* halvfranskt band
halvklotband: half-cloth binding
halvklotbd. *see* halvklot band
halvläderband: half-leather binding
halvmarokängband: half-morocco
  binding
halvmarokgbd. *see* halvmarokängband
halvnummer: half issue(s)
halvpergamentband: half-vellum
  binding
halvpergmtbd. *see* halvpergamentband
handgjord: handmade
handgjort: handmade
handkolorerad: hand-colored
handlar om: deals with
handpresstryckeri: handpress
handskrift: manuscript, handwriting
handskriven: handwritten
hänvisning: reference
här: here
hårt: hard, close
hel: entire, whole
helförgylld: entirely gilt
heliogravyr: photoengraving
helkbd. *see* helklotband
helklotband: full-cloth binding
helsida: full page
helsidesbild(er): full-page
  picture(s)
helsidesillustration: full-page
  illustration
helsidesplansch(er): full-page
  plate(s)
helskinnband: full-leather binding
hfn. *see* häfte(n)
hfr. *see* halvfranskt

hfrbd. *see* halvfranskt band
hjortskinn: buckskin, doeskin
hklot. *see* halvklotband
hög: tall
höger (högra): right-hand
högersida: right-hand page
högst: most, extremely
högt: highly, greatly
höjdformat: portrait size
hopvikt: folded
hörn: corner(s)
hörnbit: cornerpiece
hörnlagad: corner(s) repaired
hörnskada: corner(s) damaged
höst: Autumn, Fall
hundöron: dog-ears
hundra: hundred
hundrade: hundredth
huvudsakligen: mainly
huvudtitel: main title, title proper
hygglig: nice
hyst: contained

i: in
i allt: altogether
i press: in press, being printed
i st.f. *see* i stället för
i stället för: instead of
icke: not
identifieringsfält: bibliographic
  strip
ifall annat icke angives: unless
  otherwise indicated
ill. *see* illustration, illustrerad
illegal litteratur: clandestine
  literature
illuminering: illumination, coloring
illustr. *see* illustration, illustrerad
illustration(er): illustration(s)
illustratör: illustrator
illustrerad: illustrated
imitation: imitation
impressum: imprint
in-folio: in folio format
inalles: in all, a total of
inb. *see* inbunden
inbunden: bound

inciselerad: carved in
index: index
indraga: discard
indragen: withdrawn from circulation
inhäftad: inset, inserted
initial(er): initial(s)
inkl. *see* inkluderad
inklistr. *see* inklistrad
inklistrad: pasted in, glued in
inkluderad: included
inköpspris: purchase price
inkunabel(bler): incunabulum(a)
inl. *see* inledning
inlagt: loosely inserted, laid in
inledande: introductory
inledn. *see* inledning
inledning: introduction
innehåll: contents
innehåller: contains
innehållsförteckning: table of contents
inramad: framed, bordered
inre: internal, interior, inner
inskjuten: intercalated, inserted
inskrift: inscription
institution: institution
inte: not
interfol. *see* interfolierad
interfolierad: interleaved
intern: internal
intern rapport: internal report
intryckt: embossed
invikt: folded in

jämför: compare
jämn: smooth
jämte: together with
jansenistband: Jansenist binding
japanpapper: Japanese vellum
jfr. *see* jämför
jmfr. *see* jämför

kalender: calendar
kallnål: drypoint
källor: sources
kalv: calf

kalvband: calf binding
kalvskinn: calfskin
kan skaffas: in print, available
kapitälband: headband
kapitel: chapter(s)
kapitelöverskrift: chapter heading
karikatyr(er): caricature(s)
kart. *see* kartonnerad
karta: map, chart
kartbild: picture map
kartbl. *see* kartblad
kartblad: map(s)
kartografi: cartography
kartong: pasteboard, cardboard
kartongpärmar: boards
kartonnerad: in paper boards
kartskiss(er): sketch map(s)
kartusch(er): cartouche(s)
kåseri(er): talk(s), light essay(s)
katalog: catalog
kbd. *see* klotband
kedjeband: chained binding
kemigrafi: photoengraving, zincography
kiosklitteratur: cheap, sensational novels
klb. *see* klotband
klbd. *see* klotband
klipp: cut, excision
klippt: cut, damaged by excision
klot: cloth
klotb. *see* klotband
klotband: cloth binding
klotbd. *see* klotband
klotöverdrag: cloth covers
kluven: split
knapp(ar): boss(es)
knappast: hardly
knäppe(n): clasp(s)
knytband: tie(s)
knytremmar: leather ties
kodex: codex
kokbok(böcker): cookbook(s)
kollation: collation
kollationering: collation
kolofon: colophon
kolor. *see* kolorerad

kolorerad: colored
kolorering: coloring
komedi: comedy
kommentar(er): comment(s), commentary(ies)
kommenterad: commented, annotated
kompilation: compilation
kompilator: compiler
kompl. *see* komplett
komplett: complete
konfiskerad: suppressed
konkordans: concordance
konstläder: imitation leather, leatherette
konsttryck: artistic print
konsttryckpapper: fine-coated paper
kontant: cash
konto: account
kontor: office
kontroll: checking, inspection
koppardjuptryck: photogravure
kopparstick: copper engraving
koppartryck: copperplate printing
korrektur: proof
korrigering: correction
kplt. *see* komplett
kprst. *see* kopparstick
krönika(or): chronicle(s)
kungl. *see* kunglig
kunglig(a): royal
kungörelse(r): decree(s), official announcement(s)
kurvor: curved lines
kväde: verse
kvadratisk: square
kvalitet: quality
kvartal: quarter of a year

lacksigill: wax seal
läder: leather
läderband: leather-bound, leather binding
läderbd. *see* läderband
låg: low, reduced
lagad: repaired

lager: stock
lagerfläckad: foxed
lagerfläckar: foxing
lagerkatalog: catalog of books in stock
lagerlista: stock list
lagning: repair
lappad: mended
lärobok: textbook
läromedel: teaching aid(s)
lätt: light, slightly
levande kolumntitel: running head
lexikon: dictionary
likaledes: also, equally
liksom: as, like
liljor: fleurs-de-lys
limmad: glued
limmat papper: sized paper
limning: gluing
linje(r): line(s)
linjerad: ruled, lined
linneband: cloth binding
listkatalog: list catalog
lit. *see* liten
liten: small, little
litogr. *see* litografi
litrografi(er): lithograph(s)
litografierad: lithographed
litteraturförteckn. *see* litteraturförteckning
litteraturförteckning: list of references
ljus: light-colored
ljustrycksplansch(er): heliogravure plate(s)
ljustrycksplchr. *see* ljustrycksplanscher
löpande paginering: continuous pagination
lös: loose
lösblad: loose leaf(ves)
lösbladsutgåva: loose-leaf issue
lösnr. *see* lösnummer
lösnummer: separate number, issue
loss: loose, unstitched
lossnad: loosened
löst: odd, loosely

lumbeckbindning: a patented
book binding
lumppapper: rag paper
lunta: old, unwieldy volume
lyx: deluxe
lyxband: deluxe binding

m.fl. *see* med flera
m.m. *see* med mera
m.u. *see* mer utkommit
mager: thin
måhända: possibly
målad: painted
månadsskrift: monthly (periodical)
månatlig: monthly
många: many
mängd: lot, quantity
manuskript: manuscript, typescript
marg. *see* marginal
marg(er): margin(s)
marginal(er): margin(s)
marginalsiffror: marginal numbers
marinblå: navy blue
märke: mark
marknad: market
marmorerad: marbled
marmorering: marbling
marokäng: morocco
maskhål: wormhole(s)
maskstungen: perforated by worms
mästare: master(s)
mattad: tarnished, lusterless
med fettfläckar: grease-spotted
med flera: and others, etc., et alia
med mera: et cetera
medaljbeskr. *see* medaljbeskrivning
medaljbeskrivning: description of
medal(s)
medaljong: medallion
medaljplansch(er): plate(s) of
medals
medarbetare: collaborator
meddelande: bulletin, report
medelmåttig: mediocre
medeltida: medieval
medfaren: worn, faded

medföljer: accompanies
medl. *see* medlem
medl.-avg. *see* medlemsavgift
medlem(mar): member(s)
medlemsavgift: member fee
medverkan: collaboration
mellan raderna: interlinear
memoarer: memoirs
mer utkommit: more published,
incomplete set
metallfästen: metal clasps, metal
fastenings
mezzotint: mezzotint
mikrofiche: microfiche
mikrofilm: microfilm
mikroutgåva: microform edition
mindre: less, smaller
miniatyr: miniature
miniatyrbok: miniature book
minneskrift: commemorative
volume
mitt: middle
mjuk: flexible
mjukt band: flexible binding
moaré: moiré
moderniserad: modernized, brought
up to date
mögelfläck(ar): mildew stain(s)
monografi: monograph
mönster: pattern
mörkare: darker
mörkbrun: dark brown
mosaikinläggning(ar): mosaic
inlay(s)
musik: music
musikbilaga(or): music supple-
ment(s)
musiknot(er): music note(s)
mycket: very, highly

n.f. *see* ny följd
n.s. *see* ny serie
naggad: notched
något: somewhat
några: a few, a couple of
namn: name
namnregister: index of names

namnt. *see* namnteckning
namnteckning: signature (name)
näst sista: next to the last
nästan: almost
nätt: neat
nedre: lower, bottom
nedsatt: reduced
nedsmutsad: soiled
nettopris: net price
ngt. *see* något
nio: nine
nionde: ninth
nittio: ninety
nittionde: ninetieth
nitton: nineteen
nittonde: nineteenth
notering: annotation, notes
notlinje(r): line(s) for musical
  notation
nötning: use, rubbing, wear
nött: worn
novell(er): short story(ies)
novellsamling: collection of short
  stories
nr. *see* nummer
numera: now
nummer: number(s), issue(s)
numr. *see* numrerad
numrerad: numbered
ny: new
ny följd: new series
ny serie: new series
ny tryckning: reprint
ny uppl. *see* ny upplaga
ny upplaga: new edition
ny utg. *see* ny utgåva
ny utgåva: new edition, reissue
nyare: more recent
nyckelord: keyword
nyckelroman: *roman à clef*
nyckeltitel: key title
nygjort omslag: new wrapper(s)
nyinbunden: rebound, newly
  bound
nypris: list price
nyss utkommen: just published
nytr. *see* nytryck, nytryckt

nytryck: reprint(s)
nytryckt: reprinted
nytt: new, something new

o.a. *see* och andra
o.s.v. *see* och så vidare
obekant: not known
obet. *see* obetydlig
obetydl. *see* obetydlig
obetydlig(t): insignificant(ly)
object: item
obunden: unbound
ocensurerad: unexpurgated, un-
  censored
och andra: and others
och så vidare: and so forth
oclotbd. *see* originalklotband
offentl. *see* offentlig
offentlig: public
officiell: official
officin: printshop, press
offset: offset
oförändr. *see* oförändrad
oförändrad: unchanged
oinbunden: unbound
okänd: unknown
oklot. *see* originalklotband
oklotb. *see* originalklotband
oktavformat: octavo size
olimmat papper: unsized paper
oljefläckad: oil-stained
omarb. *see* omarbetad, omarbet-
  ning
omarbetad: revised
omarbetad utgåva: revised edition
omarbetning(ar): revision(s)
omfång: number of pages
omfatta: comprise
omfattad: comprised
omfattar: comprises
omkring: approximately
omnämnd: mentioned, listed
omsl. *see* omslag
omslag: wrapper(s)
omslagstitel: cover title
omsorgsfull(t): careful(ly)
omställd: transposed

omtryck: reprint(s)
onumr. *see* onumrerad
onumrerad: unnumbered
opag. *see* opaginerad
opaginerad: unnumbered
ordbok(böcker): dictionary(ies)
ordförklaring: glossary
ordinarie: ordinary
ordlista: glossary, word list
ordspråk: proverb(s)
oregelbunden: irregular
orig. *see* original
origband. *see* originalband
orighäfte. *see* originalhäfte
orighalvklotbd. *see* originalhalvklotband
orighelkbd. *see* originalhelklotband
original: original
originalband: original binding
originaletsning(ar): original etch-
ing(s)
originalhäfte(n): original issue(s)
originalhalvklotband: original half-
cloth binding
originalhelklotband: original full-
cloth binding
originalkartonnage: original boards
originalklotband: original cloth
binding
originallinneband: original linen
binding
originalomslag: original wrapper(s)
originaltryck: original printing
originaltygband: original fabric
binding
originalupplaga: first edition
originell: curious, amusing
origkart. *see* originalkartonnage
origkbd. *see* originalklotband
origlinneband. *see* originallinneband
origtygband. *see* originaltygband
ornerad: decorated
osk. *see* oskuren
oskuren: uncut
otryckt: unpublished
ouppskuren: unopened, uncut

öv. *see* översatt
ovan: above
ovanlig: unusual
ovanst. *see* ovanstående
ovanstående: above-described,
the above
över: about, concerning; above
överdragspapper: fancy paper
övers. *see* översatt, översätta,
översättning
översatt: translated
översätta: translate
översättning: translation
översikt: abstract, synopsis
översiktstabell: synoptic table
överskrift: heading, caption
översnitt: upper edge
överstrucken: crossed out
överstycke(n): headpiece(s),
frieze(s)
övertitel: general title, main title
övre: top
övrig: other, remaining

på: in, upon
paginerad: paginated
påklistrad: pasted on
pamflett(er): (controversial)
pamphlet(s)
pappband: boards
papper: paper
papper- och pappomslag: paper
and cardboard cover(s)
pappersfläckad: foxed
pappomslag: hard paperboard
cover(s)
papp-pärmar: (original) cased
binding
paraferad: initialed
parallell: parallel
parallelltitel: parallel title
parallellutgåva: parallel edition,
parallel issue
pärm(ar): board(s), cover(s)
pärmbordyr: border on sides
pärmexlibris: book stamp(s)
on sides

pärmfals(ar): joint(s)
pärmficka: pocket
pärmfileter: fillet designs on side(s)
pärmförgyllning: gilding on side(s)
pärmöverdrag: covering of sides
pärmstämpel: stamp, design on
　sides
partiband: case binding
påseende: approval
påseendesändning: consignment
　sent on approval
passepartout: passe partout
pastisch: pastiche
per kontant: cash
pergament: parchment, vellum
pergamentband: vellum binding
pergamentbd. *see* pergamentband
pergamentrygg(ar): vellum back(s)
pergrygg. *see* pergamentrygg
pergryggar. *see* pergamentrygg(ar)
periodisk skrift: periodical
perkal: calico
perkalin: buckram
personregister: index of names
pl. *see* plansch
pl.-bl. *see* planschblad
pl.-blad. *see* planschblad
pl.-s. *see* planschsida
pl.-sid. *see* planschsida
plagiat: plagiarism
planritning(ar): plan(s), design(s)
plansch(er): plate(s)
planschbild(er): plate illustrations
planschblad: plate(s)
planschpapper: plate paper
planschserie: set of plates
planschsida(or): plate(s)
platta bind: flat bands
plchr. *see* planscher
plr. *see* planscher
plschr. *see* planscher
portf. *see* portfölj
portfölj(er): portfolio(s)
porträtt(er): portrait(s)
porträttplansch(er): portrait
　plate(s)
postnummer: zip code, postal code

postum: posthumous
ppbd. *see* pappband
ppomslag. *see* pappomslag
ppr. *see* papper
pr. *see* pro
präglad: embossed
praktband: deluxe binding
praktbilder: splendid illustrations
praktverk: deluxe publication
preliminär: preliminary
prenumeration: subscription
pris: price
prisändring: change in price
prisbelönad: prizewinning
prislista: price list
privat: private
privattryck: privately printed
　publication
pro: for, per, each
prospekt: prospectus, booklet
prov: sample(s)
proveniens: origin, provenance
provisoriskt band: temporary
　binding
prydd: decorated
prydl. *see* prydlig
prydlig: neat
pseudonym(er): pseudonym(s)
publ. *see* publicerad, publikation
publicerad: published
publiceras: in press
publiceringsdatum: date of publi-
　cation
publikation: publication
punkterad: dotted, stippled
putsad: trimmed

rabatt: discount
rad: line
raderad: erased
rak: straight
råkanter: untrimmed edges
ram: frame, border
rar: rare
rariss. *see* rarissimum
rarissimum: extremely rare
råsnitt: uncut edges

rättad: corrected
rättelse(r): corrigenda, correc-
tion(s), errata
rättelseblad: errata sheet
rea: sale
realisationsböcker: book bargains
rec.-stämpel. *see* recensionsstämpel
recensionsstämpel: review-copy
stamp
red. *see* redaktion, redaktör,
redigerad
redaktion: editorship
redaktör: editor
redig. *see* redigerad
redigerad: edited
redogörelse: account, report
referat: abstract
reg. *see* register
register: index(es)
registerblad: index page(s)
rem(mar): tie(s)
remsa(or): tie(s), ribbon(s)
ren: clean
renoverad: restored, repaired
rensad: cleansed, expurgated
renskära: (to) trim
renskuren bok: trimmed book
reproduktion(er): reproduction(s)
rest: balance, remainder
restupplaga: remainders
reva(or): tear(s)
revid. *see* reviderad
reviderad: revised
rik: rich
riktpris: list price
rispa(or): tear(s), scratch(es)
röd: red
rolig: amusing, nice
roman(er): novel(s)
röntgenbilder: x-ray illustrations
rörande: dealing with
rostfläck(ar): rust stain(s)
rött: red
rubricerad: rubricated, titled
rubrik: rubric, title
rubriktitel: running title
rundad: rounded

rutmönster: checkered design
rygg: spine
ryggdekor: decorated spine
ryggfält: panel(s) on spine
ryggförgyllning: gilding on spine
ryggornerad: decorated on spine
ryggornering: ornaments on spine
ryggskylt(ar): label(s) on spine
ryggtitle: spine title, title on spine
rysk: Russian
ryssläder: Russian leather

s. *see* sida
saga: tale
saknas: lacking, missing
sakregister: subject index
sällan: rarely, seldom
sällsynt: rare
samarbete: collaboration, cooperation
saml. *see* samling
samlad: collected
samling: collection
samlingsband: collective volume,
pamphlet volume
samlingsbd. *see* samlingsband
samlingstitelblad: collective title
page
samlingsverk: collected work
samma: same
sammanbunden: bound together
sammandrag: abridgment, synopsis
sammanfattning: summary
sammetliknande: velvetlike
sammetsband: velvet binding
sammetsbd. *see* sammetsband
samt: and also
samtida: contemporary
samtidig: contemporary, simultaneous
sångbok(böcker): songbook(s)
sannolikt: probably
särskild: special, separate
särskilt: especial, especially
särtr. *see* särtryck
särtryck: offprint(s), separate(s)
schatterad: hatched, azure-tooled

se: see
sen. *see* senare
senare: later
senast: latest, last
separat: separate, separately
ser. *see* serie
serie: series
sex: six
sextio: sixty
sextionde: sixtieth
sexton: sixteen
sextonde: sixteenth
sid. *see* sida
sida(or): page(s)
sidnummer: page number
siffra(or): figure(s), number(s)
sigill: seal
signatur: initials
signerat exemplar: inscribed copy
signering: signature
silverbrokadband: bound in silver
  brocade
silverspänne(n): silver clasp(s)
sirad(e): decorated
sista: last
självbiografi: autobiography
sjätte: sixth
sjökort: nautical chart(s)
sju: seven
sjunde: seventh
sjuttio: seventy
sjuttionde: seventieth
sjutton: seventeen
sjuttonde: seventeenth
skad. *see* skadad
skadad: damaged
skådespel: play, drama
skamfilad: chafed, worn
skämt: joke(s), jest(s)
skämtbok(böcker): jokebook(s)
skandalskrift: lampoon
skår(or): (ornamental) cut(s),
  scoring
skåra(or): scratch(es), scoring
skattad: esteemed
skavd: gnawed
skick: state

skiljer sig: differs
skillingtryck: broadside
skinn: leather
skinnband: leather binding
skinnbd. *see* skinnband
skinnkapitäl: headcap
skinnryggband: bound with leather
  back
skinnryggbd. *see* skinnryggband
skiss(er): sketch(es)
skolbok(böcker): textbook(s)
skolier: scholia, critical notes
skönskrift: calligraph
skrapad: scratched
skrbd. *see* skinnryggband
skrifter: writings
skrivpapper: writing paper
skrynklad: wrinkled, crushed
skuren: trimmed, cut
skyddskartong: slipcase
skyddsomslag: jacket
skyltexemplar: display copy
skyltlåda: display case, showcase
slät: smooth
sliten: worn
slut: end
slutblad: last page
slutord: postface, postscriptum
slutvinjett: tailpiece
små: little, small
smädeskrift: lampoon
smal: narrow
smärre: minor
småskrift(er): pamphlet(s);
  miscellanea
småtryck: pamphlet(s)
smutstitel: half title
snitt(ar): edge(s)
solblekt: faded
solkad: soiled
som: like, which
sommar: Summer
sönderläst: tattered
sönderriven: torn, lacerated
söndrig: torn
sp. *see* spalt(er)
spalt(er): column(s)

spänne(n): clasp(s)
spår: trace(s)
språk: language(s)
sprängd: sprinkled
spricka(or): break(s), crack(s)
ss. *see* sidor
st. *see* stor
stående order: standing order
ställvis: in some places
stålstick: steel engraving
stämpel: stamp, tooled design
stämplar: stamps, tooled designs
standardboknummer: standard
  book number, ISBN
standardformat: standard size
standardserienummer: standard
  serial number, ISSN
starkt: much, strongly
stentryck: lithography
stilenlig: in style
stilfull: in good style, tasteful
stiliserad: stylized
stor: large
storlek: dimension, size
större: larger
strimla(or): guard(s)
studium: survey, study
stycke(n): item(s), matter
styrelse: board
styvhäftad: bound in boards
subskriberad upplaga: subscriber's
  edition
suppl. *see* supplement
supplement: supplement
sv. *see* svensk
svag: slight, weak
svart: black
svärtad: darkened
svartskinnsryggband: half black-
  leather binding
svensk: Swedish
svinläder: pigskin
svit: run, set

t.o.m. *see* till och med
tab. *see* tabell
tabell: table

tabellblad: table(s)
tal: number (e.g., ett 40-tal: some
  forty; 1800-talet: 19th century)
talr. *see* talrik
talrik: numerous
teckn. *see* teckning
tecknad: drawn
teckning(ar): drawing(s)
textblad: sheet(s) of text
textfigur(er): figure(s) in the text
textförlust: loss of text
textkom. *see* textkommentar
textkommentar: annotations,
  textual comments
textsid(or): page(s) of text
tid: time
tid. *see* tidigare
tidigare: earlier
tidning(ar): newspaper(s)
tidskrift: journal, periodical
tidstypisk: typical of the age
till och med: up to and including,
  through
till salu: on sale
tillägg: appendix(es), supple-
  ment(s)
tilläggshäfte: supplementary issue
tillägnad: dedicated
tillägnan: dedication
tillbunden: bound with
tillök. *see* tillökad
tillökad: enlarged
tillökning(ar): addition(s)
tills. *see* tillsammans
tillsammans: in all, together
tillstånd: state, permission
tillverkats: was (were) fabricated
tio: ten
tionde: tenth
tit. *see* titel
titel: title
titelark: title sheet
titelblad: title page
titelram: title border
titelsida: title page
titelstämpel: stamp on title page
titelvinjett: title vignette

titlar: titles, title pages
tjänst: service
tjock: thick
tjugo: twenty
tjugonde: twentieth
tjugu: twenty
tolfte: twelfth
tolkning(ar): interpretation(s)
tolv: twelve
tom: empty, blank
tr. *see* tryck, tryckning, tryckt
träblock: woodblock
träfritt papper: wood-free paper
trägravyr: wood engraving,
  xylography
transkription: transcription
translitteration: transliteration
träpärm(ar): wooden side(s)
trasig: tattered, damaged
träsnitt: woodcut, xylography
träsnittsplansch: plate with woodcut
tre: three
tredje: third
trenne: three, a triad of
treplansskisser: sketches on three
  planes
trettio: thirty
trettionde: thirtieth
tretton: thirteen
trettonde: thirteenth
trevl. *see* trevlig
trevlig: pleasant
troligen: probably
tryck: printing
tryckalster: printed product,
  printing
tryckfel: typographical error,
  misprint
tryckning: impression, printing
tryckningsort: place of printing
tryckort: imprint
tryckt: printed
tryckt såsom manuskript: privately printed
tryckt som manuskript: privately
  printed
tryckuppgift: imprint, colophon

tryfferad bok: grangerized book
tummad: well worn
tunga: flap
tus. *see* tusen
tusen: thousand
tv. *see* tvär
två: two
tvär: oblong
tvättad: washed
tvenne: two, a couple of
tydlig: obvious, clear
typ: type, genre, class
typisk: typical

u.å. *see* utan år, utan årtal
u.o.o.å. *see* utan ort och år
udda del: odd volume
uncial: uncial
under tryckning: (about) to be
  published
undersökning: investigation
understöd: support, subsidy
understödjare: sponsoring body
understreckad: underlined
undertitel: subtitle
undre: lower, bottom
ungefär: approximately
uniform: uniform
unik: unique
uppdrag: order
uppfodrad: mounted
uppgift(er): information
upphöjda bind: raised bands
upphovsman: author
uppk. *see* uppköptes
uppköptes: was (were) bought up
uppl. *see* upplaga
upplaga: number of copies, edition
upplysn. *see* upplysning
upplysning(ar): information
uppsats(er): essay(s), article(s)
uppslagslitteratur: reference
  literature
upptagen: listed, occupied
upptill: at the top
ur band: out of its binding
urblekt: discolored, faded
urklipp: clipping

urval: selection
utan år: without year
utan årtal: without date of publication
utan band: without binding
utan ort och år: without place and year
utarb. *see* utarbetad
utarbetad: compiled, edited
utdrag: extract
utförd: executed
utförl. *see* utförlig
utförlig: extensive, detailed
utg. *see* utgåva utgivare, utgiven
utgåva: edition, issue
utgåvenummer: number of edition
utgavs: was (were) published
utgivare: publisher
utgiven: edited, published
utgör: constitutes
utk. *see* utkom
utkast: draft
utkom: appeared, was published
utkommen: appeared, published
utl. *see* utländsk
utländsk: foreign, non-Swedish
utm. *see* utmärkt
utmärkt: excellent
utök. *see* utökad
utökad: increased, enlarged
utomordentligt: extraordinarily
uts. *see* utsåld
utsåld: out of stock, sold out
utskuren: cut out
utsökt: choice, exceptional
utstyrsel: makeup, design
uttolkning: interpretation, translation
utvidg. *see* utvidgad
utvidgad: enlarged
utvikbar: foldout

vack. *see* vacker
′vacker: nice, beautiful
välbev. *see* välbevarad
välbevarad: well preserved
vald: selected
välskband: quarter-bound

vältryckt: well printed
vanlig: common, ordinary
vanligaste: most common
vänster(stra): left-hand
vapen: arms
vapensköld: coat of arms
vår: Spring
varav: of which
värdefull: valuable
värderad: valued
variant(er): variant(s)
varibland: including, among which
varje: each
vattenfläck(ar): water stain(s)
vattenmärke(n): watermark(s)
vattenstämpel(stämplar): watermark(s)
vävband: cloth binding
vävbd. *see* vävband
vbd. *see* vävband, välskband
vecka: week
vecko-: weekly
verk(en): work(s)
verken: the works (of _____)
verkställd: executed
vers: verse, poetry
versal(er): capital letter(s), uppercase letter(s)
version: version
vikt: weight, folded
vinj. *see* vinjett
vinjett(er): vignette(s), tailpiece(s)
vinter: Winter
vitterhet: literature, belles lettres, scientific literature
vitterhetsarbete(n): work(s) of literature
vol. *see* volym
volym: volume
vyer: views
vyplansch(er): plate(s) of views

xylografi: wood engraving

ytterformat: gross size
ytterligare: further, additional
ytteromslag: dust wrapper(s)
ytterst: most, extremely, utmost